Global Economic Crisis

KDI/EWC SERIES ON ECONOMIC POLICY

The Korea Development Institute (KDI) was established in March 1971 and it is Korea's oldest and best-known research institute in the fields of economic and social sciences. Its mission is to contribute to Korea's economic prosperity by drafting socio-economic development plans and providing timely policy recommendations based on rigorous analysis. Over the decades KDI has effectively responded to rapidly changing economic conditions at home and abroad by conducting forward-looking research as well as putting forth significant efforts in formulating long-term national visions.

The East-West Center promotes better relations and understanding among the people and nations of the United States, Asia and the Pacific through cooperative study, research, and dialogue. It serves as a resource for information and analysis on critical issues of common concern, bringing people together to exchange views, build expertise and develop policy options. The Center is an independent, public, nonprofit organization with funding from the US government, and additional support provided by private agencies, individuals, foundations, corporations, and governments in the region.

The KDI/EWC series on Economic Policy aims to provide a forum for scholarly discussion, research and policy recommendations on all areas and aspects of contemporary economics and economics policy. Each constituent volume in this series will prove invaluable reading to a wide audience of academics, policy makers and interested parties such as NGOs and consultants.

Titles in the series include:

Responding to Climate Change
Global Experiences and the Korean Perspective
Edited by Chin Hee Hahn, Sang-Hyop Lee and Kyoung-Soo Yoon

Global Economic Crisis
Impacts, Transmission and Recovery
Edited by Maurice Obstfeld, Dongchul Cho and Andrew Mason

Global Economic Crisis

Impacts, Transmission and Recovery

Edited by

Maurice Obstfeld

Class of 1958 Professor of Economics, University of California, Berkeley, USA

Dongchul Cho

Professor, KDI School of Public Policy and Management, Korea

Andrew Mason

Professor of Economics, University of Hawaii at Manoa and Senior Fellow, Population and Health Studies, East-West Center, Hawaii, USA

KDI/EWC SERIES ON ECONOMIC POLICY

A JOINT PUBLICATION OF THE KOREA DEVELOPMENT INSTITUTE, THE EAST-WEST CENTER, AND EDWARD ELGAR PUBLISHING LTD

KDI

EAST-WEST CENTER
COLLABORATION • EXPERTISE • LEADERSHIP

EE

Edward Elgar

Cheltenham, UK • Northampton, MA, USA

Published by
Edward Elgar Publishing Limited
The Lypiatts
15 Lansdown Road
Cheltenham
Glos GL50 2JA
UK

Edward Elgar Publishing, Inc.
William Pratt House
9 Dewey Court
Northampton
Massachusetts 01060
USA

Reprinted 2014

A catalogue record for this book
is available from the British Library

Library of Congress Control Number: 2012935333

MIX
Paper from
responsible sources
FSC® C013056

ISBN 978 1 78100 629 0

Typeset by Servis Filmsetting Ltd, Stockport, Cheshire
Printed and bound in Great Britain by TJ International Ltd, Padstow

Contents

PART III POLICY PERSPECTIVES

Contributors

Joshua Aizenman is a Professor of Economics at the University of California at Santa Cruz.

Michael D. Bordo is a Professor of Economics at Rutgers University.

Marcos Chamon is the Senior Economist in the Research Department at the International Monetary Fund.

Menzie D. Chinn is a Professor in the Department of Economics at the Robert M. La Follette School of Public Affairs at the University of Wisconsin at Madison.

Dongchul Cho is a Professor in the KDI School of Public Policy and Management.

Barry Eichengreen is the George C. Pardee and Helen N. Pardee Professor of Economics and Political Science in the Department of Economics at the University of California at Berkeley.

Atish Ghosh is the Assistant Director in the Research Department at the International Monetary Fund.

Michael M. Hutchison is a Professor of Economics at the University of California at Santa Cruz.

Hyeon-Wook Kim is the Director of the Department of Macroeconomics at the Korea Development Institute.

Jun Il Kim is a Deputy Division Chief in the Research Department at the International Monetary Fund.

John S. Landon-Lane is an Associate Professor of Economics at Rutgers University.

Hangyong Lee is a Professor of Economics and Finance at Hanyang University.

Hangyu Lee is a Research Fellow at the Korea Development Institute.

Kyung-Mook Lim is a former Research Fellow at the Korea Development Institute.

Andrew Mason is a Senior Fellow of the East-West Center and a Professor in the Department of Economics at the University of Hawaii at Manoa.

Maurice Obstfeld is the Class of 1958 Professor of Economics at the University of California at Berkeley.

Min-Kyu Song is a Research Fellow at the Korea Institute of Finance, a former Research Fellow in the Department of Finance at the Korea Development Institute and a former Head of International Finance at the Korea Securities Research Institute.

Acronyms and Abbreviations

ARMs	adjustable-rate mortgages.
BEC	broad economic category.
BRICs	Brazil, Russia, India and China as an economic group.
CDS	credit default swap.
CIP	covered interest parity.
CPI	consumer price index.
ECB	European Central Bank.
EMEs	emerging market economies.
EMP	exchange market pressure.
FX	foreign exchange.
G7	The Group of Seven (G7) is the meeting of finance ministers from a group of seven industrialized countries with large economies: Canada, France, Germany, Italy, Japan, the United Kingdom and the United States.
G20	The Group of Twenty (G20) comprises the finance ministers and central bank governors of 19 countries. The twentieth member is the European Union, which is represented by the rotating Council presidency and the European Central Bank. The 19 countries are Argentina, Australia, Brazil, Canada, China, France, Germany, India, Indonesia, Italy, Japan, Mexico, Republic of Korea, Russia, Saudi Arabia, South Africa, Turkey, the United Kingdom and the United States of America.
GDI	gross domestic income.
GDP	gross domestic product.
GSA	government sponsored agency.
FDI	foreign direct investment.
Fed	US Federal Reserve Board.
GDP	gross domestic product.
IMF	International Monetary Fund.
KOSDAQ	Korean Securities Dealers Automated Quotations.
KOSPI	Korea Composite Stock Price Index.
M&A	merger and acquisition.
NPL	nonperforming loan.

OECD	Organisation for Economic Co-operation and Development.
OLS	ordinary least squares.
PPI	producer price index.
SIVs	structured investment vehicles.
SME	small and medium-size enterprise.
SRI	systemic funding risk indicator.
WTO	World Trade Organization.

Preface

The global economic crisis triggered in 2008 has significantly changed the economic landscapes of many countries. Some are still struggling with deep scars made by the crisis, and others that have been relatively less damaged are also suffering from stagnating global demand. The impacts of the global crisis were not limited to economic recession, but extended to the ways of thinking about how markets operate and what policies are desired. With aftershocks still in play, it may be premature to assess the overall impacts of the 2008 global crisis. A better understanding of the causes and impacts of the global crisis at the moment, however, should help shore up efforts to prepare appropriate policies for the future.

The conference on Global Economic Crisis: Impacts, Transmission and Recovery, organized by the East-West Center and the Korea Development Institute and held in Honolulu, Hawaii, in 2010, investigated the global crisis from historical, international and policy perspectives. Participants reaffirmed that lax supervision and regulation in the financial market of the advanced countries were at the center of the story, although there surely were multiple causes. They also confirmed that the bold macroeconomic policies carried out immediately after the outbreak of crisis saved the global economy from plunging into another Great Depression. Regarding the postcrisis performance across countries, they agreed that sound balance sheets were critical for resilient recoveries. In particular, the analyses of the Korean economy were greatly illuminating in this respect. Whereas Korea, with fragile balance sheets, suffered miserably upon the shock of the Asian crisis a decade ago, it survived relatively well during the recent global economic crisis thanks to improved fundamentals.

Upon publishing this volume, I would like to thank Dr Maurice Obstfeld, professor at the University of California, Berkeley, Dr Dongchul Cho, professor at the KDI School of Public Policy and Management, and Dr Andrew Mason, professor at the University of Hawaii at Manoa and senior fellow at the East-West Center, for coordinating the conference and preparing this volume for publication. I also wish to thank the paper writers, discussion participants and others involved in contributing to the success of this conference. My sincere gratitude goes to Dr Kennon Breazeale who capably managed production coordination, and the East-West Center's graphics and production services, which brought the book to a camera-ready state.

Oh-Seok Hyun
President
Korea Development Institute

1. Introduction and overview

Maurice Obstfeld, Dongchul Cho and Andrew Mason

In 2008 the global economy witnessed the most severe crash since World War II. The prolonged subprime mortgage crisis in the United States finally erupted in a global panic, triggered by the Lehman Brothers bankruptcy filing in September. A sharp collapse in international trade followed, leaving no countries immune to the sequence of economic shocks. Suddenly the era of Great Moderation was transformed into the era of Great Recession, eliciting unprecedented macroeconomic policy responses in emerging and advanced economies alike. In most advanced countries, huge budget deficits emerged as policy interest rates fell to near-zero levels.

Although the global economy began to recover in the second half of 2009, the crisis raised many questions: How different was this crisis from the previous ones? What flaws in financial markets contributed to the crisis? How important was financial globalization in exacerbating the immediate international spillovers of the crisis? How important were global imbalance and global overheating in explaining the global meltdown? Were all countries similar before the crisis in terms of major macro indicators? Did different precrisis fundamentals generate different postcrisis performances? How severe were the shocks to emerging countries such as Korea? This volume attempts to answer some of these questions, which are clearly of great importance for the future of the global economy.

Part I of the volume consists of two chapters comparing the recent crisis with earlier ones. Part II contains four chapters on international aspects of the crisis: two about financial markets and two focused on international trade. The four chapters in Part III examine macroeconomic policy responses as well as the roles of precrisis fundamentals.

PART I HISTORICAL PERSPECTIVES

In Chapter 2, "The global financial crisis: is it unprecedented?" by Michael D. Bordo and John S. Landon-Lane, the authors build upon recent literature in distinguishing among three different types of financial crises—banking crises, currency crises and sovereign debt crises—and they investigate the negative output effects of crises from 1880 to 2009.

The authors base their study of output effects on the long spans of data assembled by Angus Maddison. In analysing crisis effects since the late nineteenth century, Bordo and Landon-Lane use data from 23 countries, most of them in Western Europe, but also including Canada, Japan, the United States, Argentina, Brazil and Uruguay. When computing a measure of severity for each successive recession, the authors find that banking crises are the most damaging, because the recessions associated with them are larger and seem to inflict stronger international spillovers than do the other types of crisis. They then focus attention on individual banking crises and identify five global events: 1890–91, 1907–08, 1913–14, 1931–32 and 2007–08. The authors conclude that the recessions associated with the 2007–08 financial crisis were indeed unprecedented, in that output losses were at the *low* end in comparison with previous major banking crises.

The authors also draw policy lessons from the historical record. First, the recent crisis underscores the historical lesson that countries with sound financial systems, an effective lender of last resort and efficient financial supervision fare better in global financial crises. Second, financial innovations may increase global systemic risk, making a case for enhanced financial supervision and regulation. Finally, the fact that the recent crisis was actually one of the least costly since the late nineteenth century suggests that policymakers have learned lessons from the past global financial crises: after the Lehman collapse they followed aggressively expansionary monetary and fiscal policies, which was certainly not the case before World War II.

In Chapter 3, "Responses of the Korean economy to the global economic crisis: another currency crisis?" Dongchul Cho focuses on the behavior of Korea's financial and export markets and macroeconomic policy responses during the 2008–09 global economic crisis. His comparisons show how the Asian economic crisis of 1997–98 was similar in some ways and different in others. The stress is on fundamental changes to the Korean economy after 1997, and the ways in which those changes cushioned Korea's financial sector and exporters in 2008, allowing a rapid economic rebound in 2009. According to Cho, there was an implosion of domestic markets in the 1997–98 crisis (when contracting domestic demand caused a sharp fall in GDP, whereas export demand was still expanding). In contrast, foreign markets collapsed in the more recent crisis (when a sharp fall in external demand was the trigger, but domestic demand fell only slightly, and both rebounded quickly).

The author analyses other main differences between the two crises. As it turned out, the second crisis saw a much more rapid recovery to precrisis levels, with only a moderate and brief drop in employment. Also, the second crisis was a stand-alone currency crisis, and was not accompanied by a banking crisis. In contrast to the monetary tightening of 1997 (which aggravated the concurrent banking crisis), the Korean authorities followed a policy of monetary easing in 2008 and allowed the exchange rate to float (which in turn bolstered the expansionary monetary policy stance, as well as playing an automatic stabilizing role, without wasting foreign reserves).

Moreover, the 2008 trade shock to Korea (a 40 percent drop in export demand during the last quarter of the year) was short-lived. Exports began to recover in the first quarter of 2009 and reached precrisis level a little more than a year later, at a time when most other countries still had not recovered. One reason for the quick recovery is the large share of China in Korea's export market (24 percent, plus about 6 percent for Hong Kong); and China recovered rapidly. Moreover, Korea's market shares in China and in other regions were increasing at this time, which the author attributes to the sharp depreciation of the Korean won. Rough calculations based on regression analyses show that a depreciation of 20 percent during the crisis should result in at least a 5 to 6 percent increase in Korean exports. Thus, depreciation likely accounts for two-thirds of the differential in 2009 between the growth of Korea's exports and the growth of global trade.

However, the author emphasizes most strongly changes in the fundamentals of the Korean economy after the 1997–98 crisis and the resulting stabilizing effects during the next crisis. He argues that financial buffers in place in 2008 were critical in preventing a repetition of the 1997–98 banking crisis. Ample foreign reserves dampened the impact of sudden capital outflow in 2008 (an outflow far more massive than a decade earlier). Major companies were in a far stronger position, thanks to effective government pressure after 1997 to restructure and to lower debt–equity ratios. Korea's banks were also stronger in 2008. Finally, household debt in Korea was not a source of significant trouble, because house prices had increased far less in Korea than in Europe and the United States. He cautions, however, that prolonged expansionary policies will erode the soundness of fundamentals and therefore must be readjusted to normal settings in a timely way.

PART II INTERNATIONAL PERSPECTIVES

The first two chapters in Part II discuss financial market aspects of the international spillovers due to the crisis. Joshua Aizenman and Michael

Hutchison, in "The international financial markets and transmission of the crisis: determinants of exchange market pressure and absorption by international reserves", focus on the adverse affects of the crisis on the external positions of countries throughout the world, especially the emerging market economies. The authors analyse exchange market pressure (EMP), measured as the sum of the percentage change in the nominal exchange rate (against the US dollar) and the percentage loss of reserves during the height of the financial crisis, from August 2008 to February 2009. Korea, for example, experienced a 51.55 percent nominal depreciation of the won and an 18.70 percent loss of reserves, resulting in a total exchange market pressure (EMP) of 70.25 percent.

The vast majority of countries experienced intense EMP: 63 countries (82 percent of the sample) experienced positive EMP, whereas the values were negative for only 14 countries in the sample. Most of the countries with positive EMP experienced depreciation of their currencies against the US dollar (66 countries), although several currencies remained stable (5 countries). All countries were affected, moreover, regardless of whether they had tight restrictions on capital flows.

Rather than attempting to identify the root causes of the shock, the authors focus on two questions: (1) how the transmission of the global shock was affected by the extent of international balance sheet exposure, financial development and financial openness of the countries examined and (2) the trade-off between exchange rate depreciation and loss of international reserves in absorbing the shock, and how the choice of a point on the trade-off was determined. The results of this study highlight the importance of the ratio of total external liabilities to GDP in accounting for exchange market pressures, and of the ratio of short term external debt to international reserves in accounting for the higher relative importance of currency depreciation in accommodating the adjustment to a given degree of exchange market pressure. The findings also corroborate the notion that the 2008–09 crisis was the first global crisis in the era of modern financial globalization, affecting practically all countries (even though the exposure to exchange market pressures varied widely).

Overall, EMP was absorbed mainly by currency depreciation, and only to a lesser extent by losses of international reserves. Aizenman and Hutchison examine the trade-off between the two, with particular reference to the responses of emerging market economies. They argue that the responses of the emerging market economies were motivated more by the fear of losing reserves and less by the fear of floating. Even though these economies had built up large international reserves prior to the financial crisis, they still relied primarily on exchange depreciation rather than reserve loss to absorb most of the EMP. Aizenman and Hutchison suggest that this was possibly a deliberate choice, motivated by a desire to enhance competitiveness in the face of exceptionally weak external demand.

Averages by region show that the greatest effects were felt in Eastern Europe and Central Asia (50 percent EMP). This is not surprising, given that the subprime crisis emanating from the United States was directly linked to financial institutions in Western Europe, which in turn were tightly linked through banking ties with the more fragile economies of Eastern Europe. By contrast, Africa and the Middle East fared best as a region (with the lowest EMP at only 21 percent), followed closely by Latin America (23 percent EMP) and East Asia (nearly 26 percent EMP). When arranged in three tiers by income group, the middle-income countries fared best (28 percent EMP) and the low-income countries fared worst (33.7 percent EMP).

The data also confirm the key importance of balance sheet effects in explaining vulnerabilities and adjustments. Countries with a higher ratio of total foreign liabilities to GDP were more vulnerable to the financial crisis. Countries with large balance sheet exposure (high external portfolio liabilities exceeding international reserves) responded by allowing greater exchange rate depreciation and comparatively less reserve loss.

The second chapter of Part II, by Hangyong Lee and Min-Kyu Song, asks "How did Korean financial markets get infected by the global financial crisis?" In this chapter, the authors are particularly interested in studying how financial instability in advanced countries generated such an immediate and powerful spillover effect on the Korean economy during the global financial crisis. To address this question, the authors look at heavy short-term borrowing by Korean banks and the rapid increase of Korea's external debt prior to the start of the global crisis in 2007. The resulting high level of short-term external debt increased Korea's vulnerability to the shock. Lee and Song also investigate the subsequent large-scale capital outflows from Korea.

Quarterly data for Korea's balance of payments during 2008–09 reveal a massive net capital account deficit (US$42.6 billion) in the fourth quarter of 2008, and Korean deposit-taking institutions repaid to foreigners US$48.4 billion in short-term borrowing in the same quarter. The authors discuss comparable data for previous quarters and for 2009, when the economy began to recover and financial markets regained stability. Data on total external debt likewise show a peak in the fourth quarter of 2008, although the ratio of short-term debt to foreign exchange reserves peaks in the previous quarter. An index constructed at the Bank of Korea (the systemic funding risk indicator), however, shows that very high risk prevailed even before the start of the intense phase of the crisis (the Lehman Brothers bankruptcy in mid-September 2008).

Korea's total external debt (US$379 billion at the end of 2008) was not as large as claimed in the international press, but the reports heightened concerns about another currency crisis. The Korean government pointed out that, after deducting nonobligatory debt and debt to domestic branches of foreign banks, the Korean banks and corporations owed only US$77.5 billion, which was only about one-third of the country's foreign exchange reserves.

The authors explain the various ways in which external debt is contracted. Dividing total external debt between Korean banks and branches of foreign banks in Korea, the authors find that the share attributed to the foreign banks rose continuously from 2005 (45.1 percent) to 2009 (63.0 percent), whereas the share of the Korean banks dropped below 50 percent in 2006 and continued to decline thereafter.

The Korean government's response has been to reduce Korea's vulnerability to future shocks by introducing measures to curb excessive short-term external borrowing in normal times and sudden outflows during periods of financial instability. To decrease risk exposure in the banking system, the government is considering measures to regulate the total volume of foreign-exchange swaps by imposing a limit on the forward position, in relation to the respective bank's capital, although such a measure could seriously hamper the financing necessary for trade.

A subsection of the chapter by Lee and Song is devoted to reasons for the rapid increase in external debt between 2006 and the fourth quarter of 2008.They focus on hedging foreign exchange risks, arbitrage opportunities, domestic bond investments, lending to firms that import machinery and equipment, and the management of interest rate risks by Korean banks in a way that provided foreign bank branches with another investment vehicle.

While the first two chapters of Part II discuss financial aspects of the crisis, the remaining two analyse real aspects, international trade in particular. Menzie D. Chinn, in "Imbalances, overheating, and the prospects for global recovery", begins by asking four questions: (1) How important were global imbalances and global overheating in explaining the global crisis? (2) How did trade exposure propagate the negative shock? (3) How important was the maintenance of domestic demand in Asia (particularly in China) in protecting the global economy from an even greater downturn? (4) Are global imbalances and global overheating in need of further correction, or have they been sufficiently adjusted? The chapter is accordingly organized into sections that examine the causes of the global imbalances and their relationship to the financial crisis, the importance of trade linkages and, finally, the prospects for current account balances and overheating.

The review of recent attempts to explain the rise of global imbalances (defined as large current account balances) includes trends in saving and investment balances, the intertemporal approach, mercantilist behavior, the global saving glut and distortions in financial markets. The author presents regression analysis that tests and throws doubt on the saving glut hypothesis.

Further regression analysis examines the importance of institutions, with particular reference to the relationship between current account balances and government budget balances. Chinn cites his joint research findings with Hiro Ito as evidence against the argument that emerging market countries (especially those in East Asia) will experience lower rates of saving once they achieve higher levels of financial development and better developed legal infrastructures. He argues that more open financial markets do not appear to have any impact on current account balances for this group of countries.

Chinn also cites joint research with Jeffry Frieden and their argument that excess saving outside the United States combined with domestic financial distortions were central to the development and extent of the global crisis. Their interpretation is consistent with the view that a resumption of expanding imbalances, without removing the distortions in credit markets, will cause another crisis, albeit perhaps in some other form. He notes that much of the US government's financial regulation package has yet to be implemented and, even when it is implemented, the financial reforms are unlikely to do more than moderate the distortions. He thus concludes that policymakers should seek to mitigate large current account balances (in either direction), as a second best policy.

The author examines the deep drop in trade flows during the 2008–09 global recession, pointing out that a large component of the decline was due to the drop in exports of manufactured durable goods. It is very difficult, however, to judge the impact of trade financing, because the purported decrease in access to trade financing occurred at the same time as the general credit freeze in the global financial system. He also examines data on the drop in aggregate demand—the traditional view of how foreign demand shocks are propagated—with particular reference to China's trade. He suggests that it is useful to distinguish different channels through which the recession spread, because the spread in the industrialized economies took place earlier than in emerging markets.

Chinn presents a simple framework to analyse overheating in combination with a trade imbalance, as a starting point for discussing the prospects for rebalancing versus overheating in the global economy. He then proceeds to examine the major advanced economies (with emphasis on the United States), along with BRICs (Brazil, Russia, India and China, with emphasis on China). He concludes that there is little chance of overheating in the short term in the advanced countries (where there is greater risk of deflation), whereas the possibility of overheating is more pronounced in the emerging markets. He adds that, under current policies, rebalancing of current accounts is not proceeding and that additional measures could reinforce an adjustment to sustainable current account balances with sustainable growth.

The last chapter of Part II, by Hangyu Lee, is "The great trade collapse and contraction of exports in Korea during the global crisis". The author begins by defining what economists have called "the great trade collapse" during the 2008–09 global crisis: world trade shrank far more than world GDP, an outcome that cannot be reconciled easily with standard macroeconomic theories. The recent literature on this subject offers various candidate explanations for the trade collapse, including compositional effects (due to the high share of durables in trade), internationalized supply chains and the trade credit hypotheses. These are discussed in the chapter with a focus on Korea. Other explanations (such as inventory adjustment and protectionism) are also mentioned.

Lee argues that the compositional effect is the most relevant for explaining the collapse of Korea's exports during the crisis. According to this hypothesis, the fact that demand for durable goods is more volatile than for nondurable goods, together with the fact that durable goods account for a larger share of world trade than of world GDP, implies that world trade can be more volatile than world GDP. In the case of Korea, Lee demonstrates that durable goods exports account for about 75 percent of the contraction of the country's total exports during the crisis. By extension, he argues that any country in which durable goods account for a relatively larger share of exports is likely to experience a relatively more severe contraction of exports during a global downturn. The reduction in exports during the crisis was moderated for Korea, in contrast to other countries with similar shares of durable goods in their exports, by the large depreciation of the Korean won during 2008.

There is also a clear regional effect. The rapid recovery of emerging economies helped Korea. Export data by region show that Korea's exports to emerging Asian economies (China and ASEAN) recovered faster, more strongly and earlier than those to the advanced economies (reflecting the severe recession that continued almost to the end of 2009 in the European Union, Japan and the United States).

The author cautions against arguments for a policy response that would merely attempt to change the structure of exports (for example, by promoting the cyclically less sensitive service sector). He argues that such a policy could create serious economic distortions and thereby cause significant resource misallocations.

PART III POLICY PERSPECTIVES

The first chapter in Part III, one of the two discussing policy aspects of the crisis, is "Macroeconomic and financial policies before and after the crisis" by Barry Eichengreen. In this chapter, Eichengreen offers a set of provisional lessons concerning the roles of monetary, fiscal and regulatory policies in relation to the crisis.

First and foremost, Eichengreen argues that lax financial-sector supervision and regulation (in the advanced countries in particular) were at the center of the crisis (although the crisis had multiple causes) and that it was appropriate for postcrisis efforts by the G20 governments to focus on regulatory reform. He describes the actual accomplishments by 2010 as disappointing and falling short of measures that might otherwise have been taken by that time to strengthen prudential supervision and regulation in the wake of the most serious global financial crisis in 80 years.

Second, as a result of the crises of the 1990s, emerging markets had already learned the importance of running budget surpluses and keeping fiscal capacity in reserve. During 2007–08, by contrast, too many advanced countries entered the crisis with large budget deficits and elevated debts, and their unprecedented fiscal response created unprecedented problems of debt sustainability. Eichengreen recommends that the United States and other advanced countries take the earlier lesson to heart.

Third, Eichengreen draws attention to the importance of early and concerted intervention to resolve banking-sector problems. No aggressive fiscal stimulus will jump-start private spending in the absence of bank lending, he argues, and no banks will be lending if they need to rely on the market to recapitalize themselves. Public recapitalization is expensive and unpopular, and politicians shun it. But failing to recapitalize early will probably have serious consequences in the long run. Bad debts would ideally be recognized and written down promptly, although political and institutional factors may make this difficult.

Fourth, the author points out the lack of adequate mechanisms for international policy coordination. Countries with unused fiscal capacity could have done more to support global demand, but they failed to respond when urged to do so. Countries that entered the crisis with heavy debt loads should have been more cautious about debt sustainability and the risks of permanent damage to their economic and financial systems. Eichengreen argues that monetary easing was underutilized compared to fiscal easing, and in particular faults the European Central Bank for its reluctance to react aggressively.

Finally, the author points to the importance of longer-term historical factors. In the United States, the pendulum swung first one way and then the other: from free-market fundamentalism up to the Great Depression, to the strong oversight that ensued, then to the easing and elimination of restrictions in the final decades of the last century and now back to stronger regulation. During the latest crisis, the aggressive quantitative easing by the US Federal Reserve reflected memories of the 1930s and the Federal Reserve's poor performance in response. By contrast, the reluctance of the European Central Bank to pursue a comparable policy reflected memories of European hyperinflation in the 1920s and fear of a repetition.

The author also comments on global imbalances. Some researchers have emphasized the role of global imbalances in the crisis, but he does not. Instead, he questions whether policymakers should give priority to prevent the recurrence of these imbalances as a means of preventing renewed financial instability.

Eichengreen analyses macroeconomic policies of the G20 nations during three years (2008–10). He provides a series of graphs to compare the sizes of stimulus packages in individual G20 countries in relation to their rates of growth slowdown (where the expected tendency is found), as well as to shares of government revenue in GDP and sizes of government debts (where a weak or no relationship is found). Data on monetary policy confirm that the central banks of countries suffering the most pronounced slowdowns were the most inclined to cut interest rates, although they were not always rewarded with lower long-term real interest rates. Other data suggest that exchange rate adjustment played a positive role in global adjustment. He evaluates some of the results of fiscal stimulus by various countries (at least those apparent in mid-2010) and points out, admittedly with hindsight, weaknesses and possibly superior policy responses.

The second chapter of Part III, by Hyeon-Wook Kim, is "Macroeconomic policies of Korea to cope with the crisis". It discusses the macroeconomic policy aspect, but focuses on the case of Korea. This chapter examines macroeconomic trends, government policies, asset prices and financial markets prior to the 2008 crisis, evaluates government policies implemented during the crisis and makes related policy recommendations for the postcrisis period.

The author characterizes precrisis Korean fiscal policy as expansionary during 2003–04, close to neutral during 2005–06 and closer to contractionary in 2007. The government limited its intervention in foreign exchange during this period, which allowed won depreciation and thereby helped to buffer the external shocks of 2008. He also examines asset prices and points out that, despite the rapid expansion of household credit and sharp rise in house prices, Korea differed from the United States and European countries, because the Korean households' bubble ("credit card bubbles") burst in 2003 and was followed by economic contraction at that time. The episode was long past by 2008.

To examine the housing and stock markets more closely, Kim uses a weighted average of the house and stock price indexes to create an index of asset prices covering 1991 to 2010. The index shows that overall asset prices were usually driven by house prices during the 1990s, but that after the 1997–98 crisis, the effects of stock prices were more important (reflecting the great expansion of the stock market). The analysis shows, however, that the upward trend of asset prices starting in 2005 cannot be attributed fully to inappropriate monetary policy (although he notes that the economic situation could have been better if monetary policy had been contractionary enough to alleviate the upward pressure of asset prices).

Kim then turns to the government policy responses in 2008. The fiscal stimulus package was larger (in proportion to the size of the economy) in Korea than in any other OECD country. The author discusses the contribution of this package to Korea's GDP growth from late 2008 to 2010 and concludes that the fiscal stimulus played a successful pump-priming role during the crisis. He credits further government efforts (to implement expansionary monetary and fiscal policies) with moderating the serious contraction at the beginning of 2009 and with promoting the country's fast economic recovery. A major factor in the recovery was increasing demand from Korea's trading partners. He also examines the Bank of Korea's low-interest-rate policy, facilitated by exchange rate flexibility, which led to consumer price index inflation peaking in mid-2008 but subsequently stabilizing at about 2 to 3 percent.

The author then discusses numerous concerns about the postcrisis period and makes recommendations for an appropriate exit strategy for Korea, including more restraint of government spending, the prompt phasing out of temporary fiscal incentive measures, the expansion of the government's revenue base and structural changes in the framework of fiscal policy. In addition, in order not to allow inflationary pressure to build for too long, the central bank should begin an upward adjustment of interest rates as soon as possible.

The third chapter of Part III, by Marcos Chamon, Atish Ghosh and Jun-Il Kim, is "Are all emerging market crises alike?" It is one of two chapters in the volume on the relationship between precrisis fundamentals and crises. The authors of this chapter propose a general framework for a more unified approach to crises in emerging market economies (EMEs), based on the confluence of an underlying vulnerability and a specific crisis trigger. The vulnerability is typically a balance sheet mismatch (maturity, currency, liquidity) that may persist for many years until a crisis is triggered by a particular event. Such vulnerabilities can therefore be readily identified, provided appropriate data are available. By contrast, the event that triggers the crisis may take many different forms (economic or political, domestic or external) and is likely to be highly unpredictable. The EMEs that suffered the worst performance (that is, experienced their own domestic crises in 2008–09) were indeed those that had underlying vulnerabilities. By contrast, even EMEs that were hit hard by global financial crisis (through trade or financial links with advanced economies) came through relatively unscathed if they did not have these vulnerabilities.

The authors tabulate major EME crises by country, listing underlying vulnerabilities and plausible triggering events. They find great similarity of the underlying vulnerabilities but dissimilarity of the triggers. The underlying vulnerabilities are nearly always maturity or currency mismatches on public or private sector balance sheets. By contrast, the triggers vary widely and include political uncertainty, external shocks and perceptions about policy inconsistencies or insufficient political will.

They point out that balance sheet analysis is data intensive. They therefore propose a simpler approach of creating indicators of vulnerability that are broadly related to currency and maturity mismatches. They then define a crisis as a capital account crisis involving sudden stops in capital flows. Using this definition, they construct a table of individual crises in a 50-country sample from 1994 to 2006. They consider five potential explanatory variables for each of three sectors (external, public and financial) and present summary information on the statistical significance of the explanatory variables from their regressions.

Chamon, Ghosh and Kim use this framework to quantify vulnerabilities. By 2008, the EMEs in the sample were somewhat less vulnerable to crisis than in the past, with an average crisis probability of 4.6 percent in 2008 (compared with 5.2 percent through 2007). The time series of average EME crisis probability is plotted by region from 1995 to 2010, revealing long downward trends in Asia and Latin America during the years leading up to the 2008 crisis, in contrast to a rising trend and peak in Eastern Europe.

Contrary to the general perception that improvement of the public finances in Latin America and improvement of external indicators in East Asia were responsible for lower vulnerabilities in those regions, the authors' decomposition of factors explaining the falling vulnerability scores points mainly to improved external indicators in both regions. In Europe, it was mainly deterioration of the external indicators that resulted in higher estimated vulnerability.

Further regression analysis, examining the change in real GDP growth in 2008–09 as a function of estimated vulnerability, reveals that the expected correlation is statistically and economically significant. That is, each percentage point increase in predicted crisis probability in the index for 2008 would have lowered growth by 1.82 percentage points in 2008–09. Even controlling for other factors, which are ignored in the regression, the index continues to be highly significant.

The authors also look closely at capital flows and find that the extent of capital outflow was largely unrelated to precrisis vulnerability (although a few outlying countries stand out as exceptions). They also argue that the "indiscriminate" pattern of outflows is plausible and tends to support anecdotal evidence that the large capital outflows from Korea and Brazil, for example, occurred not because investors were worried about vulnerabilities, but because the larger and more liquid markets in these countries allowed investors to withdraw funds from them more easily than from other countries. Even taking this factor into consideration, the authors conclude that precrisis vulnerability is the most important determinant of how EMEs fared, once the crisis had been triggered.

The authors caution that crisis prediction in itself is a fool's errand, because it is most likely impossible to predict specific triggers to crises. They recommend that policy efforts instead be directed at reducing or eliminating the underlying vulnerabilities, which is the approach of current efforts for crisis prevention, such as the early warning exercise of the International Monetary Fund and Financial Stability Board.

The last chapter of the volume, "Structural fundamentals of Korean corporations: this time was different", by Kyung-Mook Lim, discusses the effects of precrisis fundamentals in Korea's corporate sector. The author of this chapter provides basic indicators to compare the performance of the Korean economy as it weathered the two crises in 1997–98 and 2008–09. During 1997–98 fixed investment declined more than 20 percent, accompanied by massive lay-offs. It took two years for investment to regain the precrisis level, at which time employment had not yet fully recovered. In the 2008–09 crisis, by contrast, fixed investment declined only modestly, and unemployment even less, and both recovered in less than a year.

To explain the rapid recovery of the Korean economy from the second crisis, the author outlines numerous factors that have been discussed in the literature, notably, effective fiscal and monetary policies and the recovery of external demand due to the rapid recovery of developing countries such as China. He then turns to the Korean corporate sector and argues that fundamental changes, made as a result of the first crisis, enabled the economy to absorb the external shock effectively, to weather the 2008–09 crisis in a different way, and to rebound quickly.

In particular, Lim focuses on the restructuring of Korea's big corporations (both financial and non-financial): the improved corporate governance and the market-monitoring mechanism that emerged from the post-1997 reforms, the decline in the high debt–equity ratio and the improved liquidity of corporations. His detailed analysis first concentrates on the longer-term change in the debt–equity ratio. Previous analysis used data from the 1990s and immediate post-1997 period to argue that the big corporations were successful in reducing their ratios under pressure from the government. Building on that work, the author uses data up to 2009 to analyse the detailed process of reducing the ratio and its effects on investment and employment. Lim also notes that market pressure (especially by foreign investors) was stronger in the second crisis than in the first, as the post-1997 capital market liberalization raised foreign ownership of listed companies to 37 percent by 2006 (compared with 13 percent in 1996).

The author uses a database originally constructed by the Korea Listed Companies Association and refined by WISEfn Corporation, which covers a sample of about 8800 companies. For comparisons of key factors such as the debt–equity ratio and liquidity, the author contrasts the entire sample with (1) the large corporate groups (*chaebols*) and (2) the remaining listed companies. The findings highlight the post-1997 successes of the Korean government in focusing on the *chaebols*.

By examining the capital structure of companies from 1990 to 2008, Lim demonstrates how the listed companies managed to reach the government's goal: a debt–equity ratio of about 200 percent (down from the precrisis level of about 400 percent for *chaebols*). This was achieved in part through aggressive efforts to reduce total debt up to 2002, along with success in issuing seasoned equity. But success was also due to a change in accounting: switching asset valuation from the historic-cost basis to the fair-market-value basis. From 2004 total debt began to rise again, but companies were able to keep the lowered debt–equity ratio relatively stable, mainly due to the rapid increase in retained earnings (continuing even through the end of the dataset in 2009), which is a reflection of improved company profitability. The author makes the point that "too big to fail" is no longer a valid argument in Korea, primarily because the debt–equity ratio of the *chaebols* (which had been much higher than that of other companies in 1997) converged to a similar level with the ratios of the other listed companies after 2002. The near-disappearance of this difference is confirmed by the regression results from a 1990–2009 dataset.

In the immediate post-2008 crisis period, neither debt–equity ratios nor debt levels changed significantly, despite the global crisis, which implies that Korean listed companies had no urgent need to reduce their debt burdens at this time, in contrast to the post-1997 period. The author suggests that the well-controlled response of the corporate sector to the 2008–09 crisis was the main factor in preventing the huge external shock of 2008–09 from being propagated to other domestic sectors, and thus that the effects of the global crisis were different this time because of the improved financial soundness of the major Korean companies.

The author also points out that the growth rate of investment in Korea was sluggish in the post-1997-crisis period, but still very high (at around 30 percent of GDP) in comparison with other OECD countries (where the average was closer to 20 percent). Although some other authors claim that the current rate is lower than the optimal level, Lim questions whether a further increase in the investment level in Korea is either possible or desirable. He also points out that the post-2003 rate has been much higher for listed Korean companies than for nonlisted ones, which implies that the sluggishness of growth is due mainly to nonlisted (mainly small and medium-size) companies (SMEs). Thus, a major remaining task for the government (albeit a politically difficult one, since the SMEs employ most of the labor force) is to expand the corporate restructuring process to include the SMEs.

CONCLUSION

We began this volume by posing many challenging questions regarding the global crisis. To those, we found some tentative answers. For example, Michael D. Bordo and John S. Landon-Lane conclude that the recessions associated with the 2007–08 financial crisis were indeed unprecedented in that output losses were at the *low* end in comparison with previous major banking crises, probably thanks to the unprecedentedly bold macroeconomic policies. As for the causes of the crisis, Barry Eichengreen argues that lax supervision and regulation (in the advanced countries in particular) were at the center of the story, although there surely were multiple causes. Marcos Chamon, Atish Ghosh and Jun-Il Kim find that different balance sheet vulnerabilities well explain different postcrisis performances across countries. This finding about the relationship between precrisis fundamentals and postcrisis performances is reconfirmed by Dongchul Cho and Kyung-Mook Lim from the comparisons of the Korean economy between the 1997–98 Asian crisis and the 2008–09 global crisis.

Of course, the results of this volume cannot deliver the final answers to all the questions addressed. At the same time, many important issues remain to be explored. For example, what sorts of unconventional monetary policies were developed and deployed during the crisis, and how effective were they? Should the crisis lead to a reassessment of fiscal policy effectiveness? What are the implications of the crisis for international liquidity and the design of the international monetary system? What are the implications of Asia's rise in the global economic landscape, particularly the rise of China, which took over the position of *buyer of last resort* from the United States over the course of the recovery? How should one understand the effect of crises on policymaking processes, apparently leading the ideology of the free market to wane and arguments for regulation to wax in prominence? In this regard, the contribution of this volume should be found in taking a step forward and inviting subsequent research in these areas.

PART I

Historical perspectives

2. The global financial crisis: is it unprecedented?

Michael D. Bordo and John S. Landon-Lane

INTRODUCTION

A financial crisis in the United States in 2007 spread to Europe and led to a recession across the world in 2007–09. Have we seen patterns like this before? Or is the recent experience novel? This chapter compares the recent crisis and recent recession to earlier international financial crises and global recessions.

First we review the dimensions of the recent crisis. We then present some historical narrative on earlier global crises in the nineteenth and twentieth centuries. The description of earlier global crises leads to a sense of déjà vu.

We next demarcate several chronologies of the incidence of various kinds of crises: banking, currency and debt crises and combinations of them across a large number of countries for the period from 1880 to 2010. These chronologies come from earlier work of Bordo with Barry Eichengreen, Daniela Klingebiel and Maria Soledad Martinez-Peria and with Chris Meissner (Bordo et al. 2001; Bordo and Meissner 2007), from Carmen Reinhart and Kenneth Rogoff's recent book (2009), and from a study by the International Monetary Fund (Laeven and Valencia 2010).[1] Based on these chronologies we look for clusters of crisis events that occurred in a number of countries and across continents. These we label global financial crises.

International financial crises inevitably are associated with recessions. We then ascertain the impact of the global financial crises identified by our cluster analysis on real output in the countries affected. To do this we first demarcate business cycle turning points in the countries affected by the global crises and then measure the accumulated output losses in the recessions associated with the identified crises. Not surprisingly, we find that the economic impact of the Great Depression dwarfed that of the recent crisis, but so did several other historic global financial crises. We consider several factors that could explain the patterns of global financial crises. These include globalization, the gold standard and whether the United States was in crisis. We conclude with some policy implications of our evidence.

DIMENSIONS OF THE RECENT GLOBAL FINANCIAL CRISIS

The collapse in the subprime mortgage market after the collapse of a major housing boom in the United States (which had been propelled by expansionary monetary policy and long standing government policies encouraging home ownership) and the plunge in values of mortgage backed securities in the United States in 2007, led to a crisis in the US shadow banking system (nonbank financial intermediaries that had issued and held mortgage backed securities) (Gorton 2010). These pressures led to liquidity shortages in the interbank wholesale markets that funded the financial sector. The crisis spread to European banks via the drying up of interbank liquidity, which led inter alia to the run on Northern Rock in the United Kingdom in September 2007 and the exposure of European banks to mortgage backed securities held in off-balance-sheet structured investment vehicles (SIVs) which led to threats to the solvency of banks in Germany, France, Belgium, the Netherlands, Italy, Switzerland and Iceland.

Although the US Federal Reserve, the European Central Bank and the Bank of England provided ample liquidity in the fall of 2007, the crisis worsened with the collapse of Lehman Brothers (in which case the US monetary authorities did an about-face after having bailed out Bear Stearns in March 2008) and the near collapse of AIG (saved by a huge bailout) in September 2008.

A credit crunch and a pause in expansionary monetary policy in early 2008 reflecting a misplaced fear of commodity price hikes leading to inflation (Hetzel 2009) led to a recession in the United States and Europe. The advanced country recession and a collapse in international trade finance greatly reduced exports from China and other emerging Asian countries, as well as the rest of the world, leading to a global downturn. In addition, several eastern European countries were hit by crisis because they were overexposed to foreign currency denominated debt. They were rescued by the International Monetary Fund (IMF).

The global crisis ended with government bailouts of insolvent banks, guarantees of the liabilities of the banking system, the provision of credit facilities to unclog financial markets and expansionary monetary and fiscal policy in many countries. The global recovery began in the summer of 2009, making the recession (which began in late 2007 in the United States and other countries) the longest (and possibly the deepest) one in the post-war era.

HISTORICAL PATTERNS IN INTERNATIONAL FINANCIAL CRISES

We provide a brief narrative of events which could be characterized as global financial crises. We also demarcate several episodes which were primarily regional rather than global crises.

We first define our terms. The essence of a financial crisis is a banking crisis (Schwartz 1986). According to Bordo et al. (2001):

> for an episode to qualify as a banking crisis, we must observe either bank runs, widespread bank failures and the suspension of deposits into currency such that the latter circulates at a premium relative to deposits (a banking panic), or significant banking sector problems (including but not limited to bank failures) resulting in the erosion of most or all of banking system collateral that are resolved by a fiscally underwritten bank restructuring.

This definition allows us to distinguish between pre-1914 banking panics, in which lender of last resort intervention was either absent or unsuccessful, and subsequent crises, in which a lender of last resort or deposit insurance was in place and the main problem was bank insolvency rather than illiquidity.[2]

Financial crises are aggravated when they lead to or are accompanied by currency crises (a speculative attack on a pegged exchange rate) and debt crises (sovereign debt defaults). International financial crises are banking crises that are often accompanied by currency crises (twin crises) or by debt crises (or by both currency and debt crises together) that occur in multiple countries and across continents. They also involve both advanced and emerging countries.

Such events are often triggered by asset price booms and busts in key countries. Stock market and property booms often burst preceding financial crises (Bordo 2003).

The world has seen a number of global financial crises since the beginning of the nineteenth century and even before (Kindleberger 1978). Before World War I they occurred in an environment of globalization—the integration of goods, labor and capital markets in which free capital mobility was often at the heart of asset booms and busts that led to crises. They also occurred under the classical gold standard, which linked countries together by fixed exchange rates. In the interwar period major financial crises occurred after the world returned to the gold exchange standard. After World War II, under the Bretton Woods system with pegged exchange rates, capital controls and extensive financial regulation, financial crises were rare, although there were frequent currency crises. Since the early 1970s, along with the switch to a floating exchange rate regime (for the advanced countries), the removal of capital controls and the liberalization of domestic financial markets, international financial crises have reappeared.

The Specie Standard Era

A number of international financial crises involving banking crises in London, the continent of Europe, the United States and Latin America occurred during the nineteenth century when most countries were on specie standards (silver, gold, bimetallism). Also in that century after the end of the Napoleonic Wars, globalization in trade and capital increased dramatically (Bordo et al. 2003). We briefly demarcate several events in the nineteenth century (before our data starts in 1880) and then the crisis events after 1880.

The first international financial crisis was the crisis of 1825 (Neal 1998; Bordo 1998). The opening up of Latin America after the overthrow of the Spanish empire led to the opening up of international trade between England and the Latin American republics and massive capital flows from London (and the continent) to finance infrastructure, mining and government. The investment was fueled by easy monetary policy by the Bank of England. Many of the ventures financed were fraudulent. This led to a boom on the London stock exchange. Once the capital outflows impinged on the Bank of England's gold reserves, the Bank rate was raised and the stock market crashed.

This led to a banking panic which was not quickly stemmed by lender of last resort action. A sudden stop of capital flow from London led to debt defaults, banking panics and currency crashes across Latin America. The panic in London spread to the continent and according to some sources, to the United States.

Banking panics and stock market crashes in London in 1837, 1839, 1847 and 1857 spilled over to the continent. The first two crises impacted the United States via the cotton trade. The 1847 crisis involved a railroad boom, stock market crash and harvest failure. The crisis was triggered by tight Bank of England policy. The 1857 crisis started in the United States with the failure of the Ohio Life Insurance Company, leading to a stock market crash and banking panic. This crisis augured the importance of the United States in future global financial crises. Major banking panics also occurred in London and Germany.

The crisis of 1873 had a global reach. According to Kindleberger (1978), it started with the collapse of a property boom in Germany and Austria, then spread through the continent and affected the United States as European investors dumped US railroad stocks. The United States had a major panic associated with a corporate governance scandal in the railroad sector (Benmelech and Bordo 2008). The collapse of that sector contributed to a serious and drawn out recession. The crisis spread to Latin America via a sudden stop, as the Bank of England raised its bank rate to offset gold outflows (Catão 2007). This led to a series of debt defaults across the region and a banking crisis in Peru (Reinhart and Rogoff 2009).

The Classical Gold Standard Era, 1880–1913

The pre-World War I classical gold standard era witnessed two major global financial crises: 1890–93 and 1907–08. In both periods banking, currency and debt crises occurred in countries across the world. In some of the countries affected, output losses were very large (Bordo and Eichengreen 1999).

In a three-year span, there were two big crises centered on 1890 and 1893, with crisis events also occurring in the intervening years.

The 1890 crisis is usually termed the Baring crisis. In the 1880s substantial capital flows from the advanced countries of Western Europe to develop the infrastructure of the periphery occurred during a period of sluggish domestic demand. Major recipients of these funds were Argentina, Uruguay and Brazil. The associated land boom financed by generous bank lending ended in a bust consequent upon the Bank of England and other European central banks raising their discount rates to stem losses in their gold reserves (Bordo 2006). The sudden stop led to a banking crisis, debt default and currency crisis in Argentina. Barings Brothers (a leading London merchant bank), which was heavily exposed to Argentine debt, became insolvent. It was rescued by a lifeboat operation (a consortium of key London banks that agreed to backstop Barings assets with a British government guarantee) orchestrated by the Bank of England, which prevented a banking panic. But panics did occur in numerous European countries and in Latin America. In addition to Argentina, a triple crisis occurred in Portugal, while the United States, Brazil and Russia had twin crises.

In an environment of continued financial stringency following the Baring crisis, a major twin crisis broke out in the United States in 1893, reflecting concerns over threats by the Free Silver movement to its continued adherence to the gold standard (Friedman and Schwartz 1963). Australia had a major banking panic at the end of a land boom financed by British capital, triggered by a decline in the terms of trade. Other countries in crisis in 1893 included New Zealand, Italy, Greece and several Latin American countries. In this period Bordo and Murshid (2001 and 2006) find evidence of both contagion between the core and periphery countries and a significant risk of a global financial crisis.

The second major global financial crisis was in 1907. A banking panic in the autumn in the United States was at the heart of it. It may have been triggered by the Bank of England discriminating against merchant banks financing US trade, following large payments by British insurance companies to cover losses stemming from the San Francisco earthquake (Odell and Weidenmier 2004). Other countries hit by banking crises included France, Italy (which had a twin crisis), Denmark, Sweden, Japan, Chile and Mexico. This crisis led to significant output losses in several countries (Bordo and Eichengreen 1999).

The last big crisis in this era was in 1914 at the outbreak of World War I, reflecting a global demand for liquidity. Massive lender of last resort operations (for example, the United States invoked the Aldrich–Vreeland Act and issued emergency currency), the closing of stock exchanges and the imposition of capital controls in many countries prevented panics in many countries.

The Interwar Period 1919–39

The interwar period is notorious for financial crises. They occurred in two waves: 1920–25 and 1929–33.

The crises of the 1920–25 period reflected the attempts globally by central banks to unwind the inflation that had built up in the war. It also reflected global imbalances reflecting shifts in the pattern of global production and agriculture. Disinflation impinged upon the balance sheets of many European countries, leading to banking crises in the Scandinavian countries, the Netherlands and Italy, as well as in Japan, Mexico and elsewhere. Some of these were twin crises. The brief global recession of 1920–22 was quite severe.

The 1929–33 great contraction is infamous as the worst of all crisis periods. It was preceded by stock market crashes in the United States and United Kingdom. A series of banking panics in the United States beginning in October 1930 were not successfully allayed by the Federal Reserve (Friedman and Schwartz 1963; Bordo and Landon-Lane 2010) and turned a serious recession into the Great Depression. The depression was transmitted around the world by the fixed exchange rate links of the gold exchange standard (Friedman and Schwartz 1963) and by the implosion of international fiduciary currency reserves built upon a thin film of international gold reserves (Bernanke 2000). Adherents to the gold exchange standard who lacked credibility were prevented by "golden fetters" from offsetting banking panics (expansionary monetary policy would have led to a speculative attack on the gold parity) which proliferated across Europe (Eichengreen 1992). Many countries across the world also were hit by debt and currency crises. Countries extricated themselves from depression only when they left the gold standard and followed expansionary monetary policy. The banking panics and deep deflation greatly worsened the real economies of countries that experienced them (Bernanke and James 1991).

Post-World War II: Bretton Woods, 1944–73

In the Bretton Woods adjustable peg regime, characterized by widespread capital controls and extensive financial regulation designed to prevent a reoccurrence of the financial chaos of the interwar period, there were very few banking crises (or debt crises). However there were frequent currency crises, as many countries were unable to align their domestic financial policies with their pegged currencies (Bordo 1993).

The Managed Float and a Return to Globalization, 1973–2010

After the breakdown of the Bretton Woods system the global financial economy reopened. In addition, in the face of high inflation many controls on the banking and financial system began to crumble. The financial crisis problem of earlier eras returned.

Banking crises erupted in both advanced and emerging countries in the 1970s. In 1974 in the United States, Franklin National Bank was bailed out, while in Germany Herstatt Bank was not. Neither of these events were classic banking crises. Other European countries witnessed significant bank failures as did other parts of the world. In the emerging countries there were scores of currency crises. However, in this decade it is difficult to discern a global financial crisis.

The 1970s was the height of the Great Inflation, the causes of which include a misplaced emphasis on the Phillips curve, the end of the gold discipline of the Bretton Woods system and the oil price shocks of 1973 and 1978. At the end of the 1970s, the United States and other advanced countries shifted to a very tight monetary policy to break the back of inflationary expectations. In addition to precipitating one of the worst post-war recessions in many countries, the tight policies also led many countries in Latin America and elsewhere to default on debts built up in the preceding inflationary era.

In the Latin American debt crisis beginning in 1982, Mexico, Argentina, Chile, Ecuador and diverse countries such as Egypt and Turkey defaulted on their sovereign debt, triggering financial difficulties for banks across the world. Many banks had lent money to the countries affected. In the United States, key money center banks such as Chase and Citibank were bailed out.

The IMF and World Bank report scores of banking crises in emerging countries in this decade. The period 1982–84 may constitute a global financial crisis.

The 1990s was characterized by three regional financial crises: in Europe 1990–91, the Tequila Crisis in 1994 and the Asian crisis of 1997–98.[3]

The liberalization of financial markets in many countries in the late 1980s led to a series of financial crises in Europe. In the Nordic countries, freeing the banks from extensive controls led to a property boom in Sweden and Finland. A bust was triggered by the European Monetary System crisis and the breakdown of the Soviet empire. These forces produced the Nordic banking and currency crisis (Jonung and Hagberg 2005). Banks also failed in Norway. Other countries such as Italy and Australia also had banking crises in this period.

Tight Federal Reserve policy in reaction to an inflation scare may have been the trigger for a massive devaluation by Mexico in 1994. This led to a banking crisis and a rescue package arranged by the United States. Other Latin countries also were hit by debt, banking and currency crises referred to as the tequila effect. Impact on the advanced countries was minimal.

The causes for the massive currency and banking crises in Thailand, Indonesia and Korea, as well as less dramatic disruption in Hong Kong, Malaysia, the Philippines and Taiwan, include overvalued currency pegs, original sin (liability dollarization), the drying up of Japanese lending after its banking crisis, corporate malfeasance and corruption. These crises had contagion effects on other emerging countries, possibly reflecting stringency in advanced country lending. Two prominent countries were Russia, which defaulted on its debt in 1998, and Brazil, which had a serious currency crisis in 1998. A threat by the Russian crisis to the advanced countries by the incipient collapse of Long Term Capital Management (LTCM, a large hedge fund greatly exposed to Russian debt), which seriously exposed the balance sheets of important counterparties (including New York money center banks) to loss, was offset by a Federal Reserve arranged rescue.

The Asian crisis had impact across many emerging countries but did not seriously impact the advanced countries. However, many have argued that it would have had serious impacts on them, if the IMF, other governments and other agencies had not provided generous rescue packages. On the other hand, others have argued that the rescues were largely bailouts, which would engender future moral hazard (Bordo and Schwartz 2000).

EMPIRICAL EVIDENCE

Identifying Global Crises

In order to quantify the effect that a global financial crisis has on a country's real economy (business cycle), we first need to identify periods of global financial distress. To do this we assemble information on three types of financial crises: banking crises, currency crises and sovereign debt crises. We have 57 countries in our sample, which runs from 1880 to 2009. Multiple sources were used to accumulate information on these three types of crises and the information obtained was aggregated into our database. The raw data on banking, currency and debt crises can be found in Figures 2.1, 2.2 and 2.3.

The sources used were Bordo et al. (2001), Bordo and Meissner (2005), Reinhart and Rogoff (2009), Laeven and Valencia (2010) and the IMF's *World Economic Outlook*. The dating of currency crises, using an intersection between an EMP index and narratives, is similar across the chronologies as is the dating of debt crises. However, there were some differences between Bordo and coauthors and Reinhart and Rogoff on the definition of banking crises. Reinhart and Rogoff's definition is generally more liberal than ours. They include as banking crises a number of episodes that we do not, such as minor banking crises in Canada in 1893 and the United Kingdom in 1991, 1994 and 1995; and they do not include some, such as the major banking panic in the United States in 1893. Also, recent work by López-Salido and Nelson (2010) show banking crises in the post-war United States that are different from either ours or Reinhart and Rogoff's. They demarcate 1973–75, 1982–84 and 1988–91 as crises, whereas Reinhart and Rogoff designate only 1984 as a banking crisis in that period. In addition Jalil (2010) demarcates several minor banking crises for the United States in the 1920s and also in the nineteenth century that neither of us demarcates. In this chapter we include all the crises reported by the different authors. We do not distinguish between major and minor banking crises.

In order to identify periods of global crisis, we first look for clusters of crises. To do so, for each year, we count the number of crises for each category. These raw counts are reported in Figures 2.4, 2.5 and 2.6.[4] Candidate global crises are then identified using a centered moving sum of order 2 of these raw counts. That is, for each period we count the number of unique crises for the current period and for the preceding and following periods as

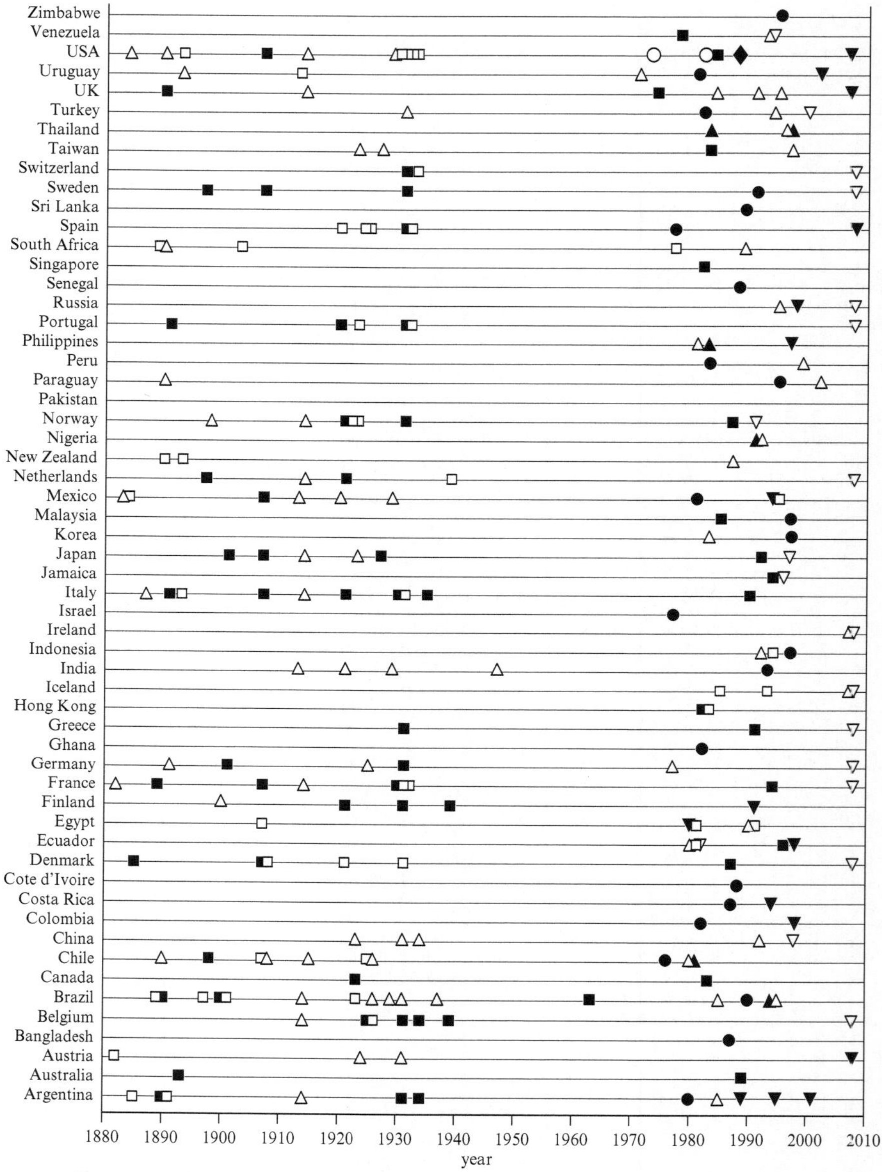

Key: □ A (Bordo et al. 2001), △ B (Reinhart and Rogoff 2009), ○ C (López-Salido and Nelson 2010), ▽ D (Laeven and Valencia 2010), ■ A+B, ▲ A+D, ▼ B+D, ● A+B+D, ◆ C+D

Figure 2.1 Banking crises dates: selected countries, 1880–2010

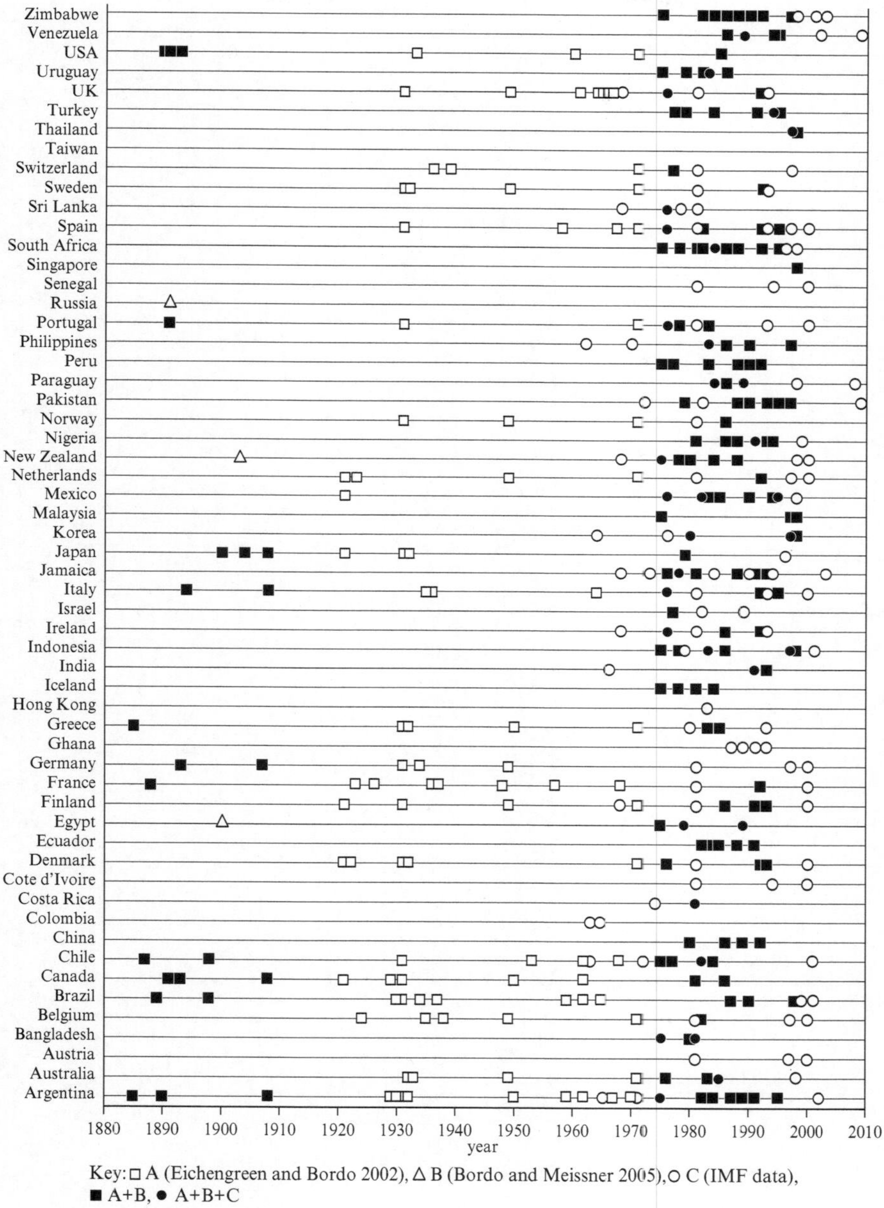

Figure 2.2 Currency crises dates: selected countries, 1880–2010

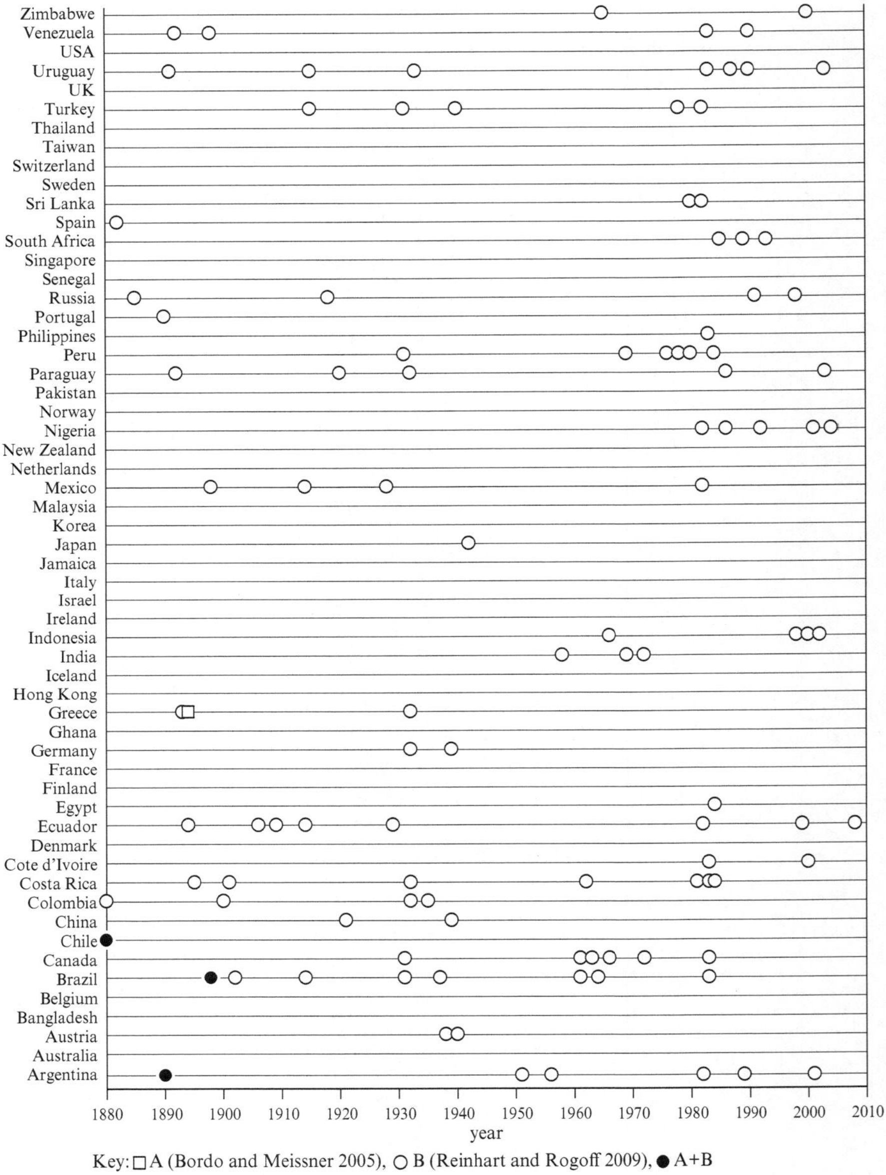

Figure 2.3 Sovereign debt crises dates: selected countries, 1880–2010

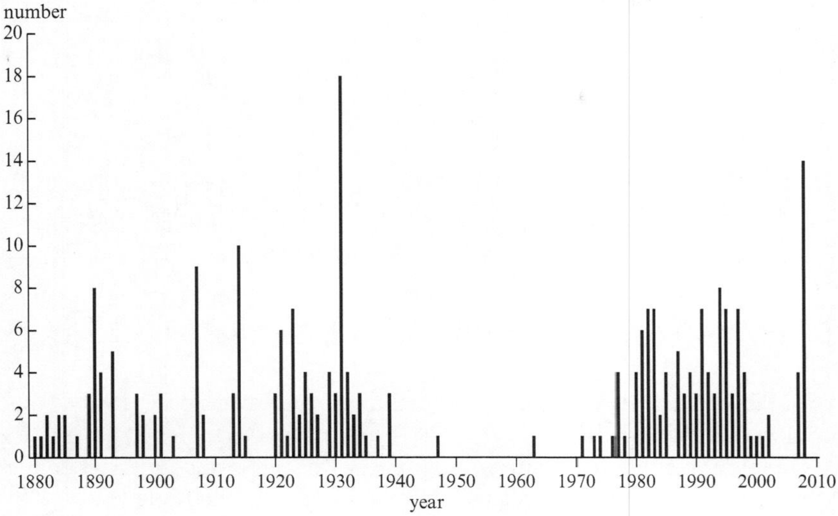

Figure 2.4 Frequency of banking crises (raw), 1880–2010

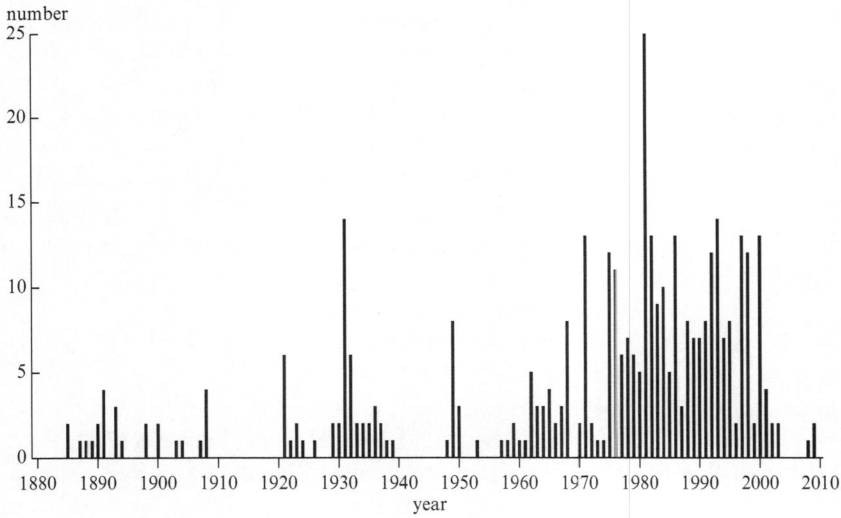

Figure 2.5 Frequency of currency crises (raw), 1880–2010

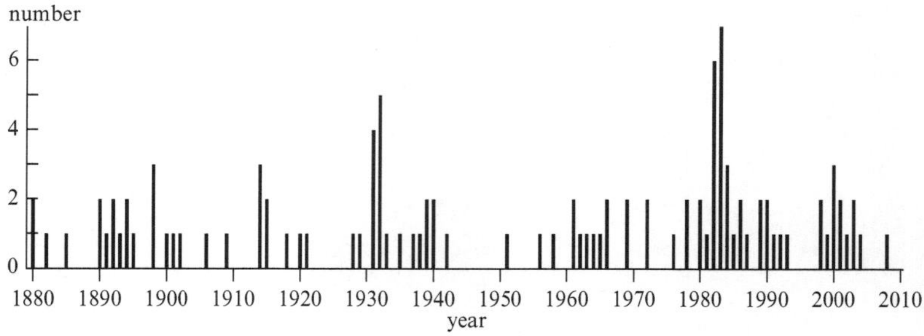

Figure 2.6 Frequency of debt crises (raw), 1880–2010

well. Peaks in the two-period moving sum series are candidates for periods of global financial crises.

One important consideration, however, is that not all countries are the same in the sense that a crisis in a large country (for example the United States) is different from a crisis in a small country (for example New Zealand) in its effect on the global economy. To account for this effect we weight each observation by the country's real GDP relative to US GDP.[5] If a banking crisis occurs in a country whose real GDP is half that of the United States, then the observation is given a weight of 0.5. This weighted count thus reflects the relative importance of the country (in terms of its size) when deciding whether a cluster of banking crises constitutes a global financial crisis.

In determining whether a cluster is a global crisis we use the following rule. First, we find a local peak of the two-period moving sum of the weighted count series, y_t. A local peak is defined to be a period (t) where

$$y_t > y_{t-1} \text{ and } y_t > y_{t+1}. \tag{2.1}$$

In case of ties, ($y_t = y_{t+1}$) then period t is chosen if $y_{t-1} > y_{t+2}$ and period $t + 1$ is chosen if $y_{t+2} > y_{t-1}$. Second, the local peak, found in (2.1), is an extreme value (thus the cluster must be large enough to be considered a rare event). And third, the countries making up the cluster must be from different geographical regions.

A peak is considered an extreme event if the weighted sum of total crises is more than three standard deviations from the mean. In order to account for outliers, the upper 10 percent of the data is first trimmed before computing the mean and standard deviation of the data. Once the cut-off is determined, we look at the boundary value of the weighted series. The crisis is considered large and rare if it is in the upper tail of the distribution

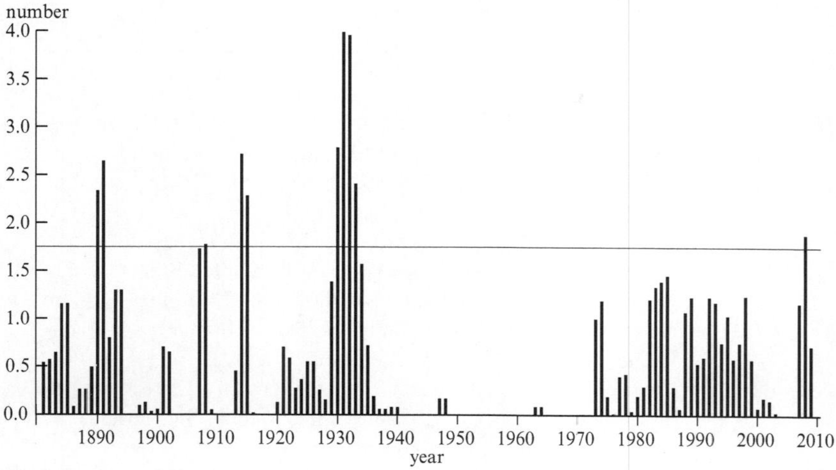

Figure 2.7 *Weighted two-period moving sum of banking crisis frequencies, 1880–2009*

and has a total combined weight that is greater than the combined output of the United States.

The preceding rule is applied to the data on banking crises, currency crises and debt crises individually. It is also applied to a combined banking and currency crisis dataset to look for global "twin" crises and to a combined banking, currency and debt crisis dataset to identify global "triple" crises, to a combined banking and debt crisis and to a combined debt and currency crisis dataset. The results are given below.

Global banking crises

The two-period weighted moving sum banking crisis series is depicted in Figure 2.7. The horizontal dashed line represents the three standard deviation threshold for (partly) determining a global crisis and is equal to 1.75. Thus the five identified global crises have a weighted sum greater than 1.75. Using the rule outlined above we found global banking crises in the following periods: 1890–91, 1907–08, 1913–14, 1931–32 and 2007–08. The countries involved in each of these global banking crises are reported in Table 2.1.

In all of the identified periods, countries from at least two (and usually more) distinct geographical regions are present. The most recent global crisis contains only countries in North America and Europe, whereas the other crises contain countries in at least three distinct geographical areas. It is also evident from Figure 2.7 that the most recent global banking crisis

Table 2.1 Global banking crises (two year window), 1890–2008

Period	Countries involved
1890–91	Argentina, Brazil, Chile, Germany, Italy, New Zealand, Paraguay, Portugal, South Africa, United Kingdom, United States
1907–08	Chile, Denmark, Egypt, France, Italy, Japan, Mexico, Sweden, United States
1913–14	Argentina, Belgium, Brazil, France, India, Italy, Japan, Mexico, Netherlands, Norway, United Kingdom, United States, Uruguay
1931–32	Argentina, Austria, Belgium, Brazil, China, Denmark, Finland, France, Germany, Greece, Italy, Norway, Portugal, Spain, Sweden, Switzerland, Turkey, United States
2007–08	Austria, Belgium, Denmark, France, Germany, Greece, Ireland, Netherlands, Portugal, Russia, Spain, Sweden, Switzerland, United Kingdom, United States

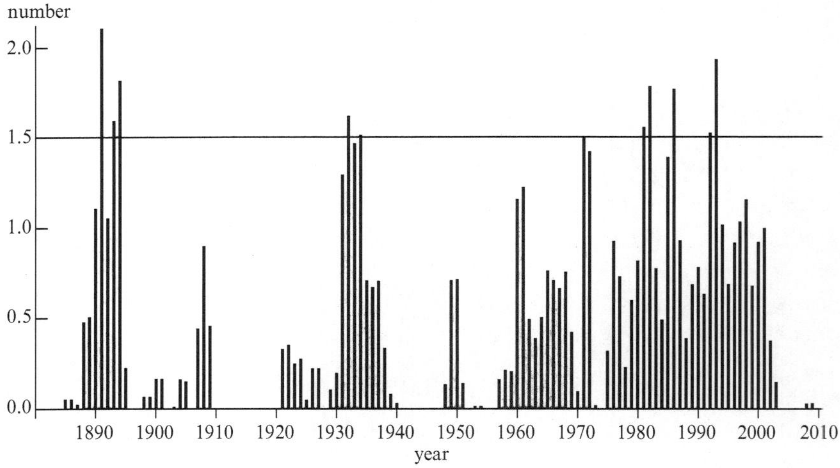

Figure 2.8 Weighted two-period moving sum of currency crisis frequencies, 1880–2009

ranks fourth in terms of the weighted sum of countries having banking crises and appears quite similar to the banking crisis of 1907–08.

Global currency crises

Figure 2.8 depicts the two period moving sum of the weighted count of currency crises, where again the weights are relative GDP in 1990 dollars. Using the same rule as described above, we identify the following periods

Table 2.2 Global currency crises, 1890–1993

Period	Countries involved
1890–91	Argentina, Canada, United States
1893–94	Canada, Germany, Italy, United States
1931–32	Argentina, Australia, Brazil, Canada, Chile, Denmark, Finland, Germany, Greece, Japan, Norway, Portugal, Spain, Sweden, United Kingdom
1933–34	Australia, Brazil, Germany, United States
1970–71	Argentina, Australia, Belgium, Denmark, Finland, Greece, Netherlands, Norway, Philippines, Portugal, Spain, Sweden, Switzerland, United States
1981–82	Argentina, Austria, Bangladesh, Belgium, Canada, Chile, Costa Rica, Cote d'Ivoire, Denmark, Ecuador, Finland, France, Germany, Ireland, Israel, Italy, Jamaica, Mexico, Netherlands, Nigeria, Norway, Pakistan, Philippines, Portugal, Senegal, South Africa, Spain, Sri Lanka, Sweden, Switzerland, United Kingdom, Uruguay, Zimbabwe
1986–87	Australia, Canada, China, Ecuador, Finland, Greece, Indonesia, Ireland, Mexico, Nigeria, Norway, Paraguay, Philippines, South Africa, United States, Uruguay, Venezuela, Zimbabwe
1992–93	China, Denmark, Finland, France, Ghana, Greece, India, Ireland, Italy, Jamaica, Netherlands, Nigeria, Pakistan, Peru, Portugal, South Africa, Spain, Sweden, United Kingdom, Zimbabwe

as global currency crises: 1890–91, 1893–94, 1931–32, 1933–34, 1970–71, 1981–82, 1986–87 and 1992–93.

The cut-off for crises to be more than three standard deviations away from the mean in this case is 1.5, thus all identified currency crises have a total weight equal to 1.5 times the size of the US economy. The countries involved in these global currency crises are reported in Table 2.2.

There are some noticeable differences in the occurrences of the currency crises compared with the global banking crises found above. The period 2007–08, where we did identify a global banking crisis, does not have a global currency crisis. In fact there are only two periods where there are both a global banking crisis and a global currency crisis. These are the 1931–32 period and the 1981–82 period.

Debt crises

Figure 2.9 depicts the weighted moving sum of the number of sovereign debt crises for the period 1880–2009. Using a threshold of three standard

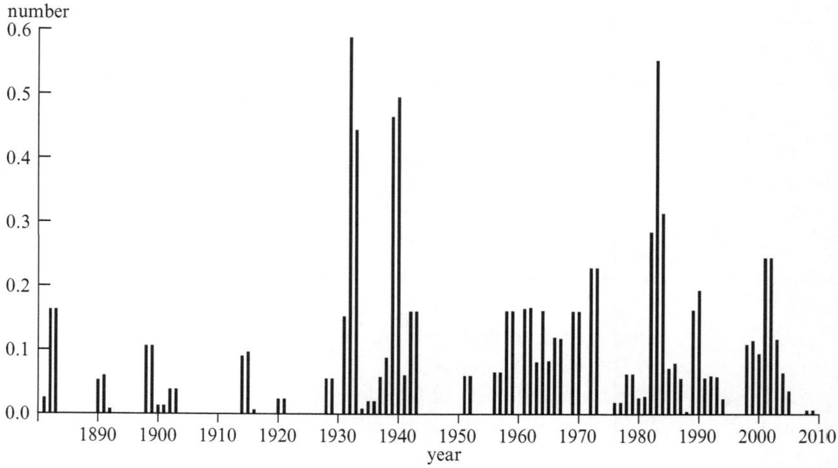

Figure 2.9 Weighted two-period moving sum of debt crisis frequencies, 1880–2009

BOX 2.1 COUNTRIES EXPERIENCING GLOBAL TWIN CRISES 1931–32

Argentina
Brazil
Denmark
Finland
Germany
Greece
Norway
Portugal
Spain
Sweden
United States

deviations above the mean, a number of peaks are identified. However, in no case was the peak large enough to be considered a global crisis; the largest peak was in 1932 and had a value of 0.58. Thus our identification does not yield any debt crisis important enough to be declared a global debt crisis. Again we do not observe any global debt crisis for the most recent period (2007–08).

Global "Twin" Crises

In the preceding sections we separately identified global crises for banking, currency and debt crisis. We found two periods where there were both

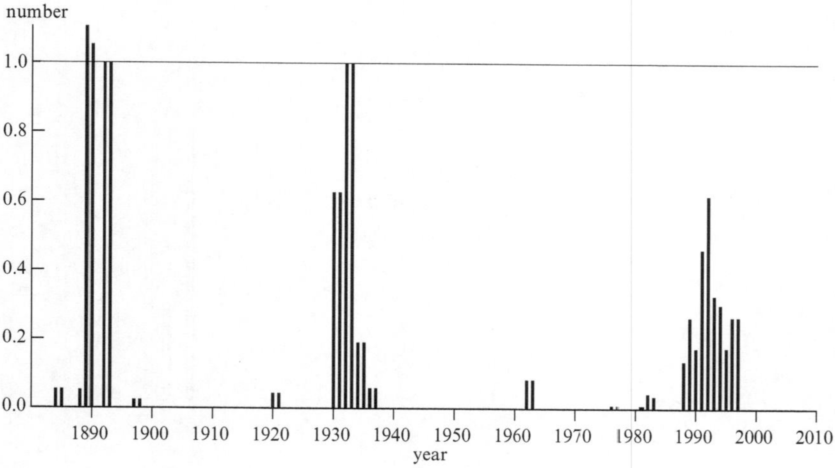

Note: Countries included in the global twin crises of 1931–32 are Argentina, Brazil, Denmark, Finland, Germany, Greece, Norway, Portugal, Spain, Sweden, and the United States.

Figure 2.10 Weighted two-period moving sum of twin banking and currency crises frequencies, 1880–2009

global banking and global currency crises. However, this approach did not check whether the countries included in each type of crisis overlapped or were different. That is, we do not know whether in these periods there were both a banking crisis and a currency crisis occurring in parallel (that is, to two different sets of countries) or in unison (that is, to the same countries). In this section we compute the weighted count of the countries having "twin" banking and currency crises concurrently (see Box 2.1). The moving sum of this weighted count of "twin" crises is depicted in Figure 2.10.

Using a threshold of three standard deviations, only one global "twin" crisis is identified: 1931–32. The two peaks around the 1890s do not constitute a global crisis, as only one country is involved in each case: Brazil for 1889 and the United States for 1893. This suggests that the other period where there is an overlap of banking crisis and currency crisis—from 1981 to 1983 (a banking crisis 1982–83 and a currency crisis 1981–82)—was a period where there were both a banking crisis and a currency crisis but that these crises affected different sets of countries.

Figures 2.11 and 2.12 show the weighted moving sum of the other twin crises (currency and debt or banking and debt), and we identify

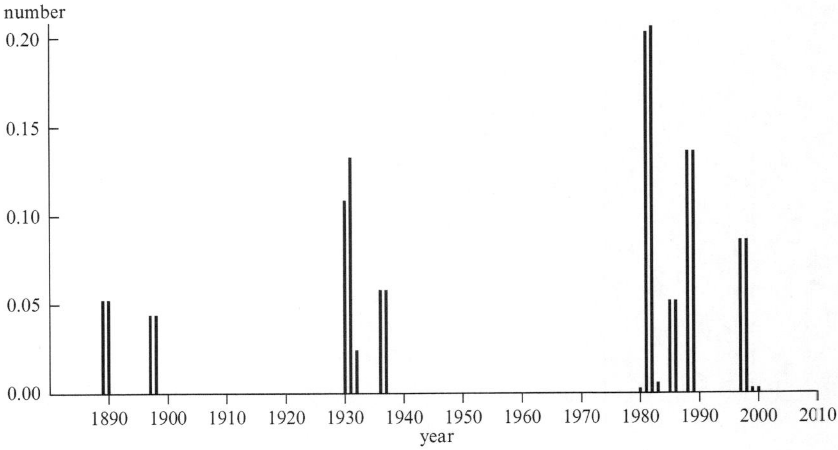

Figure 2.11 Weighted two-period moving sum of twin currency and debt crisis frequencies, 1880–2009

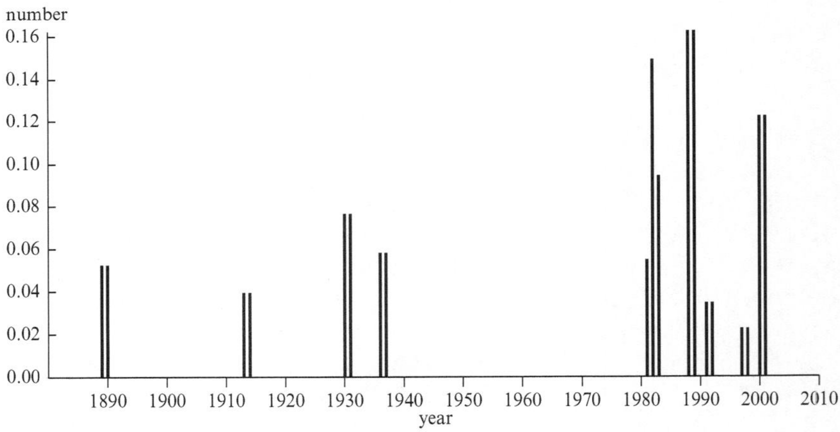

Figure 2.12 Weighted two-period moving sum of twin banking and debt crisis frequencies, 1880–2009

no periods where there were significant numbers of these types of twin crises.

Global "Triple" Crises

Previously we did not identify any periods where there were any global debt crises. In this section we compute weighted counts of countries

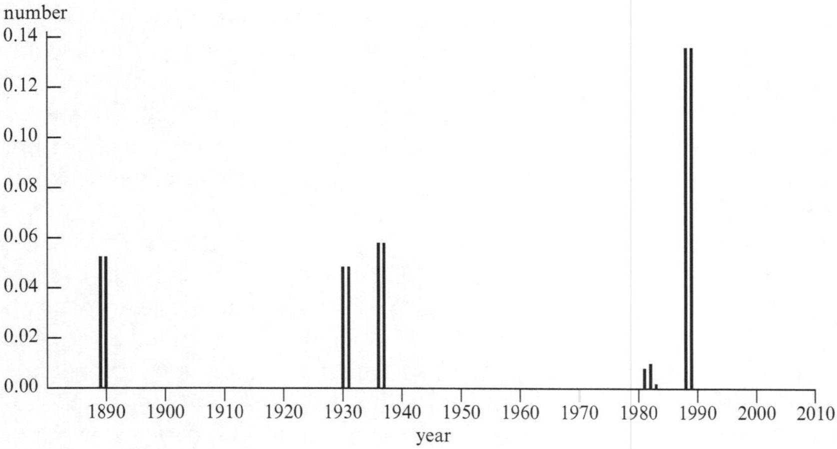

Figure 2.13 Weighted two-period moving sum of triple crisis frequencies, 1880–2009

having all three crises at once, and the moving sum of these weighted counts is depicted in Figure 2.13. Again there are no periods that we can identify where a significant number of countries had "triple" crises.

Robustness

In order to check that our findings are robust to our method, we tried a number of alternative approaches. First we used a fixed threshold to identify a global crisis rather than use the three standard deviations approach described above. Second we used a three-period moving average instead of the two-period moving average reported above. Third, we used relative per capita real income rather than relative real income as the weight. For all alternatives, the main conclusions that we draw are unaltered. The main differences between the alternative approaches are the identification of smaller crises periods when using per capita real income as the weight. All the crises periods identified above are identified using the other methods.

COMPARING AND QUANTIFYING THE CRISES

In the previous section we used informal "cluster" analysis to identify global crises. In that section we combined datasets on crises from a number of sources and counted the number of observed crises to look for clusters of crises across the world. In this section we turn our attention to quantifying the "cost" of a recession and compare these costs across the different types of crisis and noncrisis periods. In order to be consistent, we use a restricted dataset that consists of countries for which we have data that span the entire sample period from 1880 to 2009. This restricted set of countries is nonetheless quite varied and consists of countries from many regions, a variety of levels of development and a variety of levels of openness.

The countries included in this analysis are Argentina, Australia, Austria, Belgium, Brazil, Canada, Chile, Denmark, Finland, France, Germany, Italy, Japan, the Netherlands, New Zealand, Norway, Portugal, Spain, Sweden, Switzerland, the United Kingdom, the United States and Uruguay. In order to quantify the loss caused by a recession, we first date business cycles for each country by looking for peaks and troughs of real output for each country, using a common business cycle dating algorithm. We then compute the cost of each recession for each country and compare this cost across the many different types of crisis periods identified above.

The set of countries included in our analysis is kept constant over the whole sample, even though data for other countries become available over time, as we wanted to keep a consistent set of countries for the analysis and to not bias our results. If the countries to be added were chosen randomly, one would not expect the results to be affected by the addition of extra countries in the later periods, but it is fair to assume that the availability of data is not a random event and is most likely a function of a country's development. Also the aim of this exercise is to compare recessions across different crisis periods, so it is important to have a consistent set of countries across time.

Data

The data that we use is real output in constant 1990 dollars and comes from the dataset compiled by Angus Maddison.[6] This methodology is described in more detail in Maddison (2007), but nominal output for each country is first converted into 1990 local currency units and then converted into 1990 dollars using a database of international comparisons reported by the World Bank in 1990.

Identifying Cycles and Measuring Loss

In order to have a consistent set of dating rules across each country in our sample, we use the business cycle dating procedure of Bry and Boschan (1971), which was updated by Harding and Pagan (2000, 2002). Here we date the classical cycle—that is, the turning points of the level of real

Table 2.3 Peak and trough years used in empirical analysis, by country

Country	Years
Argentina	
peak years	1885, 1889, 1894, 1896, 1899, 1901, 1906, 1910, 1912, 1920, 1924, 1929, 1935, 1937, 1941, 1944, 1948, 1951, 1958, 1961, 1965, 1974, 1977, 1979, 1984, 1987, 1994, 1998, 2008
trough years	1886, 1891, 1895, 1897, 1900, 1902, 1907, 1911, 1917, 1921, 1925, 1932, 1936, 1938, 1943, 1945, 1950, 1952, 1959, 1963, 1966, 1976, 1978, 1982, 1985, 1990, 1995, 2002
Australia	
peak years	1881, 1883, 1885, 1887, 1889, 1891, 1894, 1896, 1898, 1900, 1904, 1910, 1913, 1926, 1938, 1943, 1951, 1956, 1960, 1976, 1981, 1989
trough years	1882, 1884, 1886, 1888, 1890, 1893, 1895, 1897, 1899, 1902, 1905, 1912, 1918, 1931, 1939, 1946, 1952, 1957, 1961, 1977, 1983, 1991
Austria	
peak years	1881, 1884, 1887, 1892, 1899, 1902, 1907, 1912, 1922, 1929, 1939, 1941, 1944, 1974, 1977, 1980, 1992, 2008
trough years	1882, 1885, 1889, 1893, 1901, 1903, 1909, 1919, 1923, 1933, 1940, 1942, 1945, 1975, 1978, 1981, 1993
Belgium	
peak years	1883, 1887, 1890, 1900, 1913, 1916, 1928, 1933, 1937, 1939, 1951, 1957, 1974, 1980, 1982, 1992, 2008
trough years	1884, 1888, 1891, 1901, 1915, 1918, 1932, 1934, 1938, 1943, 1952, 1958, 1975, 1981, 1983, 1993
Brazil	
peak years	1890, 1895, 1898, 1901, 1906, 1909, 1911, 1913, 1917, 1923, 1928, 1938, 1941, 1955, 1962, 1964, 1980, 1987, 1989, 1997, 2000, 2002, 2008
trough years	1894, 1897, 1900, 1904, 1908, 1910, 1912, 1914, 1918, 1925, 1931, 1940, 1942, 1956, 1963, 1965, 1983, 1988, 1992, 1999, 2001, 2003
Canada	
peak years	1882, 1884, 1888, 1891, 1894, 1903, 1907, 1913, 1917, 1928, 1944, 1947, 1953, 1956, 1981, 1989, 2007
trough years	1883, 1885, 1889, 1893, 1896, 1904, 1908, 1914, 1921, 1933, 1946, 1949, 1954, 1958, 1982, 1992
Chile	
peak years	1882, 1887, 1891, 1893, 1895, 1898, 1902, 1904, 1908, 1910, 1913, 1918, 1920, 1925, 1929, 1937, 1940, 1943, 1946, 1948, 1953, 1955, 1958, 1963, 1971, 1981, 1998, 2008
trough years	1885, 1888, 1892, 1894, 1897, 1900, 1903, 1905, 1909, 1911, 1915, 1919, 1921, 1927, 1932, 1938, 1941, 1944, 1947, 1949, 1954, 1956, 1959, 1965, 1975, 1983, 1999

Table 2.3 (continued)

Country	Years
Denmark	
peak years	1883, 1887, 1911, 1914, 1916, 1920, 1923, 1931, 1939, 1944, 1950, 1962, 1973, 1979, 1992, 2007
trough years	1885, 1888, 1912, 1915, 1918, 1921, 1925, 1932, 1941, 1945, 1951, 1963, 1975, 1981, 1993
Finland	
peak years	1883, 1890, 1898, 1900, 1907, 1913, 1916, 1929, 1938, 1943, 1952, 1957, 1975, 1989, 2008
trough years	1881, 1884, 1892, 1899, 1902, 1908, 1915, 1918, 1932, 1940, 1945, 1953, 1958, 1977, 1993
France	
peak years	1882, 1894, 1896, 1899, 1907, 1909, 1912, 1916, 1920, 1924, 1926, 1929, 1933, 1937, 1939, 1974, 1992, 2007
trough years	1885, 1895, 1897, 1902, 1908, 1910, 1914, 1918, 1921, 1925, 1927, 1932, 1935, 1938, 1944, 1975, 1993
Germany	
peak years	1885, 1890, 1900, 1913, 1918, 1922, 1928, 1939, 1944, 1974, 1981, 1989, 1992, 2001, 2008
trough years	1886, 1891, 1901, 1915, 1919, 1923, 1932, 1940, 1946, 1975, 1982, 1990, 1993, 2003
Italy	
peak years	1882, 1887, 1890, 1893, 1896, 1901, 1909, 1913, 1918, 1926, 1929, 1932, 1935, 1937, 1939, 1974, 1992, 2002, 2007
trough years	1881, 1884, 1889, 1892, 1894, 1897, 1902, 1910, 1914, 1921, 1927, 1931, 1934, 1936, 1938, 1945, 1975, 1993, 2003
Japan	
peak years	1882, 1887, 1890, 1892, 1895, 1898, 1901, 1903, 1907, 1913, 1919, 1921, 1925, 1929, 1933, 1940, 1943, 1973, 1992, 1997, 2000, 2007
trough years	1881, 1884, 1888, 1891, 1893, 1896, 1899, 1902, 1905, 1909, 1914, 1920, 1923, 1927, 1931, 1934, 1942, 1945, 1974, 1993, 1999, 2001
Netherlands	
peak years	1888, 1892, 1895, 1899, 1903, 1906, 1913, 1916, 1928, 1937, 1939, 1957, 1960, 1974, 1980, 2001, 2008
trough years	1891, 1893, 1896, 1900, 1904, 1908, 1914, 1918, 1934, 1938, 1944, 1958, 1961, 1975, 1982, 2003
New Zealand	
peak years	1881, 1884, 1887, 1890, 1892, 1896, 1900, 1903, 1907, 1911, 1914, 1920, 1923, 1925, 1929, 1938, 1943, 1947, 1950, 1954, 1959, 1961, 1966, 1969, 1974, 1976, 1984, 1987, 1989, 1997, 2007

Table 2.3 (continued)

Country	Years
New Zealand	
trough years	1883, 1885, 1888, 1891, 1894, 1897, 1901, 1904, 1909, 1913, 1918, 1922, 1924, 1927, 1932, 1941, 1944, 1948, 1951, 1955, 1960, 1962, 1968, 1970, 1975, 1977, 1985, 1988, 1992, 1998
Norway	
peak years	1881, 1885, 1893, 1897, 1902, 1916, 1920, 1923, 1930, 1939, 1941, 1957, 1981, 1987, 2008
trough years	1883, 1886, 1895, 1898, 1904, 1918, 1921, 1924, 1931, 1940, 1944, 1958, 1982, 1988
Portugal	
peak years	1888, 1890, 1893, 1900, 1904, 1907, 1912, 1914, 1916, 1923, 1925, 1927, 1929, 1934, 1937, 1939, 1941, 1944, 1947, 1951, 1973, 1982, 1992, 2002, 2007
trough years	1889, 1892, 1894, 1902, 1906, 1909, 1913, 1915, 1918, 1924, 1926, 1928, 1930, 1936, 1938, 1940, 1942, 1945, 1948, 1952, 1975, 1984, 1993, 2003
Spain	
peak years	1883, 1888, 1892, 1894, 1901, 1909, 1911, 1913, 1916, 1925, 1927, 1929, 1932, 1935, 1940, 1944, 1947, 1952, 1958, 1980, 1992, 2008
trough years	1887, 1890, 1893, 1896, 1905, 1910, 1912, 1914, 1919, 1926, 1928, 1931, 1933, 1938, 1941, 1945, 1949, 1953, 1959, 1981, 1993
Sweden	
peak years	1881, 1883, 1885, 1891, 1899, 1901, 1904, 1907, 1916, 1920, 1930, 1939, 1951, 1976, 1980, 1990, 2007
trough years	1882, 1884, 1887, 1892, 1900, 1902, 1905, 1909, 1918, 1921, 1932, 1941, 1952, 1978, 1981, 1993
Switzerland	
peak years	1881, 1886, 1888, 1890, 1893, 1899, 1902, 1906, 1911, 1915, 1920, 1929, 1933, 1938, 1940, 1948, 1951, 1957, 1974, 1981, 1990, 1994, 2001, 2008
trough years	1883, 1887, 1889, 1891, 1894, 1901, 1903, 1908, 1914, 1918, 1921, 1932, 1935, 1939, 1943, 1949, 1952, 1958, 1976, 1983, 1993, 1995, 2003
United Kingdom	
peak years	1883, 1889, 1899, 1902, 1907, 1918, 1925, 1929, 1938, 1943, 1949, 1951, 1957, 1973, 1979, 1990, 2008
trough years	1885, 1893, 1901, 1904, 1908, 1921, 1926, 1931, 1939, 1947, 1950, 1952, 1958, 1975, 1981, 1992

Table 2.3 (continued)

Country	Years
United States	
peak years	1883, 1887, 1889, 1892, 1895, 1901, 1903, 1906, 1909, 1913, 1916, 1919, 1926, 1929, 1937, 1944, 1948, 1953, 1957, 1969, 1973, 1979, 1981, 1990, 2000, 2007
trough years	1885, 1888, 1890, 1894, 1896, 1902, 1904, 1908, 1910, 1914, 1917, 1921, 1928, 1933, 1938, 1947, 1949, 1954, 1958, 1970, 1975, 1980, 1982, 1991, 2001
Uruguay	
peak years	1883, 1886, 1888, 1894, 1896, 1899, 1904, 1908, 1910, 1912, 1919, 1924, 1928, 1930, 1939, 1941, 1954, 1956, 1958, 1961, 1966, 1970, 1981, 1987, 1994, 1998
trough years	1881, 1884, 1887, 1890, 1895, 1898, 1900, 1905, 1909, 1911, 1915, 1920, 1925, 1929, 1933, 1940, 1943, 1955, 1957, 1959, 1963, 1967, 1972, 1984, 1988, 1995, 2002

output—using the following rules: the minimum length of a cycle is two years; a recession or an expansion has to be at least one year in length; and peaks and troughs must alternate. The actual peak years and trough years that we use can be found in Table 2.3.

It should be noted that we could have alternatively looked at growth cycles—turning points in the growth rate of real output—but in order to be consistent across the whole sample period of 1880–2009, we compare only classical cycles. This means that for latter periods, where the growth of real output is high, some countries have very long cycles.

There are many different approaches to quantifying the loss of a recession. Some, for example Bordo et al. (2001) and Laeven and Valencia (2010), use a measure of how long the economy took to get back to a measure of "potential" output as a measure of the severity of the recession. Harding and Pagan (2002) discuss a number of different approaches to measuring the severity of a recession, including duration (time from peak to trough), amplitude (percentage loss from peak output to trough output) and accumulated loss (the sum of the percentage differences from peak output to all output levels for each period of the recession). This last-named measure approximates out horizontally, for the duration of the recession, the area above the actual level of output and the projection of peak output. Harding and Pagan (2002) also use a measure of the steepness of the recession by measuring the difference between the actual accumulated loss and the loss if actual output followed a straight line from peak output to trough output, which they call an excess loss measure.

In our approach we use the accumulated percentage loss as our measure of the severity of a recession. This measure has the benefit of combining information about the recession's depth and duration into one number. The problem with using only amplitude or only duration is that it would be hard to compare a short but sharp recession with a long but shallow recession. Which of these recessions is worse? One would have a longer duration and the other would have larger amplitude. The accumulated percentage loss measures the total loss due to a recession as a percentage of the peak level of output and is able to compare all types of recessions. We do not use the other Harding and Pagan (2002) measure (the excess measure), as our dating rules allow for one year recessions, which would necessarily yield zero excess.

The other measures mentioned above (the ones that measure how long it takes the economy to get back to a measure of potential output) are not used either. The main reason is that we want to compare the severity of the most recent banking crisis in terms of the effect on the severity of recession during this period. As most economies in our sample had peaks in either 2007 or 2008, there are not enough data to compute this measure. Since we are not able to use this duration measure to compare the severity of recessions across the different periods with the most recent recessions, we do not report the severity measures of Bordo et al. (2001).

Results from our Comparisons

As noted above, we use a consistent classical business cycle dating algorithm to date classical business cycles for each of the 23 countries in our sample from 1880 until 2009.[7] For each recession that is identified, we compute the accumulated percentage loss of the recession compared with the counterfactual that the country stayed at peak output for the entire duration of the recession. If the last identified turning point was a peak, then we measured the accumulated loss from this peak until the end of the sample in 2009. For most countries the last identified peak was in 2007 and 2008, and there is considerable evidence that these countries troughed by 2009 (although the algorithm cannot determine this without knowing the level of output for 2010). Given that we do not know the actual trough dates for the last recession, we obviously run the risk of having truncated measures, but we do not think this is a major issue, given that most of the countries in our sample appear to have troughed by the end of 2009.

In order to account for country size, we weight each loss measure by the country's GDP relative to that of the United States. Once we compute the measure of severity for each recession, we then compare the severity of recessions over all of the sample and in particular during periods of crisis. Some summary statistical results on the severity of the recessions can be

Table 2.4 Summary statistics for weighted cumulative percentage loss in a recession

Category	Mean	Median	Interquartile range
All recessions	−1.12	−0.15	[−0.68, −0.05]
Noncrisis	−0.62	−0.10	[−0.51, −0.03]
Any crisis	−1.20	−0.15	[−0.71, −0.05]
Banking crises			
All countries	−3.03	−0.62	[−2.03, −0.17]
Crisis countries	−4.56	−0.66	[−2.39, −0.17]
Currency crises			
All countries	−1.21	−0.15	[−0.71, −0.05]
Crisis countries	−1.54	−0.33	[−1.29, −0.11]

found in Table 2.4. The statistics that are reported are the mean of the distribution, the median of the distribution, and the 25th and 75th percentiles (the interquartile range).

The first number reported in Table 2.4 is for all recessions in our sample. The mean weighted (weighted by relative GDP) accumulated percentage loss for all recessions in our sample is −1.12 percent, but it is clear that the distribution of accumulated losses is highly skewed to the left, as the median and 25th and 75th percentiles are much smaller at −0.15, −0.68 and −0.05 percents, respectively. Thus the distribution of accumulated loss of a recession is skewed to the left with a large number of large negative losses. That is, the distribution has a "fat" lower tail.

Next we report the mean, median and interquartile range for those recessions that do not overlap any of the crisis (banking, currency or debt) periods and for those that do overlap with any of the crisis periods.[8] The mean accumulated loss during a crisis period is approximately twice that for recessions that occur outside of any of the crisis windows. The median and 25th percentiles are also shifted left, suggesting that recessions during crises are worse, in terms of accumulated percentage loss, than recessions during noncrisis periods.

We next split the crisis periods into their respective types and report results for the types of crises that we identify: banking crises and currency crises. Looking first at banking crises (periods where there is a global banking crisis), we observe that the loss distribution is heavily skewed to the left, with a mean loss of around −3.03 percent and a median loss of around −0.62 percent. We also split the sample into those countries that actually have a banking crisis and those that do not (but nonetheless have a recession during a global banking crisis) and find that countries

Table 2.5 Summary statistics for weighted cumulative percentage loss: individual banking crises, 1890–2008

Crisis	Mean	Median	Interquartile range
1890–91			
All countries	−1.19	−0.52	[−1.39, −0.20]
Crisis countries	−1.91	−1.11	[−2.34, −0.39]
1907–08			
All countries	−1.12	−0.21	[−0.35, −0.12]
Crisis countries	−2.95	−0.30	[−5.70, −0.21]
1913–14			
All countries	−2.44	−0.63	[−2.31, −0.18]
Crisis countries	−2.09	−0.63	[−2.85, −0.21]
1931–32			
All countries	−6.92	−1.94	[−2.98, −0.61]
Crisis countries	−9.35	−1.18	[−2.19, −0.24]
2007–08			
All countries	−1.00	−0.51	[−1.19, −0.10]
Crisis countries	−1.08	−0.15	[−1.53, −0.10]

that have a banking crisis have slightly larger losses than countries that do not.

The pattern for the currency crises is different. Again a currency crisis is a period where there is a currency crisis. First it is clear that recessions during currency crises are not as severe as those during banking crises. There appears to be a discernable difference between those countries having a currency crisis (their recessions are worse) than those not having a currency crisis but having a recession during a currency crisis.

Comparing Individual Banking Crises

The results of the previous section suggest that banking crises are the more important crises to consider, given that recessions associated with them are large and there appears to be more spillover from crisis countries to other countries for banking crises than other types of crises. Because of this and the fact that the most recent crisis is a "pure" banking crisis, we next focus our attention on the individual banking crises that we have identified.

The results reported in Table 2.4 are for all the banking crises across all periods and it is useful to be able to compare each crisis window to each other one. This comparison is reported in Table 2.5. Here the summary statistics are reported for each crisis window identified in the fourth

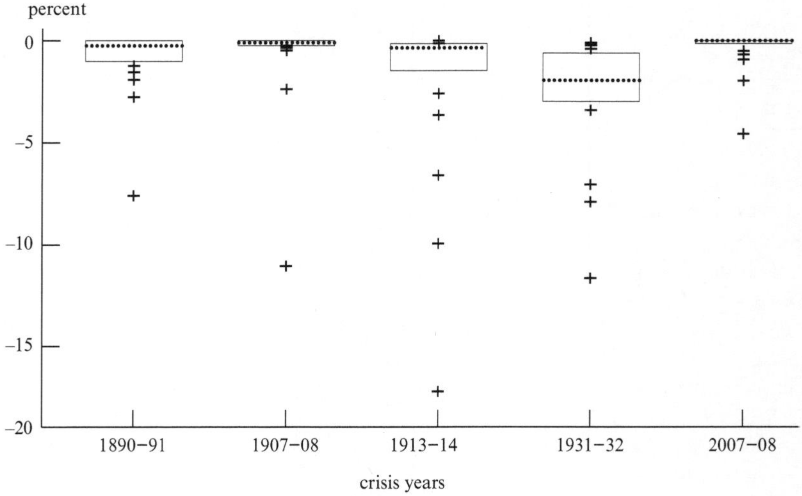

Note: For Figures 2.14 and 2.15, the left tail of the distribution for the 1931–32 crisis is cut off at -30 percent. Some observations with weighted losses less than -30 are not reported.

Figure 2.14 Distributions of accumulated percentage loss for banking crises: all countries, 1890–91 to 2007–08

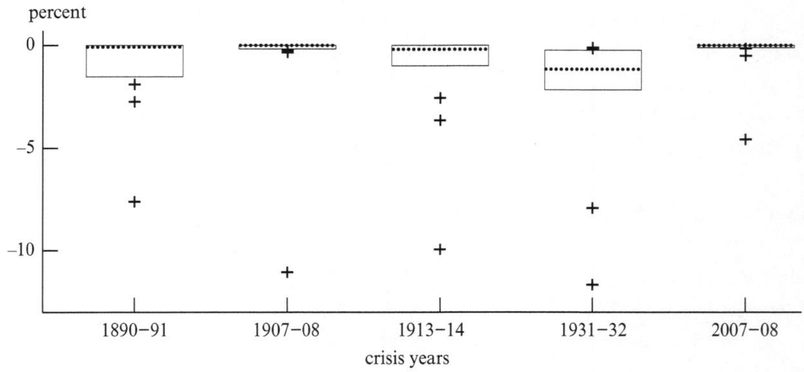

Figure 2.15 Distributions of accumulated percentage loss for banking crises: crisis countries, 1890–91 to 2007–08

section above. The results show that clearly the banking crisis of the 1930s was associated with much more severe recessions than any other crisis window. The most recent crisis has relatively small losses compared with the other major banking crises.

Another interesting point to note about the most recent crisis is that the tail of the accumulated loss distribution is not as "fat" as for the other preceding crises. Figures 2.14 and 2.15 contain boxplot graphs depicting the weighted accumulated percentage loss distributions for each of the identified banking crises windows. The boxplots graphically report the same information as Table 2.5. More importantly they also report the tail of the distribution. Each boxplot reports a box which runs from the 25th percentile to the 75th percentile. The dotted line reports the median. The closer the dotted line is to the 75th percentile (the top line of the box in this case) the more skewed the distribution. Any observations that lie outside the interquartile range are depicted with '+' symbols.

Looking at Figures 2.14 and 2.15 we see that the most recent crisis is the only crisis without a very long lower (left) tail. Alternatively, if the distribution is skewed like the other crises, the tail is much shorter. Unlike the other crises, there are no really large losses associated with the most recent crisis, with the largest accumulated loss being less than 5 percent.

The conclusions one can draw from these observations is that the recessions associated with the most recent financial crisis were indeed quite unprecedented given first that the output losses were at the low end of what we would have expected after looking at the previous major banking crises and second that we did not observe any really large negative losses (no fat left tail). This is unprecedented, given the previous experience of global banking crises.

DISCUSSION

Our empirical evidence in the preceding section indicates that since 1880 the world has witnessed five global financial (banking) crises.[9] This result is based on our aggregation of several chronologies of banking crises, where we calculate a moving sum of the weighted counts by country size and condition on crisis incidence across continents. When we add in currency crises and search for global twin crises, we find only one: in the 1930s. When we add debt crises to the total, we find that no triple global crises occurred. In terms of incidence weighted by country size, the 1930s was the worst global crisis by far, followed by the recent crisis. Although the number of countries affected by crises was lower than some of the historic crises, the presence of the United States and other major countries makes the recent crisis important in terms of the number and size of countries involved.

We also measured the output losses in global crises. We used a business cycle dating algorithm to date classical business cycles and for each recession we computed the accumulated percentage loss as our measure of the severity of a recession. We found that the distribution of recessions associated with crises was highly skewed with a fat left tail and that the mean accumulated percentage loss was higher for recessions associated with crises than those that were not associated with crises. We also found that recessions associated with banking crises were worse than those associated with currency crises, and we found that banking crises appeared to affect all countries more than currency crises. The losses during recessions associated with currency crises were larger for those countries that did have a currency crisis than for those that did not.

We then compared the five global banking crises that we identified and found that the recessions associated with the most recent crisis were quite similar in average loss to the 1907–08 crisis but not as large as in the 1890–91 and the 1913–14 crises (see Table 2.5). The other important finding is that the most recent crisis is not associated with a highly skewed loss distribution. Unlike all other banking crises, there are no really large negative losses. This result is unprecedented.

Thus, global financial crises have occurred before this one. The most recent crisis appears quite similar in its economic impact to the crisis of 1907–08 in that the recessions associated with it are small relative to other crises in history. It is certainly not the worst crisis in recent history and is most likely not the worst crisis since the Great Depression, at least with respect to output losses of recessions associated with the crisis.

Moreover, from our evidence we see that there is a clear link between international financial crises and the severity of recessions. Indeed global crises may help synchronize the business cycle (Bordo and Helbling 2010).

We summarize some possible factors that can explain the incidence of global financial crises. First, international financial crises since at least 1857 seem to occur when the United States (the largest economy since the end of the nineteenth century) is involved. One strong possible reason for the US involvement in global financial crises is that the US banking system has long been crisis prone. In the pre-1914 era this reflected two basic problems: unit banking and the absence of an effective lender of last resort. This contrasted with many of the other advanced countries, which had nationwide branch banking systems (which could more easily diversify portfolios across regions) and also had central banks (which had learned by the 1870s to act as lenders of last resort to the financial system). London was also important as a focal point for the global transmission of crises before 1914, but the Bank of England had learned to become an effective lender of last resort. England had its last banking crisis in 1866.

Since 1914 the United States has had a central bank, the Federal Reserve, which was established in large part to prevent the type of banking panics that characterized the national banking era (1865–1914). However the Federal Reserve failed in its role as lender of last resort to allay a series of banking panics in the 1930s, which it is argued precipitated the Great Depression. In addition the United States kept unit banking (in most states) after the establishment of the Federal Reserve until very recently.

The United States has, since 1865, had a dual banking system in which state banks (with lower capital and reserve requirements) have been regulated by state banking authorities, while national banks have been regulated by the federal Comptroller of the Currency. According to White (1983) this fostered regulatory competition, inefficiency and instability. Moreover for seven decades after 1914 member banks of the Federal Reserve (all national banks and some state banks) were supervised by the Federal Reserve. Since the 1930s a new patchwork of regulatory agencies has proliferated to supervise and regulate the diverse parts of the nonbank financial system. Heavy regulation may explain the absence of banking crises in the United States (as well as the rest of the world) from the 1930s to the 1970s. The lack of regulatory coordination and failures in supervision in the United States may have been a cause of the recent crisis.

Second, financial globalization seems to be an important part of the story of global financial crises. The free movement of global capital and frequent sudden stops was a key element in the global crisis environment of the nineteenth century (Bordo et al. 2010). These patterns have re-emerged in the second era of globalization since the 1970s.

Third, the international monetary regime was also important in the proliferation of crises. When the world was on the gold standard both before and after World War I, crises were transmitted by fixed exchange rates and, in the interwar period when credibility was low, "golden fetters" prevented many countries from offsetting them. Moreover, the alternating waves of inflation and deflation that reflected the automatic operation of the gold standard pre-1914 may have itself triggered financial instability leading to crises (Bordo 1990). However, today most countries (with the principal exception of the European Monetary Union) are in a managed float regime, and global financial crises are present. This suggests that increasingly tighter linkages between global financial markets and burgeoning capital flows today operate independently of the exchange rate regime.

Fourth, asset booms fueled by capital inflows and busts triggered by sudden stops were key elements in many of the international financial crises prior to World War I. In the interwar period, the 1920s stock market boom was similar in many respects to the railroad booms of the nineteenth century and was fueled by international capital flows (Eichengreen 1992; Bordo 2003). Finance for both the technology boom of the late 1990s and the recent property booms in the United States and elsewhere had an important international element manifest in the international scope of securitization and the global proliferation of derivatives.

POLICY LESSONS

What are some of the policy lessons to be learned from the historical record of global financial crises?

First, the historical record suggests that international financial crises before 1914 largely burned themselves out. Countries (such as Britain) that had effective lenders of last resort in place insulated themselves from them. Others did not and (like the United States) had to suspend convertibility of bank liabilities into currency. Also the absence of a lender of last resort in the United States and key flaws in its banking system made it an important catalyst for international crises because of its economic importance. Moreover, in this era although there was minimal policy coordination (for example between the Bank of England and the Banque de France in the 1907 crisis), it was minimal and episodic (Flandreau 1997; Bordo and Schwartz 1999). In the interwar period, the League of Nations was largely ineffective in coordinating rescues, as were other intergovernmental arrangements (Bordo and Schwartz 1999).

In the post-war period, the IMF and other agencies have dealt with currency crises and debt crises to some effect. The resolution of banking crises has been largely done by national monetary authorities. The growing problem of liability dollarization prevented lender of last resort operations in dollars in the Asian countries hit by crisis in 1997–98. Their problems were solved by massive international rescues. A similar problem arose in the aftermath of the recent crisis.

In the recent crisis the question is moot whether international policy coordination was effective. Many countries did lender of last resort actions to stem the financial crisis in their own countries. They also pursued expansionary monetary and fiscal policy. These actions likely prevented the recession from being worse. It is not clear that national authorities pursued these actions because of international arrangements. More likely they did it because they had learned some lessons from the Great Depression.

The lesson from history that countries with sound financial systems, effective lenders of last resort and efficient financial supervision and regulation fared better in global financial crises than others has held up in the recent crisis (Bordo and Meissner 2005). Countries such as Canada, Australia and New Zealand, whose banks were less exposed to mortgage backed securities, whose banks did not have structured investment vehicles and did not have underregulated shadow banking systems, largely avoided the recent crisis.

Second, what seems to be novel about the recent crisis is the extent to which financial innovation—partly in response to the supervision and regulation of the banking systems and financial markets in place in the United States and other advanced countries—led to the development of securitization, derivatives and off balance sheet entities designed to evade capital requirements. These innovations were globally linked through financial globalization. This increased global systemic risk. In earlier eras, stock (and bond) markets across countries were linked together during crises, but the linkages are much tighter today and occur across virtually all international financial markets. This development may make the case for enhanced global financial supervision and regulation to ameliorate the systemic risks—although how to achieve this in the face of the sanctity of sovereignty is problematic, to say the least. It also may make the case for capital controls. However, it is not clear that the inefficiencies of widespread capital controls and the inevitability of evading them are worth the effort.

Finally, the fact that this crisis was one of the least costly of the global financial crises suggests that perhaps policymakers in the countries affected learned some of the lessons from the past global financial crises. They followed aggressive expansionary monetary and fiscal policies. This was certainly not the case before World War II.

NOTES

1. There is considerable overlap in the different chronologies, as Reinhart and Rogoff incorporated many of the dates of Bordo and coauthors, who used IMF and World Bank chronologies for the period since the early 1970s.
2. Reinhart and Rogoff (2009:10) have a different, more liberal definition: "We mark a banking crisis by two types of events: (1) bank runs that lead to the closure, merging or takeover by the public sector of one or more financial institutions and (2) if there are no runs, the closure, merging, takeover or large scale government assistance of an important financial institution (or group of institutions) that mark the start of a string of similar outcomes for other financial institutions."
3. Japan had a major banking crisis after the bursting of property and stock bubbles in 1989. Although this likely contributed to the Asian crisis of 1997, it was not an international financial crisis.
4. As noted above in many instances multiple authors identify the same crisis. In these cases the crisis is counted only once, so as not to bias the results toward finding a global crisis.
5. Here we use GDP in 1990 dollars as reported in Maddison (2009).
6. The dataset can be found at www.ggdc.net/maddison.
7. For Argentina we have data only for 1884.
8. A recession is deemed to overlap if any of the periods of the recession overlap with any of the periods of the crisis window.
9. This number is increased to nine crises when we use a larger window in our moving sum.

REFERENCES

Benmelech, E. and M.D. Bordo. 2008. "The Financial Crisis of 1873 and 19th Century Corporate Governance". Unpublished paper, Harvard University.

Bernanke B. and H. James. 1991. "The Gold Standard, Deflation, and Financial Crisis in the Great Depression: An International Comparison". In *Financial Markets and Financial Crises*, edited by R. Glenn Hubbard, Ch. 2. Chicago: University of Chicago Press.

Bernanke, B. 2000. *Essays on the Great Depression*. Princeton, New Jersey: Princeton University Press.

Bordo M.D. 1990. "Comments on Charles Kindleberger: The Panic of 1873". In *Crashes and Panics: The Lessons from History*, edited by Eugene N. White, pp. 132–3. Homewood, Illinois: Dow-Jones Irwin.

Bordo, M.D. 1993. "The Bretton Woods International Monetary System: An Historical Overview". In *A Retrospective on the Bretton Woods International Monetary System*, edited by M.D. Bordo and B. Eichengreen, Ch. 1. Chicago: University of Chicago Press.

Bordo, M.D. 1998. "Comment on Larry Neal: The Bank of England's First Return to Gold and the Stock Market Crash of 1825". *Federal Reserve Bank of St. Louis Review*, **80** (3): 77–82.

Bordo, M.D. 2003. "Historical Perspective on Booms, Busts and Recessions, Chapter III: When Bubbles Burst". In *World Economic Outlook*, pp. 64–6. Washington: International Monetary Fund.

Bordo, M.D. 2006. *Sudden Stops, Financial Crises, and Original Sin in Emerging Countries: Déjà vu?*. NBER Working Paper 12393. Cambridge, Massachusetts: National Bureau of Economic Research. Available at www.nber.org/papers.html.

Bordo, M.D. and B. Eichengreen. 1999. "Is Our Current Economic Environment Unusually Crisis Prone?" In *Capital Flows and the International Financial System: Proceedings of a Conference Held at the H.C. Coombs Centre for Financial Studies, Kirribilli, on 9–10 August 1999*, edited by David Gruen and Luke Gower, pp. 18–74. Canberra: Reserve Bank of Australia. Available at www.rba.gov.au/publications/confs.

Bordo, M.D. and T. Helbling. 2010. *International Business Cycle Synchronization in Historical Perspective*. NBER Working Paper 16103. Cambridge, Massachusetts: National Bureau of Economic Research.

Bordo, M.D. and J.S. Landon-Lane. 2010. "The Banking Panics in the United States in the 1930s: Some Lessons for Today". Unpublished paper, Rutgers University.

Bordo, M.D. and C.M. Meissner. 2005. *The Role of Foreign Currency Debt in Financial Crises: 1880–1913 vs. 1972–1997*. NBER Working Paper 11897. Cambridge, Massachusetts: National Bureau of Economic Research. Available at www.nber.org/papers.html.

Bordo, M.D. and C. Meissner. 2007. "Financial Crises, 1880–1913: The Role of Foreign Currency Debt". In *The Decline of Latin American Economies: Growth, Institutions, and Crises*, edited by S. Edwards, G. Esquivel and G. Márquez, Ch. 4. Chicago: University of Chicago Press.

Bordo, M.D. and A.P. Murshid. 2001. "Are Financial Crises Becoming More Contagious?" In *International Financial Contagion*, edited by Stijn Claessens and Kristin I. Forbes, pp. 367–403. Boston, Massachusetts: Kluwer Academic Publishers.

Bordo, M.D. and A.P. Murshid. 2006. "Globalization and Changing Patterns in the International Transmission of Shocks in Financial Markets". *Journal of International Money and Finance*, **25** (4): 655–74.

Bordo, M.D. and A.J. Schwartz. 1999. "Under What Circumstances, Past and Present, Have International Rescues of Countries in Financial Distress Been Successful?" *Journal of International Money and Finance*, **18** (4): 683–708.

Bordo, M.D. and A.J. Schwartz. 2000. "Measuring Real Economic Effects of Bailouts: Historical Perspectives on How Countries in Financial Distress Have Fared with and without Bailouts". *Carnegie Rochester Conference Series on Public Policy*, **53** (1): 81–167.

Bordo, M.D., B. Eichengreen, D. Klingebiel and M.S. Martinez-Peria. 2001. "Is the Crisis Problem Growing More Severe?" *Economic Policy*, **32**: 53–82.

Bordo, M.D., A. Taylor and J. Williamson. 2003. *Globalization in Historical Perspective.* Chicago: University of Chicago Press.

Bordo, M.D., A. Cavallo and C. Meissner. 2010. "Sudden Stops: Determinants and Output Effects in the First Era of Globalization, 1880–1913". *Journal of Development Economics*, **91** (2): 185–364.

Bry, G. and C. Boschan. 1971. *Cyclical Analysis of Time Series: Selected Procedures and Computer Programs.* NBER Technical Paper 20. New York: distributed by Columbia University Press for the National Bureau of Economic Research.

Catão, L. 2007. "Sudden Stops and Currency Drops: A Historical Look". In *The Decline of Latin American Economies: Growth, Institutions and Crises*, edited by S. Edwards, G. Esquivel and G. Márquez, pp. 243–90. Chicago: University of Chicago Press.

Eichengreen, B. 1992. *Golden Fetters: The Gold Standard and the Great Depression, 1919–1939.* New York: Oxford University Press.

Flandreau, M. 1997. "Central Bank Cooperation in Historical Perspective: A Skeptical View". *Economic History Review*, **50**: 735–63.

Friedman, M. and A.J. Schwartz. 1963. *A Monetary History of the United States 1867–1960.* Princeton, New Jersey: Princeton University Press.

Gorton, G. 2010. *Slapped by the Invisible Hand: The Panic of 2007.* Princeton, New Jersey: Princeton University Press.

Harding, D. and A. Pagan. 2000. "Knowing the Cycle". In *Macroeconomics and the Real World*, edited by R. Backhouse and A. Salanti, vol. 1, pp. 23–41. New York: Oxford University Press.

Harding, D. and A. Pagan. 2002. "Dissecting the Cycle: A Methodological Investigation". *Journal of Monetary Economics*, **49** (2): 365–81.

Jalil, A. 2010. "A New History of Banking Panics in the United States, 1825–1929: Construction and Implications". Unpublished paper, University of California at Berkeley. Available at academic.reed.edu/economics/jalil.

Jonung, L. and T. Hagberg. 2005. *How Costly Was the Crisis of the 1990s? A Comparative Analysis of the Deepest Crisis in Finland and Sweden over the Last 130 Years.* DG ECFIN Economic Papers 224. Brussels: Directorate General for Economic and Financial Affairs. Available at ec.europa.eu/economy_finance.

Hetzel, R. 2009. "Monetary Policy in the 2008–2009 Recession". *Economic Quarterly*, **95** (2): 201–33.

Kindleberger, C. 1978. *Manias, Panics and Crashes: A History of Financial Crises.* New York: Basic Books.

Laeven, L. and F. Valencia. 2010. *Resolution of Banking Crises: The Good, the Bad, and the Ugly.* IMF Working Paper 10/146. Washington: International Monetary Fund.

López-Salido, D. and E. Nelson. 2010. *Postwar Financial Crises and Economic Recoveries in the United States.* Federal Reserve Board of Governors (mimeo).

Maddison, A. 2007. *Contours of the World Economy, 1–2030 AD: Essays in Macro-Economic History.* Oxford: Oxford University Press.

Maddison, A. 2009. *Historical Statistics of the World Economy: 1–2008 AD.* Available at www.ggdc.net/maddison.

Neal, L. 1998. "The Financial Crisis of 1825 and the Restructuring of the British Financial System". *Federal Reserve Bank of St. Louis Review,* **80** (3): 53–76.

Odell, K. and M. Weidenmier. 2004. "Real Shock, Monetary Aftershock: The 1906 San Francisco Earthquake and the Panic of 1907". *Journal of Economic History,* **64**: 1002–27.

Reinhart, C. and K. Rogoff. 2009. *This Time Is Different: Eight Centuries of Financial Folly.* Princeton, New Jersey: Princeton University Press.

Schwartz, A.J. 1986. "Real versus Pseudo Financial Crises". In *Financial Crises and the World Banking System,* edited by F. Capie and G.E. Wood, pp. 11–31. London: MacMillan.

White, E. 1983. *The Regulation and Reform of the American Banking System, 1900–1929.* Princeton, New Jersey: Princeton University Press.

3. Responses of the Korean economy to the global crisis: another currency crisis?

Dongchul Cho

INTRODUCTION

The crisis during 2008–09 was truly *global.* Enormous impacts spread throughout the world. Reinhart and Rogoff (2009, Box 16.1), for example, identified the recent crisis as one of the two *global* crises (the other being the Great Depression) from the past two centuries of financial data.

It was no surprise that Korea, too, was severely hit by the crisis. Korea was particularly susceptible to global shocks, since its financial and export sectors were opened. Asset prices plummeted, exports collapsed, a drastic economic contraction followed and even the trauma from the financial crisis in 1997 resurfaced. Sentiments in the market were propelled to the extreme, and *The Economist* (26 February 2009) ranked Korea fourth (after South Africa, Hungary and Poland) on its list of emerging economies most likely to become the next victims of the global crisis. Yet, Korea managed to recover relatively early at a relatively strong pace.

In these respects, Korea is an interesting country to study: it is an open economy, subject to global shocks and has the experience of a crisis in its past comparable to the recent one. By examining Korea's adjustment to the recent global crisis, this chapter seeks some clues to the transmission mechanism of global shocks to emerging economies and the critical factors of host countries for either mitigating or amplifying the effects of external shocks.

The chapter is organized as follows. The next section sketches the development of the recent crisis in Korea and compares it with the 1997–98 crisis. The third section examines the two transmission channels: financial and export markets. The fourth section explains Korea's macro-policy reactions to the crisis and compares them with those during the 1997–98 crisis. The final section concludes with emphasis on the roles of fundamentals in mitigating the effects of external shocks.

THE KOREAN ECONOMY DURING THE GLOBAL CRISIS PERIOD

Crisis and Recovery: A Brief Sketch

The Korean economy maintained a reasonable pace of stable growth until the third quarter of 2008. Domestic demand had somewhat slowed due to the soaring oil prices and the resulting loss of purchasing power, but exports had maintained a solid expansion. In fact, exports in the third quarter increased by 27 percent, compared with those in the same quarter of the previous year, despite the global slowdown since the subprime mortgage crisis in the United States.

However, the Lehman Brothers bankruptcy filing in September 2008 and the subsequent panic in the global financial market changed the whole environment. Enormous shocks hit Korea through the open doors of the financial and export markets. The exchange rate depreciated from around 1100 to over 1500 won per US dollar, and foreign reserves declined from US$240 billion at the end of September to US$201 billion at the end of December. Other asset markets also responded. For example, stock values collapsed by approximately 30 percent by the end of the year 2008 (Figure 3.1).

Korea's exports likewise collapsed at an incredible pace. The year-on-year growth rate of exports declined from 27.6 percent in September to 7.8 percent (−2.6 percent, month-to-month) in October and further to −19.5

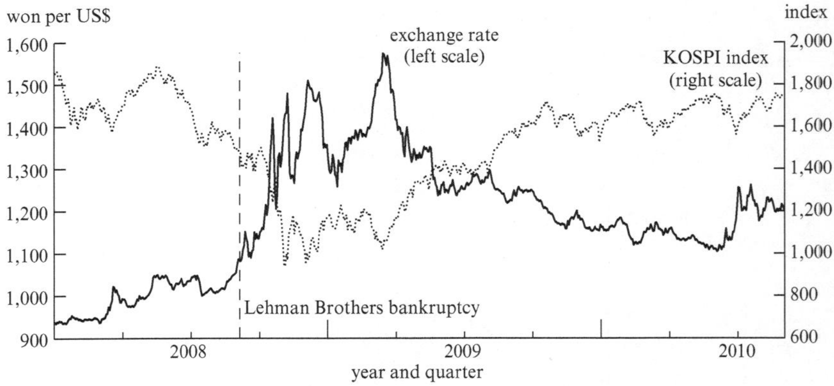

Source: Bank of Korea.

Figure 3.1 Exchange rate of the won and the Korean stock price index, 2008–10

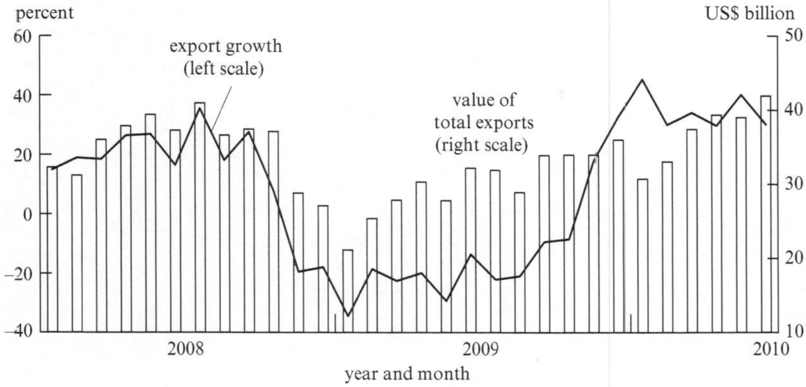

Source: Korea Customs Service.

Figure 3.2 Value and growth rate of exports from Korea, 2008–10

percent (−22.3 percent, month-to-month) in November (Figure 3.2) This collapse in export revenue raised concerns about Korea's capability to earn hard currency and aggravated investor sentiments in a currency market that was already unstable.

International forecasting institutions rushed to join the march of downgrading their outlooks for Korea. For example, the International Monetary Fund (IMF) revised its forecast on Korea's 2009 growth from 2.5 percent in November 2008 to −4.0 percent in January 2009 (Figure 3.3)—a drop of 6.5 percentage points within just two months. However, this was not particularly dramatic at that moment, compared with the revisions made by major investment banks. And most of these forecasts shared a common prediction that Korea (as well as other East Asian economies) would contract more than crisis-originating countries such as the United States.

To the surprise of many commentators, however, the Korean economy began to recover from the second quarter of 2009. After the final jitters in March, the financial market began to stabilize. Also in trade sectors, some recovery signals of export demand were detected. Having paused in the first quarter, the Korean economy began to recover at a relatively rapid pace, achieving more than 8 percent growth in a single year alone up to the first quarter 2010. Whenever relevant statistics were released, international institutions continued to revise their "forecasts" upward, until the Korean official annual growth rate of 2009 was finally announced as 0.2 percent in February 2010.

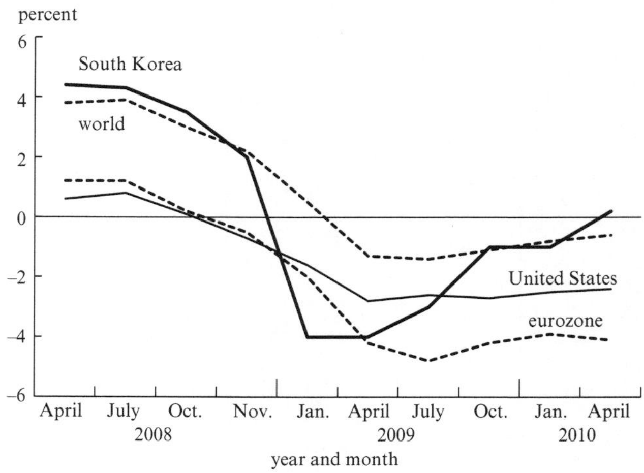

Source: IMF World Economic Outlook.

Figure 3.3 Growth rates of the European Union, Korea, the United States, and the world for the year 2009: IMF forecasts and revisions, April 2008 – April 2010

Comparison with the 1997–98 Crisis: A First Look

The early recovery of Korea may have been a surprise to many forecasters, particularly those who had memories of the deep and painful crisis triggered in 1997. On the surface, the two crises looked alike: asset values and GDP collapsed simultaneously, though the recent crisis was slightly less severe in terms of magnitude and duration. The initial adjustments in the currency value, stock price index and GDP during the recent crisis were approximately two-thirds of those in 1997 (Figure 3.4). The duration of the crisis—though the definition of "crisis" is always elusive—was also shorter this time: it took six months this time, compared with 12 months during the previous crisis, for the value of the currency to regain a level 20 percent lower than the precrisis level, and for the stock price index to regain the precrisis level. It took four quarters this time, compared with six quarters during the previous crisis, for GDP to regain the precrisis level.

The fundamental difference between the two crises, however, can be found in the responses of aggregate demand components (Figure 3.5). During the 1997–98 period, domestic demand drove the collapse of GDP, while export demand continued to expand. This time, in contrast, it was external demand that triggered the crisis, while the contraction in

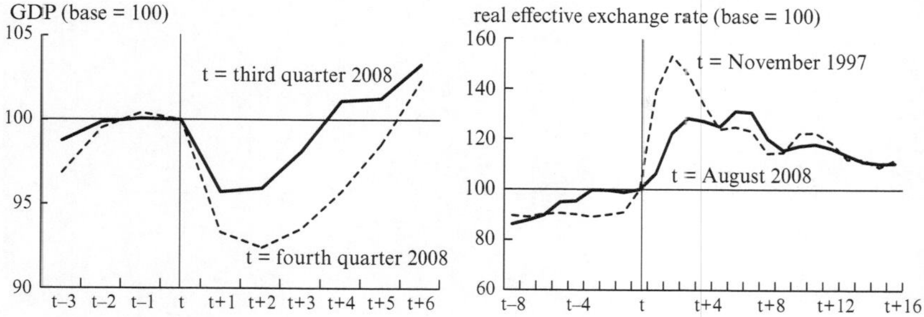

Source: Bank of Korea.

Figure 3.4 Similarities between the 1997–98 and 2008–09 crises in Korea: GDP growth and real effective exchange rate

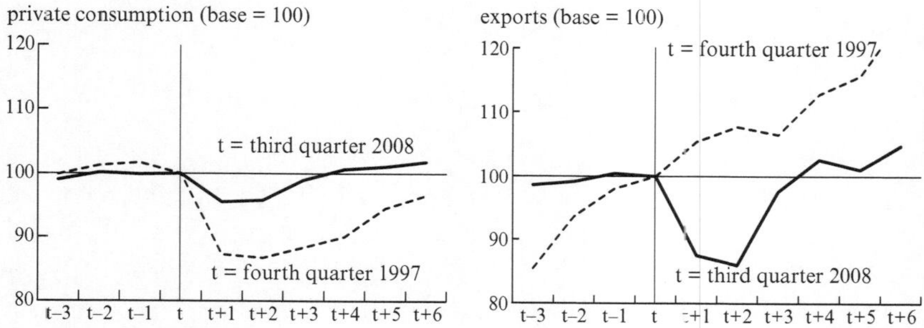

Source: Bank of Korea.

Figure 3.5 Differences between the 1997–98 and 2008–09 crises in Korea: private consumption and exports

domestic demand was relatively mild. This stark contrast in the responses of aggregate demand components clearly demonstrates that the sources of crises were different. Whereas the 1997–98 crisis was triggered by the *implosion* of domestic markets, the recent crisis was mainly triggered by the *explosion* of foreign markets.

This difference in the two crises was translated into the difference in job loss statistics—probably the most direct single indicator of society's suffering from an economic crisis (Figure 3.6). It has been shown that most short-term employment fluctuation in Korea is driven by domestic demand rather than exports.[1] Consistent with this finding, the job-loss rate during the recent crisis was contained within 1 percent (on a year-on-year basis) at its peak in May 2009, which was far milder than 7.4 percent in August 1998.

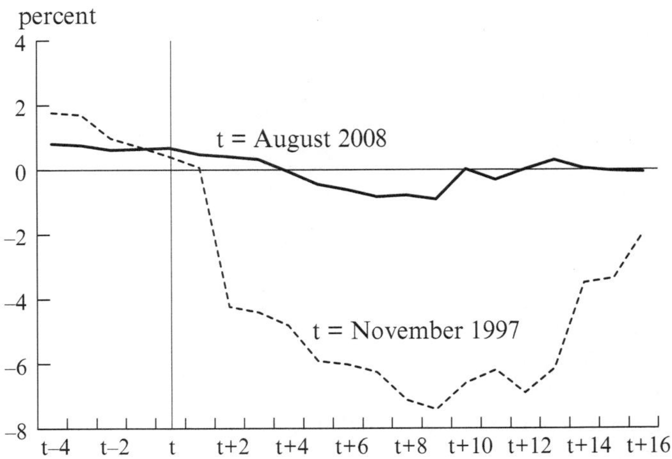

Source: National Statistics Office of Korea.

Figure 3.6 Trends of growth rates of employment in Korea: 1997–98 versus 2008–09 crises

In short, the two crises of Korea appeared similar, but their sources and impacts were quite different. The foreign-driven crisis in 2008 ended up incurring less pain than the 1997–98 crisis, which was caused by weak domestic fundamentals, particularly in financial markets.

TWO CHANNELS OF CRISIS TRANSMISSION

Financial Market: Currency Crisis, but not a Banking Crisis

Currency and domestic credit markets

The financial market was the first channel that directly transmitted the global crisis. Immediately after the Lehman Brothers bankruptcy, panicked financial institutions rushed out to secure liquidity from anywhere possible in the world. Korea, which had accumulated short-term foreign debts since 2005, was particularly susceptible to this liquidity shock (Figure 3.7). Despite having the sixth largest foreign reserves in the world, Korea's ratio of short-term foreign debt to reserves exceeded the ratios of other emerging economies in September 2008 (Figure 3.8).[2] Being an emerging economy with no hard currency, Korea was swept into the strong current of global financial panic and experienced an abrupt and massive capital outflow. The net financial capital withdrawn upon for just

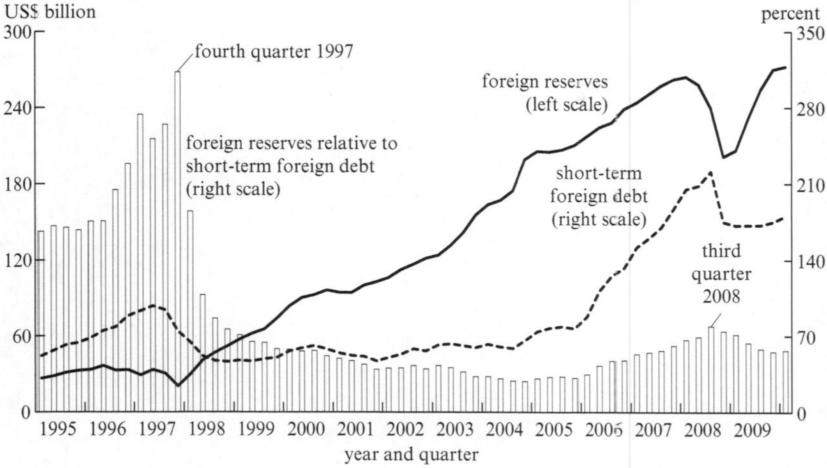

Source: Bank of Korea.

Figure 3.7 Short-term foreign debt and foreign reserves in Korea, 1995–2010

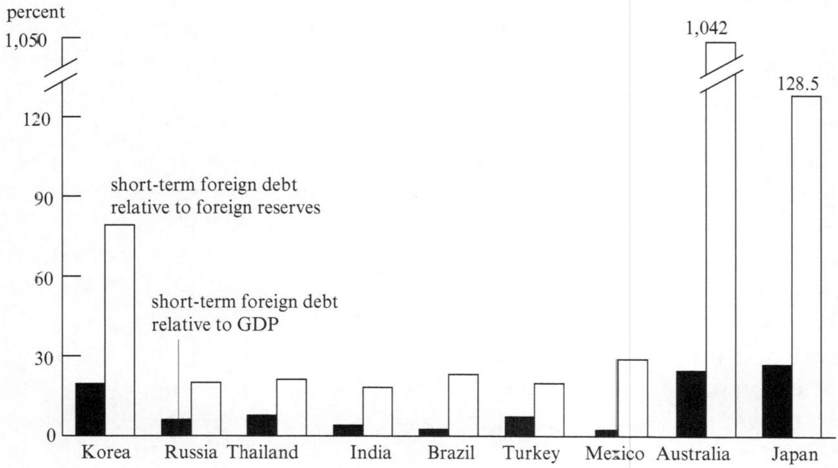

Note: Data are for September 2008.

Source: Bank for International Settlements, IMF, World Bank and Global Insight databases.

Figure 3.8 Short-term foreign debt and foreign reserves in selected countries in September 2008

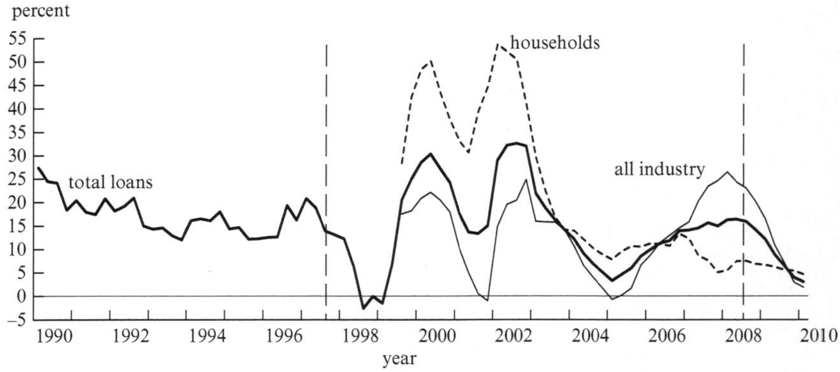

Note: Vertical lines indicate onset of crises.

Source: Bank of Korea.

Figure 3.9 Growth rates of loans by depository banks to households and industry in Korea, 1990–2010

one month (October 2008) was US$25.5 billion (more than 3 percent of annual GDP), which was far larger than the US$6.4 billion in December 1997, the worst month during the 1997–98 crisis.[3] As a result, the Korean currencey fell in value vis-à-vis the US dollar by more than 30 percent, and foreign reserves were reduced by approximately 20 percent during the three-month period from September to December 2008. By any working definition of the literature, this event should be classified as a currency crisis.[4] The stock market's adjustment during the same period, more than 20 percent, can also be classified as a crisis by some definitions.[5]

Despite the crises in asset markets, however, Korea's credit market was not greatly affected by, or largely immune to, the global crisis. Bank credits continued to increase (Figure 3.9), and no evident spikes were observed in either the ratio of nonperforming loans or the dishonored ratio of promissory notes (Figure 3.10). No major banks were bailed out by the government, and no symptoms of bank-runs were detected. By any working definition of the literature, it was far from a banking crisis.[6] In fact, this was the most marked difference from the 1997–98 crisis period when the whole financial system melted down.[7]

Financial policy reactions

Many efforts of the government contributed to relieving the tensions in the financial market. First, the government announced that it would provide temporary guarantees (until the end of June 2009, later extended to the end

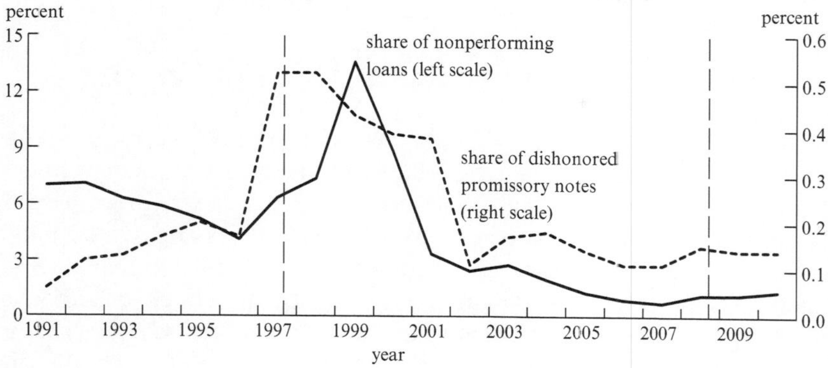

Notes:
The rate for 2010 is the first quarter.
Vertical lines indicate the onset of crises.

Source: Financial Supervisory Service of Korea and Bank of Korea.

Figure 3.10 Default rates in Korea, 1991–2010

of December 2009) on rolled-over short-term foreign debts of commercial banks, as many other governments did at that time. Although no banks ended up relying on government money, this policy must have helped mitigate concerns of international investors. The government also raised 10 trillion won (1 percent of GDP) for stabilizing bond markets (though only 5 trillion won was used up to the time the fund was dissolved) and increased capital bases of public agencies for credit guarantees. In many instances, the government allegedly relied even on moral suasions for commercial banks to roll over the loans to small and medium size enterprises. The Bank of Korea also kept pace with the government by extending its operating instruments to risky assets such as commercial bank debentures.

It is noteworthy, however, that a similar menu of policies was taken in response to the 1997–98 crisis, when Korea nonetheless plunged into a severe banking crisis. In this respect, critical factors that protected the Korean banking system must lie somewhere else.

Buffers to absorb the shocks

Typically, a currency crisis is transmitted into a banking crisis—a twin crisis—through the following channels:

- sudden reversal of foreign currency liquidity flow →
- shrinkage of bank assets in the public sector (when the exchange rate is pegged) or the private sector (when the exchange rate is floated) →

- decrease in credit supply and a surge in default →
- deterioration of banks' capital bases →
- vicious cycles of credit crunch between banks and borrowers.

Every single step toward a twin crisis was observed during the 1997–98 crisis, but the Korean economy in 2008 was equipped with better buffers at most junctures. First, an ample amount of foreign reserves helped dampen the impacts of a sudden reversal in capital flows on private banks' assets. Although the massively accumulated short-term foreign debts made the Korean economy fragile to a foreign liquidity shock, the amount of foreign reserves was still large enough to cover the whole short-term foreign debt. For example, the aforementioned government guarantee on foreign debts would not have been regarded as credible by the market, had foreign reserves not been sufficient as in 1997.

The means of supplying foreign reserves was also improved. Unlike in 1997, the government did not waste foreign reserves this time by committing to a certain level of *price* (that is, the exchange rate). Instead, the government secured additional liquidity via currency swaps with the United States and other countries, and supplied a manageable *quantity* of reserves within a closed circuit of the banking sector by auction. That is, instead of fighting the market to protect the currency value, the government concentrated its efforts on protecting the banking system by supplying foreign currency liquidity required to reduce the accumulated leverage. It was not a sheer coincidence that the decrease in foreign reserves during the crisis period from September to December 2008 (approximately US$40 billion) was almost the same as the decrease of short-term foreign debts.[8] This approach to the foreign exchange market seems to have been effective in damping the adverse impacts of capital outflows on the banking sector, while honoring the automatic stabilizing role of the exchange rate (see below).

Second, sound financial positions of firms, particularly large corporations (or *chaebols*), were crucial in absorbing the impacts from the banking system to the real economy. Since the 1997–98 crisis, Korean firms had carried out drastic restructuring, and their financial stability had significantly improved.[9] As an example, the average debt-to-equity ratio of the corporate sector fell from over 400 percent in 1997 to around 100 percent in 2008, and the interest coverage ratio rose from barely over 100 percent in 1997 to over 500 percent in 2008 (Figure 3.11). This improvement in financial buffers greatly helped Korean firms to weather the credit constraints and demand contraction posed by the global crisis.

There was some concern about household debt-leverage. As in many advanced countries, Korean households had substantially increased debts in relation to housing investment since the 1997–98 crisis. An important

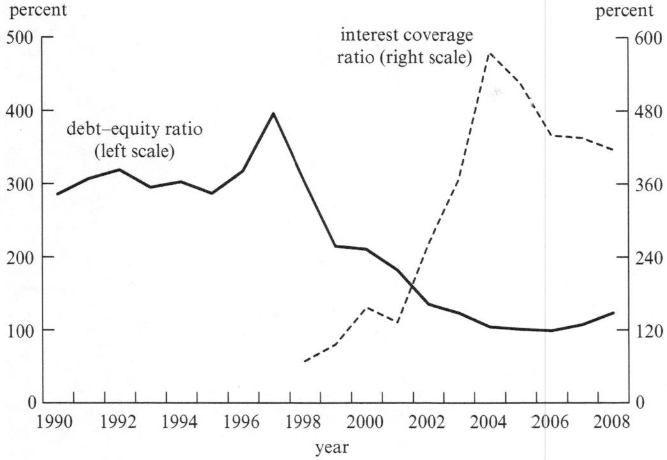

Source: Bank of Korea.

Figure 3.11 Financial buffers of Korean firms: debt–equity ratio 1990–2008 and interest coverate ratio, 1998–2008

difference, however, was that the magnitude of house price hikes in Korea was far milder than those in advanced countries during the run-up to the crisis (Figure 3.12). To the extent that the debts were backed by less bubbly assets, the associated risks were likely to be smaller. In fact, Korea's house prices were almost immune to the crisis, and household debts did not trigger any significant trouble during the crisis period.

Third, banks had also secured far better capacities to absorb shocks in 2008 than in 1997. Based on the improved Bank for International Settlements (BIS) capital adequacy ratio and return on equity, the banking sector would have been able to avoid a critical situation, even if a certain degree of defaults had taken place (Figure 3.13).

All in all, the financial buffers of each sector played critical roles in protecting Korea's currency crisis from spreading like a plague into a banking crisis. This must have helped save domestic demand, hence employment, during the recent crisis, despite enormous additional shocks that flooded into Korea through the trade channel.[10]

Export Market: Faster Recovery than other Countries

Fall and rise of Korea's exports

The magnitude of the shock through the trade channel was no smaller than that through the financial channel: approximately 40 percent

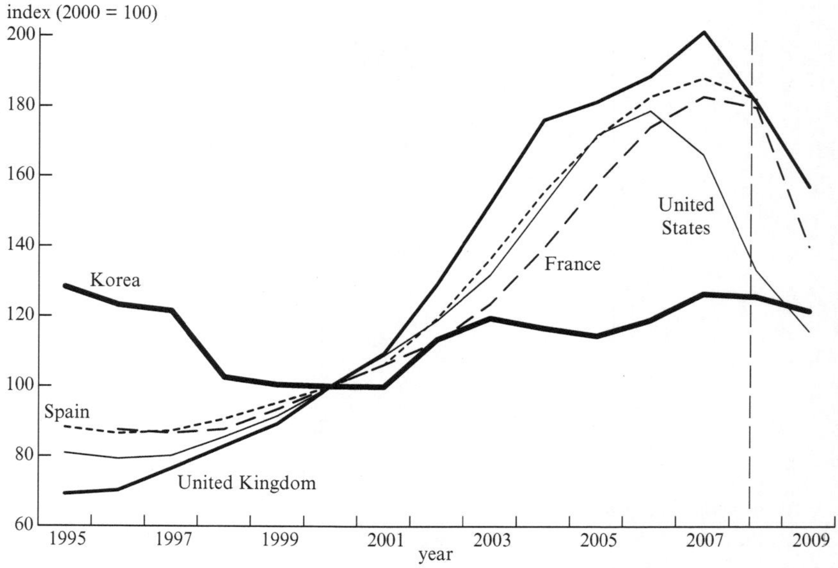

Note: The vertical line indicates the onset of the 2008 crisis.

Source: Kookmin Bank (Korea); Standard and Poor's and S&P/Shiller Case (United States); National Institute for Statistics and Economic Studies (France); Banco de Espana (Spain); and Nationwide (United Kingdom).

Figure 3.12 Trends of real house prices in selected countries, 1995–2009

of export demand evaporated during the three-month period from September to December 2008.[11] This dramatic collapse in export was a worldwide phenomenon, but served as the main ground for the extremely gloomy forecasts on the Korean economy (as well as other East Asian economies), which relied heavily on manufacturing export sectors.[12]

Having passed the trough in January 2009, however, Korea's exports began to recover along with global trade. This recovery must have benefitted from global policy coordination and demand recovery. But it is still notable that the recovery pace of Korea's exports was faster than that of other economies. By the second quarter 2010, Korea had fully recovered to the precrisis level, while most other countries had not (Figure 3.14). For the entire year 2009, Korea's exports went through a relatively milder correction (−13.8 percent) than those of global trade (−22.9 percent), raising its market share in global trade to 3.1 percent (compared with 2.8 percent in 2008).

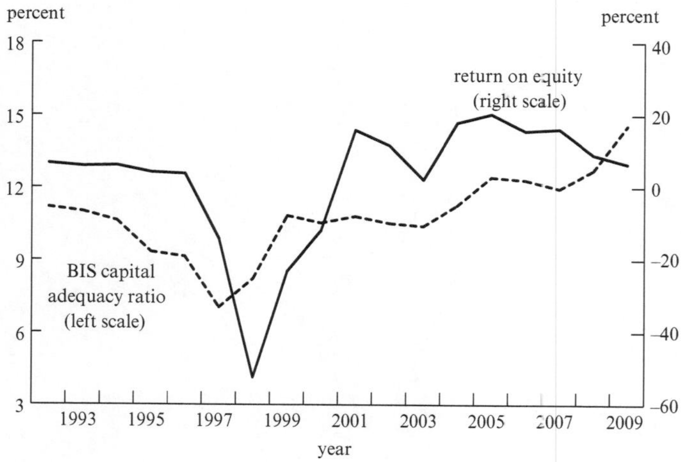

Source: Financial Supervisory Service of Korea.

Figure 3.13 Financial buffers of Korean banks: return on equity and BIS capital adequacy ratio, 1992–2009

China, the biggest trading partner of Korea

One of the reasons for the relatively fast recovery of the export sector was Korea's concentration on the China market. The share of China in Korea's export market was 24 percent (almost 30 percent including Hong Kong) in 2008, while the respective shares in the cases of the United States, the European Union and Japan were 10 percent, 13 percent, and 6 percent. Therefore, given this export structure, Korea's exports were likely to recover faster, if China's imports recovered faster than those of other regions, which in turn was a natural implication of the global rebalancing: the unwinding of global imbalance should imply a relatively small correction of final demand (domestic absorption, to be precise) in China compared with that in the United States. As long as Korea's exports to China did not entirely rely on final demand induced by the United States, or to the extent that they depended on China's autonomous domestic absorption, a relatively small correction of Korea's exports was required in the process of global rebalancing.

This composition effect, thanks to China's faster recovery alone, however, cannot fully explain the differential between the growth rates of Korea's exports and that of global trade. If Korea's market shares in China and other regions had remained the same, the growth rate of Korea's exports in 2009 would have recorded −20.8 percent—a weighted average of the import growth rates of China (−11.3 percent) and the other

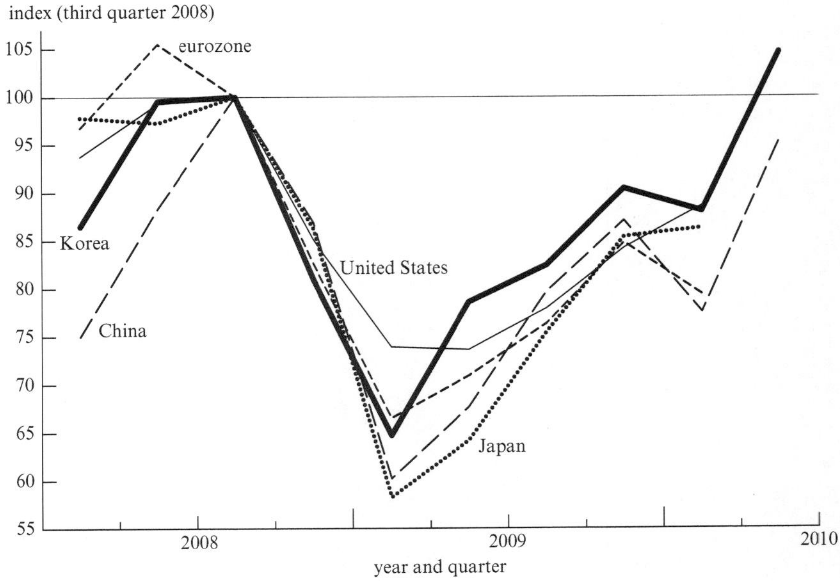

Source: Eurostat, Korea Customs Service, Trade Statistics of Japan, National Bureau of Statistics of China and US Census Bureau.

Figure 3.14 Trend of exports from selected countries, 2008–10

Table 3.1 Korea's exports, global imports and global trade, 2008–09

Item	2008	2009
Growth rate of Korea's exports (%)	–	−13.8
Growth rate of global imports (%)	–	−22.9
of which by China	–	−11.3
of which by other countries	–	−23.8
Korea's exports as a share of global trade (%)	2.7	3.0
of which to China	9.9	10.2
of which to other countries	2.2	2.4

Sources: Global Insight and Bloomberg databases.

regions (−23.8 percent)—still falling short of the realized rate (−13.8 percent). In fact, Korea's market shares did increase in both China and other regions, implying that macro-factors in addition to the China factor must have been at work (Table 3.1).

Exchange rate, an automatic stabilizer

The most likely macro-factor was the huge depreciation of the Korean won that occurred during the crisis period. Though it is always difficult to quantify precisely the effects of the exchange rate on exports, the following result from a simple regression (for monthly data from January 2000 to April 2010) can provide a first approximation:

$$\underset{}{EX_{Korea}} = \underset{(-4.31)}{-3.28} + \underset{(2.25)}{0.37 IM_{US}} + \underset{(3.48)}{0.33 IM_{Euro}} + \underset{(1.90)}{0.20 IM_{Japan}} + \underset{(8.35)}{0.25 IM_{China}}$$

$$\underset{(-0.14)}{-0.03 ER_0} - \underset{(-0.90)}{0.38 ER_{-1}} + \underset{(0.31)}{0.13 ER_{-2}} + \underset{(2.21)}{0.56 ER_{-3}} + residual \qquad (3.1)$$

where EX_{Korea} is the log-export (in U.S. dollars) of Korea, IM_i is the log-import (in US dollars) of region i and ER_t is the log of the real effective exchange rate of the Korean won.[13] A noticeable result is that the effect of IM_{China} appears smaller than that of IM_{US} or IM_{Euro}, despite the share of China (larger than that the shares of the United States or European Union) in terms of Korea's export destinations. This result suggests that a substantial portion of China's imports is induced by other regions' final demand. In fact, the relative magnitudes of the coefficients for each region appear to be similar to the relative sizes of GDP.

As for the exchange rate, it appears to take several months until its effects kick in, which seems to explain why Korea's exports began to recover from the second quarter of 2009, several months after the exchange rate shock in the fourth quarter of 2008. Yet, the accumulated elasticity with respect to the exchange rate is calculated at 0.28, with due consideration to the unpolished regression specification.[14] Applying this rough estimate, more than 20 percent of exchange rate depreciation that occurred during the crisis period could generate an export increase of at least 5–6 percent, accounting for two-thirds of the differential in growth rates between Korea's exports and global trade in 2009.

In this regard, the "currency crisis", not accompanied by a banking crisis, contributed to the faster recovery of export sectors in Korea. To put it elegantly, Korea's experience confirms the textbook prediction that a flexible exchange rate system will help to stabilize the economy automatically. And this role of the exchange rate was particularly necessary in an economy such as Korea's, open to capricious international capital flows.

MACRO-POLICY REACTIONS

Monetary Policy

Among many policy reactions to the crisis, the most contrasting in 2008 to those in 1997 was the monetary policy. In 1997 the policy interest rate was raised to almost 30 percent (a level that was more than twice the precrisis rate of approximately 12 percent), while in response to the recent crisis it was lowered to 2 percent (a level that was less than half the precrisis rate of 5.25 percent) (Figure 3.15). No doubt the monetary easing in 2008 was crucial in shielding the domestic economy from the external storm, whereas the monetary tightening in 1997 aggravated the domestic banking crisis.

More interesting than the policy effects, however, was the environment that led to different policies.[15] Most advanced countries aggressively lowered interest rates to cope with their own financial crises in 2008, while they did not in 1997. This trend in international policies lightened the Bank of Korea's burden associated with the monetary easing in 2008, despite the exchange rate depreciation.

The critical difference, however, was the foreign currency liquidity situation when the crisis was triggered. Given the near depletion of foreign

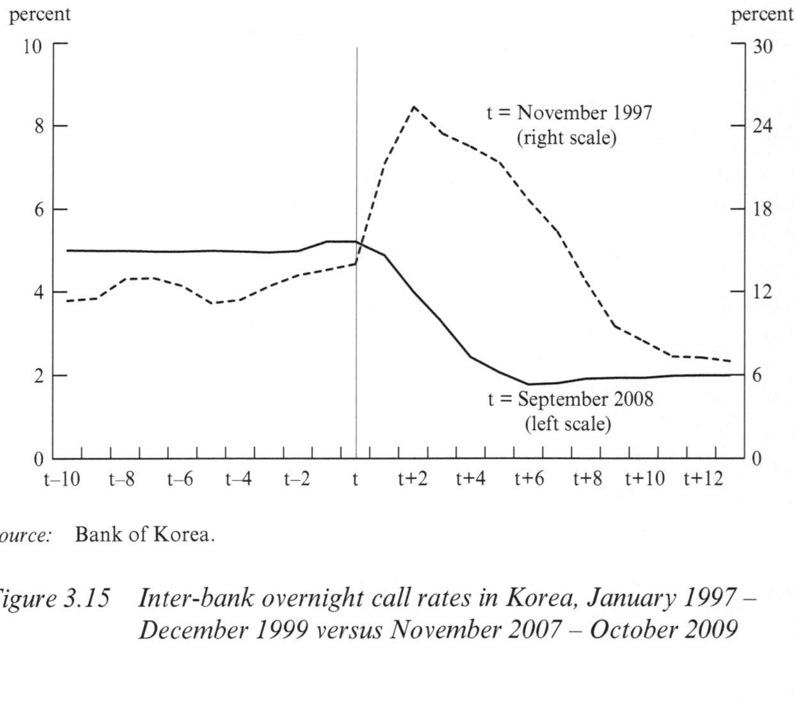

Source: Bank of Korea.

Figure 3.15 Inter-bank overnight call rates in Korea, January 1997 – December 1999 versus November 2007 – October 2009

reserves, the high interest rate policy in December 1997 may have been inevitable, but in 2008 Korea had room to maneuver on this front.[16] The most important factor that led to different foreign reserve situations was the government's approach to the foreign exchange market. In 1997, the government believed that it could, and should, control the foreign exchange market, and actually did attempt to engineer a "smooth and orderly" depreciation from the beginning. This approach merely invited currency speculation and catalyzed reserve depletion in the end. In 2008, in contrast, the government let the exchange rate adjust to the shock instead of wasting foreign reserves, which eventually saved the flexibility of monetary policy as well as the aforementioned automatic stabilizing role of the exchange rate.

Fiscal Policy

Fiscal policy reactions were not as contrasting as monetary policy reactions. In both periods, expansionary fiscal stances were assumed. The sizes of budget deficits, approximately 3 percent of GDP, were also similar.

However, the processes to similar results, *ex post*, were different. In 1997, the IMF initially recommended that the Korean government maintain a budget balance in December 1997 when fiscal stimulus was most needed. Only after severe recession had taken hold was a budget deficit allowed in 1998 and gradually expanded as the recession deepened.[17] This time, in contrast, the Korean government announced fiscal expansion as soon as the global crisis was set off, and injected the necessary stimulus. A supplementary budget of 10 trillion won (approximately 1 percent of GDP) was implemented in November 2008, and an additional supplementary budget of 28.4 trillion won (approximately 2.8 percent of GDP) was drawn up by March 2009. Considering time lags common to fiscal policy effects, the early execution of fiscal spending must have contributed to stabilizing the economy.

CONCLUSION: PUTTING THE PIECES TOGETHER

The recent crisis and subsequent recovery of Korea may have been a surprise to many forecasters. But it was a relief to most Koreans who still had vivid memories of the 1997–98 crisis. Many factors contributed to mitigating the effects of the shocks on Korea. Some factors worked in protecting the domestic banking system, and others were operated for inducing relatively fast export recovery (Figure 3.16).

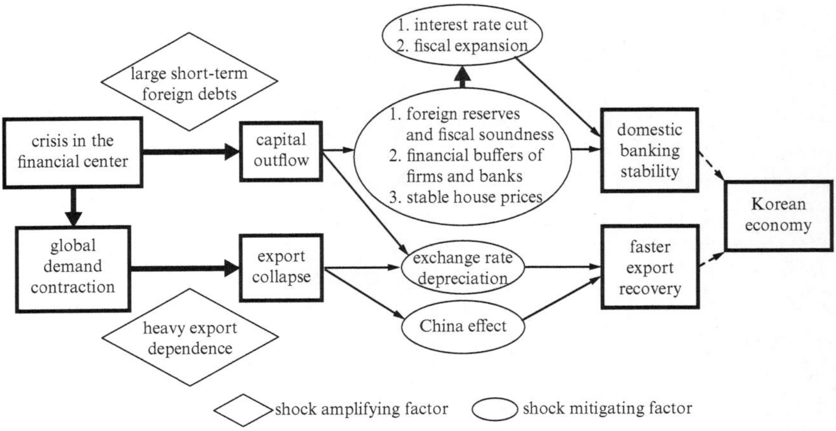

Figure 3.16 Channels of transmission of the global crisis to Korea

These factors can be broadly classified into two categories: precrisis fundamentals and postcrisis macro-policy reactions. The former includes a large amount of foreign reserves, improved financial structures of firms and banks, relatively mild house price hikes and a tradition of sound government budget, while the latter includes a foreign exchange policy that honored market forces, a monetary policy that stabilized the domestic economy and a fiscal policy that was carried out on time. Between the two categories, however, inextricable relationships exist. Sound fundamentals are necessary, though not sufficient, conditions for flexible macro-policy reactions.[18] In reverse, prolonged expansionary policies erode the soundness of fundamentals, which will eventually restrict the flexibility of macro-policies.

Korea managed successfully to recover this time, thanks to the relatively sound precrisis fundamentals achieved by the restructuring processes since the 1997–98 crisis, along with consistent macro-policies. However, if the emergency policies are not normalized on time, and if necessary restructuring is delayed, the recent success could become an ominous prelude to another crisis in the future.

NOTES

1. Shin and Kim (2008), for example, find that domestic demand, particularly private consumption, is significantly correlated with employment. This finding, though subject to simultaneity bias critiques, makes sense in that export (or manufacturing) industries are mostly capital intensive, while service industries are labor intensive.

2. Hangyong Lee and Min-Kyu Song (Chapter 5 in the present volume) explain in detail how Korea's short-term foreign debt had accumulated since 2005.
3. More than 90 percent of this capital outflow, or US$25.5 billion, is accounted for by the reduction in short-term debt, while the equity market exhibited net capital inflow.
4. The definitions of "currency crisis" in the empirical literature range from a narrow one focusing on devaluations of nominal exchange rates (Edwards and Montiel 1989 and Frankel and Rose 1996, among others) to a broader one that also considers reductions in foreign reserves and hikes in interest rates (Eichengreen et al. 1996 and Sachs et al. 1996, among others).
5. See, for example, Reinhart and Rogoff (2009).
6. Caprio and Klingebiel (1996) define a period of "financial distress" as one "when a significant fraction of the banking sector is insolvent but remains open", and Calomiris and Gorton (1991) define a "financial panic" as a time "when bank debt holders suddenly demand their debt claims into cash to an extent that the banks are forced to suspend the convertibility of their debt into cash". Demirgüç-Kunt and Detragiache (1998) define a "systemic crisis" as one in which (1) nonperforming loans accounted for at least 10 percent of total assets, (2) the cost of rescue operations was greater than 2 percent of GDP, (3) banking problems resulted in a large-scale nationalization of banks and (4) emergency measures (such as a deposit freeze, prolonged bank holidays and generalized deposit guarantees) were introduced.
7. After the 1997–98 crisis and up to the end of 2004, five of 33 major banks were closed and ten were merged. More drastic restructuring was carried out for small banks (called "merchant bank corporations"), as a result of which only one of 30 survived, while 22 were closed and seven were merged, during the same period. For this restructuring, 64 trillion won (almost 13 percent of GDP) of public money was mobilized in 1998, and 40 trillion won (almost 7 percent of GDP) was added in 2000. See Committee for Public Fund Management (2001).
8. From September to December in 2008, short-term debts were reduced by US$39.7 billion (from US$186.6 billion to US$149.9 billion), and foreign reserves were reduced by US$38.5 billion (from US$239.7 billion to US$201.2 billion).
9. Using micro-data for Korea's listed companies, Kyung-Mook Lim (Chapter 11 in the present volume) analyses in detail how Korean firms have changed their financial positions since 1998 and how they managed to cope with the recent crisis without significant disruptions.
10. See Bernanke (1983), Bernanke and Gertler (1989) and Kiyotaki and Moore (1997), among others, for the literature emphasizing the importance of credit markets on economic fluctuations. Similarly to Kaminsky and Reinhart (1999), Cerra and Saxena (2008) more recently documented that the output impact of a banking crisis was nearly twice as great as a currency crisis, using a wide set of data covering 190 countries.
11. See Hangyu Lee (Chapter 7 of the present volume) for cross-country analyses of the drastic collapse in global trade volume during this period of time.
12. A leading example is the IMF's position note by Martin Sommer (2009), which established a strong negative cross-country relationship between the growth rate of the fourth quarter of 2008 and the proportion of manufacturing industries in GDP. It is obvious that an economy more dependent on exports should be more affected by the global trade shock. However, contrary to a casual argument, this never implies that crisis-affected regions (for example, East Asia) should contract more than crisis-originating countries (for example, the United States) through trade channels. See Kato (2009) and Cho (2009) for more discussion on this point.
13. The real effective exchange rate was constructed by taking an average of nominal exchange rates deflated by CPI for 12 economies (Australia, China, Japan, France, Germany, Italy, Hong Kong, the Netherlands, Singapore, Taiwan, the United Kingdom and the United States), weighted by the trade portion of the respective country.
14. Estimates of the accumulated elasticity from different specifications range from 0.15 to 0.35.

15. Hyeon-Wook Kim (Chapter 9 in the present volume) discusses Korea's monetary and fiscal policies before and after the crisis in detail, and thus this section emphasizes the differences from the macro-policies during the 1997–98 crisis period.
16. On the verge of national default in December 1997, all of the policy measures including monetary policy were lined up to secure foreign currency liquidity rather than economic stabilization. See Fischer (1998) and Krueger (2000) for example. Under this policy priority, it was necessary, or probably inevitable, to impose a high interest rate policy. It was particularly so, given that a penalty interest rate was charged on the foreign currency loans of the Bank of Korea to commercial banks. Otherwise, commercial banks desperate for foreign currency liquidity would have rushed to borrow domestic currency at relatively low interest rates, and would have converted it into foreign currency to pay back their existing borrowings to the Bank of Korea, which could have further deteriorated the foreign exchange situation. See Lee (2011) and Cho (2010) for details of the financial market situation in Korea during the crisis period.
17. The recommended budget deficit of the IMF was expanded to 0.8 percent of GDP in the fifth agreement on 7 February 1998, 1.75 percent of GDP in the sixth agreement on 2 May, 4 percent of GDP in the seventh agreement on 24 July and finally 5 percent of GDP in the eighth agreement on 27 October. See Chopra et al. (2002) for details.
18. The monetary policy of Korea in 1997 and the recent fiscal policy of Greece may be leading examples.

REFERENCES

Bernanke, Ben S. 1983. "Nonmonetary Effects of the Financial Crisis in the Propagation of the Great Depression". *American Economic Review*, **73** (3): 257–76.

Bernanke, Ben S. and Mark Gertler. 1989. "Agency Costs, Net Worth, and Business Fluctuations". *American Economic Review*, **79** (1): 14–31.

Calomiris, Charles W. and Gary Gorton. 1991. "The Origins of Banking Panics: Models, Facts, and Bank Regulation". In *Financial Markets and Financial Crises*, edited by R. Glenn Hubbard, pp. 109–74. Chicago: University of Chicago Press.

Caprio, Gerard, Jr. and Daniela Klingebiel. 1996. *Bank Insolvencies: Cross-Country Experience*. Policy Research Working Paper 1620. Washington: World Bank.

Cerra, Valerie and Sweta Chaman Saxena. 2008. "Growth Dynamics: The Myth of Economic Recovery". *American Economic Review*, **98** (1): 439–57.

Cho, Dongchul. 2009. *The Republic of Korea's Economy in the Swirl of Global Crisis*. ADBI Working Paper 147. Tokyo: Asian Development Bank Institute.

Cho, Dongchul. 2010. "Overcoming the 1997–98 Crisis: Macroeconomic Policy Adjustments". Unpublished paper, Korea Development Institute.

Chopra, Ajai, Kenneth Kang, Meral Karasulu, Hong Liang, Henry Ma and Anthony Richards. 2002. "From Crisis to Recovery in Korea: Strategy, Achievements, and Lessons". In *Korean Crisis and Recovery*, edited by David T. Coe and Se-Jik Kim, pp. 13–104. Washington: International Monetary Fund; Seoul: Korea Institute for International Economic Policy.

Committee for Public Fund Management. 2001. *White Paper*. Seoul: Committee for Public Fund Management, Ministry of Finance and Economy. Available at www.pbfunds.go.kr. In Korean.

Demirgüç-Kunt, Asli and Enrica Detragiache. 1998. "The Determinants of

Banking Crises in Developing and Developed Countries". *International Monetary Fund Staff Papers*, **45** (1). Available at www.imf.org.

Economist, The. 2009. "Domino Theory: Where Could Emerging Market Contagion Spread Next?" *Economics Focus* (26 February 2009). Available at www.economist.com/node/13184631.

Edwards, Sebastian and Peter Montiel. 1989. "Devaluation Crises and the Macroeconomic Consequences of Postponed Adjustment". *International Monetary Fund Staff Papers*, **366** (4): 875–903.

Eichengreen, Barry, Andrew Rose and Charles Wyplosz. 1996. "Contagious Currency Crises: First Tests". *The Scandinavian Journal of Economics*, **98** (4): 463–84.

Fischer, Stanley. 1998. "The Asian Crisis: A View from the IMF". Address at the Midwinter Conference of the Bankers' Association of Foreign Trade. Available at www.imf.org/external/np/speeches/1998/012298.htm.

Frankel, Jeffrey and Andrew Rose. 1996. "Currency Crashes in Emerging Markets: Empirical Indicators". *Journal of International Economics*, **41** (3–4): 351–66.

International Monetary Fund. 2008. *World Economic Outlook 2008*. Washington: International Monetary Fund.

International Monetary Fund. 2009. *World Economic Outlook 2009*. Washington: International Monetary Fund.

Kaminsky, Graciela L. and Carmen M. Reinhart. 1999. "The Twin Crises: The Causes of Banking and Balance of Payments Problems". *American Economic Review*, **89**: 473–500.

Kato, Takatoshi. 2009. "Implications for Asia from the Global Financial Crisis and Policy Perspectives". Paper presented at the Harvard Asia Business Conference, 14–15 February 2009. Available at unpan1.un.org/intradoc/groups/public/documents/aapam/unpan035841.pdf.

Kiyotaki, Nobuhiro and John Moore. 1997. "Credit Cycles". *Journal of Political Economy*, **105**: 211–48.

Krueger, Anne O. 2000. "Conflicting Demands on the International Monetary Funds". *American Economic Review*, **90** (2): 38–42.

Lee, Kyu-sung. 2011. *The Korean Financial Crisis: Onset, Turnaround and Thereafter*. Washington: World Bank; Seoul: Korea Development Institute.

Reinhart, Carmen and Kenneth S. Rogoff. 2009. *This Time is Different: Eight Centuries of Financial Folly*. Princeton, New Jersey: Princeton University Press.

Sachs, Jeffrey, Aaron Tornell and Andres Velasco. 1996. *Financial Crises in Emerging Markets: The Lessons from 1995*. Working Paper 1759. Cambridge, Massachusetts: Harvard Institute of Economic Research.

Shin, Sukha and Heesam Kim. 2008. "An Analysis on the Recent Slowdown of Employment". *KDI Economic Outlook*, **25** (1): 153–64. In Korean.

Sommer, Martin. 2009. *Why Has Japan Been Hit So Hard by the Global Recession?* IMF Staff Position Note SPN/09/05. Available at www.imf.org.

PART II

International perspectives

4. International financial markets and transmission of the crisis: determinants of exchange market pressure and absorption by international reserves

Joshua Aizenman and Michael M. Hutchison

INTRODUCTION

This chapter evaluates how the global financial crisis emanating from the United States was transmitted globally. Our focus is on the extent that the crisis caused external pressures (exchange market pressure), measured by a combination of exchange rate depreciation and loss of international reserves, across different regions of the world and across countries with different income levels and differing levels of restrictions on international capital flows.

International financial markets were at the heart of the worldwide financial crisis that emerged in late 2007 and reaching a climax between August 2008 and February 2009. Although the crisis started with the mortgage-related (subprime) crisis in the United States, and was closely linked to banks in Western Europe holding mortgage-backed securities and derivative products, it quickly led to a global liquidity crisis that had a great and adverse affect on the rest of the world.

We focus in this chapter on the extent to which the global financial shock adversely affected the external position of countries throughout the world, but especially in emerging market economies. We measure external position by looking at changes in exchange market pressure—a combination of exchange market depreciation and loss of international reserves—as well as considering these two components separately. We are interested in two basic questions. First, how has the transmission of the global shock been affected by the extent of international balance sheet exposure, financial development and financial openness?[1] Second, given the degree of exchange market pressure, what determines the trade-off or choice between exchange rate depreciation and loss of international reserves in absorbing the shock? We sidestep in this chapter questions regarding the root causes of the crisis. These issues are covered by growing literature dealing with the precrisis trends and policies that led to the buildup of financial vulnerabilities, and ultimately to the crisis in the United States and its rapid transition to the global economy (see Obstfeld 2010 and Obstfeld and Rogoff 2010, and the references therein).

Our results highlight the importance of the ratio of total external liabilities to GDP in accounting for exchange market pressures, and the ratio of short term external debt to international reserves in accounting for the higher relative importance of exchange rate depreciation in accommodating the adjustment to a given degree of exchange market pressure. Our findings also corroborate the notion that the 2008–09 crisis was the first *global* crisis in the era of modern financial globalization, affecting practically all countries. Yet, there was a systematic variation in countries' exposure to exchange market pressures, where countries with higher ratios of total foreign liabilities to GDP and higher GDP per capita were more exposed.

The next section provides an overview of the response of emerging and developing economies to the global financial shock, with the help of summary statistics and simple correlations. The third section explains external vulnerability to financial shocks, followed by a concluding section.

RESPONSE OF EMERGING AND DEVELOPING ECONOMIES TO THE GLOBAL FINANCIAL SHOCK

Global External Responses to the Financial Crisis

Table 4.1 presents the change in exchange market pressure (EMP),[2] the exchange rate depreciation and the percentage change in international reserves during the height of the financial crisis, from August 2008 to February 2009. The table ranks countries from the highest to the lowest EMP. The EMP measure is the sum of the percentage change in the exchange rate (positive values denote percentage depreciation) and percentage loss of reserves. High values denote greater external pressure.[3] The two components of EMP are the percentage change in the exchange rate (depreciation relative to the US dollar) and the percentage in international reserves.

It is remarkable how extreme and widespread external pressures were, across groups of countries and regions, during the height of the financial

Table 4.1 Changes in exchange market pressure, exchange rates and international reserves: averages by economy, August 2008 to February 2009

Economy	Exchange market pressure (%)	Exchange rate (% change)	Foreign exchange reserves (% change)
Poland	107.98	79.51	−28.47
Zambia	96.59	60.00	−36.59
Russia	89.27	52.32	−36.95
Republic of Korea	70.25	51.55	−18.70
Sweden	69.74	49.50	−20.24
Romania	66.67	50.00	−16.67
New Zealand	63.99	44.85	−19.14
Sri Lanka	63.24	6.31	−56.93
Brazil	59.84	51.59	−8.25
Australia	59.82	46.23	−13.59
United Kingdom	56.88	40.00	−16.88
Turkey	56.78	45.69	−11.10
Jamaica	55.26	22.55	−32.72
Bulgaria	54.61	24.00	−30.61
Swaziland	54.38	37.11	−17.27
Mexico	54.34	48.41	−5.93
Czech Republic	51.30	45.05	−6.26
Mauritius	49.70	28.79	−20.91
Indonesia	48.68	31.39	−17.29
United Arab Emirates	45.88	0.00	−45.88
Colombia	44.11	42.56	−1.55
Kyrgyz Republic	41.59	17.13	−24.46
South Africa	41.42	37.11	−4.31
Cote d'Ivoire	41.18	23.47	−17.71
Ecuador	41.05	0.00	−41.05
Malaysia	40.65	13.19	−27.46
Morocco	40.33	19.67	−20.65
Hungary	40.28	58.09	17.82
Paraguay	39.37	27.68	−11.69
Euro area countries	38.96	23.44	−15.52
India	38.72	19.39	−19.33
Kenya	38.62	18.37	−20.25
Norway	37.08	36.77	−0.31
Iceland	36.85	42.43	5.58
Burkina Faso	36.46	23.47	−12.99
Latvia	35.85	22.22	−13.62
Uganda	34.52	20.68	−13.84

Table 4.1 (continued)

Economy	Exchange market pressure (%)	Exchange rate (% change)	Foreign exchange reserves (% change)
Kazakhstan	32.54	25.02	−7.52
Togo	32.04	23.47	−8.58
Georgia	31.96	19.15	−12.81
Peru	31.95	15.66	−16.29
Tunisia	30.37	23.93	−6.44
Moldova	29.45	9.78	−19.67
Canada	23.06	23.30	0.25
Venezuela, Bolivia	22.89	0.00	−22.89
Pakistan	21.81	11.72	−10.09
Singapore	18.98	12.41	−6.57
Argentina	18.41	17.55	−0.86
Switzerland	16.81	12.38	−4.43
Dominican Republic	15.55	3.32	−12.23
Uruguay	15.12	23.70	8.58
Chile	13.69	18.49	4.80
Brunei Darussalam	11.41	12.41	1.00
Republic of Yemen	11.34	0.19	−11.16
Tanzania	11.34	11.89	0.55
Qatar	11.10	0.00	−11.10
Egypt	10.31	5.47	−4.84
Nicaragua	8.44	2.88	−5.56
Guatemala	7.80	7.67	−0.13
Philippines	6.97	7.59	0.62
Denmark	3.65	23.22	19.57
Angola	3.17	0.93	−2.24
Costa Rica	3.12	2.48	−0.64
Bangladesh	−0.30	0.55	0.86
Thailand	−0.58	7.53	8.10
China	−3.63	0.00	3.63
Bolivia	−4.21	−0.99	3.23
Israel	−5.10	19.88	24.98
Saudi Arabia	−5.31	0.00	5.31
Panama	−5.42	0.00	5.42
El Salvador	−6.92	0.00	6.92
Japan	−9.99	−9.67	0.33
Hong Kong	−12.97	−0.64	12.32
Jordan	−13.09	0.00	13.09
Oman	−18.41	0.00	18.41
Kuwait	−25.33	7.41	32.74
Lebanon	−26.39	0.00	26.39

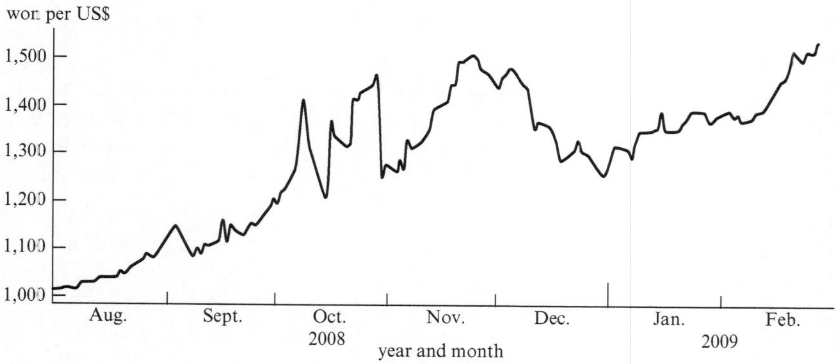

Note: Rates are based on the first days of respective months.

Figure 4.1 Depreciation of the Korean won, August 2008 – March 2009

crisis from August 2008 to February 2009. They ranged from highs experienced in Poland (108 percent), Zambia (97 percent), Russia (89 percent) and the Republic of Korea (70 percent) to negative values (a combination of appreciation and/or gain in international reserves) for economies such as Hong Kong, China, Lebanon and Saudi Arabia. Korea experienced a 52 percent depreciation of the exchange rate against the US dollar (Figure 4.1) and a 19 percent loss of reserves during the period, for a total EMP of more than 70 percent. The vast majority of economies experienced intense EMP: 63 (82 percent of the sample, where euro member countries are counted as one monetary and exchange rate entity) experienced positive EMP, and only 14 economies experienced the opposite (negative EMP values). Most of the economies with positive EMP experienced depreciation of their currencies against the US dollar (66 in the sample), although several maintained their currencies stable (5 in the sample, excluding of course the United States), whereby EMP is manifested only in international reserve losses.

Table 4.2 presents summary statistics. The sample is divided into income groups, regions and the extent of capital market restrictions. To put this into broader perspective, the average EMP for the full sample of all countries (independently of their income levels) was about 31 percent. Emerging markets and low income countries had average EMP of about 35 percent, while middle and high income countries had lower EMP rates at 28 percent and 33 percent, respectively. Emerging markets differ most from other country groups in the composition of the ratio of exchange rate to reserve loss—emerging markets absorbed much less of the EMP by losing reserves (and experienced corresponding greater exchange

Table 4.2 Subsample averages by income level, region and capital restrictions

Groups	Exchange market pressure (%)	Exchange rate (% change)	Foreign exchange reserves (% change)
Full sample (90 countries)	30.60	21.15	−9.45
Emerging markets (MSCI index)	35.31	26.72	−8.58
Income			
High	32.95	24.11	−8.84
Low	33.66	19.19	−14.47
Middle	27.96	19.41	−8.55
Middle and low	29.18	19.36	−9.82
Region			
Canada and Western Europe	37.37	26.97	−10.40
Eastern Europe and Central Asia	50.35	34.55	−15.79
East Asia	25.65	18.58	−7.07
South Asia	30.87	9.49	−21.37
Latin America	23.02	15.75	−7.27
Africa and Middle East	21.11	15.59	−5.51
High level capital restrictions			
Bond	29.45	17.20	−12.25
Bond inflow	25.97	13.66	−12.30
Equity	31.11	18.42	−12.69
Equity inflow	27.28	18.35	−8.94

Notes:
Exchange market pressure (EMP) is defined as (Δ exchange rate) − (Δ foreign exchange reserves). Percentage changes are calculated over the most severe period of global financial crisis from July 2008 through February 2009. The euro area counties in our sample are Austria, Belgium, Cyprus, Finland, France, Germany, Greece, Ireland, Italy, Malta, the Netherlands, Portugal, Slovenia and Spain. Emerging markets are defined according to the Morgan Stanley Capital International (MSCI) Emerging Market Index. Only countries that experienced positive EMP are included in the sample (except Hungary, see endnote 4), for a total of 20. Income group classification follows IMF definitions, while the following IMF regional groups have been combined: (1) North America and Western Europe and (2) the Middle East, North Africa and Sub-Saharan Africa. A high level of financial restrictions is defined as 0.75 or 1.0 for bond and equity and as 1.0 for bond inflow and equity inflow, according to the Schindler capital controls index.

rate depreciation). Specifically, the ratio of reserve loss to exchange rate depreciation is 0.32, while low income countries, with an EMP similar to emerging markets, had a ratio of 0.75. The ratio for the full sample is 0.45.

The financial crisis also hit all regions of the world, although the greatest effect was felt in Eastern Europe and Central Asia (50 percent EMP). This is not surprising, given that the subprime crisis emanating from the United States was directly linked to financial institutions in Western Europe, and Western Europe in turn was tightly linked through banking ties with the more fragile economies of Eastern Europe. By contrast, Africa and the Middle East fared best as a region with the lowest EMP (an average of only 21 percent), followed closely by Latin America (23 percent EMP).

The EMPs for the group of countries with high levels of capital restrictions of various types are also shown in Table 4.2. The countries with high levels of capital controls experienced EMP somewhat below the sample average (except for countries with a high level of equity restriction, which experienced approximately the same EMP as the sample average).

Panel studies of EMP frequently normalize the exchange rate depreciation rate and reserve loss rate, focusing on the deviations from their means, normalized by the standard deviation of the relevant series (see Levy-Yeyati and Sturzenegger 2005). As our focus is on a cross country comparison during an unprecedented global crisis, we refrain from such normalizations. As a sensitivity analysis, we compare in Box 4.1 our EMP measure and the weighted EMP used in the IMF's *World Economic Outlook* (Danninger et al. 2009). The correlation between the two measures is highly significant and equals 0.63.

In summary, the global financial crisis affected countries across the globe in all regions, at all income levels and whether or not they had tight restrictions on capital flows. Exchange market pressure was intense in most countries, mainly absorbed by exchange rate depreciation but also through substantial losses of international reserves. The widespread nature and intensity of the crisis makes this financial crisis episode the most global in nature since the Great Depression.

Emerging Market Responses to the Financial Crisis

Our main focus is on how the global financial crisis affected emerging market economies. To this end, Table 4.3 presents simple correlations of EMP with economic indicators (GDP per capita and trade openness) and financial indicators. The financial indicators cover financial development (stock market capitalization), financial openness (capital account openness), total financial account liabilities (total external liabilities as a percentage of GDP) and balance sheet exposure (short term foreign debt exceeding international reserves, as a percentage of international reserves). The correlations are calculated for the full sample of emerging markets as well as regional groupings of emerging markets: (1) Eastern Europe and

BOX 4.1 CORRELATIONS OF AUTHORS' EMP MEASURE WITH THE MONTHLY WEIGHTED EMP MEASURE OF THE IMF AND THE EMERGING MARKETS FINANCIAL STRESS INDEX (EM-FSI)

	weighted EMP (IMF)	EM-FSI
EMP, July 2008 – February 2009	0.6254***	0.3300*

Symbols *and *** indicate significant correlations at 10 and 1 percent levels, respectively. The EMP (IMF) captures exchange rate depreciations and declines in international reserves and is defined for country *i* in month *t* as

$$EMPI_{i,t} = \frac{(\Delta e_{i,t} - \mu_{i,\Delta e})}{\sigma_{i,\Delta e}} - \frac{(\Delta RES_{i,t} - \mu_{i,\Delta RES})}{\sigma_{i,\Delta RES}},$$

where Δe and ΔRES denote the month-over-month percent changes in the exchange rate and total reserves minus gold, respectively. The exchange rate is taken vis-à-vis an anchor country, as discussed in Levy-Yeyati and Sturzenegger (2005). The symbols μ and σ denote the mean and the standard deviations, respectively, of the relevant series. The index accommodates episodes of hyperinflation, defined as annual inflation rates exceeding 150 percent, by adjusting means and standard deviations for periods with and without the prevalence of hyperinflation. For each time period we aggregate the IMF EMP measure over the number of corresponding months to make it comparable to our measure. The EM-FSI comprises five components: the "banking-sector beta," stock market returns, time-varying stock market return volatility, sovereign debt spreads, and an exchange market pressure. For more information see Balakrishnan et al. (2009).

Central Asia, (2) East Asia, (3) Latin America and (4) other emerging markets. In addition, the sample is segmented into those countries with a high degree of restrictions on international bond flows (outflows and inflows), bond inflows, equity flows (outflows and inflows) and equity inflows. The Morgan Stanley Capital International (MSCI) Emerging

Table 4.3 Correlations with exchange market pressure: emerging markets

	All emerging	Regional group				High level financial restrictions			
		Eastern Europe, Central Asia	East Asia	Latin America	Other emerging	Bond	Bond inflow	Equity	Equity inflow
Trade and GDP									
GDP per capita	0.575***	−0.296	0.776	0.004	0.521	0.817**	0.947**	0.914***	0.938***
Trade openness	−0.038	0.774	−0.009	−0.535	0.587	−0.076	−0.710	−0.182	−0.663
Financial indicators									
Financial account liabilities	0.699***	0.388	0.864	0.784**	0.541	0.661**	0.601	0.630*	0.557
Balance sheet exposure	0.361	0.598	−0.620	0.425	0.270	0.363	0.310	0.423	0.306
Stock market capitalization	0.011	0.986	0.217	−0.268	0.416	0.202	0.647	0.124	0.588
Capital account openness	−0.136	−0.187	0.200	0.022	−0.816*	0.391	0.227	0.354	0.177

Notes:
Symbols *, ** and *** indicate significant correlations at 10, 5, and 1 percent levels, respectively. Emerging markets are defined according to the Morgan Stanley Capital International (MSCI) Emerging Market Index. Only countries that experienced positive EMP are included in the sample (except Hungary, see endnote 4), for a total of 20. High level financial restrictions are defined as 0.75 or above for bond and equity and as 1.0 for bond inflow and equity inflow according to the Schindler capital controls index.

Market Index is used to classify emerging markets, and only emerging markets that experienced positive EMP are included in the sample.[4] A description of variables is provided in Table 4.4.

The focus on emerging markets stems from several observations. First, these countries were the source of most of the precrisis economic growth, and most of the global population lives there. Second, the process of globalization rapidly increased the financial and trade linkages of emerging markets with the OECD countries, relative to the more limited integration of developing, nonemerging market countries. Finally, the OECD countries have had elastic access to large dollar swap lines extended by the US Federal Reserve (either directly or via the Federal Reserve's large swap line with the European Central Bank). Thereby, the OECD countries were able to meet excess demand for dollar liquidity by borrowing dollar reserves from the Federal Reserve, facilitating the adjustment deleveraging pressures. In contrast, most emerging markets were not able to rely on borrowed reserves via swap lines; thereby they were more exposed to the need to adjust abruptly to the global crisis.

Only two of the variables for the full sample of emerging markets correlate significantly with EMP. GDP per capita (0.57) and total financial account liabilities (0.70) are positively correlated with EMP and are significant at the 1 percent level. Emerging market countries with higher per capita income, generally more integrated in the global financial system, experienced more intense EMP. Emerging markets that were more burdened with total foreign debt also experienced higher levels of EMP, partly because the global liquidity shortage associated with the financial crisis made financing debt more difficult or, in some cases, impossible for several months. In addition, external balance sheet exposure is positively (weakly) correlated with EMP (0.36). Countries not able to cover their short-term portfolio debt with reserves experienced somewhat greater external vulnerability as measured by higher values of exchange market pressure.

THE TRADE-OFF BETWEEN RESERVE LOSS AND EXCHANGE RATE DEPRECIATION

We observed that countries differ markedly in their response to the financial crisis in terms of whether exchange rate depreciation or losses of reserves absorbed EMP. Are there discernable patterns in the loss of international reserves relative to exchange rate depreciation in emerging markets for a given degree of exchange rate pressure during the global financial crisis? This is measured as the loss of international reserves as a percentage of total exchange market pressure. Large values indicate that

Table 4.4 Descriptions of variables

Variable	Description	Period	Sources	Notes
Trade and GDP				
GDP per capita	GDP (US$ million)/population	2007	National Accounts Data, International Financial Statistics, IMF	GDP in domestic currency predivided by per-US$ exchange rate
Trade openness	(imports + exports)/GDP	2007	International Financial Statistics, IMF	
Commodity exports	commodity exports (US$ million)/ total exports (US$ million)	2007	Commodity Trade Statistics Database, UNSD	
Financial indicators				
Stock market capitalization	stock market capitalization/GDP	2005	Financial Structure Dataset, World Bank	For details see econ. worldbank.org/staff/tbeck.
Capital account openness	Chinn-Ito capital account openness index	2007	http://web.pdx.edu/~ito/ Chinn-Ito_website.htm	For details see web. pdx.edu/~ito/Readme_ kaopen2007.pdf.
Balance sheet exposure	[short-term debt (US$ million) – international reserves (US$ million)] / International Reserves (US$ million)	2007	International Investment Position Data, International Financial Statistics, IMF	short-term debt proxied with portfolio investment debt liabilities
Financial account liabilities	total financial account liabilities including direct investment, portfolio debt and equity liabilities, and financial derivatives (stock, % of GDP)	2007	International Investment Position Data, International Financial Statistics, IMF	
Crisis measures				
Exchange market pressure (EMP)	(% Δ exchange rate) − (% Δ foreign exchange reserves)	July 2008 – February 2009	International Financial Statistics, IMF	exchange rate: local currency/US$
Reserve loss relative to EMP	(−% Δ foreign exchange reserves)/ EMP	July 2008 – February 2009	International Financial Statistics, IMF	

countries are absorbing a high percentage of the total shock by selling international reserves.

It is not clear a priori how emerging markets would respond, in terms of using exchange rates or reserves, in absorbing an EMP shock. It would seem to be related to balance sheet exposure. If emerging markets have a high degree of short-term external debt exposure, often denominated in a foreign currency, then they may want to limit exchange rate depreciation that increases the real value of the foreign debt. This would suggest a positive value between balance sheet exposure and the ratio of international reserves to EMP. On the other hand, balance sheet exposure by definition means that short-term external liabilities are not covered by holdings of international reserves. This makes countries more vulnerable to the global financial shock and less able to stem the external crisis by using international reserves that are in relatively short supply. This argues for a negative link between balance sheet exposure and the ratio of international reserves to EMP.

Figure 4.2 shows the link between balance sheet exposure and EMP for the sample of emerging markets. There is a negative correlation of −0.36—countries with fewer reserves relative to short-term external portfolio debt rely more on exchange rate depreciation to absorb the EMP shock. Limited reserves constrain countries in how they respond to the crisis, as is consistent with the second hypothesis discussed above.

Table 4.5 reports the correlation between the fraction of EMP due to loss of reserves ($-\%\Delta$ international reserves/EMP) with balance sheet exposure in 2007, where the sample of emerging markets has been segmented by the extent of lost reserves (percentage of EMP) during the financial crisis. This analysis reveals significant heterogeneity. While for the full sample of 20 emerging markets, the correlation between balance sheet exposure and the fraction of EMP accommodated by reserves loss is negative during the crisis, this correlation is positive and significant for nine countries that accommodated their EMP by reserves losses above 30 percent. Moreover, this correlation is highly significant within the group of eight emerging markets that accommodated their EMP by reserves losses above 40 percent, illustrated in Figure 4.3. All of these countries had reserves covering more than their short-term external debt, inducing them to absorb a significant portion of their exchange market pressure by selling reserves. This was the case in Korea and Russia, among others, during the 2008–09 crisis, reflecting the use of reserves to meet balance sheet exposure of systemic banks or politically powerful agents in the first phase of the crisis.

On the other hand, countries with few reserves relative to portfolio debt are much more likely to rely on exchange rate depreciation than to

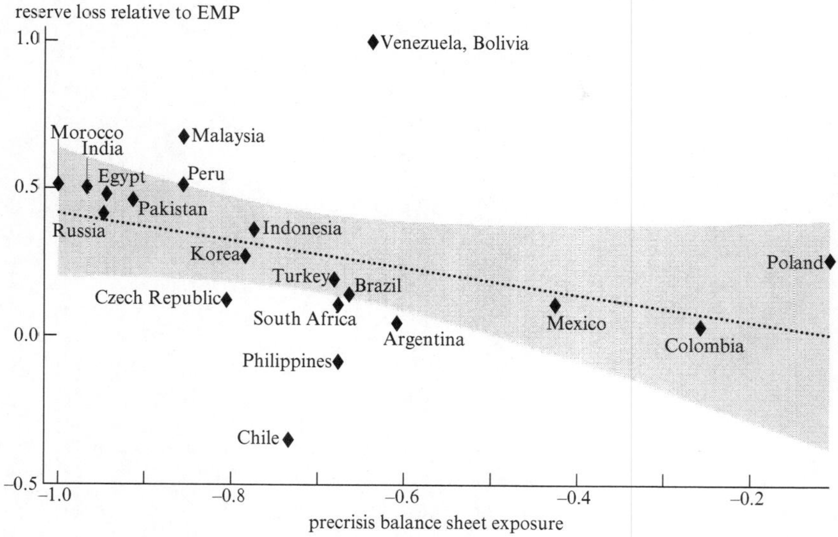

Note: The dotted line represents the linear fit, and the shaded area represents the 95 percent confidence interval. Emerging markets are defined according to the Morgan Stanley Capital International (EMSCI) Emerging Market Index. The correlation between loss of international reserves as a fraction of EMP and precrisis balance sheet exposure is −0.36 (p-value = 0.12).

Figure 4.2 International reserve losses relative to exchange market pressure and precrisis balance sheet exposure: emerging markets

Table 4.5 Correlations: shares of EMP due to loss of reserves with balance sheet exposure, 2007

(Δ international reserves)/ EMP cut-off	Correlation with balance sheet exposure	Number of countries
none	−0.3557	20
10	−0.3252	16
20	−0.1565	11
30	0.6718**	9
40	0.9142***	8

Notes:
Symbols ** and *** indicate significant correlations at 5 and 1 percent levels, respectively. Emerging markets are defined according to the Morgan Stanley Capital International (MSCI) Emerging Market Index. Only countries that experienced positive EMP are included in the sample (except Hungary, see endnote 4), for a total of 20.

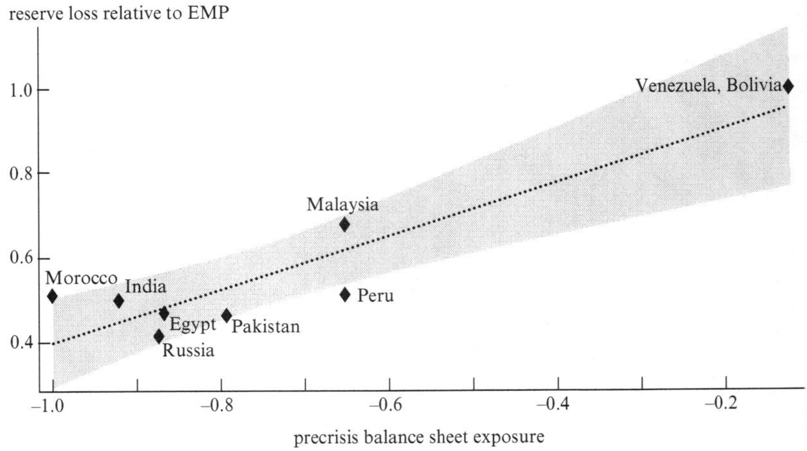

Notes:
The dotted line represents the linear fit, and the shaded area represents the 95 percent confidence interval.
The correlation between loss of international reserves as a fraction of EMP and precrisis balance sheet exposure is 0.93 significant at the 1 percent level.

Figure 4.3 Share of exchange market pressure due to loss of reserves with balance sheet exposure (2007): emerging markets with significant loss of reserves relative to EMP (40% or higher)

use scarce reserves to absorb the global financial shock. This finding is an interesting contrast to the results in Table 4.3 and suggests that the financial determinants of total vulnerability (EMP)—total financial account external liabilities—are distinct from the factors that determine the trade-off between relying on reserves rather than exchange rate depreciation—balance sheet exposure—when countries face external financial shocks.

CONCLUSIONS

The global financial crisis affected countries across the globe in all regions, at all income levels and whether or not they had tight restrictions on capital flows. The financial crisis also hit all regions of the world, although the greatest effect was felt in Eastern Europe and Central Asia. This is consistent with the notion that the subprime crisis emanating from the United States was directly linked to financial institutions in Western Europe, and Western Europe in turn was tightly linked through banking ties with the relatively exposed and fragile economies of Eastern Europe.

Emerging markets and low income countries, and particularly those countries with higher ratios of total foreign liabilities to GDP, were more vulnerable to the financial crisis. We found clear evidence that higher balance sheet exposure (higher short-term foreign debt relative to international reserves) is significantly associated with greater weight attached to currency depreciation and with lower weight attached to losing international reserves, as means of dealing with exchange market pressure during the crisis. While larger ratios of total external liabilities to GDP are clearly associated with larger EMP, a higher ratio of external short-term debt to international reserves is associated with a higher weight on price adjustment (exchange rate depreciation) and lower weight on quantity adjustment (losing reserves) as a way to accommodate a given EMP. Despite the remarkable build-up of international reserves by emerging markets during the period prior to the financial crisis, emerging markets relied primarily on exchange rate depreciation rather than reserve loss to absorb most of the exchange market pressure shock.

These findings are consistent with the observations in Aizenman and Sun (2009) regarding emerging markets' switch during the crisis from the fear of floating (Calvo and Reinhart 2002) to the fear of losing reserves during the crisis. While ratios of international reserves to GDP were high in most emerging markets before the crisis, relative to their levels in previous crises, they rarely were high enough to cover the entire external portfolio liabilities of the affected countries. Thus, countries opted to rely on exchange rate adjustment, refraining from fast depletion of their international reserves. The reluctance to rely more on reserves depletion may reflect several concerns: fear that losing reserves too fast may propagate a run on the remaining reserves, and uncertainty about crisis duration may suggest keeping reserves to deal with future market pressure. Furthermore, at times of collapsing global demand, countries are more willing to engage in competitive depreciation, as the downside of higher inflation is sharply mitigated by the global recession. Our results are also in line with Frankel and Saravelos (2010), finding that the ratio of central bank reserves to GDP in 2007 explains significantly the 2008–09 crisis incidence, where higher ratios of precrisis reserves to GDP were associated with lower exchange market pressure during the crisis. Yet, our results also suggest a key importance for the ratio of total external liabilities to GDP in accounting for higher exchange market pressure during the crisis.

Our results corroborate the notion that globally linked, national financial markets, intermediated via foreign currency markets, transmitted globally the 2008–09 financial crisis. In turbulent times, when the duration of depth of the global crisis remains unknown, emerging-market behavior has been characterized more by the fear of losing reserves and less by the fear of floating. Despite the remarkable build-up of international reserves by emerging markets during the period prior to the financial crisis, countries relied primarily on exchange rate depreciation rather than reserve loss to absorb most of the exchange market pressure shock. This could reflect a deliberate choice, possibly to gain competitiveness at times of collapsing export demand. It may also reflect market actions that moved quickly and strongly to adjust to changing circumstances, especially in emerging markets with open capital markets. The financial market crisis was followed by a global recession, suggesting that exchange rate depreciations, attempting to improve international competitiveness, can be part of the adjustment of small economies but cannot resolve global collapsing demand. Our findings also confirm the key importance of balance sheet effects in explaining vulnerabilities and adjustments. Countries with higher ratios of total foreign liabilities to GDP were more vulnerable to the financial crisis. Countries with large balance sheet exposure—high external portfolio liabilities exceeding international reserves—responded to the global shock by allowing greater exchange rate depreciation and comparatively less reserve loss.

NOTES

Acknowledgments. We are grateful to Vladyslav Sushko and Yuhan Xue for their excellent research assistance and to our discussant Ilan Noy and other participants at the 19–20 August 2010 EWC-KDI conference on Global Economic Crisis: Impacts, Transmission and Recovery. Any remaining errors are ours

1. See Eichengreen and Hausmann (2005) for studies on the impact of balance sheet exposure on financial instability.
2. See Girton and Roper (1977) and Frankel (2009) for further discussion of exchange market pressure.
3. A second EMP measure is the sum of the percentage change in the exchange rate and loss of international reserves as a percentage of the monetary base. This measure focuses on the potential monetary effects of reserve losses during the financial crisis. It gave an almost identical ranking of external market pressure and is not reported for brevity.
4. The MSCI Emerging Markets Index includes 26 economies, five of which experienced positive EMP during the period August 2008 to February 2009: China, Israel, Jordan, Taiwan and Thailand. We exclude Hungary from the group of 21 emerging markets that experienced negative EMP, because Hungary received a substantial IMF disbursement during our sample period (US$6.4 billion out of a $15.7 billion IMF stand-by agreement). This stand-by agreement significantly affected Hungary's foreign exchange reserve position and potentially the exchange rate depreciation rate. Our sample is composed of the remaining 20 emerging markets: Argentina, Brazil, Chile, Colombia, Czech Republic, Egypt, India, Indonesia, Korea, Malaysia, Mexico, Morocco, Pakistan, Peru, the Philippines, Poland, Russia, South Africa, Turkey and Venezuela.

REFERENCES

Aizenman, J. and Y. Sun. 2009. *The Financial Crisis and Sizable International Reserves Depletion: From 'Fear of Floating' to the 'Fear of Losing International Reserves'?* NBER Working Paper 15308. Cambridge, Massachusetts: National Bureau of Economic Research. Available at www.nber.org.

Calvo, G.A. and C.M. Reinhart. 2002. "Fear of Floating". *Quarterly Journal of Economics*, **117** (2): 379–408.

Danninger, S., R. Balakrishnan, S. Elikdad and I. Tytell. 2009. "How Linkages Fuel the Fire: The Transmission of Financial Stress from Advanced to Emerging Economies". In *World Economic Outlook: Crisis and Recovery*, edited by the IMF, pp.139–75. Washington: International Monetary Fund. Available at http://www.imf.org/external/pubs/ft/weo/2009/01/index.htm.

Eichengreen, B. and R. Hausmann (eds). 2005. *Other People's Money, Debt Denomination and Financial Instability in Emerging Market Economies*. Chicago: University of Chicago Press.

Frankel, J. 2009. "New Estimation of China's Exchange Rate Regime". *Pacific Economic Review*, **14** (3): 346–60.

Frankel, J. and G. Saravelos. 2010. *Are Leading Indicators of Financial Crises Useful for Assessing Country Vulnerability? Evidence from the 2008–09 Global Crisis*. NBER Working Paper 16047. Cambridge, Massachusetts: National Bureau of Economic Research.

Girton, L. and D. Roper. 1977. "A Monetary Model of Exchange Market Pressure Applied to the Postwar Canadian Experience". *American Economic Review*, **67**: 537–48.

Levy-Yeyati, E. and F. Sturzenegger. 2005. "Classifying Exchange Rate Regimes: Deeds vs. Words". *European Economic Review*, **49** (6): 1603–35.

Obstfeld, M. 2010. "The Immoderate World Economy". *Journal of International Money and Finance*, **29** (4): 603–14.

Obstfeld, M. and K. Rogoff. 2010. "Global Imbalances and the Financial Crisis: Products of Common Causes". Unpublished paper, University of California at Berkeley.

5. How did Korean financial markets get infected by the global financial crisis?

Hangyong Lee and Min-Kyu Song

INTRODUCTION

The Korean economy was hit hard by the global financial crisis. High short-term external debt resulted from excessive short-term borrowing by banks before the crisis, and the subsequent large-scale capital outflows raised concerns about another currency crisis in Korea. This chapter attempts to explain why external debt was increasing rapidly, before the September 2008 bankruptcy of Lehman Brothers, and how financial instability in advanced countries generated an immediate and powerful spillover to the Korean economy.

Korea appeared to be enjoying steady macroeconomic performance up to the time that the global financial markets were shaken by the bankruptcy announcement. Even when the subprime mortgage problems came to surface in mid-2007, the initial impact on the Korean economy was limited in scale and severity. Despite the underlying strength of the fundamentals in the Korean economy, however, vulnerability was arising from increased openness in international trade and finance. Greater openness can contribute to robust economic activities in normal times, but at the same time it can widen channels through which the shocks originating in advanced countries could be transmitted to the Korean economy.

Following the bankruptcy, financially vulnerable Korea experienced large capital outflows and serious difficulties in refinancing liabilities denominated in foreign currency. Then exports and industrial production plummeted, as a result of contracting global demand in late 2008, leading to a pronounced deceleration of economic growth. In the literature on contagion, countries can be linked through two different channels of transmission: the international trade channel and the international financial channel. Given Korea's export-oriented economic growth and fully opened financial markets, both channels played important roles in the transmission of external shocks to the Korean economy. Nevertheless, along with the global integration of financial markets, financial channels are growing in importance in transmission of shocks between economies.[1] The global financial crisis highlighted the critical role of financial markets in the propagation of adverse shocks, both in spreading shocks from one country to another and in magnifying their effects. Kohn (2008) also notes that financial linkages might now be more important than the traditional trade linkages. Cetorelli and Goldberg (2010) provide evidence on global banks' role in the transmission of the crisis to emerging market economies.

Indeed, the biggest concern raised by the media and investors was that Korea was at risk of external debt defaults and a foreign exchange liquidity problem. This concern was based on the observation that Korea's external position was highly leveraged, despite large foreign exchange reserves. For example, in a *Financial Times* (2009) report, short-term external debt on a remaining maturity basis were compared with foreign exchange reserves, giving Korea one of Asia's skimpiest coverage ratios. In this respect, a foreign exchange liquidity problem appeared to be the starting point of spillovers. This chapter attempts to explain why Korea's external debt was increasing rapidly before the bankruptcy of Lehman Brothers and how financial deleveraging in advanced countries generated an immediate and powerful spillover to the Korean economy.

FOREIGN CURRENCY SHORTAGE DURING THE GLOBAL FINANCIAL CRISIS

Capital Outflows

In the wake of the Lehman Brothers bankruptcy, the Korean won depreciated sharply, and there was a huge increase in the credit default swap (CDS) premium. Figure 5.1 illustrates the rapid deterioration in the exchange rate, as the number of Korean won per US dollar rose to 1478.5 on 29 October 2008, representing a 57.6 percent increase in won per dollar from the beginning of 2008. The CDS premium, which is a proxy for the cost of foreign currency funding, also skyrocketed to 699 basis points on 27 October 2008.

The changes in the exchange rate and CDS premium reflect the severe deterioration in foreign currency liquidity following the global financial crisis. Moreover, Figure 5.2 shows that Korea underwent reversals of capital inflows, recording a large capital account deficit of $42.6 billion in the fourth quarter of 2008. The rapid outflows of foreign capital caused a liquidity strain on the foreign exchange market, triggering a sudden rise in the exchange rate.

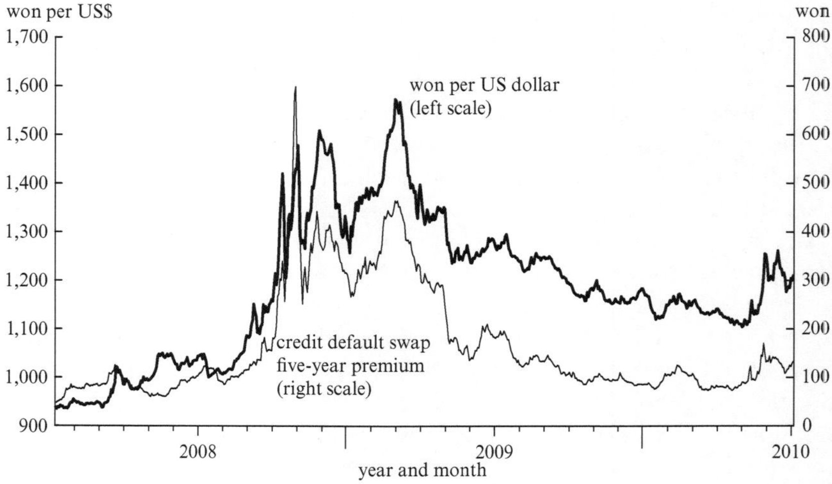

Notes:
The right-hand scale is the credit default swap (CDS) five-year premium (basis point = 0.01 percentage point).
The dataset includes working days from 2 January 2008 to 30 June 2010.

Source: Bank of Korea and Bloomberg.

Figure 5.1 Exchange rate and credit default swap premium in Korea, 2008–10

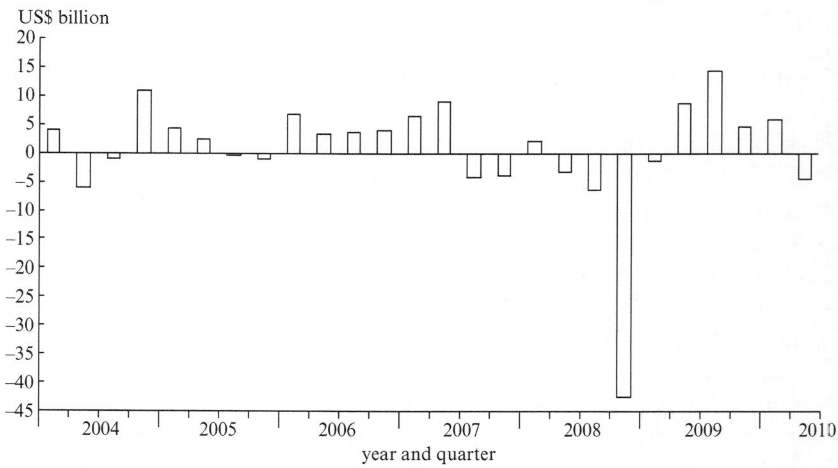

Source: Bank of Korea.

Figure 5.2 Capital account of Korea, 2004–2010

Table 5.1 Foreign currency shortage and balance of payments in Korea, 2008–09 (US$ billion)

Item	2008 Q1	2008 Q2	2008 Q3	2008 Q4	2009 Q1	2009 Q2
Current account (A)	−4.866	−0.412	−8.330	7.831	8.618	13.097
Capital account (B)	1.990	−3.161	−6.286	−42.627	−1.399	8.682
Investments	2.101	−2.934	−6.069	−43.291	−2.124	8.387
Direct investments	−5.782	−4.140	−3.661	−2.050	−2.045	−0.172
Portfolio investments	−4.402	8.357	−9.421	3.061	3.532	16.740
Derivatives	−1.250	−1.241	−3.550	−8.729	−4.894	−0.615
Other investments	13.533	−5.910	10.564	−35.572	1.283	−7.566
Other capital account	−0.110	−0.227	−0.218	0.664	0.725	0.295
A+B	−2.876	−3.573	−14.616	−34.796	7.219	21.779
Changes in reserve assets (C)	3.850	5.718	12.883	33.995	−9.017	−19.542
Errors and omissions (D)	−0.974	−2.146	1.733	0.800	1.798	−2.238
C+D	2.876	3.572	14.616	34.795	−7.219	21.780

Notes:
A positive number in the changes of reserve assets corresponds to a decrease in reserve assets. The sum of current account and capital account should be equal to the sum of changes in reserve assets and the errors and omissions, but with the opposite sign.

Source: Bank of Korea.

Table 5.1 exhibits the balance of payment in Korea with subaccounts in the capital account. It tells us which subaccount was more responsible for the foreign exchange shortage. In this chapter, the foreign exchange shortage is defined as the sum of the current account deficit and the capital account deficit, in the sense that the deficits should be financed by a decrease in reserve assets. Table 5.1 shows that the foreign exchange shortage increased to $14.6 billion in the third quarter of 2008, but the size of the current account deficit was greater than the size of the capital account deficit during that period. In the fourth quarter, despite the current account surplus, the foreign currency shortage amounted to $34.8 billion, resulting in a sharp decrease in reserve assets. In 2009, the current account continued to exhibit a surplus, and the capital account also moved back to a surplus in the second quarter.

The subaccounts in Table 5.1 show that the huge foreign currency shortage in the fourth quarter of 2008 can mostly be attributed to a large deficit in other investments. The deficit of other investments amounted to $35.6 billion among the total capital account deficit of $42.6 billion. A close look at the balance of other investments, which include trade credits,

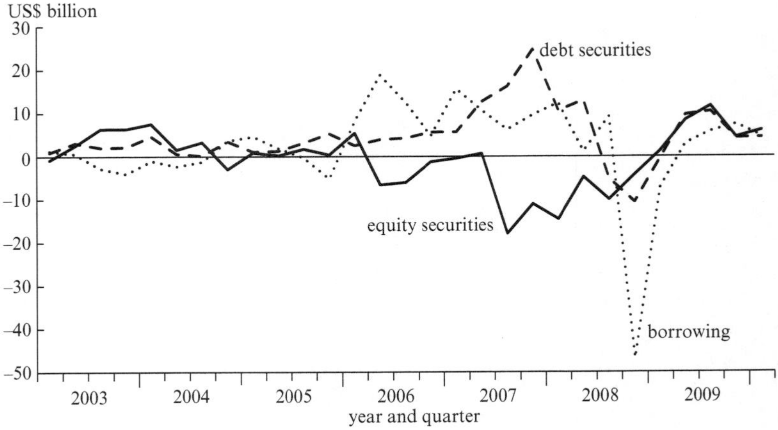

Source: Bank of Korea.

Figure 5.3 Capital outflows from Korea: equities, bonds, and borrowing, 2003–2009

loans (borrowing), currency and deposits, reveals that large capital outflows from short-term borrowing by domestic deposit-taking institutions (including foreign bank branches) were responsible for the huge deficit during the period.

In contrast, the cause of the foreign exchange shortage in the third quarter of 2008 was quite different. The balance of other investments recorded a surplus of $10.6 billion, suggesting that external borrowing continued up to the time of the bankruptcy of Lehman Brothers. The balance of portfolio investments, however, recorded a deficit of $9.4 billion. Thus, portfolio investments were the main cause of the foreign exchange shortage in the third quarter of 2008.

Although Table 5.1 outlines the balance of payments and thus the foreign exchange shortage, it does not provide information about the magnitude of capital outflows by foreign investors. To examine the capital flows across borders, we need to look at the liability side of the capital account. Figure 5.3 depicts the trend of capital flows in equity securities investments, debt securities (bonds) investments and borrowing. The data on equity investments and debt securities investments are from the liability side of portfolio investments, and the data on borrowing are from a part of the liability side of other investments in the capital account. Since the data are from the liability side of the capital account, positive values imply capital inflows (and negative values capital outflows) by foreign investors.

Several interesting aspects emerge from Figure 5.3. First, capital outflows from borrowing were most evident in the fourth quarter of 2008. In particular, short-term borrowing by deposit-taking institutions experienced a huge capital outflow of $48.4 billion in the period. Although smaller than the capital outflows from borrowing, there were also sizeable capital outflows from portfolio investments during the period. The capital outflows from equity and bond investments amounted to $4.3 billion and $10.0 billion, respectively.[2]

Second, although all three investment categories recorded capital outflows in the fourth quarter of 2008, they had earlier shown quite different trends up to the second quarter of 2008. Foreign investors had already begun to sell domestic equities in mid-2007 when subprime mortgage problems in the United States came to the surface. The capital outflows from equity investments amounted to $28.9 billion in the second half of 2007 and $29.3 billion in the first half of 2008, much larger than the capital outflows in the second half of 2008.[3]

Unlike equity investments, however, large-scale capital inflows to the domestic bond market were witnessed until the second quarter of 2008. In 2007, for example, $59.1 billion was invested in domestic debt securities. Similarly, since 2006, external net borrowing also continued to exhibit positive numbers until the third quarter of 2008. The capital inflows through borrowing amounted to $44.2 billion in 2006 and $42.0 billion in 2007. Even between the first quarter and third quarter of 2008, $22.8 billion was newly borrowed. The large-scale borrowing inevitably increased the external debt and thus raised concerns about potential currency crisis.

Third, as the Korean economy began to recover and the financial markets regained stability in 2009, all three investment categories bounced back to exhibit capital inflows. In 2009, $25.7 billion and $23.7 billion were invested in equity securities and debt securities, respectively. External borrowing also started to increase in the second quarter of 2009, amounting to $9.0 billion through the year.

External Debt

At the time of the outbreak of the global financial crisis, the media and investors raised concerns about how the Korean economy would perform, even though it was in much healthier shape than it had been during the 1997–98 East Asian crisis. In particular, there were concerns that Korea might face another foreign exchange crisis akin to the one it faced a decade earlier. Given the drought of foreign capital, some foreign investors deemed the Korean economy to be very risky because of its large external debt. For instance, *The Economist* (2009) reported the HSBC forecast that

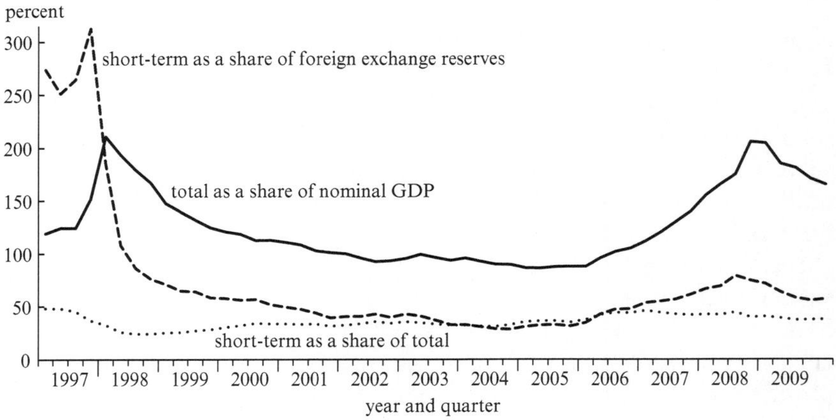

Figure 5.4 External debt of Korea: total and short-term, 1997–2010

Korea's short-term debt would exceed its shrinking reserves by the end of 2009.

Indeed, as we have seen in the previous section, the rapid increases in short-term borrowing by domestic banks since 2006 resulted in large external debt and thus made the Korean economy vulnerable to the global credit crunch.[4] The external debt was only $187.9 billion at the end of 2005, but it grew rapidly, owing to large-scale external borrowing by domestic banks (including foreign bank branches), and reached $426.1 billion in the third quarter of 2008. This level of total external debt was equivalent to 175 percent of GDP. Then the total external debt-to-GDP ratio increased to 206 percent in the fourth quarter of 2008, before decreasing steadily from 2009 onward (Figure 5.4).[5] This high debt-to-GDP ratio is comparable to the one in the 1997–98 Asian crisis (when the ratio was 210 percent in the first quarter of 1998).

Short-term external debt (with original maturity less than a year) increased more rapidly, from $65.9 billion at the end of 2005 to $189.6 billion in the third quarter of 2008. As a result, the ratio of short-term debt to total external debt was 45 percent in the third quarter of 2008, similar to the level of 48 percent reached in the first quarter of 1997. At a point when external finance becomes no longer available, Korea would have to run down its foreign exchange reserves. Therefore, international organizations and investors considered the ratio of short-term debt to foreign exchange reserves as a useful measure of the financing risk that the Korean economy would face. The ratio revealed why some foreign investors raised concerns about a potential default by Korea on its foreign debt. Despite large foreign reserves, the ratio of short-term debt to reserves increased to 79.1

percent in the third quarter of 2008. Moreover, at the end of 2008, total current external debt (debt with remaining maturity of less than a year) due in 2009 was $193 billion, which comprised short-term contracts of $150 billion and long-term debt of $43 billion due in 2009. Thus, the ratio of current external debt to foreign exchange reserves became close to one. This was what the *Financial Times* (1 March 2009) pointed out as a sign of vulnerability that might cause another currency crisis in Korea.

In responding to the concerns about external debt, the Korean government argued that a significant portion of external debt was risk-free. The government asserted that, among the total external debt of $379 billion at the end of 2008, $103 billion was nonobligatory debt, meaning that this amount was not subject to any repayment burden. For example, $39 billion was incurred as a result of advanced receipts (or unearned revenue) for shipbuilding contracts, which would be cleared from the books at the time of delivery of ships. Excluding this nonobligatory debt, the net external debt of the Korean economy came to $276 billion, significantly smaller than the claimed $379 billion. In addition, $72.4 billion of the short-term external debt of $149.9 billion was owed to domestic branches of foreign banks. Therefore, the point was made that Korean domestic banks and corporations owed only $77.5 billion, which was about a third of the foreign exchange reserves.[6]

BACKGROUND OF THE HIGH EXTERNAL DEBT

Foreign Currency Financing and Foreign Exchange Swaps

A domestic Korean bank can raise foreign currency funds in two ways: borrowing directly in the foreign currency money markets or borrowing domestic currency and converting the proceeds into foreign currency through a foreign exchange (FX) swap. When a Korean bank raises US dollars in an FX swap, it exchanges Korean won for dollars at the foreign exchange spot rate, while contracting to exchange in the reverse direction on the maturity date at the foreign exchange forward rate. Because the counterparties of Korean banks in FX swaps are most likely foreign bank branches, they are interconnected.

The Korean economy was hit hard by the global financial crisis. High short-term external debt resulted from excessive short-term borrowing by banks before the crisis, and the subsequent large-scale capital outflows raised concerns about another currency crisis in Korea. This chapter attempts to explain why external debt was increasing rapidly, before the September 2008 bankruptcy of Lehman Brothers, and how financial

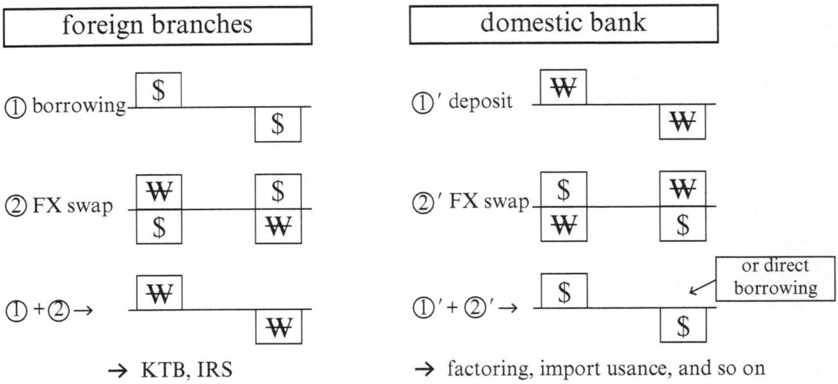

Notes:
KTB = Korean Treasury Bond.
IRS = interest rate swaps.

Figure 5.5 Flows of borrowed foreign funds between foreign bank branches and Korean banks

instability in advanced countries generated an immediate and powerful spillover to the Korean economy.

Figure 5.5 illustrates how foreign bank branches and Korean banks are interconnected through FX swaps. It shows the position changes of foreign bank branches (left panel) and Korean banks (right panel) in three steps. In each step, the left rectangle represents a transaction at time t and the right rectangle represents a transaction at $t+s$ (that is, a maturing date of borrowing or FX swap). A rectangle above the horizontal axis denotes capital inflows while a rectangle below the axis denotes capital outflows. Currency units of transactions are marked inside the rectangles.

The first step at the top of the left panel shows that foreign bank branches borrow in US dollars (inflows) and repay the principal and interest in the future (outflows). Likewise, the first step of the right panel illustrates Korean banks' financing (for instance, deposits) and repayment in Korean won. In the second steps (middle of both panels), foreign bank branches (or Korean banks) convert the US dollars (or Korean won) into Korean won (or US dollars) in an FX swap for a short-term contract. Similarly, foreign bank branches and Korean banks can enter into currency swap agreement for a long-term contract. As a result, foreign bank branches (or Korean banks) end up with funds denominated in Korean won (or in US dollars) as depicted in the third steps (bottom of both panels).[7] The third steps (without the first and the second

Table 5.2 External debt from borrowing by the banking sector in Korea, 2003–09

Item	2003	2004	2005	2006	2007	2008	2009
External debt							
Total (US$ billion)	46.1	47.0	51.2	96.2	135.4	112.6	120.2
Korean banks							
US$ billion	25.0	24.6	28.1	43.3	55.0	42.5	44.5
share of total (%)	54.3	52.3	54.9	45.1	40.7	37.8	37.0
Foreign bank branches							
US$ billion	21.0	22.4	23.1	52.9	80.3	70.1	75.7
share of total (%)	45.7	47.7	45.1	54.9	59.3	62.2	63.0
Change in external debt (%)							
Total	4.8	0.9	4.2	45.0	39.2	−22.8	7.6
Korean banks	2.0	−0.4	3.5	15.2	11.7	−12.5	2.0
Foreign bank branches	2.8	1.4	0.7	29.8	27.5	−10.3	5.6

Source: Bank of Korea.

steps) illustrate cases in which foreign bank branches raise funds directly in Korean won and Korean banks borrow money directly in US dollars.

Finally, foreign bank branches invest the proceeds in won-denominated domestic bonds or interest rate swaps, while Korean banks use the fund for loans to importing firms, factoring for exports and so on. The previous section shows that both external borrowing and bond investments had increased substantially since 2006. The financing mechanism in Figure 5.5 suggests that external borrowing and bond investment can be positively correlated, to the extent that foreign bank branches invest in domestic bonds.

Who, then, was more responsible for the increase in external debt in the banking sector: Korean banks or foreign bank branches? Table 5.2 outlines the domestic banking sector's external debt between 2003 and 2009. The total external debt of the banking sector rose from $51.2 billion in 2005 to $96.2 billion in 2006 and to $135.4 billion in 2007. The dramatic increase in external debt mainly came from the sharp rise in borrowing by foreign bank branches. The net increases in the external debt owed to foreign bank branches were $29.8 billion in 2006 and $27.5 billion in 2007. In contrast, Korean banks raised new external capital of $15.2 billion in 2006 and $11.7 billion in 2007. In 2005, the share of Korean banks in the total external debt of the banking sector was 54.9 percent, but it fell to 45.1 percent in 2006 and 40.7 percent in 2007. Interestingly, although Korean banks had less external debt before the Lehman Brothers bankruptcy, they

Table 5.3 Orders received by Korean shipbuilding firms and foreign currency forward contracts, 2003–09

Item	2003	2004	2005	2006	2007	2008	2009
Ship orders received (A, US$ billion)	23.9	31.8	31.3	61.7	97.5	71.8	18.3
Forward contracts (B, US$ billion)	4.5	12.5	16.8	35.3	53.3	41.7	16.1
B/A (%)	18.7	39.3	53.8	57.1	54.6	58.0	87.6

Source: Bank of Korea.

experienced a larger withdrawal of funds (decrease of external debt) than foreign bank branches in 2008.

Why did external borrowing increase so rapidly? The following discussion reviews the underlying factors that may have contributed to the rapid increase in external debt through the mechanisms described above.

Hedging Foreign Exchange Risks and Banks' Foreign Exchange Positions

Among the factors that led banks to increase external borrowing since 2006, one of the most frequently suggested is the increase in demand for foreign currency forward contracts by domestic exporting firms and domestic asset management firms.[8] If an exporting firm does not wish to be exposed to exchange rate risk over a period of time, it opens a forward contract with a Korean bank. Then the Korean bank is left with the exposure to exchange rate risk in the future. Thus, the bank borrows foreign currency and exchanges it into domestic currency in the spot market, to hedge the risk in its forward position. These transactions inevitably increased external debt.

The most notable exporting firms that actively entered into foreign currency forward contracts were shipbuilding firms. Because of the large size of the shipbuilding contracts and the long time interval between an order and a delivery, the shipbuilding firms in Korea are exposed to high exchange rate risks and thus have a great incentive to hedge them. Indeed, the ship orders received by Korean firms, which have the largest market share in the world market, rose by 97.3 percent (to $61.7 billion) in 2006 and by 58.0 percent (to $97.5 billion) in 2007. At the same time, the amount of forward contracts by shipbuilding firms rose to $35.3 billion in 2006 and $53.3 billion in 2007 (Table 5.3).

The increase in the external debt caused by the shipbuilding firms' forward contracts, however, would be reduced at the maturity date of the forward contracts. If shipbuilding firms deliver the foreign currency to banks, with the payment received from the importers at the maturity date, the banks can use the proceeds for the repayment of the external debt. This is the reason why the Korean government argued that the external debt in Korea was overly exaggerated.[9]

In addition to hedging demand by shipbuilding firms, domestic asset management firms also entered into forward contracts on a large scale in 2006 and 2007, as foreign investments by domestic residents increased. Investments in foreign securities rose from only $1.5 billion in 2005 to $13.1 billion in 2006 and $27.2 billion in 2007. For a substantial part of these investments, asset management firms entered into forward contracts, contributing to an increase in external debt.

Arbitrage Opportunity and Domestic Bond Investments

As described in the previous subsection, external borrowing by foreign bank branches and their investment in bond markets started to rise simultaneously in 2006. At that time, Korean banks either borrowed external funds directly or entered FX swaps with foreign bank branches in order to adjust foreign exchange positions. If they used FX swaps to raise foreign currency, the foreign bank branches were left with Korean won funds. Thus, it is not surprising that, with the proceeds, the foreign bank branches began to increase investments in domestic bonds. From the perspective of foreign bank branches, which had access to foreign capital at relatively low cost, FX swaps and bond investments seemed to provide a good, profitable investment opportunity.

Another aspect that might explain the increase in bond investments is the existence of arbitrage opportunities. In general, an arbitrage opportunity is measured by the deviation from covered interest parity conditions (CIP), which is defined as the interest rate differential minus the forward discount rate in FX swap markets.[10] Alternatively, it can be expressed as a difference between the domestic government bond yield and the currency swap rate (or FX swap rate) as illustrated in Figure 5.6.[11] It could be true that the excessive forward demand for foreign currency by shipbuilding firms and asset management firms put pressure on the currency swap rate to decrease. Given the domestic and foreign interest rates, the pressures could generate deviations from covered interest rate parity conditions and thus higher expected returns on bonds.

However, it is not clear that the arbitrage opportunity is enough to explain the foreign bank branches' investments in bonds. Until the second quarter of 2007, the deviation from CIP was not large. In 2006, it was only 0.20 percent for a three-month investment and 0.28 percent for a one-year

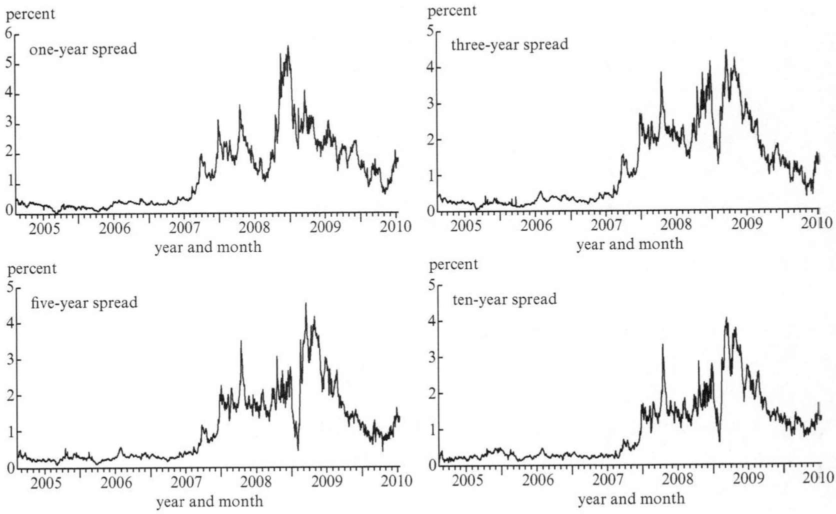

Figure 5.6 Spreads between yields of Korean Treasury Bonds and the currency swap rate in Korea, 2005–10

investment. Moreover, if we take into account transaction costs, the actual arbitrage opportunity could be minimal.

The deviation from CIP, however, began to widen considerably from the third quarter of 2007 (Table 5.4). For a three-month investment, for example, it increased to 1.41 percent in the third quarter and 2.77 percent in the fourth quarter of 2007. During the period from the third quarter of 2007 to the second quarter of 2008, the pressures on the FX swap market continued, as domestic banks attempted to secure US dollar funding to support domestic firms. At the same time, as argued by Baba et al. (2008), the nonresident foreign banks appeared to become much more cautious about lending US dollars because of heightened counterparty risk and their own need to preserve funds on hand. The liquidity problem in the foreign exchange market stemmed from the unfavorable demand and supply conditions, which likely contributed to further deviations from the CIP conditions.

Despite the large arbitrage opportunity, the foreign bank branches' investments in the bond market actually decreased in mid-2007. In addition to the credit crunch triggered by the US subprime mortgage problem, foreign bank branches appeared to face a binding constraint on Korean bond investments (the Korea limit).[12] Instead, the nonresident foreign investors increased their investments in bonds significantly, probably to exploit the widened arbitrage opportunities. In fact, their net investments

Table 5.4 *Domestic bond investment in Korea by foreign bank branches and nonresident foreign investors and arbitrage opportunity, 2006–08*

Item	2006				2007				2008	
	Q1	Q2	Q3	Q4	Q1	Q2	Q3	Q4	Q1	Q2
Investments (US$ billion)										
Foreign bank branches	0.83	9.73	6.02	1.17	16.79	−1.22	−2.41	0.68	3.57	−5.17
Nonresident foreign investors	0.17	0.41	0.64	0.12	1.82	2.13	12.68	19.87	7.10	8.60
Total	1.00	10.14	6.66	1.29	18.61	0.91	10.27	20.55	10.67	3.43
Arbitrage opportunity (% deviation from CIP)										
3 months	0.10	0.26	0.24	0.18	0.30	0.55	1.41	2.77	2.04	1.84
1 year	0.16	0.29	0.34	0.35	0.31	0.44	1.10	1.78	2.07	1.97

Source: Bank of Korea.

in bonds amounted to $12.68 billion in the third quarter and $19.87 billion in the fourth quarter of 2007, compared with $2.13 billion in the second quarter.

Other Domestic Factors in the Banking System

Since the mid-2000s, Korean banks have attempted to expand competitively. Facing sluggish bank deposits, Korean banks increased bond issuance with fixed coupon rates, and used the proceeds to expand mortgage lending with variable interest rates.[13] Then, to deal with the interest rate risks, Korean banks entered into interest rate swap agreements with foreign bank branches. Since all the Korean banks faced similar situations, foreign bank branches must be the counterparty of interest rate swaps. In interest rate swaps, Korean banks agreed to pay foreign bank branches cash flows equal to interest at a variable rate, while the foreign bank branches agreed to pay Korean banks cash flows equal to interest at a predetermined fixed rate on a notional amount for a number of periods. Interest rate swaps allow Korean banks to manage interest rate risks and also to provide foreign bank branches with another important investment vehicle. To finance funds of domestic currency for interest rate swaps, foreign bank branches borrowed money from abroad and used FX swaps. Unlike their bond investments, however, their interest rate swaps are closely related to the lending behavior of Korean banks.

Another important expansionary area of Korean banks is export–import finance, which includes foreign currency lending to firms that import machinery and equipment as well as factoring of export exchange bills and import usance. The share of long-term borrowing by foreign bank branches was only 3.7 percent at the end of the third quarter of 2008. In contrast, among the total external debt from borrowing by Korean banks, 14.6 percent was long-term debt, which suggests that, in part, Korean banks raised foreign currency funds to support the imports of machinery and equipment.

IMPACTS OF FOREIGN CAPITAL OUTFLOWS ON THE DOMESTIC FINANCIAL SYSTEM

An FX swap can be viewed as a simple lending and borrowing transaction between financial institutions. The only difference is the currencies involved in the transactions. That is, an FX swap is effectively equivalent to a transaction when foreign bank branches lend foreign currencies to Korean banks and at the same time borrow Korean won from Korean

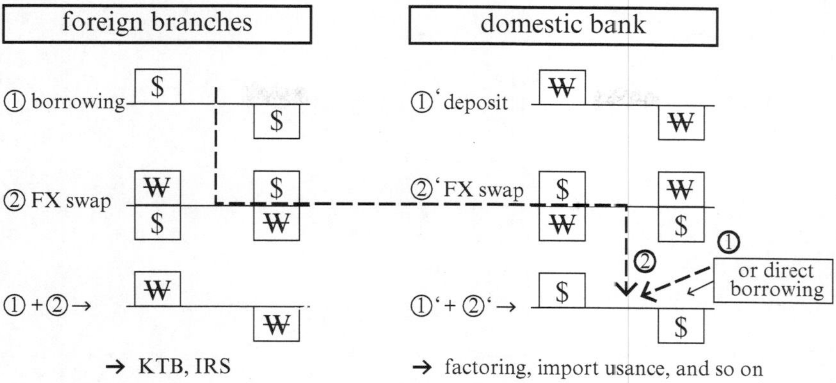

Notes:
KTB = Korean Treasury Bond.
IRS = interest rate swaps.

Figure 5.7 Channels of transmitting foreign liquidity shocks

banks. In the crisis, foreign banks in the advanced countries, hit by an adverse liquidity shock, reduced their cross-border lending and also reduced funding to their foreign branches in support of the head office balance sheet. The retreat of foreign banks' lending led to a severe dislocation of the FX swap market and caused funding difficulties for Korean banks. Therefore, when liquidity conditions tightened in foreign countries, Korean banks suffered from the foreign currency liquidity problem, not only in direct borrowing but also in indirect funding through FX swaps. Figure 5.7 illustrates the two channels by which foreign shocks were transmitted to Korean banks. Indeed, as Ceterolli and Goldberg (2010) point out, international banking linkages are viewed as having spread the profound difficulties from the financial crisis that began in advanced countries to emerging economies, including Korea.[14]

Building on Upper and Worms (2004) and others, Lee (2010) attempts to measure financial systemic risks in Korea stemming from FX swaps with foreign bank branches. He calibrates foreign currency loan transactions by using end uses of foreign currencies and direct sources of foreign currencies.[15] To elaborate, let b_{ij} denote the foreign currency borrowing of bank i from bank j, let v_{ik} be the foreign currency borrowing of bank i from the exogenous sector k, let u_{ki} be the foreign currency loans of bank i to the external sector k and let the foreign currency short (long) position of bank i be $s_i > 0 (s_i < 0)$. Then the balance sheet of bank i implies that the total uses of foreign currency funds must be equal to the total sources of foreign currency funds:

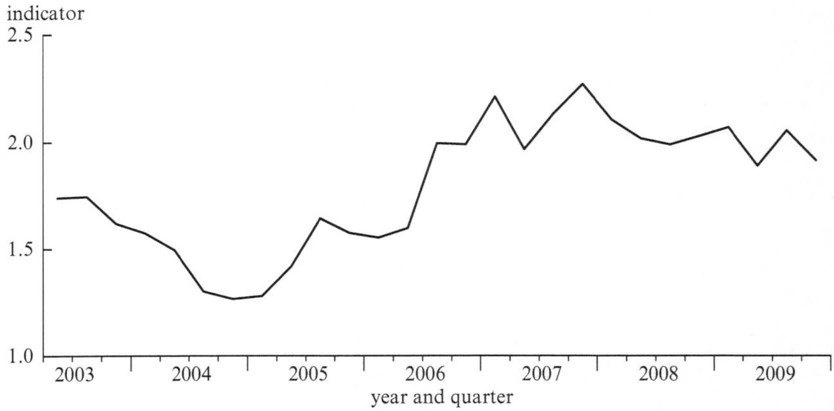

Source: Adapted from Lee (2010).

Figure 5.8 Systemic funding risk indicator in the Korean banking industry, 2002–09

$$\sum_{j=1}^{N} b_{ji} + \sum_{k=1}^{M} u_{ki} + s_i = \sum_{j=1}^{N} b_{ij} + \sum_{k=1}^{M} v_{ik} \equiv x_i \tag{5.1}$$

where N is the number of banks in the banking system, M is the number of external sectors which include nonfinancial firms and x_i is total liabilities of bank i. Here, what we can observe from each bank is that $\Sigma_{k=1}^{M} u_{ki}$, $\Sigma_{k=1}^{M} v_{ik}$ and x_i, b_{ji} are calibrated using a modified version of Schneider and Zenios (1990). Then b_{ji} indicates the interbank foreign currency lending exposures of the Korean banks.

Under additional assumptions, Lee (2010) calculates the amount of foreign currency assets directly or indirectly liquidated by each bank when it is unable to roll over one unit of external borrowing. With these measures, he constructs a systemic funding risk indicator (SRI) and argues that it shows the extent of amplification impact of the external liquidity shock on the banking system due to the interconnectedness.

Figure 5.8, adapted from Lee (2010), shows that the SRI jumped in 2006 when FX swap transactions increased along with the sharp rise of foreign bank branches' external borrowing. Because, by construction, the SRI should be equal to one if there is no interbank transaction of foreign currencies, the higher values of the SRI since 2006 suggest increased interconnectedness in foreign currency funding. Since the SRI is constructed under the assumption that the banking system is hit by unitary foreign currency liquidity shocks at each point of time, it does not tell us the actual

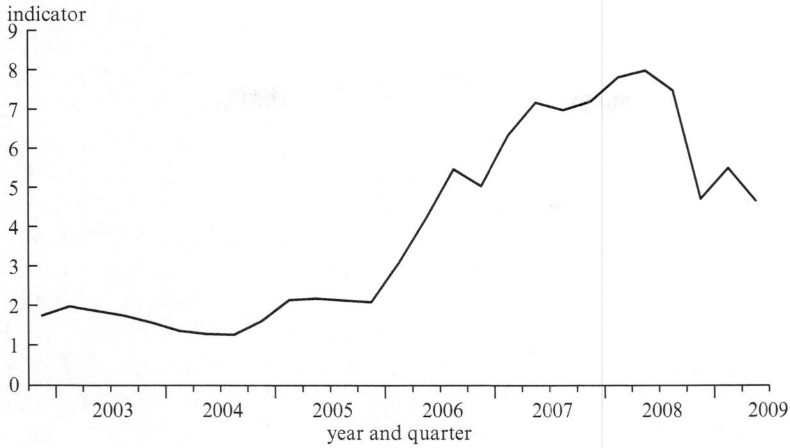

Source: Adapted from Lee (2010).

Figure 5.9 Adjusted systemic funding risk indicator in Korea, 2002–09

magnitude of risks that the banking system might face. To measure more realistic foreign currency funding risks, the size of the shocks is adjusted by multiplying the level of external debt. Figure 5.9, also adapted from Lee (2010), shows that the adjusted SRI peaks in the second quarter of 2008, suggesting that very high risk prevailed just before the Lehman Brothers bankruptcy.

CONCLUDING REMARKS

The extent of the international financial integration became painfully evident to Korea during the recent global crisis, with the insecurity of international financial markets spreading foreign currency funding pressure to the domestic banking system. High short-term external debt, resulting from excessive short-term borrowing by banks, reinforced the immediate and powerful international transmission of shocks into the domestic economy and raised concerns about another currency crisis in Korea.

To reduce the future vulnerability of the foreign exchange market to external shocks, the Korean government began to prepare comprehensive measures to curb any excessive rise in short-term external debt during normal times and sudden outflows during periods of financial instability. Since the early 2000s, several restrictions on foreign currency liquidity have existed in the banking sector. For example, Korean banks should maintain short-term assets denominated in foreign currency at a level of more than 85 percent of short-term debt denominated in foreign currency. But this restriction on the short-term foreign currency liquidity ratio was not effective during the recent crisis. Korean banks were making short-term loans to nonfinancial firms in such a way that the firms could roll over the loans and, therefore, the liquidity ratio could be met. The banks, however, could not call in the loans during the crisis period. Therefore, the government refined the restriction in that, for example, banks should hold a certain portion of safe assets among the short-term assets denominated in a foreign currency.

Another important measure that the Korean government is planning to adopt is to directly regulate the total size of FX swap transactions by imposing a limit on forward positions, depending on the individual bank's capital. This new regulation is expected to decrease risk exposures in the banking system but may have serious adverse effects on trade financing.

NOTES

1. Van Rijckeghem and Weder (2001) emphasize the importance of the financial channel in contagion among emerging market economies. Hong and Lee (2009) find that financial linkages better explain the synchronizations of contractions in domestic credits and stock prices between advanced countries and emerging market countries.
2. When the crisis hits, a plunge in stock prices and a spike in the foreign exchange rate occur simultaneously, doubling the losses to the foreign investors. This may have limited foreign capital outflows from domestic stock markets in the fourth quarter of 2008.
3. Foreign investors' shareholding out of total market capitalization was 30.1 percent in 2000. Then it increased to an unprecedented level of 42.0 percent in 2004. Capital outflows from equity investment, however, reduced the ratio of shareholding to 28.9 percent in 2008.
4. In this chapter, the term "domestic banks" refers to domestic Korean banks and foreign bank branches operating in Korea.
5. In the fourth quarter of 2008, the total external debt slightly decreased, but GDP declined even more, resulting in an increase in the ratio of external debt to GDP.
6. The Korean government also argued that, after taking into consideration nonobligatory debts, the actual amount of the current external debt was roughly $124 billion.
7. Combining cash flows of the first and second steps generates the cash flows in the third step.
8. Korea has a structural problem in the imbalance of forward contracts. Korean manufacturing exporting firms receive the revenues in US dollars but pay the cost in Korean won. Thus, they are eager to hedge exchange rate risks. In contrast, crude oil importing firms, which account for the largest share of imports, do not need to fully hedge the risks. They import crude oil in US dollars and also export refined products in US dollars. In addition, they can pass changes in the exchange rate through to domestic prices.
9. Global contraction in demand in 2008 and 2009, however, could have caused cancellation of orders, which led shipbuilding firms to over-hedge.
10. Specifically, the deviation from CIP is $(i-i^*) - ((F-S)/S)$, where respectively i and i^* are the domestic and foreign interest rates, and F and S are the forward and spot rates.

11. The bond investments by foreign investors were heavily concentrated in Korean government bonds and the Monetary Stabilization Bonds issued by the Bank of Korea. In 2007, government bonds and Monetary Stabilization Bonds accounted respectively for 66.1 percent and 31.0 percent of the total bond investments by foreign investors.
12. In part, foreign bank branches also sold the bonds to their headquarters because of the scheduled change in tax schemes in Korea.
13. In Korea, the high ratio of banks loans to bank deposits was another important concern, because this ratio is one of the measures of the vulnerability of banking systems. In fact, the global financial crisis exposed the vulnerability of Korean banks that relied on wholesale funding, especially in a currency other than the domestic currency.
14. Many studies document that systemic risks of financial institutions tend to increase as they are more interconnected. Allen and Babus (2009) provide an excellent survey.
15. This approach is taken because it is difficult to observe official statistics of FX swap transactions among banks.

REFERENCES

Allen, F. and A. Babus. 2009. "Networks in Finance". In *Network Challenge: Strategy, Profit, and Risk in an Interlinked World*, edited by P.R. Kleindorfer, Y. Wind and R.E. Gunther, pp. 367–82. Upper Saddle River, New Jersey: Wharton School Publishing.

Baba, N., F. Packer and T. Nagano. 2008. "The Spillover of Money Market Turbulence to FX Swap and Cross-Currency Swap Markets". *BIS Quarterly Review*, (March): 73–86.

Cetorelli, N. and L. Goldberg. 2010. *Global Banks and International Shock Transmission: Evidence from the Crisis*. NBER Working Paper 15974. Cambridge, Massachusetts: National Bureau of Economic Research.

Economist, The. 2009. "Domino Theory: Where Could Emerging Market Contagion Spread Next?" *The Economist* (28 February 2009).

Financial Times, The. 2009. "Korea's Debt". *The Financial Times* (1 March 2009).

Hong, K. and H. Lee. 2009. "Co-movement of Recessions across Countries: An Empirical Study on GDP, Domestic Credit and Stock Price". *Journal of Insurance and Financial Studies*, **20** (3): 125–60. In Korean.

Kohn, D.L. 2008. "Global Economic Integration and Decoupling", Speech at the International Research Forum on Monetary Policy, Frankfurt, Germany, 26 June 2008.

Lee, S.H. 2010. *Measuring Systemic Funding Liquidity Risks in the Interbank Foreign Currency Lending Market*. Working Paper 418. Seoul: Bank of Korea.

Schneider, M.H. and S.A. Zenios. 1990. "A Comparative Study of Algorithms for Matrix Balancing". *Operations Research*, **38** (3): 439–55.

Upper, C. and A. Worms. 2004. "Estimating Bilateral Exposures in the German Interbank Market: Is There a Danger of Contagion?" *European Economic Review*, **48** (4): 827–49.

Van Rijckeghem, C. and B. Weder. 2001. "Sources of Contagion: Is it Finance or Trade?" *Journal of International Economics*, **54** (2): 293–308.

6. Imbalances, overheating and the prospects for global recovery

Menzie D. Chinn

INTRODUCTION

As policymakers contemplate the prospects for the world economy, and what policy measures should be undertaken to promote sustainable growth, several questions arise. First, how important were the global imbalance and global overheating in explaining the global crisis of 2008–09? Second, how did trade exposure propagate the negative shock? Third, how important was sustained domestic demand in Asia (particularly China) in protecting the global economy from experiencing an even greater downturn? Fourth, are the global imbalance and global overheating being corrected, or have they been sufficiently adjusted?

It might appear that one could move forward on the policy front without addressing the first question. In my opinion, this is a flawed perspective; without tackling the sources of the financial crisis and the ensuing global "great recession", one cannot fully determine the appropriate course of action, in terms of rebalancing the global economy, so that we avoid a recurrence of unsustainably expanding current account balances, or overheating or falling to deflation. Hence, the first question is hardly academic, and indeed the answer is essential to answering the fourth question.

The answers to the other questions speak to the pace and nature of the global economic recovery. In particular, while trade links (the second question) were a particularly visible means by which the reduction in aggregate demand was transmitted, I do not think that was the only, or even a key, propagation channel. In particular, with respect to the other core developed economy, the repricing of risk, as well as the freeze in financial markets, was as important or even more important to spurring the great recession. Reversal of these trends will thus play out in the recovery. The extent to which the Chinese stimulus sustained world output in 2008–09 is an important question. The answer to that question carries implications for the prospects for sustaining world aggregate demand as China seeks to retrench in terms of credit and fiscal stimulus, going forward.

In this chapter, I first address the causes of the global imbalances and the relationship of those imbalances to the financial crisis. I then investigate the importance of trade linkages. The next section is devoted to a lengthy assessment of the prospects for current account balances and overheating.

DID IMBALANCES CAUSE THE CRISIS?

Potential Explanations for the Imbalances

In order to answer the question of whether the "imbalances" caused the crisis, one first has to take a stand on the sources of the imbalances.

In the years from 1998 to 2008, economists focused their attention on the causes and consequences of the expanding current account deficits and surpluses. The pattern of current account balances was interesting from an economic standpoint, in that it did not appear to conform to what would be predicted by standard economic theories. The balances were troubling from a policy standpoint, in that they were unprecedentedly large by postwar standards.

Throughout the first decade after 2000, the United States ran enormous current account deficits. China, the rest of East Asia, and the oil exporting countries ran correspondingly large current account surpluses, as shown in Figure 6.1. In 2008–09, these current account balances drastically reversed, albeit incompletely, as a global financial crisis engulfed the world economy. The proximity of the two events naturally leads to the question whether the two phenomena are related, or are causal in nature.

In this section, I review the various explanations for the rise of global imbalances, defined as large current account balances. These explanations include (1) trends in saving and investment balances, (2) the intertemporal approach, (3) mercantilist behavior, (4) the global saving glut and (5) distortions in financial markets. Note that the explanations are not mutually exclusive.

The saving–investment approach takes the perspective from the national saving identity, which states that the current account is equal to the budget balance and the private saving-investment gap. This is a tautology, unless one imposes some structure and causality.

One particularly simple variant of this approach relies upon assuming that the shocks primarily hit the government sector. Then changes in the budget balance are quasi-exogenous, and the current account consequently responds. The inspiration for this perspective is the mid-1980s experience with the Reagan era tax cuts and defense build-up. During that

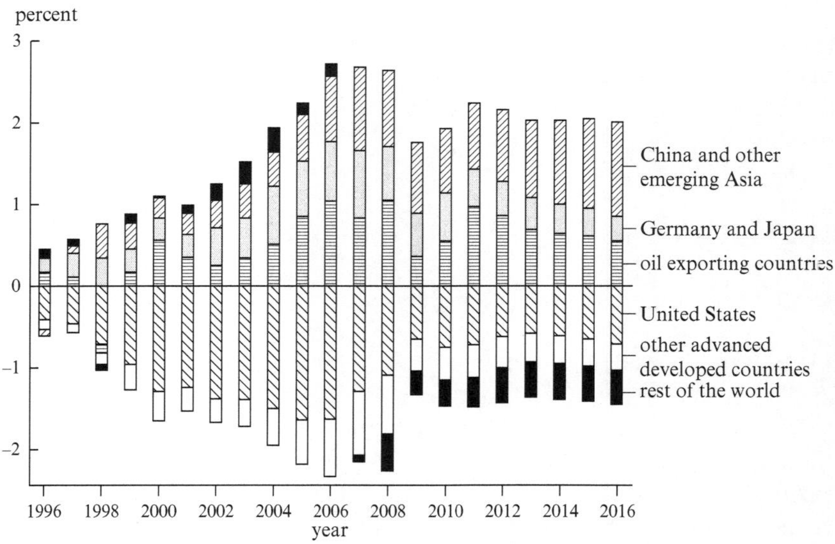

Note: The 2009–2015 data are IMF projections.

Source: IMF, *World Economic Outlook*, April 2011.

Figure 6.1 Current account balances as a share of world GDP, 1996–2016

episode, the budget deficit and current account deficits both yawned to unprecedentedly large magnitudes, inspiring the term "the twin deficits".

Upon inspection, the simple interpretation of the twin deficits clearly does not hold beyond the mid-1980s and 2001–04. Of course, other types of shocks perturb the economy, and once one allows for shocks to the other components of aggregate demand, or to the supply side, then no such positive correlation need hold at all times. However, that does not deny the validity of that view during the last decade.[1]

A systematic approach involves modeling the current account by explicitly focusing on the determinants of private investment and saving, and adding those variables to the budget balance. Chinn and Ito (2007, 2008) provide a sample of developed and developing countries over the period 1971 to 2004, using nonoverlapping five-year averages of the data. (The regression analysis controls for a similar set of variables as used in Chinn and Prasad 2003.) They find that government budget balances, initial net foreign asset positions and, for developing countries, indicators of financial deepening are positively correlated with current account balances. Among developing countries, they also find that higher terms of trade volatility are associated with larger current account surpluses (or smaller deficits). Greater macroeconomic uncertainty apparently increases domestic saving and also has a slightly negative impact on investment. The degree of openness to international trade appears to be weakly associated with larger current account deficits among developing countries.[2] Note that because they include average gross domestic product (GDP) growth and initial net foreign assets in the regressions, the saving-investment approach is consistent with some aspects of the intertemporal approach (discussed below).[3]

Their key finding is that the budget balance is an important determinant of the current account balance for industrial countries; the coefficient for the budget balance variable is 0.15 in a model controlling for institutional variables. A series of robustness checks yields the results that a 1.0 percentage point increase in the budget balance leads to a 0.1 to 0.5 percentage point increase in the current account balance.[4] For the United States, their analysis confirms the view that it is a saving drought—not investment boom—that is contributing to the enlargement of current account deficits, although there is some evidence of anomalous behavior in the 2001–04 period. For the East Asian countries, Chinn and Ito find some evidence that the current account balances are somewhat larger than predicted by their empirical models.

Chinn and Ito extend their analysis by accounting for endogeneity in two ways. First, they use an instrumental variables approach, and second they replace the budget balance with the cyclically adjusted budget balance.[5] In both cases, the coefficient on the budget balance rises considerably, ranging from 0.45 to 0.49. The US current account deficit in 2001–04 was significantly different from that predicted by the model, but just barely. China's current account was within the 95 percent prediction band.

The intertemporal approach is the mainstay of the rigorous approach to explaining current account imbalances. In this perspective, consumption today is to equal a share of the present discounted value of future expected net output, or net wealth. Hence, changes in consumption are due solely to changes in either the interest rate, or changes in expectations about future net output due to productivity shocks or reductions in investment and government spending.

The US experience of the late 1990s can therefore be rationalized by an anticipation of a future productivity boom that induces an immediate increase in consumption, resulting in a current account deficit.[6] In the context of America in the 2000s, to consume more now means to import more and export less. The deficits leading up to the financial crisis of 2008–09 are more difficult to fit into this approach. A large proportion of capital flowing to the United States takes place in the form of purchases of US government securities—not purchases of American stocks or direct investment in its factories, as it did in the years leading up to 2000. Moreover, the heavy involvement of foreign central banks in purchasing US assets suggests that the profit motive was not behind the ongoing flows to the United States.[7]

A formal test of the intertemporal approach, as applied to the recent US experience, was conducted by Engel and Rogers (2006). They model the current account as a function of the expected discounted present value of its future share of world GDP relative to its current share of world GDP (where the world is the advanced economies). The key difficulty in testing this approach is in modeling expected output growth; using a Markov-switching approach, they find that the United States is not keeping on a long-run sustainable path.[8] However, using survey data on forecasted GDP growth in the G7 countries, their empirical model appears to explain the evolution of the US current account remarkably well.

Another prominent view attributes the East Asian surpluses to explicitly mercantilist behavior. From this perspective, the developing countries of East Asia have followed an export led development strategy. That strategy resulted in rapid growth; however, starting in the mid-1990s, current account surpluses evolved into current account deficits, as investment boomed.

In the wake of the 1997 financial crisis, investment levels collapsed, while saving rates remained relatively high. Currencies depreciated sharply in the region; however, over time, East Asian central banks maintained their currencies at fairly weak levels. For some observers, this observation is sufficient to explain the relatively large and persistent current account surpluses in the region. One difficulty with this explanation is that the export led development path has been in place for decades; the explanation for the sharp break post-1997 is missing.[9]

Note that while the model explains half of the current account imbalances, it does not explain the other side: namely, why it is that the United States, United Kingdom and specific other developed countries ran substantial deficits.

In a series of papers, Dooley et al. (2003, 2008) interpret the US current account deficit as the outcome of concerted mercantilist efforts by East Asian state actors. In this context, the financing of America's trade (and budget) deficit is an explicit quid pro quo for continued access to American markets. Their explanation argues that the entire panoply of government interventions is aimed at supporting exporting industries.

There are problems with this thesis, too. Most notable is the mysterious aspect of timing: East Asian savings began flowing to the United States in 2003. Why not earlier, if the mercantilist impetus had been there all along? For a thorough critique, see Prasad and Wei (2005).

An alternative interpretation for the large scale reserve accumulation has been attributed to the self-insurance or precautionary demand. Foreign exchange reserves can reduce the probability of an output drop induced by capital flight or sudden stop. This self-insurance motivation rose substantially in the wake of the East Asian crises; this point was verified by Aizenman and Marion (2003).[10] Aizenman and Lee (2007) evaluated the relative importance of the various motivations by augmenting the conventional specifications for reserve holdings with proxy variables associated with the mercantilism approach and the self-insurance and precautionary demand approach. While variables associated with both approaches are statistically significant, the self-insurance variables play a greater economic role in accounting for recent trends.

The "global saving glut" explanation has been expounded by Bernanke (2005), Clarida (2005a, 2005b) and Hubbard (2005). This argument views excess saving from Asian emerging market countries, driven by rising savings and collapsing investment in the aftermath of the financial crisis (and to a lesser extent Europe), as the cause of the US current account deficit. More recently, the burgeoning surpluses of the oil exporters, ranging from the Persian Gulf countries to Russia, have moved to the fore as sources of excess saving. From this perspective, the US external imbalance is a problem made abroad; the lack of well-developed and open financial markets encourages countries with excess savings to seek financial intermediation in well-developed financial systems such as the United States. Hence, a solution may arise only in the longer term, as better developed financial systems mitigate this excess savings problem.

Caballero et al. (2008a) model the saving glut explanation as a shortage of assets in the developing world. Mendoza et al. (2009) model financial development as the increase in the degree of enforcement of financial contracts.

The strongest point in favor of the saving glut hypothesis is the observation of a widening current account deficit in the United States, combined with low real world interest rates. However, the saving glut versus twin deficits view is not an either-or proposition. An expansionary fiscal policy in the United States, combined with an investment drought in East Asia, would yield the observed increase in current account imbalances, while at the same time resulting in a drop in the real interest rate. Thus, a simple open economy macro model can explain the recent rise in US current account deficits, East Asian current account surpluses and the recent fall in global interest rates, without resort to exotic demand for high quality assets, or the like.

In order to formally test the saving glut hypothesis, one can evaluate whether financial development and institutional development explain the

Table 6.1 *Current account regressions, 1971–2004*

Variable	Dependent variable: five-year average of current account (% of GDP)				
	−1	−2	−3	−4	−5
	full	IDC	LDC	LDCWA	EMG
Government budget balance	0.150	0.160	0.150	0.242	0.219
	[0.068]**	[0.086]*	[0.081]*	[0.092]***	[0.076]***
Lane's NFA (initial)	0.049	0.063	0.047	0.050	0.043
	[0.005]***	[0.011]***	[0.005]***	[0.006]***	[0.009]***
Relative income	0.027	0.059	0.032	0.090	0.100
	[0.019]	[0.025]**	[0.085]	[0.090]	[0.082]
Relative income squared	0.016	−0.212	0.008	0.118	0.073
	[0.029]	[0.080]***	[0.096]	[0.105]	[0.092]
Relative dependency ratio (young)	−0.060	0.021	−0.071	−0.075	−0.013
	[0.020]***	[0.073]	[0.025]***	[0.025]***	[0.022]
Relative dependency ratio (old)	−0.205	0.001	−0.313	−0.241	−0.347
	[0.061]***	[0.081]	[0.093]***	[0.098]**	[0.106]***
Financial development (PCGDP)	0.001	−0.006	0.005	0.013	0.003
	[0.008]	[0.010]	[0.013]	[0.014]	[0.013]
TOT volatility	−0.013	0.063	−0.017	−0.006	−0.016
	[0.019]	[0.058]	[0.020]	[0.018]	[0.019]
Average GDP growth	−0.151	−0.101	−0.161	−0.145	−0.187
	[0.141]	[0.207]	[0.155]	[0.117]	[0.115]
Trade openness	0.003	0.037	−0.003	−0.008	−0.005
	[0.009]	[0.011]***	[0.010]	[0.011]	[0.010]
Oil exporting countries	0.046	–	0.047	0.039	0.028
	[0.013]***	–	[0.013]***	[0.011]***	[0.013]**
Observations	502	132	370	235	210
Adjusted R-squared	0.42	0.5	0.39	0.53	0.49

Notes:
Robust standard errors are in brackets.
Symbols *, ** and *** indicate significant at 10, 5 and 1 percent, respectively.
The estimated coefficients for the time-fixed dummies and constant are not shown.
EMG = emerging economies. IDC = industrialized countries. LDC = less developed countries. LDCWA = less developed countries without Africa.

Source: Chinn and Ito (2008).

pattern of imbalances, using the framework laid out in the third section below. The estimation results are reported in Table 6.1, extracted from Chinn and Ito (2008).[11]

One noteworthy aspect of Table 6.1 relates to the financial deepening variable. Only in the industrial countries' current account regressions does it exhibit a negative coefficient, though statistically insignificant. With these results, one may not be able to conclude that more developed financial markets lead to decreased current account balances, as posited by the adherents of the global saving glut thesis.

Because the economic environmental factors may affect the way in which financial development might affect saving and investment, we include interaction involving these variables: interactions between the financial development and legal variables (*PCGDP* × *LEGAL*), interactions between the financial development and financial openness variables (*PCGDP* × *KAOPEN*) and interactions between legal development and financial openness (*LEGAL* × *KAOPEN*). The financial and legal interactions effect is motivated by the conjecture that deepening financial markets might lead to higher saving rates, but the effect might be magnified under conditions of better developed legal institutions. Alternatively, if greater financial deepening leads to a lower saving rate or a lower investment rate, that effect could be mitigated when financial markets are equipped with highly developed legal systems. A similar argument can be applied to the effect of financial openness on current account balances.

In order to examine the importance of institutions, Chinn and Ito augment their basic model specification with variables aimed at capturing institutional factors: namely, the legal development variable (*LEGAL*), financial openness (*KAOPEN*) and associated interaction terms (including those with *PCGDP*). Table 6.2 displays results from panel ordinary least squares (OLS) regressions with institutional variables. They obtain several notable results.

Despite the inclusion of institutional variables and their interactions, the significantly positive relationship between current account and government budget balances is detected in almost all sample groups, as in Table 6.1 from the previous analysis. The point estimate on budget balances is a statistically significant 0.15 for the industrialized countries group—about the same as in the previous estimation—implying that the coefficient on the budget balance for the IDC group is robust to inclusion of institutional variables. (Note that a ±2 standard error confidence interval encompasses values as high as 0.34.) The estimated coefficients on budget balances remain close to that reported in Table 6.1, the other sample groups.[12]

Second, financial development is found to have different, and nonlinear, effects on saving and investment. Chinn and Ito use the estimates from Table 6.2 to identify the countries for which financial development would reduce the current account. With only Hong Kong and Singapore categorized as economies in East Asia at the highest tenth percentile in legal development and highest tenth percentile in financial openness, only they

Table 6.2 Current account regressions with institutional factors, 1971–2004

Variable	Dependent variable: five-year average of current account (% of GDP)				
	−1	−2	−3	−4	−5
	full	IDC	LDC	LDCWA	EMG
Government budget balance	0.159	0.154	0.168	0.251	0.230
	[0.065]**	[0.095]*	[0.079]**	[0.091]***	[0.075]***
Lane's NFA (initial)	0.049	0.069	0.047	0.051	0.041
	[0.005]***	[0.011]***	[0.005]***	[0.006]***	[0.009]***
Relative income	0.062	0.058	0.115	0.160	0.216
	[0.028]**	[0.028]**	[0.096]	[0.106]	[0.103]**
Relative income squared	0.032	−0.097	0.057	0.157	0.166
	[0.038]	[0.120]	[0.102]	[0.121]	[0.111]
Relative dependency ratio (young)	−0.061	−0.027	−0.076	−0.099	−0.044
	[0.018]***	[0.082]	[0.022]***	[0.030]***	[0.023]*
Relative dependency ratio (old)	−0.200	0.099	−0.368	−0.331	−0.529
	[0.058]***	[0.098]	[0.096]***	[0.114]***	[0.127]***
Financial development (PCGDP)	−0.008	0.010	−0.043	−0.038	−0.082
	[0.009]	[0.012]	[0.032]	[0.040]	[0.038]**
Legal development (LEGAL)	−0.003	0.002	−0.017	−0.02	−0.018
	[0.004]	[0.007]	[0.008]**	[0.009]**	[0.010]*
PCGDP × LEGAL	−0.003	−0.035	−0.021	−0.025	−0.037
	[0.004]	[0.015]**	[0.011]*	[0.012]**	[0.016]**
Financial openness (KAOPEN)	−0.001	−0.002	0.002	0.005	0.008
	[0.003]	[0.003]	[0.007]	[0.008]	[0.010]
KAOPEN × LEGAL	0.002	0.012	0.002	0.002	0.005
	[0.001]*	[0.003]***	[0.002]	[0.002]	[0.003]
KAOPEN × PCGDP	−0.003	0.002	0.000	0.002	−0.002
	[0.005]	[0.009]	[0.007]	[0.008]	[0.009]
TOT volatility	−0.013	0.100	−0.015	−0.002	−0.003
	[0.017]	[0.054]*	[0.018]	[0.019]	[0.022]
Average GDP growth	−0.123	−0.036	−0.090	−0.107	−0.132
	[0.087]	[0.243]	[0.096]	[0.124]	[0.118]
Trade openness	0.006	0.046	0.005	0.000	0.004
	[0.009]	[0.014]***	[0.013]	[0.014]	[0.014]
Oil exporting countries	0.041	–	0.040	0.035	0.025
	[0.013]***	–	[0.013]***	[0.012]***	[0.013]*
Observations	471	126	345	234	203
Adjusted R-squared	0.47	0.55	0.46	0.54	0.51

Notes:
Robust standard errors are in brackets.
Symbols *, ** and *** indicate significant at 10, 5 and 1 percent, respectively.
The estimated coefficients for the time-fixed dummies and constant are not shown.
EMG = emerging economies. IDC = industrialized countries. LDC = less developed countries. LDCWA = less developed countries without Africa.

Source: Chinn and Ito (2008).

would experience a reduction in their current account balances as financial development proceeds. For the majority of Asian emerging market countries that are categorized as middle or lower level in terms of legal development and financial openness, they will experience an *increase* in the ratio of national savings to GDP if financial markets develop further. Given these results, Chinn and Ito conclude that financial development reduces the level of current account balances, especially for Asian emerging market countries, but that effect is achieved, not through a reduction in saving rates, but through increased levels of investment.

In sum, Chinn and Ito's results present evidence against the argument that emerging market countries, especially those in East Asia, will experience lower rates of saving once these countries achieve higher levels of financial development and better developed legal infrastructure. In addition, more open financial markets do not appear to have any impact on current account balances for this group of countries.

Ito and Chinn (2010) examine whether their results are sensitive to the use of alternative indicators of financial development—namely, measures of equity, bond and insurance market activity—as well as to different aspects of financial development such as the cost performance, size and activeness of the industry. They find that credit to the private sector and stock market capitalization appear to be equally important determinants of current account behavior. While increases in the size of financial markets induce a decline in the current account balance in industrial countries, the reverse is more often the case for developing countries, especially when other measures of financial development are included. They also find that a greater degree of financial openness is typically associated with a smaller current account balance in developing countries.

Chinn et al. (2012) find that the US current account is overpredicted in the 2006–08 period, while the Chinese current account is underpredicted—in both cases by (barely) statistically significant amounts. Hence, there is some role for factors that are not accounted for in our models. One of those is financial deregulation, and the inducement of a "bubble" or boom–bust cycle delinked from fundamentals. This observation is directly linked to my interpretation of the role of the global imbalances in the financial crisis.

Imbalances and the Financial Crisis

Some observers have taken to claiming the saving glut caused the crisis, by inducing a search for yield and excessive leverage, or risk taking, or both. This view is succinctly summarized in Council of Economic Advisers (2009:22–3) as follows.

- The roots of the current global financial crisis began in the late 1990s. A rapid increase in saving by developing countries (sometimes called the "global saving glut") resulted in a large influx of capital to the United States and other industrialized countries, driving down the return on safe assets. The relatively low yield on safe assets likely encouraged investors to look for higher yields from riskier assets, whose yields also went down. What turned out to be an underpricing of risk across a number of markets (housing, commercial real estate and leveraged buyouts, among others) in the United States and abroad, and an uncertainty about how this risk was distributed throughout the global financial system, set the stage for subsequent financial distress.
- The influx of inexpensive capital helped finance a housing boom. House prices appreciated rapidly earlier in this decade, and building increased to well above historic levels. Eventually, house prices began to decline with this glut in housing supply.

In this interpretation, the trigger is excess saving associated with the inflows. What is missing from the story is the explanation for why the capital had to flow to the United States.[13] In contrast, Obstfeld and Rogoff (2009) argue:

> We too believe that the global imbalances and the financial crisis are intimately connected, but we take a more nuanced stance on the nature of the connections. In our view, both originated primarily in economic policies followed in a number of countries in the 2000s (including the United States) and in distortions that influenced the transmission of these policies through U.S. and ultimately through global financial markets.

Financial market distortions in the developing world led to the excess of saving; financial distortions in America pulled those flows to America. These financial distortions have been highlighted in a number of analyses of the financial crises. Irrationality, or waves of excess optimism and pessimism, is stressed by Akerlof and Shiller (2009). Stiglitz (2010) stresses the credit market imperfections associated with asymmetric information. Rent seeking and regulatory capture dominate the discussion by Johnson and Kwak (2010). Interestingly, excess saving from East Asia does not appear as a causal factor in any of these accounts. Roubini and Mihm (2010:80–82) and Chinn and Frieden (2009, 2011) argue that excess rest-of-world saving combined with domestic financial distortions was central to the development and extent of the crisis.

The Chinn-Frieden interpretation is consistent with the view that a resumption of expanding imbalances without dealing with the distortions in credit markets would cause a repetition, albeit in some other form. While the United States has begun addressing some of those market distortions in the form of a comprehensive financial regulation package, much of the actual regulation remains to be implemented. Even then, it is unlikely that the financial reforms will do more than moderate the distortions. Hence, going forward, policymakers should seek to mitigate large current account balances (in either direction), as a second best policy.[14]

THE GLOBAL RECESSION: PROPAGATION AND RESILIENCE

The global recession of 2008–09 was marked by a tremendously deep drop in trade flows—much more pronounced than the decrease in production. Even more remarkable, this trade drop was proportionately deeper than the one that occurred during the Great Depression (Eichengreen and O'Rourke 2010). The decline in growth rates in the value of goods exports is shown in Figure 6.2, for the world, for advanced countries and for the emerging markets and less developed countries (using International Monetary Fund definitions).[15]

Note that one can barely distinguish between the export growth of the advanced and the emerging market economies.

As discussed by Levchenko et al. (2010), it is typical for trade flows to drop more steeply than output during recessions. This is in part because trade is concentrated in manufactured goods (relative to overall output), particularly in manufactured durable goods. In the Great Recession, durable goods sectors were particularly hard hit. Eaton et al. (2010) provide evidence that almost all of the decline in world trade can be attributed to this effect. Hence, a large component of the decline in trade was due to this compositional effect.

Another component, the size of which is disputed, arose from the impact of difficulty in accessing trade financing. While there was anecdotal evidence of this effect, and there were several initiatives under the auspices of the G20 to mitigate difficulties in accessing trade financing, most of the empirical studies have failed to precisely measure the impact. That being said, it is very difficult to identify the impact of this factor, exactly because the purported decrease in access to trade financing occurs at exactly the same time as a general credit freeze in the global financial system.[16]

Finally, there is the drop in trade flows due to the drop in aggregate demand; this is the traditional view of how foreign demand shocks are

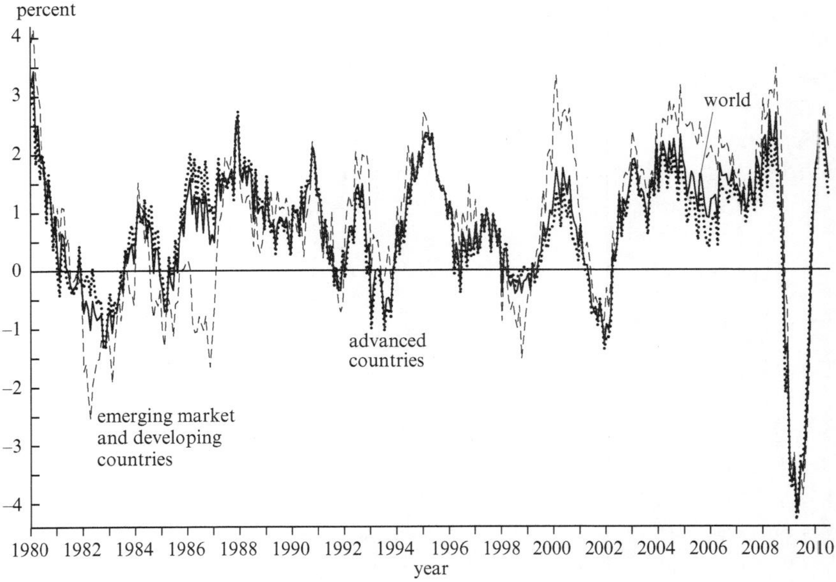

Note: Growth rates are calculated as log differences.

Source: IMF, International Financial Statistics, and author's calculations.

Figure 6.2 Annual growth rates of exports, in nominal dollars for the world, advanced countries and emerging-market and less-developed countries, 1980–2010

propagated. Certainly, Chinese exports fell substantially during the global recession, as illustrated in Figure 6.3.

On an annualized basis, Chinese exports dropped as much as 30 percent in nominal terms. How much of an impact this drop had on the Chinese economy is subject to some dispute, as the value-added content of Chinese exports is much less than 100 percent. Estimates range from 30 percent to 50 percent.[17] Even at the low end of value-added content, this implies something on the order of a $125 billion reduction in aggregate demand.[18]

Regardless of the value-added in Chinese exports, since China is at the end of a production chain centered in Asia, the reduction in Chinese exports would obviously have been propagated to the rest of the region. This explains why, in part, overall Asian output (excluding Japan) contributed less to overall world growth than China itself did. Surely, in the absence of the tremendous stimulus program that took place, Chinese and hence world output would have been less. It is not clear to me how much

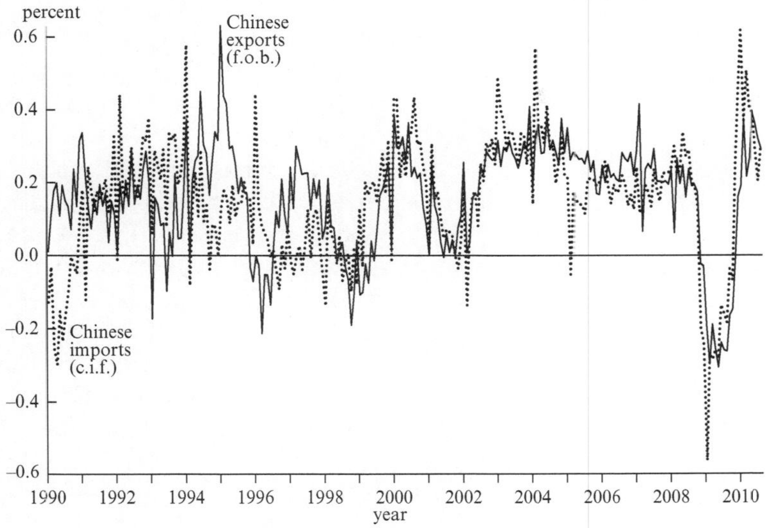

Source: IMF, International Financial Statistics, and author's calculations.

Figure 6.3 Annual growth in Chinese exports and imports, in USD, calculated log-differences, 1990–2010

less world output would have been, due to decreased Chinese demand for final imports.

The preceding discussion pertains to the propagation of shocks to the rest of the world, and in particular East Asia. One of the interesting aspects of the financial crisis of 2008 is that it was centered in the core advanced countries. The crisis started in the United States, propagated to Europe by way of the difficult-to-value and problematic derivatives on the books of European banks, and then by the freeze in credit markets in the wake of the Lehman bankruptcy.

It seems useful to distinguish, then, between how the recession spread to the other advanced countries versus to the emerging market and developing countries. In fact, one of the interesting things remarked upon by the International Monetary Fund (IMF 2009) was the fact that financial stress seemed to propagate to the industrial countries rapidly, starting in 2008. Only toward the end of 2008 did financial stress indicators begin to rise for the emerging markets.

Despite elevated stress, growth did not slow down in most of those countries as a result of financial stress, with the exception of Eastern and Southern Europe. The IMF (2009) expands upon some of the reasons why this occurred.

HAVE THE IMBALANCES BEEN CORRECTED? IS OVERHEATING STILL A THREAT?

A Framework for Analysis

In order to discuss whether a given economy has achieved a situation where, over the medium term, the current account balance is at a level that is sustainable, and yet output is close to potential GDP, it is useful to appropriate a device from an earlier time, namely the Swan diagram, which relates internal and external balance to combinations of the exchange rate and government spending. This approach was appropriate for a time when exchange rates were policy tools (because they were fixed) and the concern was with the Keynesian equilibrium condition that aggregate demand equaled production. In order to update the framework, I work with two equilibrium conditions:

$$Y^{AS} = Y^{AD} = \alpha_1 G + \alpha_2 (M/P) \tag{6.1}$$

$$0 = TB = \beta_1 G + \beta_2 (M/P) \tag{6.2}$$

where $\alpha_1 > 0$, $\alpha_2 > 0$, $\beta_1 < 0$, $\beta_2 \lesseqgtr 0$, G is government spending and M/P is real money supply. These two variables could be more broadly interpreted as measures of fiscal impulse and of monetary stimulus *broadly defined*, respectively.

Equation (6.1) states that equilibrium is given by output equaling potential output, where potential output is exogenously given. This is obviously a long run condition since, in the short run, prices are predetermined. Equation (6.2) is an external equilibrium condition, where the trade balance is set to zero for simplicity. In general, it could be set to a constant, which is exogenously set (and possibly changing over time). Note that there is one ambiguously signed coefficient, namely β_2. I will assume, for purposes of discussion, that $\beta_2 > 0$ and that the trade balance responds positively to an exchange rate depreciation that results from an expansion in the money supply.

These equilibrium conditions can be interpreted in Figure 6.4 as follows. The BB curve is sloped upward, while the YY curve is sloped downward. Points to the right of the BB curve indicate deficits, while points to the right of the YY curve indicate output in excess of potential. Countries can then be categorized as falling into four combinations of categories: (1) overheating with a trade surplus, (2) overheating with a trade deficit, (3) slack with a trade surplus and (4) slack with a trade deficit. Changes in government spending could typically restore

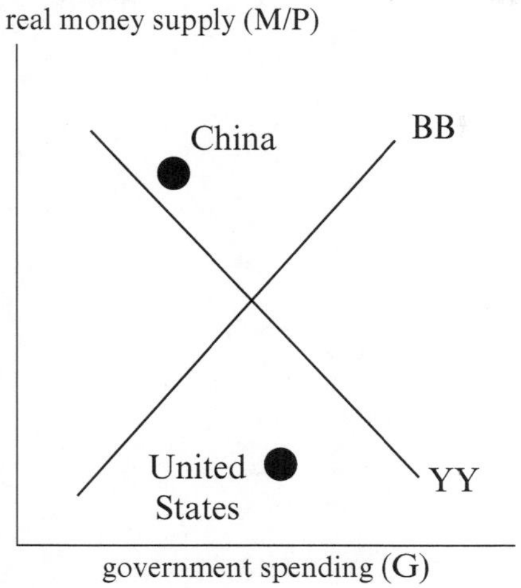

Figure 6.4 Internal and external balance

either internal and external equilibrium, but not both (except by good fortune). Similarly, monetary policy can achieve only one or the other equilibrium condition. Both instruments are needed to achieve both targets.

In Figure 6.4, I plot what are commonly viewed positions of the United States (slack with a trade deficit) and China (above potential GDP with a trade surplus). It is important not to take the graph as a fully fledged characterization of economic situations; rather it highlights the difficult choices that face certain economies. For the United States, greater fiscal stimulus could achieve full employment, but at the cost of a worsening of the trade deficit. Monetary policy in combination with some fiscal retrenchment could achieve internal and external equilibrium.

This does not seem like a difficult problem, on solely technical grounds. However, an important complication arises if we do not know what the value of potential GDP is. A decrease in potential GDP shows up as a shift inward in the YY curve. This effect is shown in Figure 6.5. If US policymakers were aiming for internal and external equilibrium (by using expansionary monetary policy and contracting fiscal policy), but misinterpreted the new level of potential output, the United States would then end up in a position of overheating the economy.

This simple observation motivates the evaluation of where each of the major economies of the world are currently, and where they are likely to be over the short to medium term (the short run being ignored in this framework).

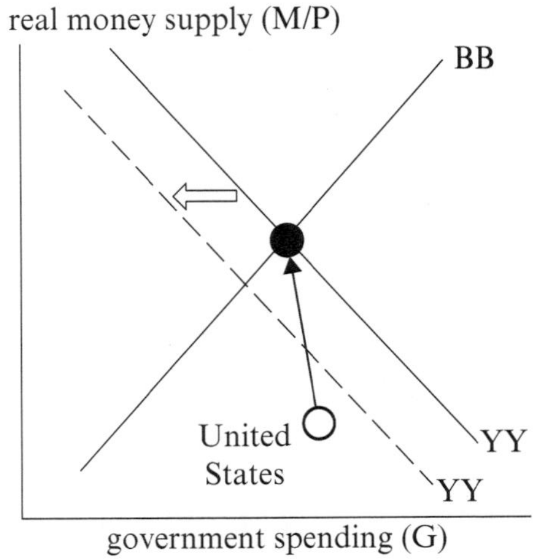

Figure 6.5 *Internal and external balance with a reduction in potential GDP*

Prospects for Rebalancing versus Overheating: The Major Economies

The United States is the key to rebalancing the world economy. As the single largest economy, and the one that has been conducting an unsustainable path, developments in that country will have the largest single impact on the world economy. Figure 6.1, with the accompanying IMF projections, demonstrates that the recent global recession has only brought a temporary respite from unsustainable current account deficits. Let us first consider the ratios of current accounts to GDP projected for the United States, the euro area and Japan, shown in Figure 6.6.

What is clear is that, without drastic changes in exchange rates and the domestic composition of output in the United States, the current account is slated to rise slightly to about −3.5 percent. What about the euro area and Japan? Without clear evidence of structural change in Japan, the IMF is projecting continued surpluses. The euro area remains at approximate balance. In other words, if rebalancing is to proceed apace, we cannot rely upon the rest of the advanced industrial countries to contribute a lot to the adjustment process. This is even more true in the wake of the sovereign debt concerns in Europe. Southern European countries are going to implement programs of fiscal consolidation. Even more worrisome, the countries that have fiscal space—namely Germany and to a lesser extent France—are also embarking upon no further programs to stimulate the economy. Certainly, there are no moves to encourage additional private consumption.

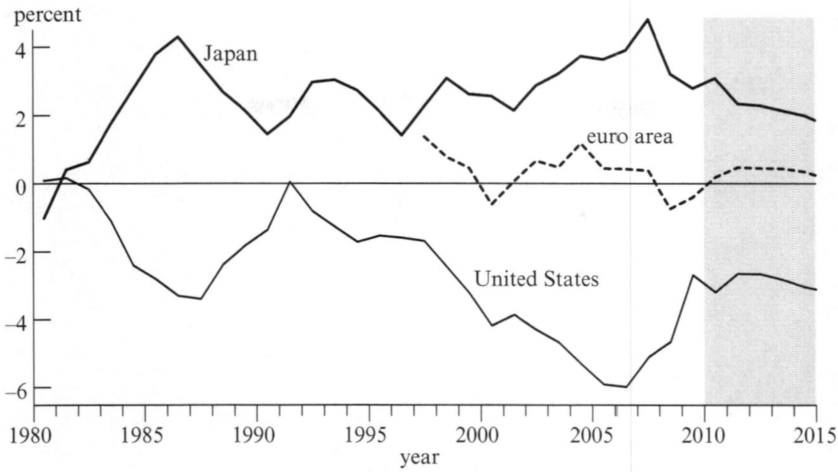

Note: Shaded area denotes forecasts.

Source: IMF, *World Economic Outlook* (October 2010).

Figure 6.6 Current account as a share of GDP, for the United States, the euro area and Japan, 1980–2015

Japan is recovering from a very deep drop in output relative to potential. With the output gap deeply negative (Figure 6.7), and deflation already entrenched, the prospects of "overheating" in Japan are nil. Somewhat more controversially, I doubt that there are realistic prospects for overheating in the euro area. With the output gap mired at nearly 4 percentage points of GDP, and a very slow recovery to potential forecast, it seems highly unlikely that inflation will surge. US inflation is also projected by the IMF to be muted, which is not surprising, given the large amount of slack in the economy.

It would be a mistake to put too much faith in the IMF projections, not because of any failings of the IMF economists, but because calculating potential GDP, and hence the output gap, is an enterprise fraught with hazards. This is particularly true during periods of substantial structural change, such as we have just experienced. For instance, the Organisation for Economic Co-operation and Development (OECD 2009) has reduced estimates of 2010 potential GDP growth by 0.4, 0.8 and 0.5 percentage points. These revisions are shown in Table 6.3, adapted from that study; but those revisions themselves are subject to considerable uncertainty.

Because the US economy is implementing the largest fiscal and monetary stimulus, the US case bears closer scrutiny.

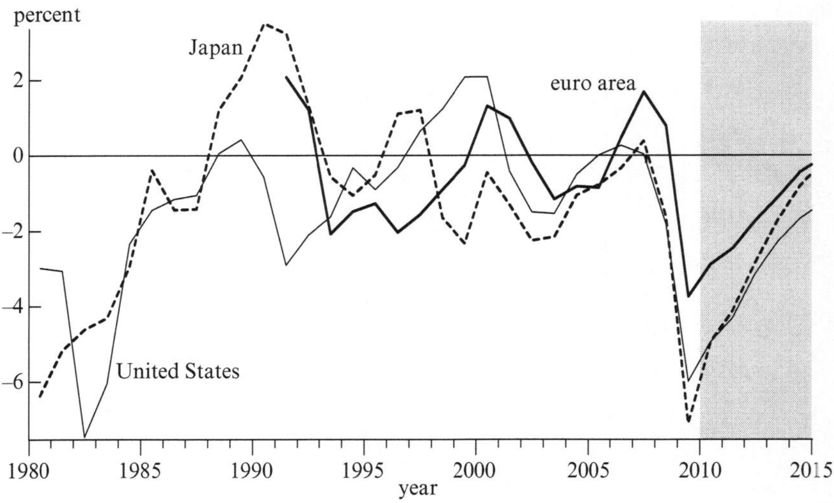

Note: Shaded area denotes forecasts.

Source: IMF, *World Economic Outlook* (October 2010).

Figure 6.7 Output gaps as a share of GDP for the United States, the euro area and Japan, 1980–2015

Table 6.3 Revisions in 2009 by national authorities in selected countries to potential output during 2007–11

Country and institution	Growth revision in 2009 (% points)				
	2007	2008	2009	2010	2011
United States: Congressional Budget Office	–	–	−0.1	−0.4	−0.2
Euro area: European Commission	−0.4	−0.4	−0.8	−0.8	–
Germany: Deutsche Bundesbank	–	–	−0.5	−0.1	0.0
Japan: Bank of Japan	–	–	−0.5	−0.5	−0.5
United Kingdom: HM Treasury	–[a]	–[a]	–[a]	–[a]	–
Italy: Italian Treasury	−0.4	−0.3	−1.0	−0.8	−0.9
Canada: Bank of Canada	–	–	−1.2	−1.0	−0.6

Note: Phased in 5 percent reduction level of potential output in the United Kingdom from the third quarter of 2007 to the third quarter of 2010. En-dashes (–) indicate data not available.

Source: Adapted from OECD (2009: Box 4-1).

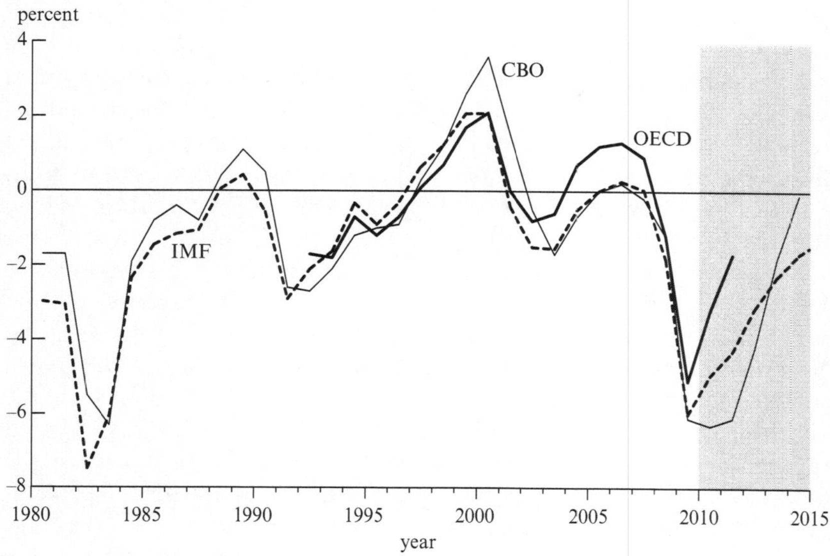

Note: Shaded area denotes forecasts.

Sources: IMF, *World Economic Outlook* (October 2010), CBO (May 2010) and OECD Economic Outlook (May 2010).

Figure 6.8 Output gap for the United States, from IMF, CBO, and OECD, 1980–2015

First, given the concerns about overheating, Figure 6.8 shows the US output gap measures from the IMF (displayed earlier in Figure 6.7), the OECD and the US Congressional Budget Office (CBO). The discrepancy between the various measures highlights the uncertainty mentioned earlier. The OECD's May 2010 estimate indicates a 2010 output gap of only about −3.2 percentage points of GDP, while the CBO indicates a much greater extent of slack, at −6.3 percentage points.[19]

The fact that there is so much discrepancy between the IMF, OECD and CBO measures is somewhat distressing, given that they are all based roughly on a production function approach. On the other hand, there is a wide degree of discretion in estimating and forecasting the inputs into the potential GDP (labor force, capital stock, technology), so perhaps we should not be too surprised.

The fact that the IMF output gap is smaller in absolute value than the CBO's might explain why the IMF is more set upon an early withdrawal of stimulus and fiscal consolidation. That being said, in my opinion, the downward revision in the IMF's estimate of the output gap of more than a percentage point (from −2.0 to −3.2, from April to October 2010) lessens the urgency to retrench.

The debate regarding the output gap is linked to the unemployment gap, and the natural rate of unemployment. There has been substantial argument that, with the large changes in the composition of output, the labor market mismatch has increased; consequently the natural rate has increased. The argument is persuasive, given the large proportion of long term unemployed—the highest on record.

Early estimates, such as Valletta and Cleary (2008) and Rissman (2009), did not find much evidence that structural unemployment has risen. More recent estimates, based on different methodologies, do find an increase in the structural rate of unemployment. Weidner and Williams (2011) work off Okun's Law to calculate an increase of 2.8 percentage points from the fourth quarter of 2007 to the first quarter of 2010. A more micro based approach is adopted by Dowling et al. (2010), who directly address the skills mismatch issue. They estimate the natural rate has risen 1.5 percentage points, while Valletta and Kuang (2010) estimate a 1.25 percentage points increase. Clearly, the unemployment gap uncertainty mirrors the output gap uncertainty.

Despite the uncertainty regarding the exact magnitude of the output gap and unemployment gap, I think it notable that there is no indication that there are rising inflationary expectations. Figure 6.9 displays the mean forecasts for inflation. Even at the ten-year horizon, expectations have barely budged. If anything, fears of *deflation* have risen. Hence, there is little danger of the US economy overheating; I suspect that a similar characterization applies to other advanced economies.

The rebalancing issue is harder to assess, in part because rebalancing depends upon what happens in the rest of the world. However, given the current constellation of exchange rates, particularly with respect to China, and the failure of Europe to expand rapidly, it is hard to see how a greater adjustment than what the IMF projects can occur. In addition, the United States has not taken any of the requisite steps to reduce its dependence upon oil; hence it remains very susceptible to widening of the current account deficit as the oil prices rebound. The importance of oil is highlighted in Figure 6.10.

Nonetheless, there are two points of optimism. The first relates to the domestic overheating issue, as well as the rebalancing issue. That is, US households appear to be retrenching more than had been earlier anticipated; household saving rates have not declined, according to the most recent statistics. The mirror image of this is that aggregate demand will not have an upward push from domestic sources, so slack is even more likely than overheating. This also means that imports—at least for consumer

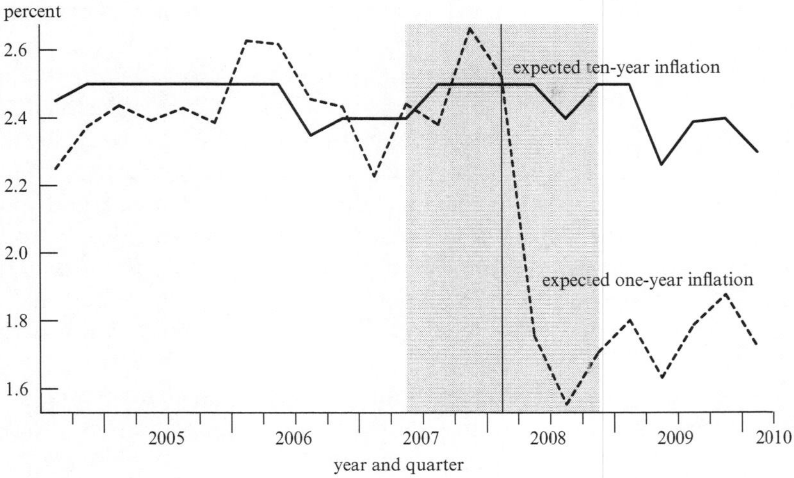

Notes:
Observations pertain to mid-quarter month.
Shaded area denotes recession dates.

Source: Philadelphia Fed Survey of Professional Forecasters.

Figure 6.9 One year expected CPI inflation and ten year expected inflation, 2005–10

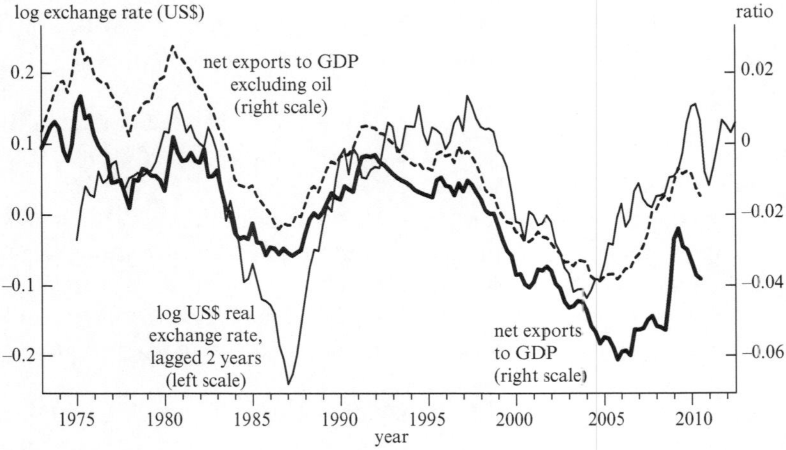

Sources: Bureau of Economic Analysis, Federal Reserve Board and author's calculations.

Figure 6.10 Log real exchange rate of the US dollar lagged two years and net exports to GDP (including and excluding oil), 1973–2012 goods—will not pick up as much as otherwise. That will help the external accounts.

The other point of optimism is that price elasticities might be higher than we think. That means the scope for trade balance adjustment (if the Chinese allow more rapid appreciation, and the rest of East Asia follows) is greater than currently allowed for. In Chinn (2010), I reinvestigate the elasticities associated with US trade flows and find that, particularly on the export side, export price elasticities are closer to unity than to 0.5, which I found in my earlier work. Import elasticities, after proper disaggregation, also appeared to be higher than detected in work from the early 2000s. That set of findings is in line with work by the IMF (2007).

The implication of this last set of findings is that rebalancing might be more feasible than anticipated, if the US dollar exchange rate is allowed to depreciate further. This depends critically upon China, as Chinese currency appreciation will allow much of the rest of the de facto dollar area to appreciate as well.

Prospects for Rebalancing versus Overheating: The BRICs

The current account balances of Brazil, Russia, India and China (together called the BRICs), and associated IMF projections, are depicted in Figure 6.11. The most notable of these are Russia's, which is projected to slide to zero by 2015, and China's, which is projected to resume expansion. The trade balance proportion is slated to stay relatively constant at its 2010 level; the net factor income proportion expands as receipts on foreign assets increase.[20]

Since the IMF does not report potential GDP for the emerging and developing countries, in Figure 6.12, I have graphed the output gaps as reported by the World Bank.[21]

Prior to the global recession, output gaps were noticeable, at roughly 3 percentage points in 2007. Forecasted output gaps for 2010 are all in the positive range, save for Russia, which exhibits a lot of slack, attributable to the large slump in energy prices. One worrisome feature is the trajectory of the output gap for India, which is predicted to rise to above 5 percentage points by 2012.

According to the IMF, inflationary pressures will be well maintained. This pattern is not quite consistent with the output gap measurements from the World Bank, especially with regard to India. Given the uncertainty surrounding the estimation of these particular countries' prospects, and identifying the proper potential GDP series, it seems to me that this is where our greatest worries about overheating reside.

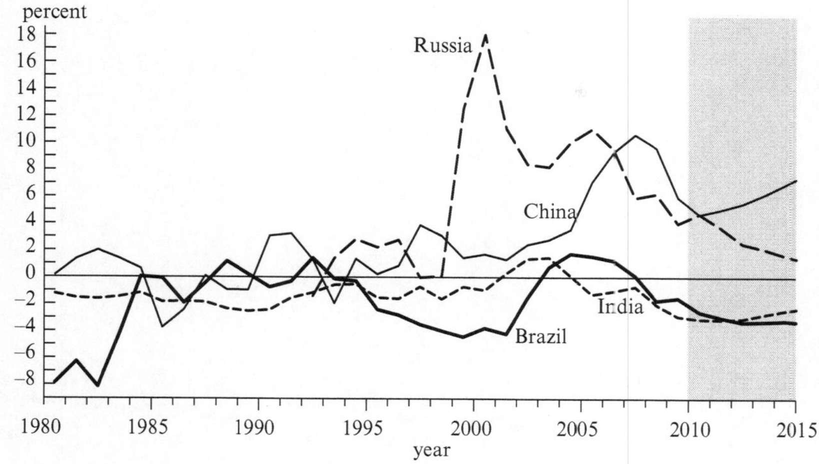

Note: Shaded area denotes forecasts.

Source: IMF, *World Economic Outlook* (October 2010).

Figure 6.11 *Current account as a share of GDP, for Brazil, Russia, India and China, 1980–2015*

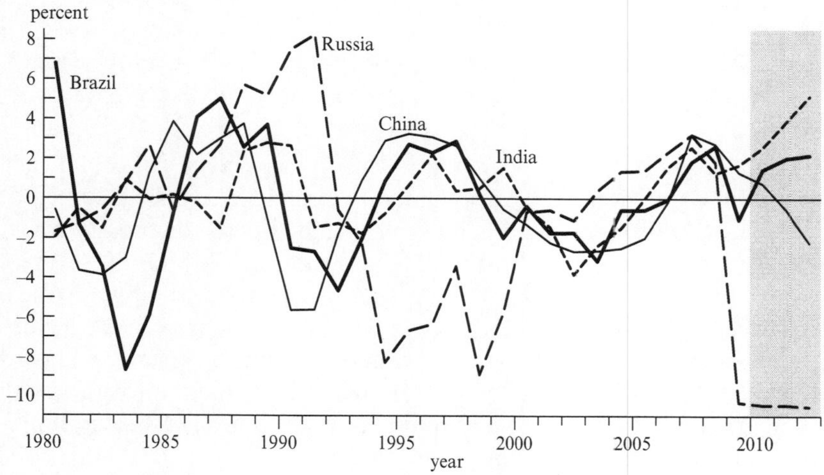

Note: Shaded area denotes forecasts.

Sources: World Bank data as of June, 2010; personal communication.

Figure 6.12 *Output gaps as a share of GDP, for Brazil, Russia, India and China, 1980–2015*

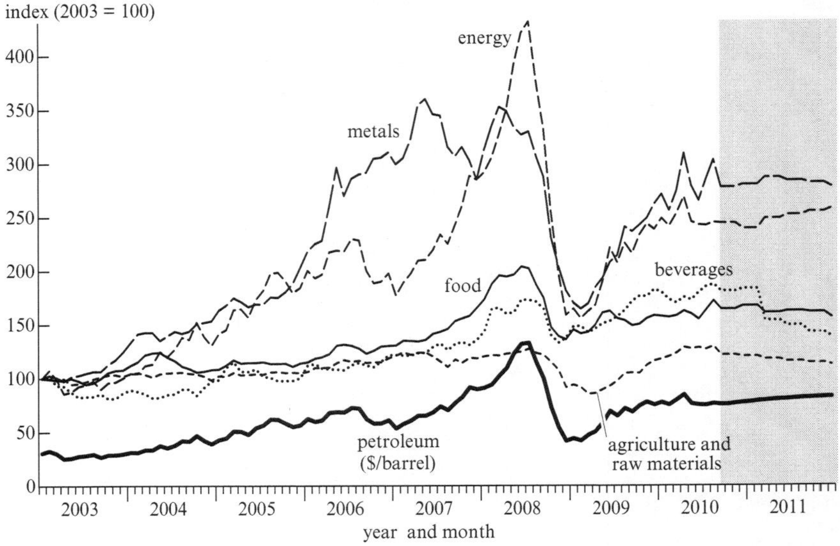

Notes:
The Y-axis units for the price of petroleum are US dollars per barrel.
The shaded area denotes forecasts made in 2010.

Source: Adapted from IMF, *World Economic Outlook*, October 2010, Figure 1-19.

Figure 6.13 Commodity price indexes for energy, food, agricultural raw materials, metals, beverages and petroleum, 2003–2011

Since Russian aggregate demand is sensitive to energy prices, and the other BRICs are sensitive to commodity prices in terms of aggregate supply shocks, it seems worthwhile to consider where commodity prices are right now. According to the IMF's outlook in March 2010, there seemed to be little movement forecasted in these prices (Figure 6.13). However, typically, these forecasts predict little of the movement in subsequent commodity prices. Hence, I would say that the biggest wild card is energy prices; a movement upward in this price would improve Russian prospects, while pushing down output gaps in the other BRICs and simultaneously pushing up inflation.

Like the United States, China merits additional discussion because of its central role in the current account imbalances. The analysis can proceed along two fronts. The first is the conventional elasticities approach, where the impact of Chinese currency revaluation is assessed in a very partial equilibrium approach. The second is a more general one, where one views the current account (really the trade balance) as the outcome of saving and

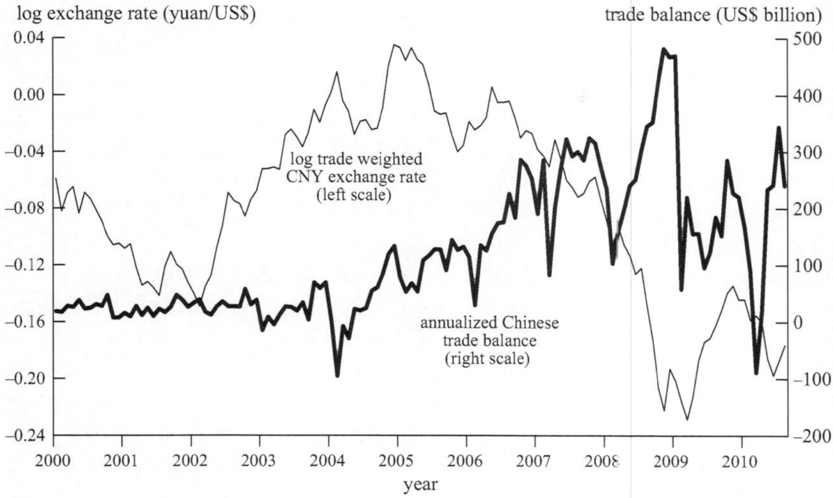

Note: A downward trend of the yuan represents appreciation.

Sources: IMF, *International Financial Statistics* and author's calculations.

Figure 6.14 Log real effective exchange rate of the Chinese yuan and the annualized trade balance of China, 2000–10

of investment and government budget decisions. The latter approach does not necessarily exclude the former; rather it changes the focus.

I will turn first to the role for exchange rate changes on the trade balance. The motivation for the interest can be easily seen by inspecting the Chinese trade balance and the real exchange rate, in Figure 6.14.

Before the surge in the Chinese trade surplus, few academic studies aimed at estimating Chinese trade elasticities, at least over the relevant period. Many of the studies used data spanning the 1980s, which arguably pertained to an economy substantially different from that of the 1990s and 2000s—see for example Cerra and Dayal-Gulati (1999) and Cerra and Saxena (2000). With respect to the recent debate, one widely cited estimate from Goldman Sachs was for a Chinese export price elasticity of 0.2 and an import price elasticity of 0.5—relatively low.

Garcia-Herrero and Koivu (2007) examine data over the 1995–2005 period, breaking the data into "ordinary" and "processing and parts" imports and exports, and relate Chinese exports to the world, imports and the real effective exchange rate, augmented by a proxy measure for the value-added tax rebate on exports, and a capacity utilization variable. In both import and export equations, the stock of foreign direct investment

(FDI) is included. One notable result they obtain is that for Chinese imports, the real exchange rate coefficient has a sign opposite to the one anticipated in the full sample. Additionally, they find that post-WTO entry, Chinese income and price elasticities for exports rise considerably. On the import side, no such change is obvious with respect to the pre- and post-WTO periods.

Marquez and Schindler (2007) argue that the absence of useful price indexes for Chinese imports and exports requires the adoption of an alternative model specification. They treat the variable of interest as world (import or export) trade shares, broken down into "ordinary" and "parts and components". Using monthly Chinese imports data from 1997 to July 2006, they find ordinary trade-share income "elasticities" ranging from −0.021 to −0.001 (in other words, the coefficients are in the wrong direction) and price "elasticities" from 0.013 to 0.021. The parts and components price elasticities are in the wrong direction, and statistically significantly so. Interestingly, the stock of FDI matters in almost all cases. Since the FDI stock is a smooth trend, it is not clear whether to attribute the effect explicitly to the effect of FDI, or to other variables that may be trending upward over time, including productive capacity.

For export shares (ordinary goods), they find income elasticities ranging from 0.08 to 0.09, and price elasticities ranging from 0.08 to 0.068. For parts and components export shares, the income coefficient ranges from a 0.042 to 0.049. Their preferred specification implies that a 10 percent real appreciation of the Chinese yuan reduces the Chinese trade balance between US$75 billion and US$92 billion.

Thorbecke and Smith (2010) do not directly examine the implications for both imports and exports, but do focus on the impact of yuan appreciation on exports, taking into account the integration of the production chain in the region. Using a sample of 33 countries over the 1994–2005 period, and a trade-weighted exchange rate that measures the impact of how bilateral exchange rates affect imported input prices, they find that a 10 percent yuan appreciation in the absence of changes in other East Asian currencies would result in a 3 percent decline in processed exports and an 11 percent decline in ordinary exports. If other East Asian currencies appreciated in line with the yuan, then the resulting change in the processed exports would be 9 percent.

Cheung et al. (2010) trade equations over the 1993–2006 period, using the Stock–Watson (1993) dynamic OLS regression method. The import and export data are examined as aggregates, and as series disaggregated into ordinary trade and processing and parts trade. The data are converted into real terms using a variety of deflators, including the US consumer price index (CPI), the producer price index (PPI) for finished goods and country specific Chinese price indexes due to Gaulier et al. (2006), as well as (for Chinese exports) Hong Kong re-export indexes. They use the IMF's CPI deflated trade-weighted index. For a supply side variable for Chinese exports, they use the capital stock in manufacturing. This capital stock measure was calculated by Bai et al. (2006).

The results are less than definitive; the estimated income and price coefficients are not typically statistically significant, although they point in the right direction. Only the supply variable coefficient is statistically significant.

As suggested by Marquez and Schindler (2007), the differing behavior of ordinary and processing exports suggests that aggregation is inappropriate. For ordinary exports, one finds that the rest-of-the-world activity is not a good predictor of exports, while the price variable is an important determinant. Using either Gaulier et al. (2006) or Hong Kong unit value indexes, one finds an export elasticity of approximately 0.6. At the same time, a 1 percent increase in the Chinese manufacturing capital stock induces between a 2.2 and a 2.5 percent increase in real exports.

Cheung et al. (2010) find that aggregate Chinese imports appear to respond strongly to income, and in the expected direction. On the other hand, they replicate Marquez and Schindler's results with regard to the price elasticity. A weaker yuan induces greater imports, rather than less. This is true also for ordinary imports. Only when moving to parts and processing imports does one obtain some mixed evidence, and there the results are still toward finding a wrong-signed coefficient. These results pertain to data prior to the global recession; the variation—or lack of variation—in the series is probably partly responsible for obtaining these perverse or nonconclusive results.

Ahmed (2009) has used data that spans the recent recession and sharp drop-off and rebound in Chinese imports and exports (from the first quarter of 1996 to the second quarter of 2009). Using first differences specifications corresponding to his equations (6) and (7), he finds that (in the long run) a 1 percentage point increase in the annual rate of appreciation of the real exchange rate would have a cumulative negative effect on real export growth of 1.8 percentage points, which is statistically significant. A 1 percentage point increase in foreign consumption growth would increase export growth by 5.9 percentage points, which is also statistically significant, and appears to be an implausibly large effect. Also, a 1 percentage point increase in the growth rate of the FDI capital stock, comparable to the supply shift term in Cheung et al. (2010), raises export growth by a cumulative and statistically significant 0.3 percentage points.

In practical terms, the difference in impacts is substantial. Consider estimates of China's export elasticities. Ahmed (2009) finds that after four years, a 20 percent yuan appreciation induces a US$400 billion decrease in Chinese exports. In contrast, Cheung et al. (2010) find a US$50 billion impact.

Most recently, Cline (2010) has come out with new estimates indicating an equally large impact from Chinese revaluation. He backs out an implied export elasticity of 1.27, assuming that the import price elasticity is unity. In dollar terms, he calculates that a 1 percent appreciation induces a US$45 billion decrease in the Chinese current account balance. This is a substantially larger impact than obtained by Ahmed (2009).[22]

In contrast to the earlier debates regarding China's burgeoning current account surplus, most economists now accept that exchange rate adjustment in and of itself would not be sufficient to shrink the Chinese current account balance to more sustainable levels. The results in Chinn and Ito (2007, 2008), discussed in the second section above, highlight the fact that fiscal policy could do additional work. And certainly there is scope for additional government spending, given the relatively low ratio of government debt to GDP. However, the cross section analysis conducted by Chinn and Ito could not get at some of the factors of specific import for the Chinese economy. After all, in their studies, the Chinese current account surplus was underpredicted—not by a statistically significant amount, but by a couple of percentage points. This outcome was a function of the underprediction of national saving.

That means that we need to focus on the determinants of the private saving–investment balance as a critical factor, in addition to elasticities and income, as suggested in a simple Keynesian–Mundell-Fleming framework.

Kuijs (2005) stressed corporate saving as the main culprit in the surge in the early 2000s. Prasad (2009) has focused on both corporate and household saving, while Ma and Yi (2010) argue that currently all three of the components of saving—government, household and corporate—have been abnormally high and rising.

The biggest medium term issue seems to be the decreasing share of labor income in Chinese GDP. This phenomenon, combined with the relatively high household saving rate, means that merely trying to raise the household saving rate (by improving the social safety net, and by increasing access to consumer credit) cannot in and of itself solve the problem. Hence, rebalancing involves a rebalancing of the domestic shares of income, away from capital.

This point has become increasingly central as the debate has moved to whether wage rates are rising. Those familiar with the Lewis (1954) and Fei–Ranis (1964) model of development will recall that as wages rise, the share of income going to capital decreases. If the propensity to save of labor is less than that of capitalists, then the saving rate should decline (Kroeber 2010). It might be that this process is happening as a natural outcome arising from the exhaustion of labor close to the coastal provinces. Even if that is true, the process of raising household savings (in aggregate terms, not just as a share of household income) can be accelerated by aggressive government action—although even the most aggressive action will take years to have a substantive impact.

In sum, there is scope for government policy to accelerate rebalancing. In the short term, this involves faster currency appreciation.[23] Over the longer term, it involves allowing state owned enterprises to pay dividends, reducing the monopoly power of the state owned corporations, and accelerating the development of a social safety net and provision of social services (which will reduce incentives for household saving, while decreasing government saving).

CONCLUSION

This tour of the world economy has necessarily given short shrift to many important aspects of the rebalancing and overheating debate. The key points I glean from this analysis is that there is little chance of overheating in the short term in the United States or other advanced countries. Rather, the greater downside risk is of deflation. On the other hand, with the likelihood of a two-speed global recovery becoming ever more apparent, the possibility of overheating is more pronounced in the emerging markets.

Rebalancing of current accounts is not proceeding apace—at least not with the current policies in place. Continued consumer retrenchment in the United States will aid in adjustment to a smaller US current account deficit, but Northern European fiscal retrenchment is not helpful. In addition, the failure of the Chinese to implement more rapid currency appreciation means that the quickest means of effecting some adjustment has been put on hold. Yet additional measures, described in Chinn et al. (2011), could further reinforce adjustment to sustainable current account balances with sustainable growth.

NOTES

Acknowledgments. I thank the discussant Hangyu Lee and other participants at the EWC–KDI conference on Global Economic Crisis: Impacts, Transmission, and Recovery, at the East-West Center, 18–19 August 2010, for helpful comments. I thank Jamus Jerome Lin for providing data, and Yin-Wong Cheung, Eiji Fujii and Hiro Ito, for allowing me to cite joint work.

1. See for instance Chinn (2005). A dissenting view is Truman (2005).
2. They also find limited evidence to support the patterns of evolutions in current accounts predicted by the stages-of-development hypothesis. Other potentially important variables such as indicators of capital controls (Chinn and Ito 2006) and average GDP growth, however, appear to bear little systematic relationship with current account balances.
3. Gruber and Kamin (2007) obtain similar results for a smaller panel of 61 countries spanning the 1982–2003 period. They find that including a crisis dummy for the East Asian countries statistically explains those countries' current account balances. However, their results do not shed light on the source of US deficits. Hence, while the stylized facts are relevant to the question at hand, they pertain to the period before the appearance of global imbalances.
4. Smaller estimates of the fiscal impact are reported by Bussière et al. (2005), Corsetti and Müller (2006) and Gruber and Kamin (2007).
5. For the instrumental variables approach, they use a dummy for the left-wing government, political constraint (democracy) index, military spending as a ratio to GDP, yearly changes in unemployment rates and regional dummies. The "trend" budget balance is estimated using the high pass filter.
6. See Pakko (1999) for an early interpretation in this vein. Note that the empirical evidence for the theoretical model underpinning this argument is weak; see Nason and Rogers (2006).
7. There are numerous ways in which to account for intertemporal effects in current account dynamics. Chinn and Lee (2009) apply a structural vector autoregression approach, which allows for transitory and permanent shocks to drive the current account and the real exchange rate. Using the same approach as in Lee and Chinn (2006), they examine the United States, the euro area and Japan, and find that a large share of the 2004–07 US current account is inexplicable using their model.
8. Engel and Rogers use data over the 1790–2004 period for one of their sustainability tests. The survey-based tests rely upon a shorter sample, 1994–2004. Choi et al. (2008) allow for different rates of discount, and can replicate the pattern of imbalances in a two-country model.
9. Gagnon (2011) shows that current account balances are highly correlated with central bank official intervention.
10. See also Aizenman and Lee (2007) and Jeanne and Rancière (2006).
11. Since these results are sensitive to the inclusion of the African countries, Chinn and Ito also report separate sets of results with and without the African countries included, for the developing country sample. They also report separate results for an emerging market group that differs somewhat from the developing country sample.
12. Gruber and Kamin (2009) report similar results.
13. Caballero et al. (2008a, 2008b) view the link from inflows to crisis through the prism of the asset shortage interpretation.
14. Clearly, this is a rejection of the Greenspan (2005) doctrine that associates larger current account deficits and surpluses with greater optimizing in the face of increased capital mobility.
15. Note that these are nominal values of trade. Deflating by unit value indexes (keeping in mind all the problems with such indexes) halves the percentage point drop during the Great Recession. The greater comovement is partly attributable to vertical specialization. See Chinn (2010) for a discussion of how vertical specialization drives a wedge between measured trade and trade in value added.
16. See Mora and Powers (2009) for an evaluation of the trade credit hypothesis, while Iacovone and Zavacka (2009) assess the hypothesis that bank credit constraints hit the export-oriented manufacturing firms the hardest, thus explaining the sharp drop in trade.
17. Dean et al. (2007) provide an estimate of 30 percent, based upon the vertical specialization model of Hummels et al. (2001). Arguing that that approach is inappropriate when

the usage of input is due to tax incidence reduction, Koopman et al. (2008) estimates 50 percent domestic valued added for 2006 exports.

18. The calculations are as follows: Chinese exports in 2008 were about US$1.4 trillion. Assuming 30 percent value added in Chinese exports then suggests about US$420 billion in 2008 export value added. The 30 percent reduction then implies a reduction in aggregate demand of US$126 billion. Since actual Chinese GDP in 2008 was US$4.519 trillion, this implies a reduction in aggregate demand through export demand reduction of about 2.8 percent. If value added is 50 percent, then the impact was about 4.7 percent.
19. Output gaps can also be measured by time series methods, such as the high pass filter and band pass filter. These measures indicate smaller output gaps, at roughly 2 and 1 percentage points, respectively. Since both the high pass and band pass filters are subject to end-point distortions, I forecast forward six years starting from 2010, and then apply the filter to the entire data series.
20. The World Bank's (2010a) *China Quarterly Report* (June) indicates a 2 percentage points GDP gap between the trade balance and the current account by 2015.
21. These are production function based measures of potential GDP, similar to those developed by the OECD for their advanced country measures. A description is contained in the World Bank (2010b: Box 2.8).
22. Cline's specification is a regression of the current account to GDP ratio on the log real exchange rate, the growth differential between China and the rest-of-the-world, and a time trend, over the 2000–2010 period. The adjusted R-squared is 0.89, but no diagnostics are provided for serial correlation, heteroskedasticity and so on.
23. There has been some debate whether such appreciation endangers China's growth too much. On one side is Dani Rodrik (2008). On the other side are the IMF (2010) and Eichengreen and Rose (2010).

REFERENCES

Ahmed, Shaghil. 2009. *Are Chinese Exports Sensitive to Changes in the Exchange Rate?* International Finance Discussion Paper 987. Washington: Board of Governors of the Federal Reserve System.

Aizenman, Joshua and Jaewoo Lee. 2007. "International Reserves: Precautionary versus Mercantilist Views, Theory and Evidence". *Open Economies Review*, **18** (2): 191–214.

Aizenman, Joseph and Nancy P. Marion. 2003. "The High Demand for International Reserves in the Far East: What's Going On?" *Journal of the Japanese and International Economies*, **17** (3): 370–400.

Akerlof, George A. and Robert J. Shiller. 2009. *Animal Spirits: How Human Psychology Drives the Economy and Why It Matters for Global Capitalism.* Princeton, New Jersey: Princeton University Press.

Bai, Chong-En, Chang-Tai Hsieh and Yingyi Qian. 2006. "Returns to Capital in China". *Brookings Papers in Economic Activity*, 2006-2 (fall): 61–88.

Bernanke, Benjamin, 2005. "The Global Saving Glut and the U.S. Current Account". Remarks at the Sandridge Lecture, Virginia Association of Economics, Richmond, Virginia, 10 March.

Bussière, Matthieu, Marcel Fratzscher and Gernot J. Müller. 2005. *Productivity Shocks, Budget Deficits and the Current Account.* ECB Working Paper 509. Frankfurt: European Central Bank.

Caballero, Ricardo, Emmanuel Farhi and Pierre-Olivier Gourinchas. 2008a. "An

Equilibrium Model of 'Global Imbalances' and Low Interest Rates". *American Economic Review*, **98** (1): 358–93.

Caballero, Ricardo, Emmanuel Farthi and Pierre-Olivier Gourinchas. 2008b. "Financial Crash, Commodity Prices, and Global Imbalances". *Brookings Papers on Economic Activity*, 2008-2 (fall): 1–68.

Cerra, Valerie and Anuradha Dayal-Gulati 1999. *China's Trade Flows: Changing Price Sensitivities and the Reform Process.* IMF Working Paper 99/01. Washington: International Monetary Fund.

Cerra, Valerie and Sweta Chaman Saxena. 2000. *An Empirical Analysis of China's Export Behavior*. IMF Working Paper 02/200. Washington: International Monetary Fund.

Cheung, Yin-Wong, Menzie Chinn and Eiji Fujii. 2010. "China's Current Account and Exchange Rate". In *China's Growing Role in World Trade*, edited by Robert Feenstra and Shang-Jin Wei, pp. 231–71. Chicago: University of Chicago Press for NBER.

Chinn, Menzie. 2005. *Getting Serious about the Twin Deficits.* Council Special Report 10. New York: Council on Foreign Relations.

Chinn, Menzie. 2010. *Supply Capacity, Vertical Specialization and Trade Costs: The Implications for Aggregate U.S. Trade Flow Equations.* Unpublished paper (June); revision of NBER Working Paper 11719 (October 2005).

Chinn, Menzie, Barry Eichengreen and Hiro Ito. 2011. "Rebalancing Global Growth". In *Ascent after Decline: Regrowing Global Economies after the Great Recession*, edited by Otaviano Canuto and Danny M. Peiziger. Washington: World Bank.

Chinn, Menzie and Jeffry Frieden. 2009. "Reflections on the Causes and Consequences of the Debt Crisis of 2008". *La Follette Policy Report*, **19** (1): 1–5.

Chinn, Menzie and Jeffry Frieden. 2011. *The Lost Decades: The Making of America's Debt Crisis and the Long Recovery*. New York: W.W. Norton.

Chinn, Menzie and Hiro Ito. 2006. "What Matters for Financial Development? Capital Controls, Institutions, and Interactions". *Journal of Development Economics*, **82**: 163–92.

Chinn, Menzie and Hiro Ito. 2007. "Current Account Balances, Financial Development and Institutions: Assaying the World 'Savings Glut'". *Journal of International Money and Finance*, **26** (4): 546–69.

Chinn, Menzie and Hiro Ito. 2008. "Global Current Account Imbalances: American Fiscal Policy versus East Asian Savings". *Review of International Economics*, **16** (3): 479–98.

Chinn, Menzie and Jaewoo Lee. 2009. "Three Current Account Balances: A 'Semi-Structuralist' Interpretation". *Japan and the World Economy*, **21**: 202–12.

Chinn, Menzie and Eswar Prasad. 2003. "Medium-Term Determinants of Current Accounts in Industrial and Developing Countries: An Empirical Exploration". *Journal of International Economics*, **59** (1): 47–76.

Choi, Horag, Nelson C. Mark and Donggyu Sul. 2008. "Endogenous Discounting, the World Saving Glut and the U.S. Current Account". *Journal of International Economics*, **75** (1): 30–53.

Clarida, Richard. 2005a. "Japan, China, and the U.S. Current Account Deficit". *CATO Journal*, **25** (1): 111–14.

Clarida, Richard. 2005b. "Some Thoughts on 'The Sustainability and Adjustment of Global Current Account Imbalances'". Speech given at the Council on Foreign Relations, 28 March.

Cline, William. 2010. *Renminbi Undervaluation, China's Surplus, and the US Trade Deficit*. Policy Brief 10-20. Washington, DC: Peterson Institute for International Economics.

Congressional Budget Office (CBO). 2009. *The Effects of Automatic Stabilizers on the Federal Budget*. Washington: Congressional Budget Office.

Corsetti, Giancarlo and Gernot J. Müller. 2006. "Twin Deficits: Squaring Theory, Evidence and Common Sense". *Economic Policy*, **21** (48): 597–638.

Council of Economic Advisers. 2009. *Economic Report of the President, 2009*. Washington, DC: US Government Printing Office.

Dean, Judith M., K.C. Fung and Zhi Wang. 2007. *Measuring the Vertical Specialization in Chinese Trade*. Office of Economics Working Paper 2007-01-A. Washington, DC: US International Trade Commission.

Dooley, Michael, David Folkerts-Landau and Peter Garber. 2003. *An Essay on the Revived Bretton Woods System*. NBER Working Paper 9971. Boston, Massachusetts: National Bureau of Economic Research.

Dooley, Michael, David Folkerts-Landau and Peter Garber. 2008. "Direct Investment, Rising Real Wages, and the Absorption of Excess Labor in the Periphery". In *G-7 Current Account Imbalances: Sustainability and Adjustment*, edited by Richard Clarida, Ch. 3. Chicago: University of Chicago Press for NBER.

Dowling, Thomas, Marcello Estevão and Evridiki Tsounta. 2010. *The Great Recession and Structural Unemployment*. United States: Selected Issues Paper, IMF Country Report 10/248. Washington: International Monetary Fund.

Eaton, Jonathan, Sam Kortum, Brent Neiman and John Romalis. 2011. *Trade and the Global Recession*. NBER Working Paper 16666. Cambridge, Massachusetts: National Bureau of Economic Research.

Eichengreen, Barry and Kevin H. O'Rourke. 2010. *A Tale of Two Depressions: What Do the New Data Tell Us?* London: Centre for Economic Policy Research. Available at www.VoxEU.org.

Eichengreen, Barry and Andrew Rose. 2010. "27 Up: The Implications for China of Abandoning Its Dollar Peg". Unpublished paper, University of California, Berkeley.

Engel, C. and J.H. Rogers. 2006. "The U.S. Current Account Deficit and the Expected Share of World Output". *Journal of Monetary Economics*, **53** (5): 1063–93.

Fei, John C.H. and Gustav Ranis. 1964. *Development of the Labor Surplus Economy: Theory and Policy*. Homewood, Illinois: Richard D. Irwin, Inc.

Gagnon, Joseph 2011. *Current Account Imbalances Coming Back*. Working Paper 11-1. Washington: Peterson Institute for International Economics.

Garcia-Herrero, Alicia and Tuuli Koivu. 2007. *Can the Chinese Trade Surplus Be Reduced through Exchange Rate Policy?* BOFIT Discussion Papers 2007-6. Helsinki: Bank of Finland.

Gaulier, Guillaume, Françoise Lemoine and Deniz Ünal. 2006. *China's Emergence and the Reorganization of Trade Flows in Asia*. CEPII Working Paper 2006-05. Paris: Centre d'Études Prospectives et d'Informations Internationales.

Greenspan, Alan. 2005. "Current Account". Paper presented at the Advancing Enterprise 2005 Conference, London, 4 February.

Gruber, Joseph and Steven Kamin. 2009. "Do Differences in Financial Development Explain the Global Pattern of Current Account Imbalances?" *Review of International Economics*, **17** (4): 667–88.

Gruber, Joseph and Steven Kamin. 2007. "Explaining the Global Pattern of Current Account Imbalances". *Journal of International Money and Finance*, **26**: 500–522.

Hubbard, R.G. 2005. "A Paradox of Interest". *Wall Street Journal* (23 June).

Hummels, David, Jun Ishii and Kei-Mu Yi. 2001. "The Nature and Growth of Vertical Specialization in World Trade". *Journal of International Economics*, **54**: 75–96.

Iacovone, Leonardo and Veronika Zavacka. 2009. "Banking Crises and Exports: Lessons from the Past for the Recent Trade Collapse". In *The Great Trade Collapse: Causes, Consequences and Prospects*, edited by Richard Baldwin, Ch. 13. London: Centre for Economic Policy Research. Available at www.voxeu.org.

International Monetary Fund (IMF). 2007. "Exchange Rates and the Adjustment of External Imbalances". In *World Economic Outlook 2007*, edited by the IMF, Ch. 3. Washington: International Monetary Fund.

International Monetary Fund (IMF). 2009. "How Linkages Fuel the Fire: The Transmission of Financial Stress from Advanced to Emerging Economies". In *World Economic Outlook* (April 2009), edited by the IMF, Ch. 4. Washington: International Monetary Fund.

International Monetary Fund (IMF). 2010. "Getting the Balance Right: Transitioning Out of Sustained Current Account Surpluses". In *World Economic Outlook* (April 2010), edited by the IMF, Ch. 4. Washington: International Monetary Fund.

Ito, Hiro and Menzie Chinn. 2010. "East Asia and Global Imbalances: Saving, Investment, and Financial Development". In *Financial Sector Development in the Pacific Rim*, edited by Takatoshi Ito and Andy Rose, pp. 117–60. Chicago: University of Chicago Press for the National Bureau of Economic Research.

Jeanne, Olivier and Romain Rancière. 2006. *The Optimal Level of International Reserves for Emerging Market Economies: Formulas and Applications*. IMF Working Paper WP/06/229. Washington: International Monetary Fund.

Johnson, Simon and James Kwak. 2010. *13 Bankers: The Wall Street Takeover and the Next Financial Meltdown*. New York: Vantage Books.

Koopman, Robert, Zhi Wang and Shang-Jin Wei. 2008. *How Much of Chinese Exports Is Really Made in China? Assessing Domestic Value-Added When Processing Trade Is Pervasive*. NBER Working Paper 14109. Boston, Massachusetts: National Bureau of Economic Research.

Kroeber, Arthur. 2010. "Economic Rebalancing. Twin Peaks: Fiscal and Financial Reform". *China Economic Quarterly*, **14** (2): 19.

Kuijs, Louis. 2005. *Investment and Saving in China*. World Bank Working Paper WPS3633. Washington: World Bank.

Lee, Jaewoo and Menzie Chinn. 2006. "Current Account and Real Exchange Rate Dynamics in the G7 Countries". *Journal of International Money and Finance*, **25**: 257–74.

Levchenko, Andrei A., Logan Lewis and Linda L. Tesar. 2010. "The Collapse of International Trade During the 2008–2009 Crisis: In Search of the Smoking Gun". *IMF Economic Review*, **58**: 214–53.

Lewis, W. Arthur. 1954. "Economic Development with Unlimited Supplies of Labor". *Manchester School of Economic and Social Studies*, **22**: 139–91.

Ma, Guonan and Wang Yi. 2010. *China's High Saving Rate: Myth and Reality*. BIS Working Paper 312. Basel: Bank for International Settlements.

Marquez, Jaime and John W. Schindler. 2007. "Exchange-Rate Effects on China's

Trade". *Review of International Economics*, **15** (5): 837–53. Also published as International Finance and Discussion Papers 861 (Washington: Federal Reserve Board, 2006).
Mendoza, Enrique G., Vincenzo Quadrini and Jose-Victor Ríos-Rull. 2009. "Financial Integration, Financial Deepness and Global Imbalances". *Journal of Political Economy*, **117** (3): 317–416.
Mora, Jesse and William M. Powers. 2009. "Did Trade Credit Problems Deepen the Great Trade Collapse?" In *The Great Trade Collapse: Causes, Consequences and Prospects*, edited by Richard Baldwin, Ch. 14. London: Centre for Economic Policy Research. Available at www.voxeu.org.
Nason, James M. and John H. Rogers. 2006. "The Present Value Model of the Current Account Has Been Rejected: Round Up the Usual Suspects". *Journal of International Economics*, **68**: 159–87.
Obstfeld, Maurice and Kenneth Rogoff 2009. "Global Imbalances and the Financial Crisis: Products of Common Causes". Paper presented at the Asia Economic Policy Conference, Federal Reserve Bank of San Francisco, Santa Barbara, California, 18–20 October.
Organisation for Economic Co-operation and Development (OECD). 2009. *Economic Outlook 85*. Paris: Organisation for Economic Co-operation and Development.
Pakko, Michael R. 1999. "The U.S. Trade Deficit and the 'New Economy'". *Federal Reserve Bank of St. Louis Review*, **81** (5): 11–20.
Prasad, Eswar. 2009. *Rebalancing Growth in Asia*. Working Paper 15169. Cambridge, Massachusetts: National Bureau of Economic Research.
Prasad, Eswar and Shang-Jin Wei. 2005. *The Chinese Approach to Capital Inflows: Patterns and Possible Explanations*. IMF Working Paper 05/79. Washington: International Monetary Fund.
Rissman, Ellen R. 2009. "Employment Growth: Cyclical Movements or Structural Change?" *Chicago Fed Economic Perspectives*, 2009 (4th quarter): 40–57.
Rodrik, Dani. 2008. "The Real Exchange Rate and Economic Growth". *Brookings Papers on Economic Activity*, 2008-2 (fall): 365–412.
Roubini, Nouriel and Stephen Mihm. 2010. *Crisis Economics: A Crash Course in the Future of Finance*. New York: Penguin Press.
Stiglitz, Joseph E. 2010. *Freefall: America, Free Markets, and the Sinking of the World Economy*. New York: W.W. Norton.
Stock, James H. and Mark W. Watson. 1993. "A Simple Estimator of Cointegrating Vectors in Higher Order Integrated Systems". *Econometrica*, **61** (4): 783–820.
Thorbecke, Willem and Gordon Smith. 2010. "How Would an Appreciation of the Renminbi and Other East Asian Currencies Affect China's Exports?" *Review of International Economics*, **18** (1): 95–108.
Truman, Edwin. 2005. "Budget and External Deficits: Not Twins but the Same Family". Paper presented at the Symposium on the Revived Bretton Woods System: A New Paradigm for Asian Development? Federal Reserve Bank of San Francisco, February.
Valletta, Robert and Aisling Cleary. 2008. "Sectoral Reallocation and Unemployment". *FRBSF Economic Letter*, 2008-32 (17 October). Available at www.frbsf.org.
Valletta, Robert and Katherine Kuang. 2010. "Is Structural Unemployment on the Rise?" *FRBSF Economic Letter*, 2010-34 (8 November). Available at www.frbsf.org.

Weidner, Justin and John C. Williams. 2011. *Update of "How Big Is the Output Gap?"*. San Francisco: Federal Reserve Bank of Francisco. Posted 7 July 2011, available at www.frbsf.org/publications/economics/letter/2009/el2009-19-update.pdf.

World Bank. 2010a. *China Quarterly Report (June)*. Beijing: World Bank.

World Bank. 2010b. *Global Economic Prospects*. Washington, DC: World Bank.

7. The great trade collapse and contraction of exports from Korea during the global crisis

Hangyu Lee

INTRODUCTION

During the 2008–09 global crisis, an unpleasant fact unfolded for many international economists. A large body of literature reported that world trade shrank far more than world GDP did during the crisis and argued that this fact cannot be easily reconciled with standard international macroeconomic theories such as Backus et al. (1995). The phenomenon is called "the great trade collapse", reflecting the unprecedented size of contraction in world trade, and the jargon has become popular among international economists. Responding to this unpleasant fact, many international economists have proposed various explanations for it.[1] Among them, the compositional effect, the internationalized supply chain and the trade credit hypotheses have been most frequently discussed in related literature.[2]

The compositional effect hypothesis notes differences between durable goods and nondurable goods and emphasizes a special role of durable goods in generating volatility of trade flow. It is a well known fact among macroeconomists that demand is more volatile for durable goods than for nondurable goods. Also, it has recently been reported that durable goods account for a larger share of world trade than of world GDP. The direct implication of these differences between two types of goods is that world trade can be more volatile than world GDP.

The presence of an internationalized supply chain provides another hypothesis. It is based on the observation that the production process has been involved increasingly with the vertical trading chain across many countries over time. According to Hummels et al. (2001), the trade flow related to so-called vertical specialization accounts for 21 percent of total exports of ten OECD countries and four emerging market countries, and it grew almost 30 percent between 1970 and

1990.[3] Given its quantitative importance, the internationalized supply chain can be considered another mechanism that can generate a sudden collapse in world trade. This is because, if only one part of the chain is gone, for some reason such as financial distress, the whole chain will break down and the whole of the related trade flows can then disappear altogether.

Finally, the trade credit hypothesis notes empirical evidence that financial distress in the banking sector affected trade flows adversely through reduced availability of external finance on exporters, including trade credit in past financial crises.[4]

Korea experienced a severe contraction in exports during the global crisis, just as other countries did. The growth rate of exports dropped to −17.5 percent on average during the fourth quarter of 2008 and the first quarter of 2009. To identify the main factors contributing to the severe contraction of Korean exports during this period, this chapter evaluates these hypotheses about the great trade collapse, with regard to the Korean experience, and tries to identify the factors that contributed most to the unexpected large drop in Korea's exports.

The main finding of this chapter is that the compositional effect hypothesis is the most relevant for understanding the collapse of exports in Korea during the crisis. In fact, Korea is one of the countries with a very high share of durable goods in its exports, amounting to about 65 percent immediately before the crisis. During the crisis, exports in this category experienced more severe contraction than exports of nondurable goods, and about 75 percent of the contraction of total exports came from the collapse of durable goods exports.

By contrast, the other hypotheses do not seem so relevant for the Korean case. A decomposition of total exports into intensive and extensive margins shows that the greater part of the exports contraction in Korea was generated through the intensive margin, and this fact implies that the internationalized supply chain related to the exporting sector of Korea kept working without serious interruption, even during the crisis. Also, broad evidence on the trade credit market in Korea suggests that the overall condition of the trade credit market did not deteriorate enough to induce such a large drop in trade flows.

Another main result of this chapter comes from a simple cross-country comparison with regard to the relationship between the share of durable goods exports and the drop of exports during the current crisis. The cross-country comparison suggests that a country with a higher share of durable goods exports is likely to experience harsher contraction of exports from a negative global demand shock. The empirical evidence presented in this chapter adds to the empirical findings and emerging consensus of recent literature on the great trade collapse, such as Baldwin (2009), Bems et al. (2010) and Levchenko et al. (2009), which identify the compositional effect as a major driving force generating the recent trade collapse. Also, it supports recent theoretical literature, such as Boileau (1999), Erceg et al. (2006) and Engel and Wang (2009), which emphasizes the special role of durable goods in generating realistic volatilities of trade flows in the framework of international macroeconomic models.

The next section briefly reviews recent trends of Korea's trade. The third section investigates broad data on Korean exports, to identify the main source of the large drop in Korean exports during the crisis and to show that the compositional effect hypothesis is the most relevant one in understanding the Korean experience. The final section concludes with a brief summary of the main results of this chapter and a discussion of policy implications and remaining issues.

RECENT TRENDS OF THE REAL ECONOMY AND TRADE IN KOREA

The recent global recession was on a scale that was unprecedented since the Great Depression of the 1930s. Like other countries, Korea experienced a severe contraction of its real economy and trade, and fell into a recession in the fourth quarter of 2008 (see Figure 7.1). The recession

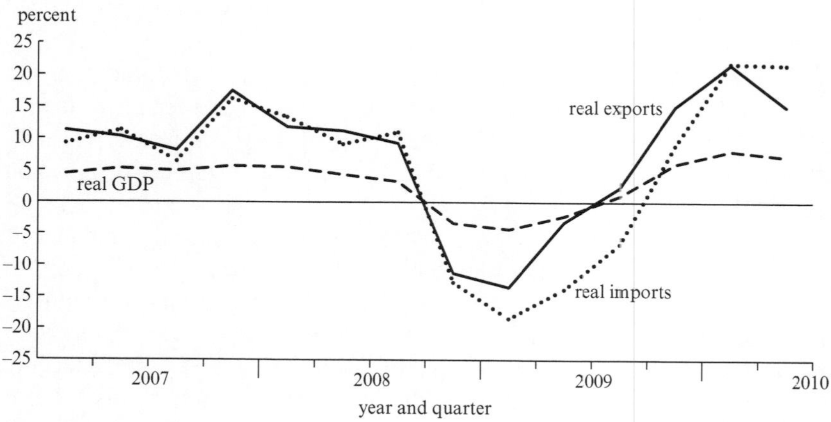

Source: Bank of Korea.

Figure 7.1 Growth rates of GDP and trade in Korea, 2007–10

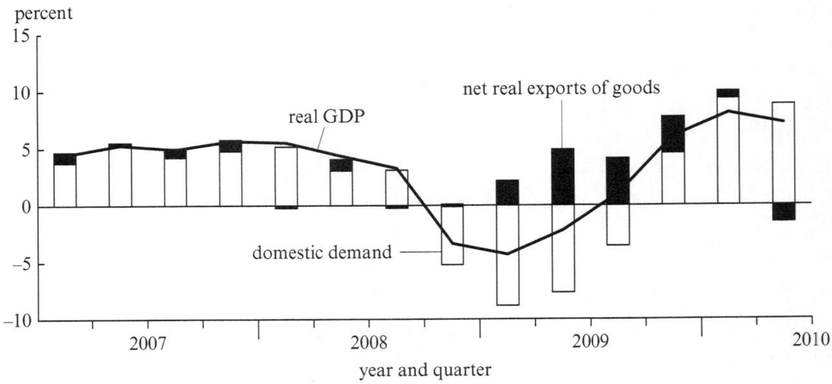

Source: Bank of Korea.

Figure 7.2 Contributions of domestic demand and net exports of goods to GDP growth in Korea, 2007–10

lasted through the next quarter and then, from the second quarter of 2009, both GDP and trade began to recover.

An interesting observation from Figure 7.1 is that the retrenchment of imports was much deeper and lasted longer than that of exports. The growth rates of exports and imports had been quite similar until the fourth quarter of 2008 but started to diverge from the first quarter of 2009. The relatively severer retrenchment of imports resulted in a large trade surplus, and the surplus contributed significantly in mitigating the negative effect of the drastic fall in domestic demand.

Figure 7.2 illustrates the contributions of domestic demand and net exports of goods to real GDP growth. It is clear that the trade surplus played an important role in the recovery of the real economy in Korea. It significantly offset the negative effect of depressed domestic demand on real GDP, particularly in 2009.

The earlier recovery of exports in Korea during the crisis is believed to have benefited from the relatively fast recovery of emerging economies, particularly China. As Figure 7.3 shows, the regional discrepancy between advanced and emerging economies widened as the recovery of the world economy from the great recession proceeded. Emerging economies, particularly emerging Asia, displayed much faster and stronger recovery from the second quarter of 2009 than advanced economies.

Reflecting the regional discrepancy in the recovery process, regional exports of Korea also followed quite different paths. More specifically,

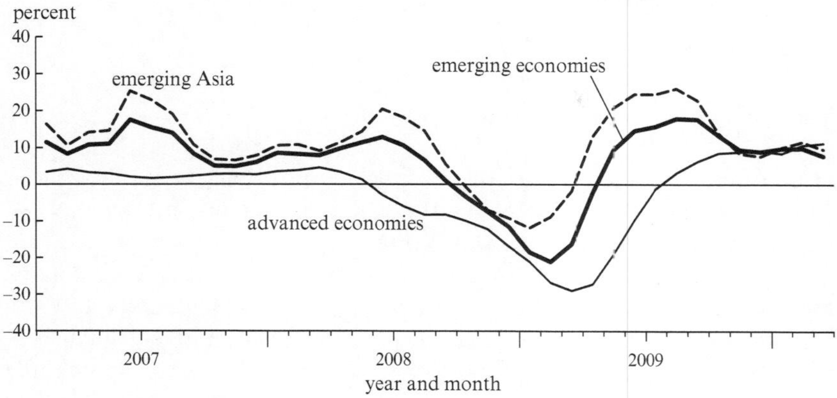

Source: International Monetary Fund, *World Economic Outlook*.

Figure 7.3 Growth rates of industrial production in emerging Asia, emerging economies, and advanced economies, 2007–10

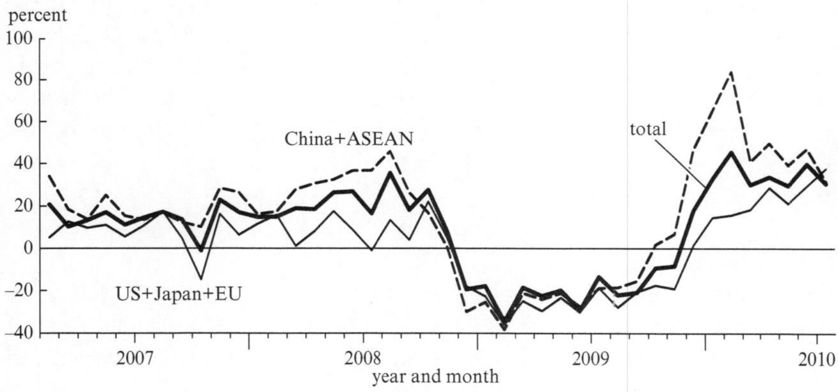

Source: Korea Customs Service.

Figure 7.4 Korean exports by region, 2007–10

as Figure 7.4 indicates, exports to China and the ASEAN countries started to recover at a fast and strong pace from the second half of 2009 and led the recovery of total exports thereafter. On the other hand, exports to advanced economies such as the United States, Japan and the European Union experienced severe retrenchment almost until the end of the year.[5]

MAIN CAUSES OF THE CONTRACTION OF EXPORTS FROM KOREA

The Compositional Effect Hypothesis

In explaining the great trade collapse, the compositional effect hypothesis emphasizes the special role of durable goods in magnifying the effect of global demand shocks on the world trade volume. It is a well known fact among macroeconomists that demand for durable goods is more volatile than demand for nondurable goods. In addition, as Baldwin (2009) and Wang (2010) indicate, durable goods account for a relatively small proportion of world GDP but a large proportion of world trade. From these facts, it is natural to expect that a global demand shock can deliver disproportionate effects: that is, the response of world trade to a demand shock is expected to be much bigger than that of world GDP.

The compositional effect hypothesis can deliver a testable cross-country implication as well. This is because shares of durable goods exports vary significantly across countries and, as a result, total exports will respond quite differently to a global demand shock. For example, given a negative demand shock such as the recent global crisis, a country in which durable goods account for a higher share of exports is expected to experience a bigger reduction in its exports than a country in which durable goods account for a lower share of exports. To test the implication of this hypothesis, with respect to the recent global crisis, a simple cross-country comparison can be made.

Cross-country comparison

For the cross-country comparison, a dataset was constructed based on the shares of durable goods exports and real export growth rates of 23 major countries. Each country's share of durable goods exports was obtained and calculated from the UN Comtrade database, which provides disaggregate trade series based on the broad economic classification code on an annual basis (see Box 7.1). Each country's share of durable goods is measured as an average of the share during 2005 to 2007. Data on each country's nominal exports, obtained from the International Monetary Fund's DOT database, were deflated with a proper deflator available for each country to calculate the growth rates of real exports.[6] To highlight the effect of durable goods, the exports growth rates were measured as averages of monthly year-to-year growth rates during the fourth quarter of 2008 and the first quarter of 2009, when the crisis was at its peak (see Table 7.1).

Figure 7.5 illustrates the relationship between the share of durable goods in exports and the real export growth rate during the crisis. As predicted

BOX 7.1 UN BROAD ECONOMIC CLASSIFICATION CODE AND DURABLE–NONDURABLE GOODS CLASSIFICATION

Broad Economic Classification (BEC)	Author's classification of goods
1 food and beverages	nondurable
11 primary	nondurable
111 mainly for industry	nondurable
112 mainly for household consumption	nondurable
12 processed	nondurable
121 mainly for industry	nondurable
122 mainly for household consumption	nondurable
2 industrial supplies	nondurable
21 primary	nondurable
22 processed	nondurable
3 fuel and lubricants	nondurable
31 primary	nondurable
32 processed	nondurable
321 motor spirit	nondurable
322 other	nondurable
4 machinery, capital equipment (except transport) and accessories thereof	durable
41 machinery and other capital equipment except transport	durable
42 parts and accessories	durable
5 transport equipment and accessories thereof	durable
51 passenger motor cars	durable
52 other	durable
521 industrial	durable
522 nonindustrial	durable
53 parts and accessories	durable
6 consumer goods	–
61 durable	durable
62 semidurable	nondurable
63 nondurable	nondurable
7 goods, n.e.s.	nondurable

Note: The UN Broad Economic Classification code is available on the website of the UN Comtrade database.

Table 7.1 Share of durable goods exports 2005–07 and growth rates of real exports and exchange rates 2008–09 of 23 major economies (%)

Economy	Share of durable goods	Growth of real exports	Change of real exchange rate
Argentina	13.45	−9.28	1.11
Australia	10.57	23.39	22.29
Brazil	26.36	−4.32	11.50
Canada	34.64	−9.32	14.91
China	51.90	−13.14	−12.44
Hong Kong	57.47	−15.10	−2.75
France	45.26	−5.31	4.59
Germany	53.85	−14.98	4.53
India	17.07	2.58	8.03
Indonesia	16.69	4.66	11.54
Italy	43.39	−17.90	3.53
Japan	68.63	−26.28	−18.17
Malaysia	55.43	−11.19	0.86
Mexico	55.04	−7.38	18.35
Philippines	62.53	−21.93	−4.04
Republic of Korea	65.28	−4.80	44.31
Russian Federation	4.53	−16.77	0.71
Singapore	59.90	−13.78	−5.10
South Africa	22.54	−1.46	24.91
Thailand	48.63	−17.76	0.71
Turkey	34.76	−9.17	9.81
United Kingdom	44.55	−9.65	32.89
United States	53.12	−11.45	0.00

Notes: The shares of durable goods are averages for 2005–07. The real exports growth rates and changes in the real exchange rates are for the fourth quarter 2008 through the first quarter 2009.

Sources: UN Comtrade database; IMF International Financial Statistics; Global Insight database.

by the hypothesis, the figure displays a clear negative relationship between the shares of durable goods exports and real exports growth rate, although there are some exceptional cases such as Russia.[7] For instance, Japan (whose share of durable goods exports was the highest among countries in the dataset before the crisis) experienced the severest exports reduction. Japan's real exports growth rate during the fourth quarter of 2008 and first quarter of 2009 was −26.3 percent. By contrast, Australia (where the share

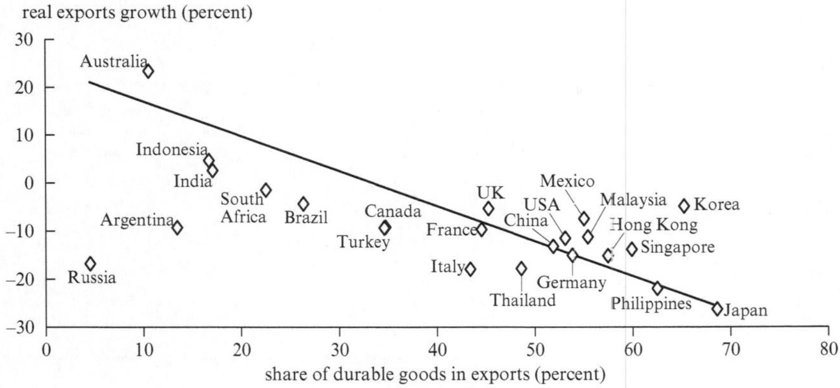

Sources: Comtrade Data Base (UN), Direction of Trade Data Base (IMF), International Financial Statistics (IMF), and Global Insight.

Figure 7.5 Exports of durable goods by select countries: real growth versus export share, fourth quarter 2008 to first quarter 2009

was only about 10 percent before the crisis) enjoyed an exports growth rate of 23 percent.

For a more formal analysis, two simple regression equations were applied to the same dataset. The explained variable is the real exports growth rate, and the share of durable goods exports is included as an explanatory variable in both equations. The real exchange depreciation rate is included only in the second equation.[8] The results of the regression analyses are reported in Table 7.2. Again, the results indicate that a tight negative relationship exists between the share of durable goods exports and the reduction of total exports during the current global crisis. The coefficient of the share of durable goods exports is estimated as −0.32 when only the share of durable goods exports is considered as an explanatory variable, and it is slightly increased to −0.26 when both the share and real exchange rate depreciation rate are considered as explanatory variables. In both cases, the coefficient is statistically significant at the 1 percent significance level. In sum, these results imply that, on average, a country with a higher share of durable goods exports (higher by 10 percentage points) experienced a greater reduction in total export growth (lower by about 3 percentage points) during the crisis.[9]

As a robustness test, a similar cross-country comparison can be made with the information technology (IT) bubble, which burst in 2001. It is widely believed that there was a mild global recession and synchronized drops of aggregate demand around the world at that time. So, if the

Table 7.2 Regression of total export growth rate on share of durable goods exports and real exchange rate depreciation rate

Variables	Regression I	Regression II
Share of durable goods	−0.32 ***	−0.26 ***
	(0.09)	(−0.08)
Real depreciation rate	–	0.33 **
	–	(0.11)
Constant	3.85	−0.86
	(4.18)	(3.85)
Adjusted R-squared	0.33	0.52

Notes: Numbers in parentheses are standard errors. Symbols *** and ** indicate statistical significance at 1 and 5 percent levels, respectively.

Sources: UN Comtrade database; IMF Direction of Trade database; IMF International Financial Statistics; Global Insight database.

compositional effect hypothesis is truly valid, a similar negative relationship is expected to emerge also in the bursting of the IT bubble. To verify this conjecture, similar data from the same 23 countries can be analysed in relation to the IT bubble. In this case, the shares of durable goods exports are measured as the value in 2000 just before the bubble burst, and real exports growth rates are measured as the value in the fourth quarter of 2001. Figure 7.6 is a scatter diagram based on the dataset. As the figure clearly shows, a similar negative relationship between the two variables emerges again. This additional cross-country comparison suggests that the validity of the compositional effect hypothesis might be quite robust.

The empirical evidence from these cross-country comparisons adds to the existing empirical findings and emerging consensus of recent literature on the great trade collapse, such as Baldwin (2009), Bems et al. (2010), and Levchenko et al. (2009). They emphasize that the compositional effect of durable goods was a main driving force in generating the recent great trade collapse. In addition, the present analysis supports recent theoretical literature, such as Boileau (1999), Erceg et al. (2006) and Engel and Wang (2009), which emphasizes the special role of durable goods in generating realistic volatilities of trade flows in the framework of international macroeconomic models.

Crucial role of durable goods exports in recent fluctuations of Korean exports

As discussed above, a key implication drawn from the cross-country comparisons is that a country with a higher share of durable goods among

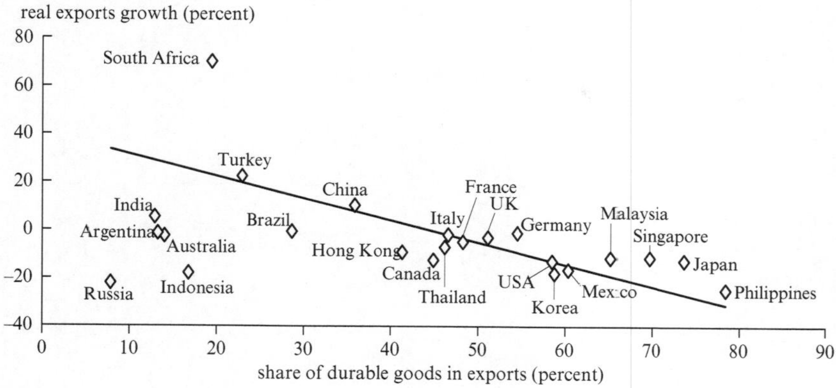

Sources: Comtrade Data Base (UN), Direction of Trade Data Base (IMF), International Financial Statistics (IMF), and Global Insight.

Figure 7.6 Exports of durable goods by select countries: real growth versus export share, fourth quarter 2001

its exports is likely to experience a severer reduction in exports due to a negative demand shock. In this sense, the contraction of Korean exports during the crisis can be regarded as a natural consequence of the global recession, reflecting a heavy concentration on durable goods before the crisis. As observed in Figure 7.5, Korea is among the countries with the highest shares of durable goods in their exports, amounting to about 65 percent just before the crisis.

To investigate how durable goods exports contributed to the large fluctuation of exports in Korea during the crisis and recovery, I decompose monthly exports data into durable goods and nondurable goods. To classify durable and nondurable goods, I convert monthly exports data using the conversion table of the six-digit harmonized system (HS) code to the UN broad economic categories (BEC) code.[10] Then, I assess the durability of each category and classify it based on the assessment.[11] Figures 7.7 and 7.8 are based on this decomposition.

From Figures 7.7 and 7.8, it is clear that the high share of durable goods exports plays a crucial role in the large drop of exports in Korea. As Figure 7.7 shows, the fall in the growth rate of durable goods exports was much deeper than that of nondurable goods exports during the crisis. During the period from the fourth quarter of 2008 to the first quarter of 2009, when the crisis was at its peak, the durable goods exports (exports of ships excluded) recorded an average growth rate of −27.0 percent while, that of nondurable goods (oil-related exports excluded) recorded only

Source: Korea Customs Service.

Figure 7.7 Exports of durable and nondurable goods by Korea: growth rates 2008–09

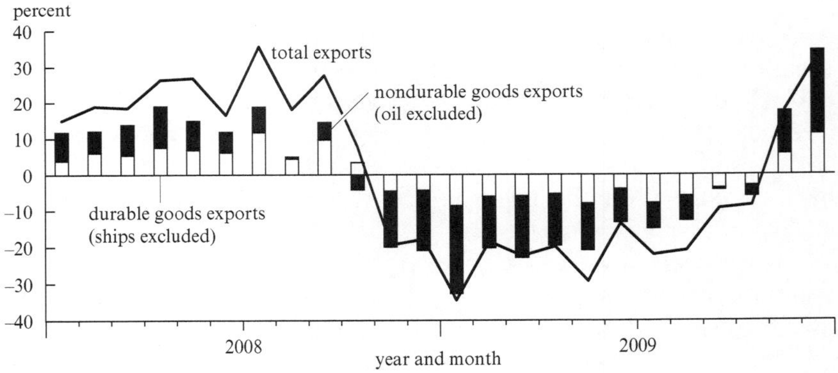

Source: Korea Customs Service.

Figure 7.8 Contributions of durable and nondurable goods to total export growth in Korea, 2008–09

−15.2 percent.[12] Figure 7.8 measures the contribution of each component to the reduction of total exports and shows that more than three-quarters of the drop in total exports is attributable to the collapse of durable goods exports during the period.

It is also interesting to observe that the compositional effect worked in exactly the opposite direction as the world economy started its

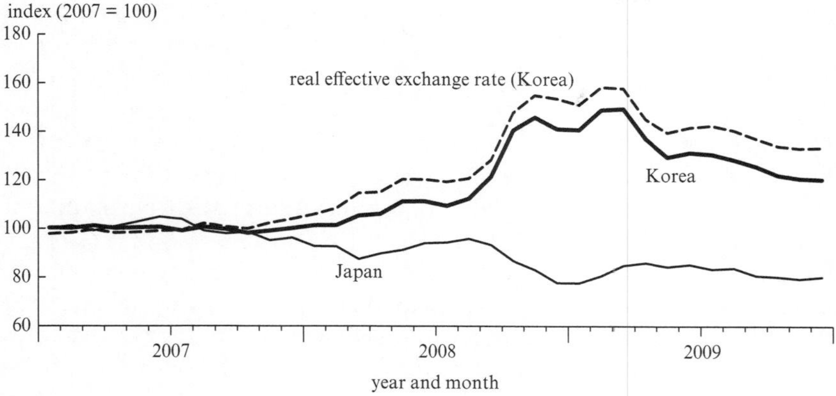

Source: International Financial Statistics (IMF) and Korea Customs Service.

Figure 7.9 Real exchange rates of the Korean won and Japanese yen to the US dollar, 2007–09

recovery process and world demand recovered from severe recession. As shown in Figures 7.7 and 7.8, durable goods exports led the recovery of Korean exports from the second half of 2009. The growth rate of durable goods exports had been higher than that of nondurable goods during the period, and the greater part of the exports growth was due to the rapid expansion of durable goods exports in the last quarter of 2009.

In sum, it can be concluded from those observations that the high share of durable goods exports of Korea and the compositional effect are key elements in understanding the fluctuation of Korean exports.

Exchange rate depreciation moderating the contraction of Korean exports

Returning to Figure 7.5, another interesting observation is that the fall of Korean exports was quite moderate compared with other countries with a similar level of share of durable goods exports, particularly Japan. While Japan and Korea had quite similar shares of durable goods exports before the crisis, Japan experienced a far deeper fall of exports than Korea during the crisis. During the fourth quarter of 2008 and first quarter of 2009, the real exports growth rate of Japan was −26.3 percent while that of Korea was only −4.8 percent.

One potential factor contributing to this large discrepancy can be found in Figure 7.9, which illustrates movements of the real exchange rates to the US dollar of the Korean won and Japanese yen from 2007 to 2009.

The figure shows that the two countries followed starkly different paths of real exchange rates from the onset of the global crisis. During the crisis, the Korean won experienced a rapid depreciation in both nominal and real terms, due to the turmoil in the foreign exchange market driven by large capital outflows. The depreciation rate of the real exchange rate to US dollar amounted to almost 50 percent at the peak of the global crisis. By contrast, the Japanese yen appreciated from beginning of the crisis, and the appreciation rate reached about 20 percent during the fourth quarter of 2008 and the first quarter of 2009.

Considering the magnitude of the divergence between these currencies, it can be argued that the large depreciation of the Korean won moderated the reduction of Korean exports during the crisis, in comparison with reductions experienced by other countries with a similar share of durable goods exports.

Internationalized Supply Chain Hypothesis

As Hummels et al. (2001) document, the production process has been involved increasingly with the vertical trading chain across many countries over time. According to their estimates, that type of trade flow, the so-called vertical specialization, accounts for 21 percent of total exports of ten OECD countries and four emerging market countries, and it grew almost 30 percent between 1970 and 1990.[13]

Given its quantitative importance, the internationalized supply chain can serve as a source of sudden collapse of world trade. This is because, if only one part of the chain is gone, for some reason such as financial distress, the whole chain will break down, and the whole related trade flow can disappear at the same time.

In order to examine whether the internationalized supply chain had influence on the contraction of exports in Korea during the crisis, I investigate trends of the intensive and extensive margins of Korean exports to the ten major trading partners during the crisis, similar to the studies by Schott (2009), Wakasugi (2009), and Bernard et al. (2009).[14] However, it is admitted that the definitions of intensive and extensive margins are quite coarse, compared with those in related literature such as Bernard et al. (2009). This is because the number of export products and values at firm level are not available in Korea. Hence, the extensive margin is defined as the number of products at a disaggregate level of the six-digit HS code whose exports values are positive. The intensive margin is simply defined as the total value of exports divided by the number of products.[15] The results are summarized in Tables 7.3 and 7.4.

As observed from Table 7.3, it is difficult to find any evidence of significant variation of the extensive margin in Korean exports during the crisis.

Table 7.3 Extensive margin: number of export products

Year	Quarter	Total	China	China and Hong Kong	India	Indonesia	Thailand	Vietnam	Czech Republic	Slovakia	Netherlands	Poland	United States
2007	average	4104	3122	3270	1477	1764	1652	2035	423	393	935	658	2448
2008	1	4126	3060	3194	1480	1804	1712	2101	477	435	963	700	2458
	2	4152	3193	3333	1545	1824	1702	2154	506	458	965	702	2498
	3	4182	3186	3341	1564	1812	1682	2144	484	449	981	687	2496
	4	4185	3136	3293	1512	1769	1710	2253	504	462	963	707	2544
2009	1	4148	3088	3233	1495	1722	1628	2183	471	424	920	674	2496
	2	4178	3147	3299	1575	1852	1684	2293	494	470	927	688	2491
	3	4184	3172	3319	1614	1842	1745	2345	540	464	946	737	2551
	4	4171	3199	3371	1626	1848	1760	2352	579	470	974	766	2494

Source: Korea Customs Service data.

Table 7.4 Intensive margin: export value per product (US$ thousand)

Year	Quarter	Total	China	China and Hong Kong	India	Indonesia	Thailand	Vietnam	Czech Republic	Slovakia	Netherlands	Poland	United States
2007	average	22,623	6564	7693	1117	818	679	705	568	1728	1201	1333	4673
2008	1	24,102	7204	8270	1314	841	807	1065	540	1828	1340	1518	4517
	2	27,575	8229	9489	1463	1087	885	1057	352	1937	1217	1448	4932
	3	27,499	8032	9379	1635	1291	1005	901	388	2500	2071	1671	4619
	4	22,239	5574	6616	1465	1185	702	603	408	1424	1982	1259	4491
2009	1	17,942	5344	6352	1061	595	594	604	391	1514	1192	1261	3328
	2	21,628	6652	7725	1307	805	599	781	358	1726	1052	1472	3810
	3	22,653	7511	8768	1268	931	659	803	341	1751	1089	1510	3848
	4	24,927	7954	9268	1427	958	796	917	391	1854	1464	1529	4023

Source: Korea Customs Service data.

The extensive margin remained almost the same, before and during the crisis, at both the total and the individual country levels. For example, the extensive margin in total exports increased in the fourth quarter of 2008 and first quarter of 2009 by 2.0 percent and 1.1 percent, respectively, compared with the average value in 2007. By contrast, the intensive margins plummeted drastically during the fourth quarter of 2008 and first quarter of 2009, at both the total and the individual country levels. The intensive margin of total exports decreased in the fourth quarter of 2008 and first quarter of 2009 by 1.7 percent and 20.7 percent, respectively, compared with the average value in 2007.

This result clearly indicates that the contraction of exports in Korea during the crisis took place mainly through the intensive margin rather than the extensive margin and that the international production chain related to the Korean export sector is robust enough to endure such a large negative shock as this global crisis.

In addition, it is notable that the result is consistent with existing related literature. More specifically, according to Bernard et al. (2009), the variation of extensive margin is related mainly to trade growth and intensive margin is more associated with cyclical fluctuations of trade. Subsequently, Schott (2009) and Wakasugi (2009) reported that a similar pattern can be observed in both US and Japanese trade data.

Considering all this evidence together, it can be concluded that the internationalized production chain hypothesis might be a minor factor in the collapse of the world trade as well as Korean exports during the current crisis.

Trade Credit Hypothesis

The last potential explanation of the great trade collapse examined in this chapter is related to trade credit. The trade credit hypothesis was originally based on literature reporting that financial distress in banking sectors had affected trade flows adversely through the reduced availability of external finance for exporters, including trade credit in past financial crises.[16] So, the original idea of the hypothesis is associated with financial instruments broader than trade credit. However, the majority of analysis in the recent literature on the issue has been limited to trade credit. The analysis of the trade credit hypothesis in this chapter will likewise be limited to investigating changes in the overall condition of the trade credit market in Korea during the crisis.

Figure 7.10 shows of the trends from 2006 to early 2010 in the purchase of export bills and the issuance of import usances by domestic banks in Korea. Both series are scaled to corresponding trade flows. So, if the overall condition of the trade credit market deteriorated severely due to financial

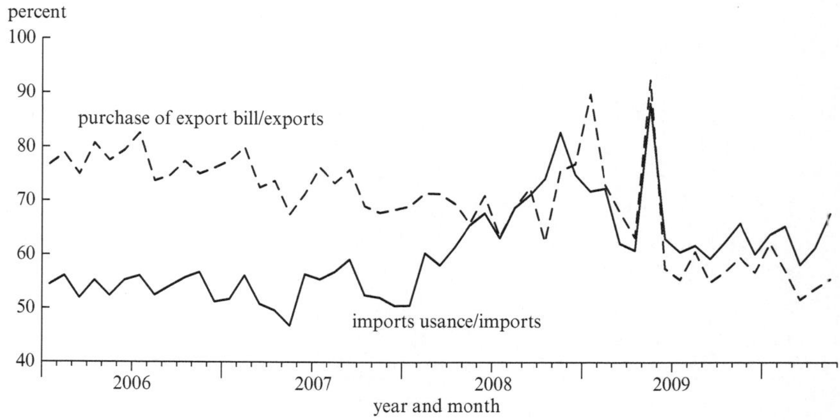

Source: Financial Supervisory Service and Korea Customs Service.

Figure 7.10 Trade credit extended by domestic banks in Korea, 2006–10

market distress and it hindered trade flows, those ratios are expected to fall or at least stay at levels similar to those before the crisis. Contrary to the expectation, however, as shown in the figure, both ratios increased during the crisis, particularly during the fourth quarter of 2008 and the first quarter of 2009. The direct implication is that the amount of trade credit did not slow down (or else slowed more moderately than exports and imports), which can be regarded as evidence that the overall trade credit market operated quite well in Korea, even during the severe financial crisis.

Further evidence can be found in Figure 7.11, which shows the trends of the discount rate in Korea applied to new trade bills from 2007 to early 2010. While the credit spread between corporate bonds and Korea's Treasury bonds widened during the crisis, the discount rate stayed at around the precrisis level. This implies that the market evaluation of the riskiness of trade bills did not change much compared with other financial instruments related with corporate sectors.

Although it has to be admitted that simple observations about Figures 7.10 and 7.11 cannot make any strong argument, it can be concluded from the observations that the overall availability of trade credit in Korea did not deteriorate so significantly as to induce a large drop in trade flows.

This well-functioning performance of the trade credit market during the crisis can be attributed in part to an active policy response. The Korean government and Bank of Korea announced in November 2008 that they would provide US$16 billion designated solely for trade credit through related financial institutions, including commercial banks, to prevent

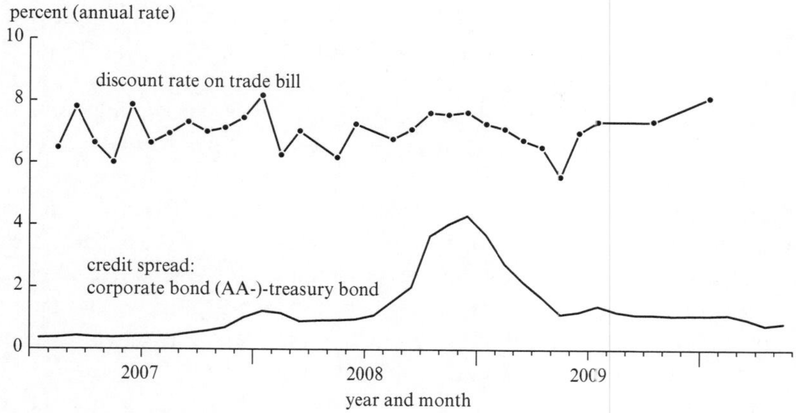

Source: Financial Supervisory Service and Bank of Korea.

Figure 7.11 Discount rates on trade bills and credit spread in Korea, 2007–10

severe slackness in the trade credit market and a trade collapse as a consequence.[17]

SUMMARY AND DISCUSSION

This chapter tries to identify the factor that contributed most to the unexpected large drop in Korean exports during the crisis, by evaluating several hypotheses on the great trade collapse with reference to the Korean experience. The main results can be summarized as follows. First, the compositional effect hypothesis is the most relevant for explaining the collapse of Korean exports during the crisis. The contraction of export goods was severer for durable goods than for nondurable goods, amounting to about 75 percent of total contraction. Second, the cross-country comparisons presented in this chapter suggest that a country with higher share of durable goods exports is likely to experience harsher contraction of exports because of a negative demand shock. This empirical evidence contributes to the growing literature on the great trade collapse and to literature emphasizing the special role of durable goods in generating realistic volatilities of trade flows in the framework of international dynamic stochastic general equilibrium models.

A key implication of this chapter is that the high share of durable goods in Korea's exports is a potentially main source of volatility in Korea's export sector and possibly in the whole economy even in the future. In other words, given the high sensitivity of Korea's exporting sector to fluctuations in the world economy due to the high share of durable goods, the spill-over into the Korean economy of an external shock can be magnified through trade channels.

Reflecting this concern, arguments are increasingly heard in Korea that, for enhancing the stability of the economy, a policy response is necessary to change the structure of the economy to make it less sensitive to external shocks. To this end, the proponents recommend that the government follow a strategy of promoting industries that are less sensitive to external economic conditions, such as the service industry.

It should be emphasized, however, that some important points may be missing from this argument. First, as economics textbooks teach, trade flows can reflect fundamentally comparative advantages across countries, and the comparative advantages can be outcomes of efficient resource allocations based on resource endowments and optimal decisions by economic agents. In this sense, the high volatility of trade flows in Korea can be regarded as a natural consequence of the given economic structure, which is already optimal in the sense of comparative advantage. Thus, if the government excessively pursues an industrial policy measure for promoting the stability of the economy, the only outcome may be serious economic distortions generating resource misallocations.

Second, it is also worth noting that it is still unclear whether the volatilities of exporting sectors can lead directly to large fluctuations of the whole economy or not. As recent literature on intermediate goods trade emphasizes, the share of value-added components in total exports can be quite small due to the increasingly fragmented industrial production chain. This means that the whole economy can remain stable in spite of the high volatility of the exporting sector. Hence, to determine whether the high volatility in the exporting sector can be a serious risk factor to the whole economy, it is necessary first to measure the exposure of an economy to changes in foreign demand from the value-added perspective, considering the quantitative importance of the increasing trade in intermediate goods.

Further research should be pursued in this direction. Recent work such as Bems et al. (2010) and Johnson and Noguera (2009) provide helpful insights for further studies, in that they measure external exposures in a more realistic way by combining trade flow and input–output table data.

NOTES

Acknowledgments. I am grateful to Menzie Chinn, Maurice Obstfeld, Joshua Aizenmann, Michael Hutchison and my colleagues at KDI for valuable comments. Also, I thank Rangmi Myoung for superb research assistance. All remaining errors are mine.

1. Baldwin (2009) provides an excellent survey of literature on the great trade collapse.
2. Besides these hypotheses, inventory adjustment and protectionism have also been suggested as explanations for the world trade collapse. See Alessandria et al. (2010) for the inventory argument.
3. For various implications of vertical specialization for the world trade and international business cycle, see Yi (2003), Kose and Yi (2006), and Giovanni and Levchenko (2010).
4. For details, see Amiti and Weinstein (2009) and Iacovone and Zavacka (2009).
5. Many experts believe that Korean exports have benefited significantly from the domestic stimulus policy adopted by the Chinese government. The extent to which this stimulus policy has contributed to the recovery of the Korean economy is certainly an interesting research issue, one that is beyond the scope of this chapter.
6. In most cases, the export price index obtained from International Financial Statistics is used as a deflator, but for some cases in which export price indexes are not available, the producer price index or the wholesale price index in dollar terms obtained from Global Insight are used.
7. Considering large commodity price fluctuations around the crisis, it would be better to exclude some countries such as Russia, whose exports concentrate heavily on the commodity sector. To do so, however, will inevitably involve some arbitrariness, and I therefore chose to use all the samples and report results to avoid such arbitrariness.
8. The real exchange rate is each country's currency to the US dollar, and the base year is 2005. It would be better to use the real effective exchange rate instead of the real exchange rate to US dollar, but doing so may reduce the sample size significantly due to limited data availability.
9. As Menzie Chinn commented at the 2010 EWC-KDI conference, the regression analyses leave much room for further investigation. However, I will leave it for future research.
10. The conversion table between the HS and the BEC codes is available at the website of the UN Comtrade database.
11. For detailed information about the classification, see Box 7.1.
12. Ship exports are excluded because, since shipbuilding usually takes a long time and it is planned so far in advance, it is difficult to take ship exports into account in a timely way, to reflect current changes in world economic conditions.
13. For various implications of vertical specialization for world trade and the international business cycle, see Yi (2003), Kose and Yi (2006) and Giovanni and Levchenko (2010).
14. I selected ten countries based on the size of direct investments abroad and exports to the destination country.
15. The definitions of intensive and extensive margins of exports used in this chapter are quite similar with those in Wakasugi (2009).
16. For details, see Amiti and Weinstein (2009) and Iacovone and Zavacka (2009).
17. Similarly, based on the fact that US cross-border bank financing bounced back earlier than bank financing from other sources, Mora and Powers (2009) argue that, due to massive policy responses, trade finance declined only moderately despite global credit market crunches.

REFERENCES

Alessandria, G., J.P. Kaboski and V. Midrigan. 2010. *The Great Trade Collapse of 2008–09: An Inventory Adjustment?*. NBER Working Paper 16059. Boston, Massachusetts: National Bureau of Economic Research.

Amiti, M. and D.E. Weinstein. 2009. *Exports and Financial Shocks*. NBER Working Paper 15556. Boston, Massachusetts: National Bureau of Economic Research.

Backus, D., P. Kehoe and F. Kydland. 1995. "International Business Cycles: Theory and Evidence". In *Frontiers of Business Cycle Research*, edited by T.F. Cooley, pp. 331–56. Princeton, New Jersey: Princeton University Press.

Baldwin, R. 2009. "The Great Trade Collapse: What Caused It and What Does It Mean?". In *The Great Trade Collapse: Causes, Consequences, and Prospects*, edited by Richard Baldwin, introductory chapter. London: Centre for Economic Policy Research. Available at www.voxeu.org.

Bems, R., R.C. Johnson and K. Yi. 2010. *Demand Spillovers and the Collapse of Trade in the Global Recession*. IMF Working Paper WP/10/142. Washington: International Monetary Fund.

Bernard, A.B., J.B. Jensen, S.J. Redding and P.K. Schott. 2009. "The Margins of US Trade". *American Economic Review: Papers & Proceedings*, **99** (2): 487–93.

Boileau, M. 1999. "Trade in Capital Goods and the Volatility of Net Exports and the Terms of Trade". *Journal of International Economics*, **48**: 347–65.

Engel, C. and J. Wang. 2009. *International Trade in Durable Goods: Understanding Volatility, Cyclicality, and Elasticities*. Working Paper. Madison, Wisconsin: University of Wisconsin at Madison.

Erceg, C.J., L. Guerrieri and C. Gust. 2006. *Trade Adjustment and the Composition of Trade*. Working Paper. Washington: Board of Governors of the Federal Reserve System.

Giovanni, J. and A.A. Levchenko. 2010. "Putting the Parts Together: Trade, Vertical Linkages, and Business Cycle Comovement". *American Economic Journal: Macroeconomics*, **2**: 95–124.

Hummels, D., J. Ishii and K. Yi. 2001. "The Nature and Growth of Vertical Specialization in World Trade". *Journal of International Economics*, **54**: 75–96.

Iacovone, L. and V. Zavacka. 2009. "Banking Crises and Exports: Lessons from the Past for the Recent Trade Collapse". In *The Great Trade Collapse: Causes, Consequences, and Prospects*, edited by Richard Baldwin, Ch. 13. London: Centre for Economic Policy Research. Available at www.voxeu.org.

Johnson, R. and G. Noguera. 2009. *Accounting for Intermediates: Production Sharing and Trade in Value Added*. Working Paper. Berkeley, California: University of California at Berkeley.

Kose, M.A. and K. Yi. 2006. "Can the Standard International Business Cycle Model Explain the Relation between Trade and Comovement?". *Journal of International Economics*, **68**: 267–915.

Levchenko, A.A., L. Lewis and L.L. Tesar. 2009. *The Collapse of International Trade during the 2008–2009 Crisis: In Search for the Smoking Gun*. RSIE Discussion Paper. Ann Arbor, Michigan: Research Seminar in International Economics, University of Michigan at Ann Arbor.

Mora, J. and W. Powers. 2009. "Did Trade Credit Problems Deepen the Great

Trade Collapse?". In *The Great Trade Collapse: Causes, Consequences, and Prospects*, edited by Richard Baldwin, Ch. 14. London: Centre for Economic Policy Research. Available at www.voxeu.org.

Schott, P.K. 2009. "US Trade Margins during the 2008 Crisis". In *The Great Trade Collapse: Causes, Consequences, and Prospects*, edited by Richard Baldwin, Ch. 15. London: Centre for Economic Policy Research. Available at www.voxeu.org.

Wakasugi, R. 2009. "Why Was Japan's Trade Hit So Much Harder?". In *The Great Trade Collapse: Causes, Consequences, and Prospects*, edited by Richard Baldwin, Ch. 23. London: Centre for Economic Policy Research. Available at www.voxeu.org.

Wang, J. 2010. "Durable Goods and the Collapse of Global Trade". *Economic Letter* (Federal Reserve Bank of Dallas), **5** (2).

Yi, K. 2003. "Can Vertical Specialization Explain the Growth of World Trade?". *Journal of Political Economy*, **111** (1): 52–102.

PART III

Policy perspectives

8. Macroeconomic and financial policies before and after the crisis

Barry Eichengreen

My charge in this chapter is to analyse the roles of monetary, fiscal and regulatory policies in the run-up to, midst of and aftermath of the crisis. This focus directs attention to the following questions:

- How important in the genesis of the crisis were lax supervision and regulation of financial institutions, perverse incentives in financial markets, the stance of monetary and fiscal policies and global imbalances?
- What explains variations in the policy response across countries?
- Should we rethink the efficacy of the policy response in the light of the problems that developed subsequently in Europe and elsewhere?

My focus is on the Group of 20 (G20) countries. The crisis also had a powerful impact on other, generally poorer economies whose experience is certainly deserving of attention.[1] But, then, a single chapter cannot cover everything.

FINANCIAL POLICIES IN THE RUN-UP TO THE CRISIS

It has become fashionable, even commonplace, to blame outside factors for the crisis in the United States. Alan Greenspan has argued that the crisis had its roots in the end of the Cold War.[2] Others have attributed the crisis to the rise of China, which unbalanced global markets by significantly augmenting the global labor supply with workers with an inordinate inclination to save (Bernanke 2010).

While factors such as these may have played an enabling or compounding role, the root causes of the crisis, in my view, lay at home, in the United States. Those root causes were an ideology of market fundamentalism and the policies flowing from it.[3] The idea that markets get it right and governments only get in the way—what I refer to here as market fundamentalism—is a powerful current in American thought. That ideology was dealt a blow by the Great Depression, which forged a consensus that markets are intrinsically unstable and require strong oversight. But historical memory does not last forever, and by the 1970s the generation that lived through the 1930s had begun to pass. Even before the Reagan revolution, American antiregulationist ideology had reasserted itself, and the policy pendulum had begun to swing in the other direction with the removal of Regulation Q ceilings on interest on the deposits and the elimination of regulatory restrictions on stockbrokers' commissions. The Reagan Administration pushed the deregulatory envelope, albeit more in the nonfinancial than the financial sphere. In the second half of the 1990s, the Clinton Administration and Greenspan Federal Reserve Board (Fed) then rejected proposals for regulating financial derivatives.[4] This was followed after the turn of the century by Bush policies, weakening oversight of the financial services industry and limiting the resources provided the overseers.

The upshot was a situation where mortgage brokers were allowed to originate subprime mortgages in the absence of meaningful regulatory oversight. Banks were permitted to minimize costly capital cushions and raise leverage to dangerous heights. They were allowed to further economize on the need for capital by shopping for ratings on complex derivative instruments concocted from those subprime mortgages. They were able to enhance those ratings further by wrapping the resulting securities in credit default swaps obtained from lightly regulated and poorly capitalized nonbank financial firms such as the American International Group. None of this was socially redeeming business practice, as we now appreciate. But the temptation was irresistible, given the heads-I-win tails-you-lose structure of executive compensation and absence of adequate regulatory oversight.

Given their inadequate resources, it is not surprising that the Securities and Exchange Commission and other regulators were unable to detect even blatant frauds such as Harry Madoff and Kenneth Starr,[5] much less sophisticated efforts at regulatory arbitrage such as Lehman Brothers' Repo 105 transactions.[6] There is a perennial "bloodhounds and greyhounds problem" in financial markets: the highly incentivized private greyhounds run very fast, and the regulatory bloodhounds attempting to stay on their trail strain to keep up. This imbalance is especially pronounced in periods such as the recent decade, when financial structures and practices are changing rapidly. But it does not help to put the bloodhounds on a starvation diet.

The limited resources with which the regulators were provided encouraged them to acquiesce in the privatization of their supervisory and regulatory functions. Where they had once placed bank assets into buckets by risk and set capital requirements accordingly, they now allowed banks to rely on their own models to gauge risk and capital adequacy. Where banks lacked models, the regulators allowed them and their customers to use letter grades assigned to their securities by the rating agencies.

Both practices were problematic. Banks had obvious incentive to tweak their models to limit the estimated likelihood of a significant loss on their portfolios, since this limited the capital they had to hold and elevated their profits. If it also heightened the risk of failure, well, that was someone else's problem. That their models of the returns on and covariances of complex derivative securities were estimated on short spans of data—covering only periods when, inter alia, housing prices were going up—was similarly not of concern. The mathematization of risk-management protocols derived from finance-theoretic tools encouraged false confidence in these practices. The fact the models were based on restrictive assumptions—necessarily in order to make them tractable—was easily forgotten. That they were linear representations of a nonlinear world was dismissed as being of second-order importance.

The rating agencies were no better. Advising an originator on how to structure an instrument so as to secure an investment-grade rating, and then rating the same security bred conflicts of interest. The agencies allowed themselves to be played off against one another by issuers shopping for ratings. Market participants alarmed by these practices had nowhere to turn, given the entry barrier posed by the Nationally Recognized Statistical Rating Organization status conferred by the US Securities and Exchange Commission and required in order for credit ratings to be used for regulatory purposes. Asian readers will no doubt feel a sense of *schadenfreude* about all this scorn being heaped on the rating agencies.[7] Their grim self-satisfaction may recede, however, when they ask themselves exactly what the alternative is for issuing ratings and setting capital requirements.[8]

THE GLASS-STEAGALL ACT AND THE GOVERNMENT SPONSORED AGENCIES

At this point is necessary to say something about a set of more specialized issues, starting with the elimination of the Glass-Steagall restrictions on mixing commercial and investment banking.[9] It is fashionable to question whether the Gramm-Leach-Bliley Act revoking the last vestiges of Glass-Steagall had much to do with the crisis. Gramm-Leach-Bliley was itself a response to the fact that banks had long since discovered ways around Glass-Steagall. And it was investment banks already specialized in the origination and distribution of complex securities, not deposit-taking commercial banks freed up by the elimination of Glass-Steagall, that played the central role in originating and distributing complex mortgage-related securities, had the highest levels of leverage and took the hardest fall.[10]

In fact the role of Gramm-Leach-Bliley was still significant, if subtler in its effects. Together with the regulatory arbitrage that contributed to their demise, the removal of the Glass-Steagall restrictions intensified the competition between the commercial and investment bank subsectors. It allowed commercial banks, with preferential access to funding courtesy of the Federal Deposit Insurance Corporation insurance on their deposits, to move into activities that had traditionally been the preserve of the investment banks.[11] The latter responded by taking on more risk in the effort to maintain their customary return on capital.[12] The explosive growth of leverage and excessive reliance on short-term funding that were two weak links in the financial chain reflected these competitive dynamics.

Another US policy pointed to by some critics is explicit and implicit subsidies for home ownership and, thereby, for housing finance, which encouraged the dubious mortgage-related financial activities implicated in the crisis. Out of the American ideal of the Jeffersonian farmer (the idea that American political and social values rested on the bedrock that every early adult, or at least every white male adult, owned his own farm) grew the notion that a man's home, even if mortgaged to the hilt, was his castle. The housing crisis of the 1930s led to the creation of the government-sponsored Federal National Mortgage Association (Fannie Mae), which purchased Federal-Housing-Authority-financed mortgages and financed its activities by selling quasi-government-guaranteed long-term bonds to insurance companies and pension funds. In the 1960s Fannie was cloned to create Ginnie Mae and Freddie Mac as a way of enhancing the financing capacity of the government sponsored agencies (GSAs) while limiting the direct burden on the federal budget. Fannie and Freddie were exempted from state and local taxes and received a line of credit from the US Treasury. By the 1990s they were borrowing directly on capital markets to finance activities that included not just purchasing mortgages but also packaging them into residential-mortgage-backed securities. This was the raw material used by J.P. Morgan and others to construct collateralized debt obligations.

In 1992 the ironically named Federal Housing Enterprise Safety and Soundness Act then encouraged Fannie and Freddie to expand their operations, which they did by obtaining regulatory authorization to hold less capital than other financial institutions. Freddie and Fannie were mandated to devote additional resources to low-income housing. By 2000, as a result, the share of low-income-housing-related underwriting activities in their new investments had reached 50 percent. The Bush Administration pushed the mandate up to 54 percent in 2004. The Community Investment Act of 1977, enforced more vigorously in the 1990s than before, required commercial banks to similarly channel more mortgage finance to low-income households: as Rajan (2010:36) put it with black humor, "to find creative ways of getting people who could not afford homes into them". This political encouragement and the incentives it created, it is argued, fostered the growth of the subprime mortgage market at the epicenter of the crisis.

Political pressure mixed with financial innovation is a toxic brew. But the story of the financial crisis as an unintended consequence of a policy of subsidizing low-income housing lends itself to exaggeration. For one thing, the subprime lending boom was overwhelmingly underwritten by nonbank lenders not subject to the Community Reinvestment Act or by banks lending outside of their own community assessment areas. For another, there is the fact that Freddie Mac and Fannie Mae were least active in the 2005–07 period when the housing market took off, this being when the GSAs' accounting scandals came to light.[13] To say that Freddie and Fannie then responded aggressively in order to maintain their market shares is not the same as saying that they were driving the market. According to the Federal Reserve Board (2008), at most 6 percent of subprime lending was connected to the Community Reinvestment Act. Finally, there is the fact that many of the same excesses and problems were evident in the commercial real estate market, where affordable-income mandates did not apply.

All this suggests that while policies channeling excessive finance into affordable housing did not help, a wider credit boom and more pervasive incentive problems were at work.

THE ROLE OF GLOBAL IMBALANCES

While there is little question that lax regulation and skewed incentives were at the heart of the crisis, some authors have placed equal emphasis on global imbalances. A first argument for the importance of global imbalances is that they lowered the required return on US Treasury securities and, by implication, on the residential-mortgage-backed securities and associated derivatives that were close substitutes. But empirical studies suggest that this effect was limited. The largest estimate of which I am aware, by Warnock and Warnock (2009), suggests that the impact on ten-year treasury yields was on the order of 90 basis points. Other estimates (such as Craine and Martin 2009) make the impact just half that. No question, lower yields encouraged investors to stretch for yield by moving into riskier assets. They encouraged portfolio managers to add risk in order to meet historical benchmarks. But it is important to think of not only signs but magnitudes. In other words, it is hard to imagine that the financial crisis would have been fundamentally different had long-term rates in the United States been 50 or even 90 basis points higher while everything else remained the same.

Moreover, emphasizing the US current account deficit and corresponding foreign surpluses reflects a focus on net capital flows, where gross flows were larger and growing more quickly.[14] If the concern is not with the level of US interest rates but with flows of finance into toxic mortgage-related securities, then foreigners were fully capable of buying into this market (or into markets for other assets that were substitutes, like the US Treasury market, pushing other investors into mortgage-related securities) without their countries running current account surpluses. In a world of international capital mobility, it was only necessary for US investors to take equal-size positions in foreign markets.[15] In fact, barely a third of the increase in the gross external liabilities of the United States in 2002–07 can be explained in an accounting sense by the country's cumulative current account deficits. While current account imbalances and capital mobility are related, much of the literature implicating imbalances in the crisis unhelpfully emphasizes the former to the exclusion of the latter.

A good indication of this is the fact that European banks were substantial enablers of the subprime crisis, in the sense that they ended up holding large numbers of subprime-related structured credit products. Europe did not run a significant current account surplus with the United States. Two-way trade in assets, in conjunction with lapses in supervision and regulation—and not global imbalances—explains this fact.

A subtler argument made by Obstfeld and Rogoff (2009) is that global imbalances and the excesses resulting in the financial crisis were jointly determined by the stance of policy. In the early stages of the debate it was fashionable to indict US fiscal policy and specifically the deterioration in the budget balance following the Bush tax cuts of 2001–02. Public dissaving meant national dissaving, widening the current account deficit. By artificially goosing the US economy, the budget deficit goosed the housing market. But much subsequent literature has questioned the link between fiscal policy and global imbalances; it has challenged the "twin deficits hypothesis", showing that, even if there was a link, it was less than tight.[16] Similarly, while fiscal policy was part of the broad policy backdrop to the housing boom, it is hard to assign it a leading role. And while the fact of large preexisting deficits limited the authorities' options when the crisis struck and raised questions about medium-term fiscal sustainability, this is different from saying that fiscal policy caused global imbalances and the crisis.[17]

More recently, debate has focused on the role of monetary policy in the crisis. US monetary policy was too loose in 2003–04, it is alleged, when the Fed's discount rate was significantly below the levels suggested by the Taylor rule. Global imbalances may not have been responsible for the decision to cut rates so sharply in 2001, but they enabled the Federal Open Market Committee to keep them at low levels by providing a steady demand for Treasury bills and bonds, low yields on those instruments notwithstanding. At its maximum in 2004, the gap between the level of interest rates predicted by the Taylor rule and the policy rate of the Federal Reseve Board (Fed) was 300 basis points. US households responded to the availability of cheap credit by going on a spending binge. This was the driver for both the housing boom and global imbalances, or so it is alleged.[18]

With benefit of hindsight we can say that the Fed overestimated the danger of a Japan-style deflation. It overreacted by cutting rates so aggressively and leaving them low, even once the economy began recovering in 2003. With hindsight we can similarly say that policymakers should have worried more about the decline in personal saving, since this behavior was predicated on an increase in housing and other financial wealth that was illusory. Tightening more quickly would have damped down the increase in asset prices, encouraging saving that would have limited global imbalances, while at the same time working to discourage the development of housing-related risks. If this meant that the US economy would have expanded somewhat more slowly after the trough in late 2002, then this was a price worth paying.

Hindsight is 20/20. In addition, there are grounds for questioning whether a somewhat higher level of short-term rates (short-term rates being those under the control of the central bank) would have made that much difference for conditions in housing markets. The main channel through which short-term rates affected housing was adjustable-rate mortgages, whose low entry rates might have lured more unsuspecting buyers into the market. Between 2001 and 2004, the gap between the rates on adjustable-rate mortgages (ARMs) keyed to the one-year interest rate and conventional 30-year mortgages nearly doubled, as did the share of new mortgage borrowers opting for ARMs. The question is whether the impact on the housing market was substantial. Bernanke (2010) objects that, although the gap between rates on ARMs and conventional mortgages grew over time, it was never large. Greenspan (2010) observes that ARM originations peaked two years before the housing market, the implication being that they could not have been responsible for the bubble.

None of this is to deny a role for global imbalances in the crisis. But it is to question whether the priority for policy, and specifically policymakers concerned to prevent renewed financial instability, should be to seek to prevent their recurrence.[19]

RESPONSE

It took three quarters, from the summer of 2007 to the spring of 2008, for the US crisis to spread to the rest of the world. In addition to the sheer fact of a US recession, there was the impact on banking systems (mainly in Europe) and on trade (mainly in Asia and Latin America). Why European banks should have been infected is no mystery. Feeling the intensification of competition (in their case owing to the Single Market rather than the elimination of Glass-Steagall), they were even more highly leveraged than their US counterparts and heavily invested in structured financial products. In some countries (Spain, Ireland and the United Kingdom, for example), they were also deeply implicated in local housing booms.

It is less clear why trade should have collapsed so dramatically, faster even than output and faster than in the 1930s. The main explanation appears to be that a substantial fraction of trade was in parts and components related to the production of "postponeables" (big ticket items on which consumers and firms temporarily stopped spending when uncertainty spiked).[20] Disruptions to the availability of trade credit also mattered, especially in the aftermath of Lehman Brothers' failure, but their effects were less persistent.[21] Thankfully, overt and murky protectionism made only a minor contribution to the slump in trade.[22]

By the summer of 2008, the world economy was tracking the Great Depression. In contrast to that earlier historical episode, the policy response was quick and powerful. That the advanced countries responded with aggressive monetary and fiscal easing is unsurprising; officials were acutely aware of the dangers of inaction (Wessel 2009). More striking is the quick and substantial reaction of emerging markets. In part this reflected the fact that there now existed, for the first time, venues like the G20 to communicate the need for a coordinated response that avoided free riding and beggar-thy-neighbor policies. At least as importantly, it reflected the fact that emerging markets had kept their powder dry. Their fiscal positions were strong, making it possible to increase public spending without exciting fears about fiscal sustainability. Currency and maturity

Table 8.1 Discretionary measures of G20 countries scaled by GDP, 2008–10

Item	2008	2009	2010
G20 PPP-GDP weighted average	0.5	1.8	1.3
Advanced G20			
all advanced countries	0.6	1.6	1.2
United States	1.1	2.0	1.8
European Union G20 average	0.1	1.0	0.8
Japan	0.4	1.4	0.4
Emerging and developing G20			
all emerging and developing countries	0.4	2.0	1.4
China	0.4	3.2	2.7
G20 discretionary impulse	0.5	1.2	−0.5

Note: The data reflect the budgetary cost of crisis-related discretionary measures in each year compared with the 2007 baseline, based on measures announced through early March 2010. They do not include (1) "below-the-line" operations that involve acquisition of assets (including financial sector support) or (2) measures that were already planned as spring 2010 adjustments in Europe to previous plans. Data for the G20 discretionary impulse represent changes from the previous year.

Source: IMF (2009).

mismatches had been reduced, so that depreciation of exchange rates did not threaten financial stability.[23] Because central banks had built credibility, cutting interest rates did not automatically excite fears of inflation. Large war chests of foreign reserves enabled central banks to support the exchange rate where necessary, to provide dollar funding and otherwise to reassure investors.

The United States moved first, applying the largest stimulus of any country in 2008 (Table 8.1). By 2009, however, the stimulus applied by G20 emerging market members matched that of the United States, scaled by GDP. It is worth reminding oneself in the light of subsequent events that the fiscal stimulus applied by EU G20 members was relatively small all through the period.[24]

Figure 8.1 shows that there was some tendency for the countries experiencing the sharpest slowdowns to apply the largest stimulus packages, as might be expected. But there is a tremendous amount of dispersion around the average relationship. To cite some obvious cases, the fiscal stimulus packages applied by the United States and China were even larger than can be accounted for by the extent of their downturns, while those of Italy and the United Kingdom were smaller than might have been expected.[25] A popular conjecture is that these variations can be explained, in part, by the

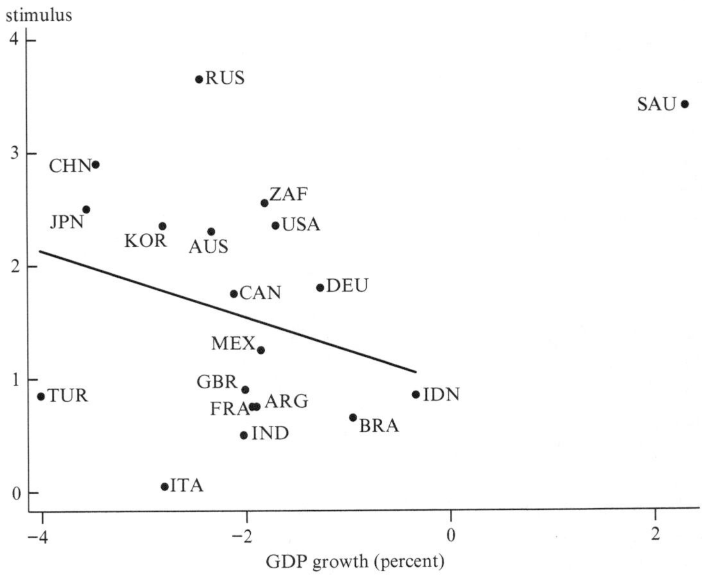

Notes:
The figure includes all G20 countries for which data are available. Saudi Arabia as an outlier is excluded when the least squares regression line is calculated.
Stimulus = discretionary fiscal stimulus as a percentage of average 2009–10 GDP.
GDP growth = change in GDP between 2007 and 2008.

Source: Fiscal stimulus data from the IMF's Fiscal Monitor, May 14, 2010 (http://www.imf.org/external/pubs/ft/fm/2010/fm1001.pdf, accessed on August 28, 2010). GDP growth data from IMF's World Economic Outlook Database, October 2009 (http://www.imf.org/external/pubs/ft/weo/2009/02/weodata/index.aspx, accessed on May 24, 2010).

Figure 8.1 Growth 2007–08 and subsequent discretionary fiscal stimulus in G20 countries

size of the public sector: countries with a larger share of tax-related revenues in GDP had more scope for ramping up public spending or cutting taxes. Figure 8.2 shows, however, that this was not the case. Figure 8.3, on the other hand, suggests that countries entering the crisis with relatively high levels of debt applied less fiscal stimulus, as might have been expected. The relationship in question is, however, relatively weak; this is one way of understanding which countries got into trouble subsequently, and why.

Figure 8.4 provides the analogous picture for monetary policy. It confirms that the central banks of countries suffering the most pronounced growth slowdowns had the greatest inclination to cut interest rates. The

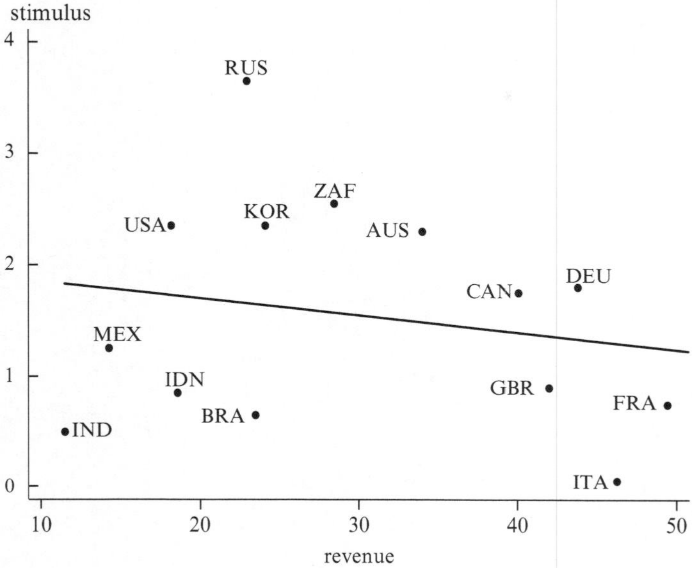

Notes:
The figure includes all G20 countries for which data are available.
Stimulus = discretionary fiscal stimulus as a percentage of average 2009–10 GDP.
Revenue = government revenue as a percentage of average 2007–08 GDP.

Source: Fiscal stimulus data from the IMF's Fiscal Monitor, May 14, 2010 (http://www.imf.org/external/pubs/ft/fm/2010/fm1001.pdf, accessed on August 28, 2010). Government revenue data from the website of the Inter-Agency Group on Economic and Financial Statistics (http://www.principalglobalindicators.org, accessed on May 24, 2010). GDP data from IMF's World Economic Outlook Database, October 2009 (http://www.imf.org/external/pubs/ft/weo/2009/02/weodata/index.aspx, accessed on May 24, 2010).

Figure 8.2 Size of government 2007–08 and subsequent discretionary fiscal stimulus in G20 countries

other thing that stands out from this figure is the aggressive response, by international standards, of the Fed, whether for doctrinal reasons or in reflection of the relatively early eruption of financial problems in the United States.[26]

Figure 8.5 shows, however, that the countries cutting policy rates aggressively were not always rewarded with lower long-term real interest rates. This is a reminder of the limited power of conventional monetary policy in a severe slump. In an environment of actual or expected deflation, central banks may be constrained by the zero bound on nominal rates, and policy rates operating on the short end of the term structure will influence the long-term rates on which investment decisions depend, only

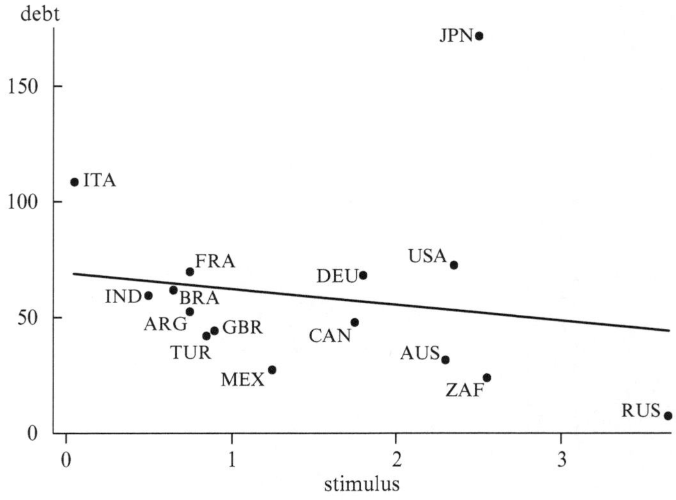

Notes:
The figure includes all G20 countries for which data are available.
Debt = government debt as a percentage of average 2007–09 GDP.
Government debt data for Argentina, Australia, Brazil and South Africa are 2007–08 averages.
Stimulus = discretionary fiscal stimulus as a percentage of average 2009–10 GDP.

Sources: Fiscal stimulus data from the IMF's Fiscal Monitor, May 14, 2010 (http://www.imf.org/external/pubs/ft/fm/2010/fm1001.pdf, accessed on August 28, 2010). GDP data from the IMF's *World Economic Outlook* database, October 2009 (http://www.imf.org/external/pubs/ft/weo/2009/02/weodata/index.aspx, accessed on May 24, 2010). Government debt data from website of the Inter-Agency Group on Economic and Financial Statistics (http://www.principalglobalindicators.org, accessed on May 23, 2010) for Australia, Brazil, France, Germany, Italy, Mexico, Russia, South Africa, the United Kingdom and the euro area; Reserve Bank of India's *Handbook of Statistics on the Indian Economy*, the Department of Finance Canada, Instituto Nacional de Estadística y Censos (Argentina), the Ministry of Finance of Japan, the Economist Intelligence Unit for Turkey and the US Department of the Treasury, Bureau of the Public Debt.

Figure 8.3 Public debt 2007–09 and discretionary fiscal stimulus in G20 countries

insofar as they succeed in influencing expectations about future conditions and policy (recall the Fed's "low for long" commitment).

Figure 8.6 can be read as suggesting that exchange rate adjustment played a positive role in global adjustment to the crisis. Real exchange rates depreciated the most in G20 countries experiencing relatively large falls in output, crowding in exports, other things being equal. Since inflation rates were not all that different, much of this adjustment was

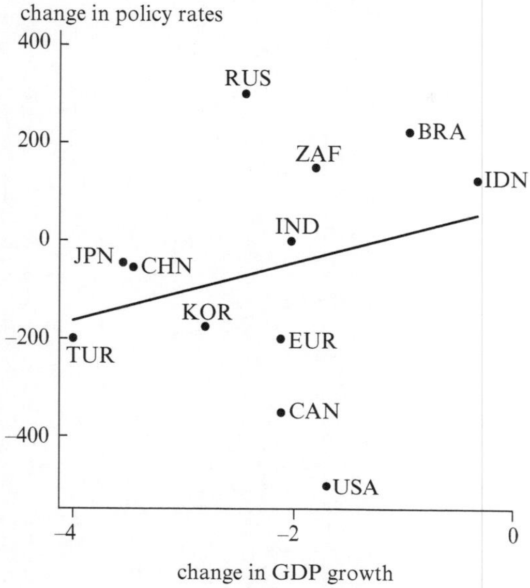

Notes:
The figure includes all G20 countries for which data are available. The United Kingdom as outlier is excluded when least squares regression line is calculated. The change in policy rates is in basis points between September 2007 and January 2009. Change in GDP growth is the percentage change between 2007 and 2008.

Figure 8.4 Growth 2007–08 and monetary policy response in G20 countries

accomplished by changes in nominal rates. The United Kingdom, which saw a sharp depreciation of sterling, is a case in point.

RETHINKING THE RESPONSE

With the passage of time, the stimulus measures widely credited with averting "Great Depression 2.0" do not come off as looking quite so positive. The resurgence of financial volatility in Europe in 2010 and contagion to other countries, together with drastic fiscal cuts auguring sharp reductions in public-sector support for aggregate demand, suggest that policymakers simply kicked the can down the road. They averted a larger collapse in aggregate demand in 2007–09 only by laying the groundwork for a further collapse in 2010 once investors awoke to problems of sovereign debt sustainability, forcing fiscal retrenchment by now dangerously

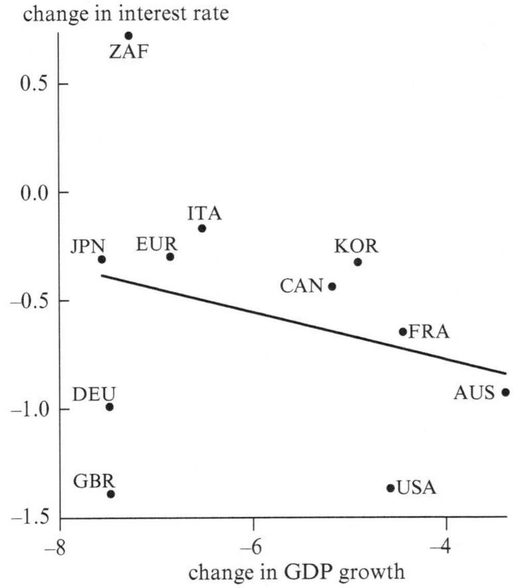

Notes:
The figure includes all G20 countries for which data are available. Russia and Mexico as outliers are excluded when the least squares regression line is calculated.
The interest rate is the percentage change in the long term real interest rate between 2007 and 2009. Change in GDP growth is the percentage change between 2007 and 2009.

Figure 8.5 Growth 2007–09 and change in long-term real interest rates in G20 countries

indebted governments. They socialized the bad debts of the financial and nonfinancial sectors by taking them onto the public-balance sheet, transforming a problem of private debt sustainability into a problem of public debt sustainability, but without resolving the underlying issues.

It is easy to be critical, but hard, even with benefit of hindsight, to say what exactly should have been done differently. A first hypothesis is that governments should have been more aware of potential problems of debt sustainability and should have exercised more restraint in applying the fiscal stimulus. As a blanket statement, this is hard to accept. In the United States, there are no signs that the US$787 billion stimulus was too large. It replaced at most a third of the private spending vaporized in the crisis. It was not enough to prevent the unemployment rate from rising into the double digits. It showed no sign of raising immediate concerns about the sustainability of the public debt. There was no upward pressure on Treasury yields: in mid-August 2010, ten-year yields were 2.59 percent,

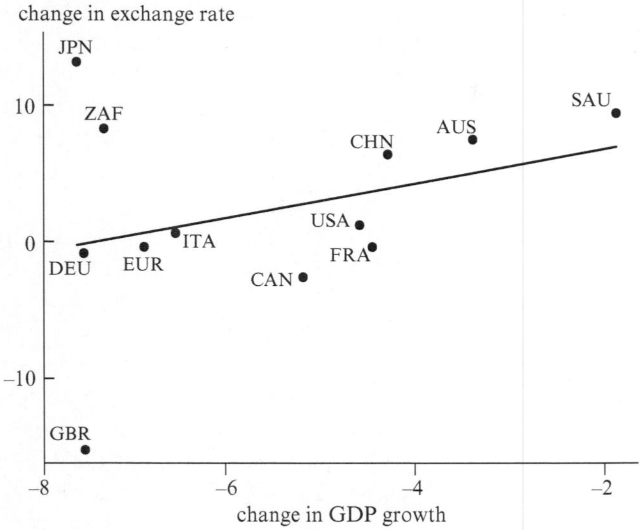

Notes:
The figure includes all G20 countries for which data are available. Russia as an outlier is excluded when the least squares regression line is calculated.
The exchange rate is the percentage change in the real effective exchange rate between January 2008 and January 2010. GDP growth is the percentage change between 2007 and 2009.

Figure 8.6 Growth 2007–09 and the change in real effective exchange rate in G20 countries

down from 3.17 percent a year before. There were no downgrades on US sovereign debt from the rating agencies.[27] All this suggests that—had we known then what we know now or, alternatively, in the absence of political constraints—even more fiscal stimulus would have been better. A number of other countries (China, Germany) were similarly in a position to provide considerable fiscal support for spending because they entered the crisis with their powder dry (with relatively low levels of debt).

A second hypothesis is that the fiscal response should have been more discriminating. Countries that entered the crisis with heavy debt loads should have been more cautious before undertaking additional deficit spending. They should have recognized that they were apt to run up against problems of debt sustainability relatively quickly, because their inherited debts were heavy and also because the denominator of the debt/GDP ratio was now likely to grow more slowly, due to the permanent damage to their economies and financial systems. But in the heat of battle, everyone laid on massive fiscal stimulus, regardless of whether or not they were really in a position to do so.

Of course, to avoid weakening global growth even further, less deficit spending by heavily indebted countries should have been accompanied by more deficit spending by other countries in a better position to undertake it. Additional international coordination would have been required, in other words. The call for coordinated fiscal stimulus was taken up by the G20, whose communiqués regularly made the case. But the size of national stimulus packages was, in the end, left to national authorities. G20 communiqués prior to the spring of 2010 said nothing about the desirability of countries with debt-sustainability issues doing less while their more lightly indebted counterparts did more. And even had the national leaders assembled by the G20 acknowledged this point, one can question whether legislatures would have followed where they led. Would the US Congress have supported an even larger stimulus on the ground that the United States needed to do more because heavily indebted countries in Europe needed to do less? That domestic politics can be an obstacle to international policy coordination is a well established fact.[28] It would have posed a significant obstacle in this context.

A third critique is that the fiscal authorities should have done more to detail their exit strategies. Explaining and credibly committing to timely exits would have enhanced confidence, encouraged private spending and reduced the magnitude of the demand shortfall that the fiscal authorities had to fill. Less deficit spending in the future would have meant lower interest rates in the future, which, operating through the term structure, would have meant lower interest rates now, encouraging private spending. To be sure, insofar as interest rates were already near zero, this mechanism would have helped less than otherwise. But one can still imagine that credible plans for eliminating exceptional deficits would have bolstered private confidence and spending, permitting the fiscal authorities to do less.

A fourth critique is that governments did too little to restructure and recapitalize banking systems, allowing sovereign and private debt problems to jeopardize the stability of financial systems. In the United States, the Obama Administration's strategy of relying on stress tests and self-recapitalization, as opposed to quick nationalization and reprivatization, made for less bank lending than would have been the case otherwise. The situation was even worse in Europe. In Germany, banks' ratio of capital to assets was still barely 5 percent in 2010, in contrast to 12 percent in the United States. In Spain, the authorities were reluctant to openly acknowledge the need to shrink the number of *cajas* (regional savings banks) until fully two years into the crisis. In Ireland, panicked authorities extended a blanket guarantee on not just bank deposits but on all bank debt, effectively taking obligations to bank bondholders onto the public balance sheet. This created renewed difficulties when the guarantees approached their expiration date.[29] It allowed questions about sovereign debt sustainability, when these began to be asked in 2010, to infect banking systems continent-wide. If we know one thing about banking crises, it is that the longer their resolution is delayed, the more costly they become.[30] In all these cases, we see how delay in resolving banking problems and questions about fiscal sustainability fed on one another in a vicious spiral.

More generally, it can be argued that the mistake was not moving more quickly to write down bad debts. In some countries (Portugal, the United States, Spain) problems of excessive indebtedness were associated not so much with public as with private debts. Nonviable real estate loans and their corporate equivalents should have been restructured more quickly, as they were in Korea after 1998. This would have both reduced uncertainty and moderated the depressing effects of debt overhangs. The problem was that mass restructuring is easier said than done. The bankruptcy courts would have been swamped. Where mortgage, car and student loans had been securitized, restructuring was even more complex, and often the loan servicer had little incentive to facilitate the process. Restructuring bad loans would have forced banks to realize additional losses, which would have required additional recapitalization. Voting publics objected to proposals for selective relief, which would have written down the mortgages of homeowners under water but would not have benefitted their more prudent neighbors who had bought smaller houses with smaller loans. Schemes for across-the-board relief, for their part, would have been prohibitively costly. All this encouraged forbearance rather than recognition of losses. A social planner might have done things differently, but that was not the political reality.

A final critique is that countries should have relied more on monetary easing and less on fiscal easing. Had central banks done more to support aggregate demand, especially in Europe, it would have been possible for governments to do less. Where the monetary authorities pulled out all the stops, as in the United States and United Kingdom, pursuing unconventional policies and engaging in quantitative easing, it is hard to imagine how they could have done more. But, unlike the Fed and the Bank of England, the European Central Bank (ECB) was reluctant to push interest rates to near zero and engage in quantitative easing, arguing that it needed to keep interest rates in positive territory so that it still had room to reduce them if conditions deteriorated still further. It was reluctant to engage in direct purchases of government bonds, given that this would likely mean purchasing the bonds of the most heavily indebted governments with the least liquid markets, exposing the central bank to accusations of favoritism and creating moral hazard.[31] More than anything, it was reluctant to initiate and defend a policy that could be seen as printing money and thereby exciting German fears of inflation.

Given subsequent problems, and the fact that the ECB was ultimately forced to turn to direct government bond purchases anyway, it is hard to avoid the conclusion that it would have been better for Europe, already in 2009, to rely less on fiscal stimulus and more on aggressive monetary stimulus.[32] It is not as if Europe's problems of fiscal sustainability were unrecognized at that date.[33] If the result had been a weaker euro already in 2009—the standard result of a mix of tighter fiscal and looser monetary policies—this would have been part of the solution to the festering crisis.

Similar points can be made about the United States and the Fed. If not in 2009, then in 2010 the Federal Reserve Board came under pressure from regional reserve bank presidents sitting on the Federal Open Market Committee to raise interest rates, or at least to refrain from further quantitative easing. In the absence of more aggressive balance-sheet expansion by the Fed, the Obama Administration felt compelled in the summer of 2010 to propose US$60 billion of extensions of the 2009 stimulus bill to limit the danger of the economy slipping back into recession. These extenders did not reassure those concerned with the country's medium-term fiscal outlook, in the Congress and elsewhere. Even if there was no sign of a European-style sovereign debt crisis, there is an argument that it would have been better for the country to rely on monetary expansion and less on fiscal expansion.

SOME CONCLUSIONS

As in the case of the Asian crisis of 1997–98, we will be debating the causes and consequences of the 2007–10 global financial crisis for years. While evaluations will continue to evolve along with events, no doubt, it is not too early to begin drawing some provisional lessons.

First, while this crisis, like all crises, had multiple causes, at its center were problems of lax supervision and regulation, in the advanced countries in particular. It is appropriate therefore that postcrisis efforts in the United States and at the level of the G20 should focus on regulatory reform. Unfortunately, accomplishments here are less than meet the eye. In the United States, nothing has been done to downsize big banks.[34] The role of the credit rating agencies in regulatory decisionmaking has not been eliminated. It will still be possible for the banks to trade bespoke credit default swaps over the counter. Other than abolishing the Office of

Thrift Supervision, nothing has been done to consolidate the fragmented process of supervisory oversight. Macro-prudential supervision will be by committee, which sounds suspiciously like no effective macro-prudential supervision at all. The new financial consumer protection agency is in limbo: it is in the Fed but not of the Fed.[35] It can be argued that financial reform is ongoing—that the Dodd–Frank bill is not the last act in the play—but many observers will be underwhelmed by this opening.

At the level of the G20, there is still no agreement on what should be the priority: a bank tax, an executive compensation tax, new restrictions on hedge funds and private equity funds or a ban on short selling. While there has been much discussion of further reforms of the Basel II framework, there has been no progress in implementation. The discussion paper released in July 2010 suggests that recommendations for significantly higher capital requirements have been watered down, provides no specifics on the measures that will be taken to correct the procyclical bias of the capital adequacy regime, does less than proposed in late 2009 to improve the quality of capital, sets the new leverage requirement (ratio of capital to unweighted assets) at Bear Stearns levels (33 to 1) and proposes waiting as long as seven years to implement new liquidity requirements. Efforts to construct a proper resolution regime for systemically significant financial firms at the global level have barely begun. This may be too negative an assessment. But it is hard to contain one's disappointment that more was not done to strengthen prudential supervision and regulation in the wake of the most serious global financial crisis in 80 years.

Second, the crisis is a reminder of the value of keeping one's fiscal powder dry. Too many advanced countries entered the crisis with large budget deficits and elevated debts. An unprecedented crisis justified an unprecedented fiscal response, but against a backdrop of fiscal profligacy, it also created unprecedented problems of debt sustainability. From the crises of the 1990s, emerging markets learned the importance of running budget surpluses and keeping fiscal capacity in reserve. One can only hope that the advanced countries, including the United States, now take that lesson to heart.

Third, the crisis underscores the importance of early and concerted intervention to resolve banking-sector problems. Banks with impaired balance sheets relying on the market to recapitalize themselves will not be lending. And in the absence of bank lending, even aggressive fiscal stimulus will not jump-start private spending. The political impediments to early intervention are considerable. Public recapitalization is expensive and unpopular, which encourages politicians to shun it in the short run. But this is something that is apt to come back and bite them in the long run.

Fourth, the crisis reminds us that mechanisms for international policy coordination remain inadequate. It would have been better in 2008–09 if countries with unused fiscal capacity had done more to support global demand, enabling those will less unused capacity to do less.[36] At the June 2010 G20 meeting in Busan, US Treasury Secretary Geithner urged Germany, China and other countries with unused fiscal capacity not to cut fiscal support willy-nilly, enabling other, mainly European, countries with pressing budgetary problems to get on with the task of fiscal consolidation and preventing the reemergence of global imbalances.[37] Once again, the sentiment was admirable, but the response was nonexistent.

Fifth, the response to the crisis is a reminder of the importance of coordinating monetary and fiscal policies. In the United States, the reluctance of Congress to recognize the need for fiscal stimulus (recall the first failed TARP vote) forced the Fed to do more than anyone was comfortable with, financially or politically. In Europe, the reluctance of the ECB to engage in quantitative easing pushed governments into doing more—often more than they were capable of doing safely. Then the inability of European governments to agree on a concerted response to the second phase of the crisis in 2010 forced the ECB to abruptly reverse its position on direct bond purchases, something that did nothing to enhance the credibility of policymakers.

But to imagine different policies is to ignore the deep-seated historical factors that shaped the response. The Fed's aggressive quantitative easing reflected memories of the 1930s and the influence of Friedman and Schwartz's interpretation of the Fed's culpability in that episode.[38] Recall then Governor Bernanke's speech on the occasion of Friedman's ninetieth birthday: "You're right, Milton. We did it. We're very sorry. But thanks to you, we won't do it again."[39] The ECB's reluctance to pursue comparable policies similarly reflected memories in Europe, and in Germany specifically, of the hyperinflation of the 1920s.[40] History casts a long shadow, whether for better or worse.

NOTES

Acknowledgment. Thanks to Gisela Rua for help with the figures in this chapter.

1. See IMF (2009a).
2. Which in his view changed the geopolitical and economic balance (Greenspan 2010).
3. Like any capsule description, this one does not cover anything. I attempt to provide a fuller analysis below.
4. A partisan if entertaining account is Johnson and Kwak (2010).
5. The financial advisor, not the former solicitor general.

6. The failure to detect and correct the Madoff fraud is recounted in Markopolos (2010).
7. After their own experience in 1997–2008.
8. Random assignment of customers to rating agencies by a clearing house as recommended by Senator Al Franken and antiquated Basel I style rules?
9. In 1999.
10. Starting with Bear Stearns.
11. Can you say "proprietary trading"?
12. In principle, it also would have been possible to return capital to the shareholders—to downsize the firm—but this would have been less rewarding both financially and in terms of ego gratification for their CEOs.
13. Causing the two GSAs to adopt a more conservative posture.
14. See Lane and Milesi-Ferretti (2007) and Whelan (2010).
15. Or for foreign investors to sell other safer US securities already in their possession.
16. A useful review of the literature is Bartolini and Lahiri (2006). An update using data through 2009 is provided by Chinn et al. (2010).
17. For more on this aspect, see the next section.
18. By Taylor (2007), among others.
19. I return to this below.
20. See Eaton et al. (2010). The postponeables terminology is from Baldwin and Taglioni (2009).
21. Partly because official export-credit agencies and the multilaterals stepped in to replace private finance.
22. See Kee et al. (2010).
23. There were exceptions, such as Korea and Hungary, where special circumstances resulted in substantial mismatches, but there exceptional swaps by the Fed and the ECB, respectively, prevented matters from degenerating excessively.
24. Of course, large variations are hidden within the EU G20 average, and the G20 does not include such EU countries as Greece, Portugal and Ireland. Spain (Table 8.1) is another matter.
25. The UK case might seem anomalous, given the magnitude of and attention devoted to the country's subsequent deficits; note, however, that the data here consider discretionary fiscal measures alone.
26. On the roots of these potential doctrinal differences, see below.
27. Not yet, that is.
28. See Frankel (1988), among others.
29. Only subordinated debt remained unguaranteed. The authorities might have opted for less expensive measures, such as guarantees for new lending or the early injection of preference or ordinary shares; in the event this was not done. See Honohan (2009) for discussion.
30. See Laeven and Valencia (2008).
31. Bini-Smaghi (2009) articulates these fears.
32. Not to mention in early 2010.
33. Buiter (2009) is a prescient warning that makes the connection with the case for quantitative easing.
34. The recently passed Dodd–Frank bill contains a provision limiting individual US banks' assets to 10 percent of total financial assets, but this is unlikely to affect even the largest financial institutions (except possibly Bank of America).
35. It has been placed in the Fed mainly in order to avoid any direct budgetary implications of its operation. Moreover, a committee of bank regulators will have the power to veto any decision taken by the new agency as damaging to the banks.
36. Recall that mainstream models suggest positive cross-border spillovers from fiscal stimulus, making possible this kind of hypothetical adjustment.
37. See Geithner (2010).
38. Friedman and Schwartz (1965).
39. Bernanke (2002).
40. So my reading of Trichet (2007) suggests.

REFERENCES

Baldwin, Richard and Dalia Taglioni. 2009. "The Great Trade Collapse and Global Imbalances". *VoxEU* (27 November). London: Centre for Economic Policy Research. Available at www.voxeu.org.

Bartolini, Leonardo and Amartya Lahiri. 2006. "Twin Deficits, Twenty Years Later". *Current Issues in Economics and Finance*, **12** (October). New York: Federal Reserve Bank of New York.

Bernanke, Ben. 2002. Remarks by Governor Ben S. Bernanke on the Occasion of Milton Friedman's Ninetieth Birthday. 8 November. Available at www.federalreserve.gov.

Bernanke, Ben. 2010. "Monetary Policy and the Housing Bubble". Speech at the Annual Meeting of the American Economic Association, Atlanta, 3 January. Available at www.federalreserve.gov.

Bini-Smaghi, Lorenzo. 2009. "Conventional and Unconventional Monetary Policy". Speech to the International Center for Monetary and Banking Studies, Geneva, 28 April. Available at www.ecb.int.

Buiter, Willem. 2009. "Fiscal Dimensions of Central Banking: Part II". *VoxEU* (24 March). London: Centre for Economic Policy Research. Available at www.voxeu.org.

Chinn, Menzie, Barry Eichengreen and Hiro Ito. 2010. "Global Rebalancing and Economic Growth". Unpublished manuscript, University of Wisconsin, Madison; University of California, Berkeley; and Portland State University (July).

Craine, Roger and Vance Martin. 2009. "Interest Rate Conundrum". *B.E. Journal of Macroeconomics*, **9**: 1–27.

Eaton, Jonathan, Samuel Kortum, Brent Neiman and John Romalis. 2010. "Trade and the Global Recession". Unpublished manuscript, Booth School of Business, University of Chicago (May).

Federal Reserve Board. 2008. "Staff Analysis of the Relationship between the CRA and the Subprime Crisis". Unpublished manuscript, Board of Governors of the Federal Reserve System (21 November).

Frankel, Jeffrey. 1988. *Obstacles to International Economic Policy Coordination*. Princeton Studies in International Finance. Princeton, New Jersey: International Finance Section, Department of Economics, Princeton University.

Friedman, Milton and Anna Jacobson Schwartz. 1965. *The Great Contraction, 1929–1933*. Princeton, New Jersey: Princeton University Press.

Geithner, Timothy. 2010. Letter to G20 Finance Ministers (4 June). Available at www.forexyard.com/en/news/TEXT-Geithner-letter-to-G20-finance-ministers-2010-06-05T035051Z.

Greenspan, Alan. 2010. "The Crisis". *Brookings Papers on Economic Activity*, (spring): 201–61.

Honohan, Patrick. 2009. "Resolving Ireland's Economic and Banking Crisis". *Economic and Social Review*, **40**: 207–31.

International Monetary Fund. 2009a. *Global Economic Policies and Prospects*. Note by the Staff of the International Monetary Fund for the Group of Twenty Meeting of the Ministers and Central Bank Governors, London, 13–14 March 2009. Available at www.imf.org (March).

International Monetary Fund. 2009b. *Economic Impact of the Crisis on the Poorest Economies*. Washington: International Monetary Fund.

Johnson, Simon and James Kwak. 2010. *13 Bankers*. New York: Pantheon.
Kee, Hiau Looi, Cristina Neagu and Alessandro Nicita. 2010. "Did Protectionist Policy Cause the Trade Collapse?" *VoxEU* (1 June). London: Centre for Economic Policy Research. Available at www.voxeu.org.
Laeven, Luc and F. Valencia. 2008. *Systemic Banking Crises: A New Data Base*. Working Paper 08/244. Washington: International Monetary Fund.
Lane, Philip and Gian-Maria Milesi-Ferretti. 2007. "The External Wealth of Nations, Mark II". Unpublished manuscript, Trinity College Dublin and International Monetary Fund.
Markopolos, Harry. 2010. *No One Would Listen: A True Financial Thriller*. New York: Wiley.
Obstfeld, Maurice and Kenneth Rogoff. 2009. "Global Imbalances and the Financial Crisis: Products of Common Causes". Paper presented to the Federal Reserve Bank of San Francisco Economic Policy Conference, Santa Barbara, 18–20 October.
Rajan, Raghuram. 2010. *Fault Lines: How Hidden Fractures Still Threaten the World Economy*. Princeton, New Jersey: Princeton University Press.
Taylor, John. 2007. Housing and Monetary Policy. Remarks prepared for presentation to the policy panel at the Symposium on Housing, Housing Finance and Monetary Policy organized by the Federal Reserve Bank of Kansas City, Jackson Hole, Wyoming (August).
Trichet, Jean Claude. 2007. Short Address at the Gala Dinner for the 50th Anniversary of the Bundesbank (20 September). Available at www.ecb.int.
Warnock, Frank and Virginia Warnock. 2009. "International Capital Flows and U.S. Interest Rates". *Journal of International Money and Finance*, **28**: 903–19.
Wessel, David. 2009. *In Fed We Trust*. New York: Pantheon.
Whelan, Karl. 2010. *Global Imbalances and the Financial Crisis*. Policy Note, Directorate General for Internal Policies: Economic and Monetary Affairs. Brussels: European Parliament.

9. Macroeconomic policies of Korea to cope with the crisis

Hyeon-Wook Kim

INTRODUCTION

The global financial crisis that began in 2008 has been characterized as the greatest economic turmoil since the Great Depression of the 1930s. Amid this crisis, the Korean economy experienced a period of sudden contraction followed by fast recovery. A severe credit squeeze shook global financial markets, causing a contraction of every economy in the world. Korea was no exception, due to its high dependency on the export sector. Consequently, Korea's financial markets, including the foreign exchange market, were thrown into a state of near panic, and the growth rate for the fourth quarter of 2008 plunged to −4.5 percent.

The Korean economy successfully bottomed out from the recession triggered by the crisis, and the pace of recovery was faster than anticipated. The assessment of Korea's recovery, both in Korea and abroad, was remarkably positive within a year of the onset of the crisis, and subsequently the economy entered a stabilization phase, normalizing the pace of recovery. It became obvious that the recovery was based on the stabilization of the global financial market and the improvement of the world trade environment, as each country implemented unprecedented expansionary policies to respond to the recession. In Korea, the process of restructuring, which had been carried out steadily since the financial crisis of 1997–98, gave the economy enhanced capacity to respond to the crisis sector by sector and prevented a prolonged recession. In addition, the Korean government's comprehensive and timely implementation of policies contributed to making the recovery faster than expected, as acknowledged by Korean and foreign economists and by international organizations such as the International Monetary Fund and the Organisation for Economic Co-operation and Development (OECD).

This chapter reviews the macroeconomic policy in Korea before and after the 2008–09 crisis and evaluates the effects of fiscal and monetary policies implemented to cope with the crisis. A complete assessment is not possible yet, because it is too early to conduct analysis on the fundamental changes in the Korean economy or to accurately address questions such as whether the private sector has recovered completely and whether the crisis lowered the potential growth rate of the economy. Therefore, this chapter is a preliminary study and a general overview of the consequences of the global financial crisis and Korea's policy responses.

Taking into account these limitations, the second section of this chapter reviews the Korean economy and its policy environment before the onset of the crisis in 2008. The third section provides an overview of the policy responses of the Korean government during the crisis, assesses the impact of fiscal stimulus on GDP growth rates and briefly assesses the Bank of Korea's monetary policy of a super-low interest rate. The concluding section focuses on the exit from the recent crisis and implications for future policy directions.

POLICY ENVIRONMENT BEFORE THE CRISIS

Macroeconomic Trends and Policies in Korea, 2005–07

Although the Korean economy experienced some difficulties in the first years of the new century, steady growth was predicted for the remainder of the decade. The economy was expected to overcome negative impacts after the household credit bubble burst in 2003. Following the severe slump in 2003 and 2004, domestic demand seemed to be on a stabilized growth trend from 2006. The slump in private consumption continued due to the deterioration in terms of trade in the first half of 2006, but private consumption appeared to be improving gradually, as the oil price growth slowed. Equipment investment had been stagnant, due to a downward adjustment in the balance sheet status of credit-card companies and partly due to the deterioration in terms of trade, but it, too, was resuming a steady pace of growth from 2006.

Korea's exports had remained sluggish since the global IT bubble burst in the early 2000s, but subsequently they showed signs of improvement, growing faster than domestic demand mainly due to the rapid economic expansion of China. In addition, the strong recovery of the US and euro-zone economies served to stabilize overseas demand, supporting exports in regaining their rapid growth pace. As the global economy maintained steady growth in 2007, the Korean economy likewise made somewhat faster progress than anticipated in 2007, and Korea's terms of trade, in contrast to 2005 and 2006, appeared to be stabilized in 2007, significantly narrowing the gap between the gross domestic product (GDP) and the

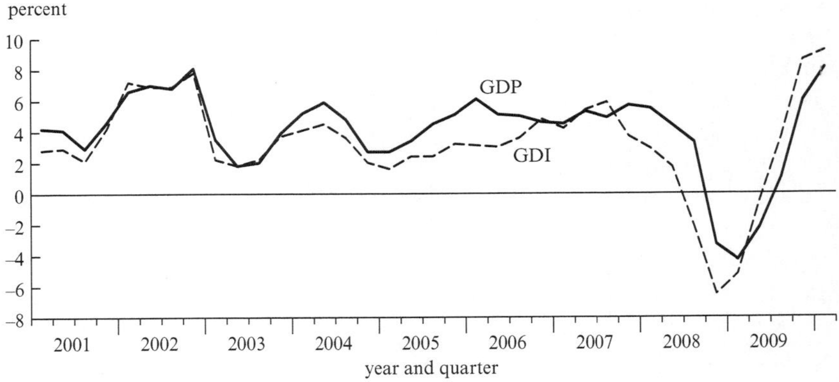

Source: Bank of Korea.

Figure 9.1 GDP and GDI growth rates in Korea, 2001–10

gross domestic income (GDI) growth rates (Figure 9.1). This stabilization in the terms of trade led to an improvement in business sentiment, reflected in the consumer sentiment index, and to steady growth of corporate equipment investment.

Accordingly, as a stable growth pattern emerged from a balanced improvement in exports and domestic demand, Korea's overall macroeconomic policy stance appeared to be normalized. Above all, the fiscal policy was set to keep the consolidated government budget in balance over the business cycle, thus ensuring the proper functioning of its automatic stabilizing role. In particular, fiscal expenditure had been curbed so that the favorable condition of tax revenue in such a well performing economy in 2007 would lead to long-run fiscal soundness. Analysis using the fiscal impulse as in Figure 9.2 confirms the changes in fiscal policy: an expansionary stance between 2003 and 2004, close to a neutral stance between 2005 and 2006, and a stance much closer to contractionary in 2007.

The monetary policy of Korea also had been implemented in a way to reduce the degree of accommodation gradually even before 2006, in response to the trend toward improvement of the real economy. The Bank of Korea undertook a five-step upward adjustment of the call rate target, by 25 basis points at each step, from October 2005 to August 2006 (Figure 9.3). The raising of the call rate target in this way was intended to eliminate gradually the side effects arising from the past period of continual low interest rates, as well as to counter preemptively the upward pressures on prices driven by the sharp rise in oil prices. In 2007, as inflation pressure

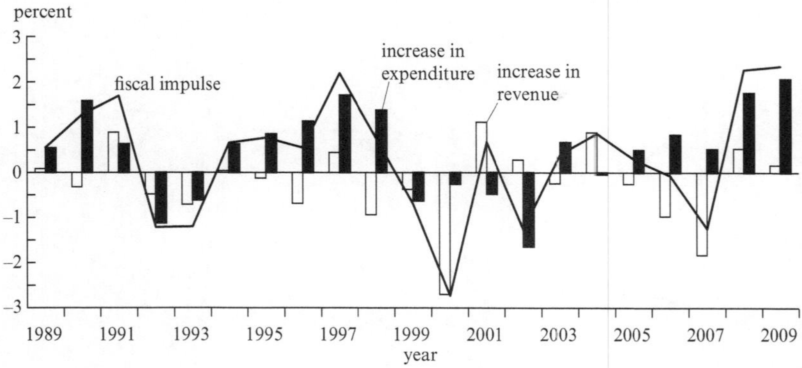

Notes:
Fiscal impulse (FI) is a measure to compute the changing impact of the budget stance of the economy with business cycle adjustment.
The FI indicator implies that the fiscal policy stance of current year is expansionary or contractionary, compared with that of previous year, when it is computed as positive or negative, respectively.

Source: Ministry of Finance and Strategy.

Figure 9.2 Fiscal impulse in Korea, 1989–2009

from aggregate demand was growing, the Bank of Korea raised the target rate by 50 basis points to 5.0 percent.

Moreover, the Korean authorities limited their intervention in the foreign exchange market by maintaining a policy of allowing the won exchange rate to be determined flexibly by supply and demand conditions of the foreign exchange market.[1] This flexibility in the exchange rate and the resulting appreciation of the won served to buffer the impacts of changes in external conditions on the domestic economy and to establish an independent monetary policy for macroeconomic stability. In other words, the continued appreciation of the Korean won up to 2007 was a result of large inflows of foreign capital under the flexible exchange rate system, and it also played the role of limiting additional expansion of foreign exchange liquidity.[2]

Asset Prices and Financial Markets in Korea, 2005–07

Several studies on the global financial crisis pointed to the expansionary monetary policy of advanced economies (particularly in the United States after the IT bubble burst) as the main culprit behind the crisis (Adrian and Shin 2008; Blanchard et al. 2010; Reinhart and Rogoff 2009a,b).

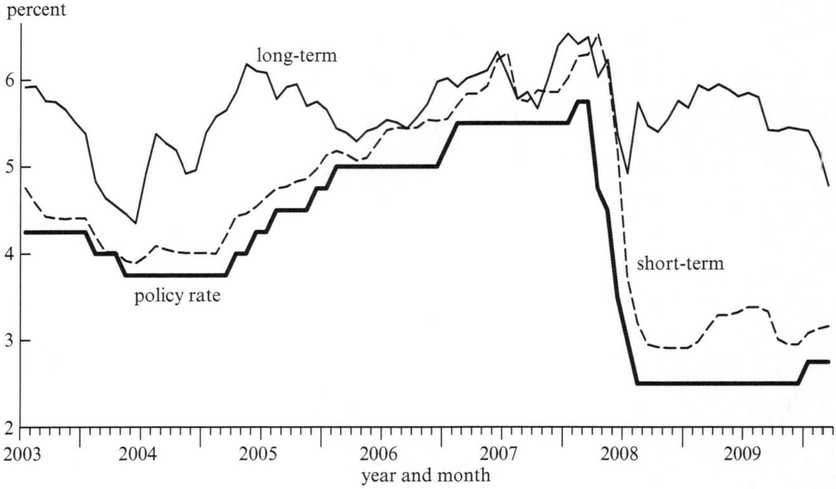

Notes:
Long-term interest rates are those of 10-year government bonds.
Short-term interest rates are the 91-day CD rate.

Source: Bank of Korea.

Figure 9.3 Interest rates in Korea, 2004–10

According to these studies, the low interest rate policy, which prevailed for a long time (see Figure 9.4) in response to the economic slowdown after the IT bubble burst, left investors with an appetite for high risk products. These conditions gave rise to high-risk investments and also encouraged the wide distribution of these products, which eventually heightened the risks in the financial sector. The low interest rate policy has also been cited as a major factor contributing to house price bubbles, combined with insufficient financial supervision and inadequate credit rating on the spread of investment products related to housing finance. In the end, these bubbles burst, throwing the global financial market and world economies into a crisis of severe credit crunch and economic slowdown.

Korea likewise pursued an expansionary monetary policy, as a means of responding to the economic slowdown after the economic crisis of the late 1990s in Korea and the bursting of the IT bubble in advanced economies. This stance resulted in a rapid expansion in household credit and a sharp rise in house prices. In this regard, Korea appears to have experienced some negative effects of its monetary policy, just as the more advanced economies did. Excessive liquidity was an underlying factor

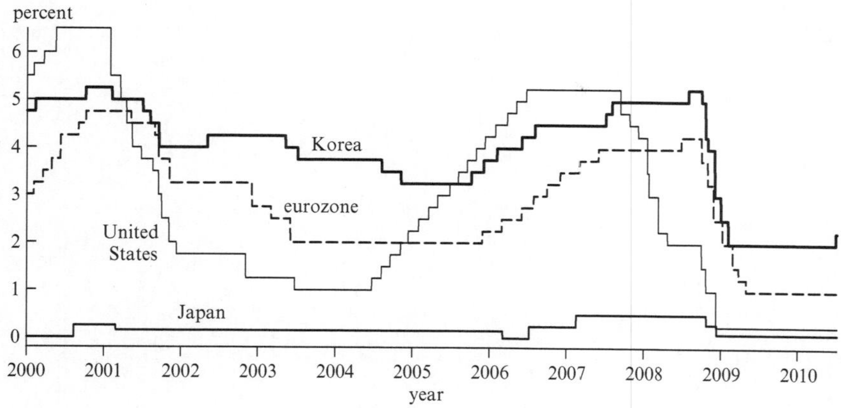

Source: International Monetary Fund.

Figure 9.4 Key target interest rates of selected countries, 2000–2010

behind the surge in Korean house prices. However, it should be noted that the Korean household credit bubble burst in 2003, with ensuing economic contraction. Also, the monetary policy expansion and the house price growth were relatively smaller in magnitude in Korea than in the United States and Europe, which were at the epicenter of the 2008–09 crisis. For this reason, it seems reasonable to argue that the conditions and consequences of monetary policy naturally turned out very differently in Korea.

In Korea as in other advanced countries, asset prices surged immediately before the outbreak of the global financial crisis. Although the Bank of Korea adjusted the call rate target upward from 3.25 percent to 5.0 percent, Korea's nominal house prices rose by 20 percent from 2005 to 2007, and the stock exchange index (KOSPI) rose by 118 percent. At first glance, the house-price growth looks much smaller than the stock-price growth. But considering the aggregate market value of houses and the differences in the degree of price fluctuations, the house-price growth was high enough to influence the overall asset prices in Korea.[3]

To examine the relation between asset price volatility and changes in Korea's monetary policy, a simple index of asset prices can be devised, consisting of the weighted average of the house price index and the stock price indexes (the KOSPI and KOSDAQ markets), using their respective aggregate market values as weights. As shown in Figure 9.5, overall asset prices were usually led in the 1990s by the fluctuations in house prices. The increasing effects of stock price fluctuations on overall asset prices can be observed after the crisis of 1997–98, however, which seems to reflect the

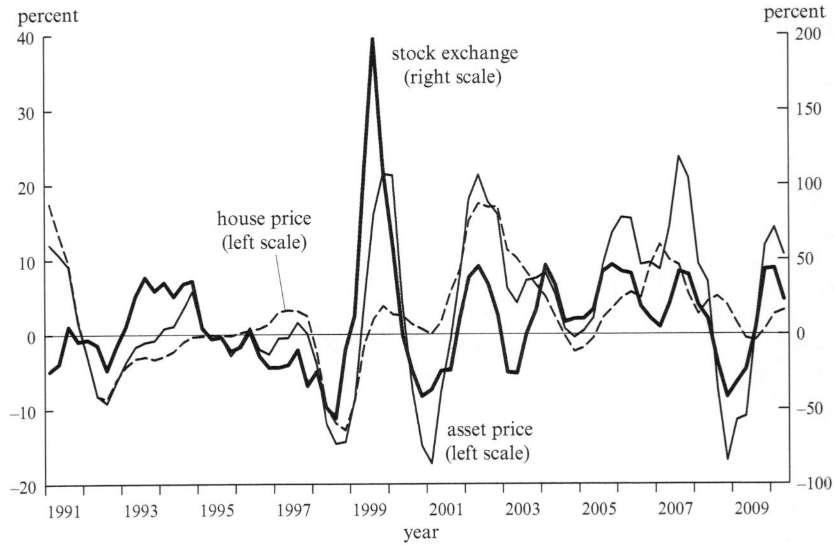

Note: The right-hand scale is based on the KOSPI index.

Source: Bank of Korea.

Figure 9.5 Change in asset prices in Korea, 1991–2010

expanded relative size of Korea's stock market. Figure 9.5 also shows that the rise in asset prices lasted for a long period prior to the global financial crisis of 2008–09. The upward trend of asset prices, which started in 2005 with the simultaneous recovery signs of stock and house prices, maintained a year-on-year growth rate of more than 10 percent in each quarter until late 2007.

Nevertheless, it is not quite clear that the upward trend in asset prices can be attributed to inappropriate monetary policy in Korea, as it was in the epicenter of the 2008–09 crisis. Although the Bank of Korea increased interest rates gradually, starting in October 2005, such a monetary policy reaction might not be strong enough to stabilize asset prices. To examine this, the following simplified version of the Taylor rule equation can be estimated for the Korean economy and compared with the observed target call rate of the Bank of Korea and the rate implied by the Taylor rule:[4]

$$\text{target call rate} = \underset{(13.97)}{3.72} + \underset{(2.56)}{0.19}\ \text{output gap} + \underset{(2.30)}{0.79}\ \text{inflation rate} + \text{residual}$$

$$\text{adjusted } R^2 = 0.17$$

Figure 9.6 Predicted asset values and residuals in Korea from Taylor Rule estimation, 2000–2010

For the output gap, the percentage difference is calculated between seasonally adjusted quarterly series of real GDP and real potential GDP, with the assumption that the annual potential growth rate is 4.6 (the average annual growth rate of the Korean economy during the period from 2001 to 2008). The inflation rate is calculated as the percentage growth of the core consumer price index (core CPI). The sample period of regression is set for the period after 2000 considering that the Bank of Korea first began to announce the call rate target in the second quarter of 1999. All estimated coefficients in the equation are statistically significant at the 5 percent level. The *t*-statistics of estimated coefficients are reported in parenthesis.

The predicted values from the estimated equation above and the residuals are reported in Figure 9.6. The predicted value from the estimated equation can be interpreted as "rule-based" monetary policy and the residual as "discretionary" monetary policy. A positive residual indicates tight monetary policy relative to the rule, while a negative residual indicates relatively loose policy. In Figure 9.6, it can be seen that, despite the Bank of Korea's series of interest rate increases from the second half of 2005, monetary policy remained loose until 2007, in the sense that the target call rate was lower (or not significantly higher) than the rate implied by the Taylor rule. According to the figure, it seems that the Bank of Korea's contractionary monetary policy stance was not strong enough to fully cope with the changes in economic conditions.

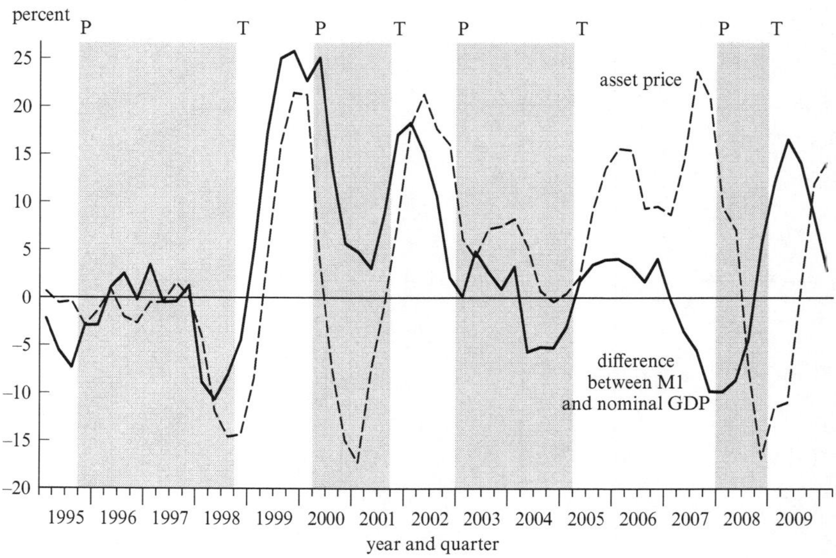

Note: The difference in growth rates is calculated as the growth rate of M1 minus the growth rate of nominal GDP. P and T indicate the peak and trough, respectively, of the business cycle, and the shaded areas are periods of contraction.

Figure 9.7 Growth rates of M1, GDP and asset prices in Korea, 1995–2010

The relation between the monetary aggregates and asset prices suggests that the asset price rise during the period 2005 to 2007 might stem from the changes in monetary policy conditions. The growth rates of asset prices in Korea have been moving closely in line with monetary aggregates, particularly M1 (narrow money, see Kim 2009 for details). Figure 9.7 indicates that the higher the year-on-year growth rate of M1 above the nominal GDP growth rate, the faster the asset prices tend to rise. M1 comprises mainly the funds of the household and corporate sectors, which need to be employed in the short term. In other words, in a case where M1 grows much faster than the growth caused by the fluctuations of real economic activity, there would be an increase in wandering short-term liquidity – which refers to liquidity moving fast toward seemingly more profitable investment opportunities emerging in certain asset markets. For example, in the period where Korea's monetary policy was being eased excessively after the economic crisis of the late 1990s, the short-term liquidity in the nonfinancial private sector rose much faster than real economic activity and flowed into the stock and housing markets.

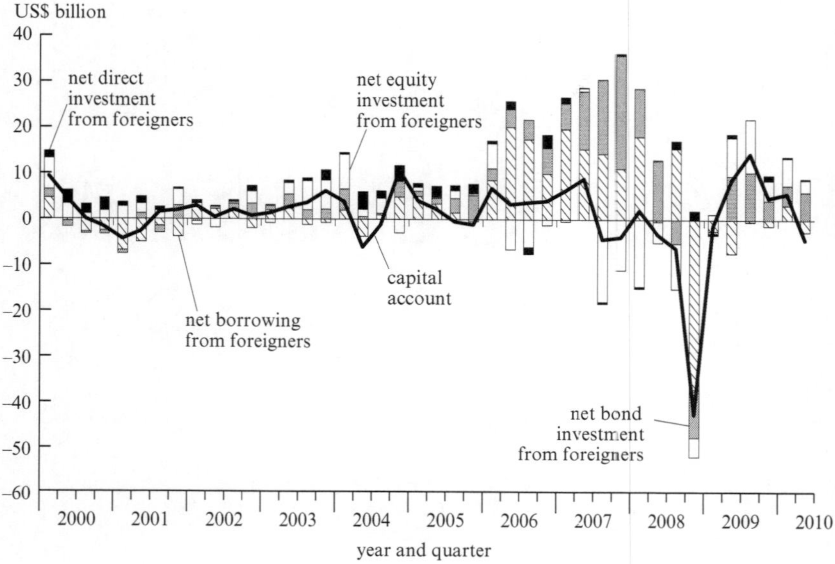

Source: Bank of Korea.

Figure 9.8 Foreign capital flows in Korea, 2000–2010

raising asset prices at a rapid pace. This trend may have continued into the mid-2000s.

The rise in asset prices after 2005 appears to move somewhat differently, however, compared with the rise in short-term liquidity seen by the growth rate gap between M1 and the nominal GDP. As a result of the gradual step-by-step rise in the base interest rate by the Bank of Korea beginning in October 2005, the growth rate of M1 was maintained at a level not much different from the rise and fall of real economic activity. In 2007, the short-term liquidity even showed a downward trend, while asset prices maintained a significantly high growth rate until early 2008 before the rapid drop due to the global financial crisis.

This difference can be attributed in part to the sharp rise in capital inflows driven by the global liquidity expansion and stock market boom. As Figure 9.8 shows, foreign capital surged into Korea from 2006, mainly through short-term loans and bond market investments. Figure 9.9 also shows that the external debt of Korea increased sharply in 2006 and 2007, due to the inflows of foreign capital and, in particular, the external debt increase in 2006 was extremely concentrated in short-term borrowing from foreign banks. In addition, there is a possibility that, along with the

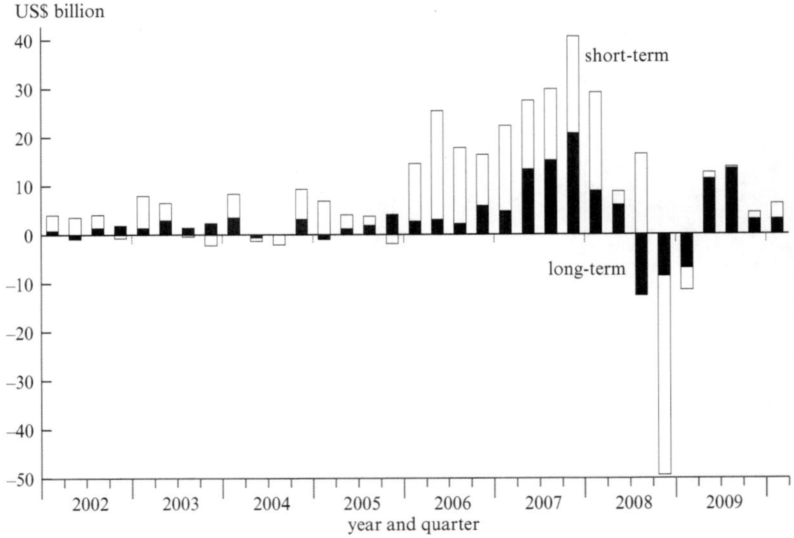

Notes:
Figures are based on changes during the period.
Short-term external debt includes liabilities in money market instruments, trade credits, loans, and deposits of foreigners.
Long-term external debt includes liabilities in bonds and notes.

Source: International Investment Position, the Bank of Korea.

Figure 9.9 Short-term and long-term external debt of Korea, 2002–10

foreign capital inflows, the investment sentiment of domestic investors improved due to expectations about a global stock market synchronization, significantly weakening the effect of contractionary monetary policy through the adjustment of the policy interest rate.

The increased liquidity from the foreign capital inflows through short-term borrowing may have been invested in nontraditional short-term financial investment products such as certificates of deposit of banks and money market funds of nonbank financial institutions, the return on which used to be higher than that of traditional products.[5] As these investment products are not included in M1, it is possible that the rise and fall in M1 might not clearly identify the fluctuation in short-term liquidity in the domestic financial market.[6] This may be a reason why the growth rate of M1 showed a declining trend, while overall short-term liquidity was expanding through the foreign capital inflows and triggered the persistent rise of asset prices.

Given the increased short-term liquidity brought by the massive inflow of foreign capital, Korea's monetary policy stance was not contractionary enough to respond effectively to the economic circumstances. Although the monetary policy cannot be identified as the main culprit in the crisis, Korea's economic situation could have been better if the policy rate had been adjusted enough to be effective in alleviating the upward pressure of asset prices.

THE CRISIS AND THE POLICY RESPONSES IN KOREA

Global Financial Crisis and Initial Policy Responses in 2008

The year 2008 began with a moderate downturn in the Korean economy, at the end of the expansionary phase that had continued until the end of 2007. The downturn was noticeable in domestic demand rather than in the export sector. The sluggish domestic demand in the first half of 2008 was mainly due to the decline of the real purchasing power of the economy, reflected in the decline of the GDI growth rate. Even so, GDI growth was faster than GDP growth, which was impacted by the rise in oil prices and the consequent worsening in the terms of trade.[7]

Korea's exports, by contrast, maintained a high growth rate of around 20 percent until the third quarter of 2008, owing to exports to emerging market economies and to an increase in export prices. By this time the negative impact on exports of the won's appreciation had weakened, reflecting greater quality competitiveness of Korean export goods.[8] At the same time, however, the current account surplus was declining. The surplus in the balance of goods account was reduced by the rise in imports due to the rising oil prices. And there was a large deficit in the balance of services account, influenced by an increase in overseas travel because of the appreciated Korean won. In particular, the surge in oil prices, combined with the increase in imports of crude oil, impaired the current account, which reached a deficit of US$14 billion during the first three quarters in 2008, after recording a surplus of US$6 billion in 2007.

As the global financial market became severely strained from September 2008, the Korean economy contracted rapidly. The Korean financial market was relatively more exposed to foreign capital and was thus affected more severely than other emerging markets were. The won experienced its sharpest depreciation ever, with the market in panic, while the plunge of Korean stock prices was just as bitter as it was in other markets. Such a sensitive reaction of the exchange market was quite unexpected, considering that Korea's foreign reserves exceeded US$250 billion in

June 2008. In retrospect, it appears that the overreaction was caused by doubt among market agents about the liquidity of Korea's official foreign reserves, which reminded them of the trauma during the crisis in 1997, when the liquid assets in the official foreign reserves became almost completely depleted. However, the more fundamental cause appears to be the short-term external debt ratio, which was higher than the ratios in other emerging markets.

Recognizing the importance of stability in the foreign exchange market, in the midst of worsening financial market conditions, the government announced comprehensive measures on 19 October 2008, which included an official guarantee of US$100 billion to external debt payment and a supply of US$30 billion to banks and exporters in urgent need of foreign exchange. The measures also made urgent use of domestic liquidity through the central bank's purchase of government bonds or premature redemption of monetary stabilization bonds. In addition, the Bank of Korea introduced a competitive swap auction facility on 20 October. On 27 October, it also slashed the key interest rate from 5 percent to 4.25 percent and the interest rate on the Aggregate Ceiling Credit Program from 3.25 percent to 2.5 percent and raised the upper limits on the program, while increasing open market operations and broadening the range of assets eligible for them to enhance bond market conditions and alleviate the credit crunch of small and medium-size enterprises.

Plentiful domestic liquidity helped to calm fears of a credit crunch in the financial market, but it also lowered the short-term interest rate and thus added to the depreciation pressure on the Korean won. Market agents seem, moreover, to have purchased foreign currencies, thus leveraging the domestic liquidity supplied by an array of measures, which caused further pressure on the Korean won.

Under those circumstances, the announcement on 29 October 2008 that the Bank of Korea had signed a currency swap contract with the US Federal Reserve Board amounting to US$30 billion made a big contribution to the stabilization of the foreign exchange market in Korea.[9] The Bank of Korea also agreed on 12 December 2008 to expand the currency swap arrangement with the Bank of Japan, from US$3 billion to US$20 billion, and announced a currency swap contract to be signed with the People's Bank of China.

Despite a variety of policy measures implemented to stabilize the financial market, the household and corporate sectors still suffered from the crunch. The uncertainty about the financial market caused domestic consumption and investment to deteriorate further, dragging down stock and house prices and increasing the cost of financing. At the same time, the diffusion of the global financial crisis was undermining the emerging economies as well as the advanced ones, damaging the export demand. Korea witnessed a sharp decline in its exports, and the economy went into recession rapidly.

Macroeconomic Policy Responses to the Crisis

In 2009, the Korean government made determined efforts to avoid a plunge of the economy, by implementary expansionary monetary and fiscal policies, in addition to the various measures already announced to stabilize the financial market.

The Bank of Korea maintained the key interest rate at the lowest level (2.0 percent) by downgrading twice (0.5 percentage point each on 9 January and 12 February 2009). The efforts to stabilize the financial market were continued, such as setting up the Bank Recapitalization Fund to supplement the recapitalization of banks in February 2009, in addition to the Bond Market Stabilization Fund already established in December 2008.

In the case of fiscal policies, the government began in the second half of 2009 to expand the fiscal budget by more than 50 trillion won (more than 5 percent of GDP). These measures included 4.4 trillion won in tax refunds (on oil consumption among others) and 4.6 trillion won of fiscal spending based on a supplementary 2008 budget. In 2009, further tax cuts (10.2 trillion won) followed, along with additional fiscal spending: 11.4 trillion won in the revised fiscal budget and 17.2 trillion won in a supplementary budget. The government established a system to take effective and bold measures in a prompt manner; calling the administration an "economic emergency government" and holding "emergency meetings" almost every week.[10]

The government's proactive policy responses contributed to moderating the serious contraction in the economy from the beginning of 2009 and to the fast recovery of the economy after the second quarter of 2009. And yet, under the worst external conditions ever faced, the Korean economy began to show signs of gradual recovery, with a quarter-to-quarter GDP growth rate of 0.2 percent in the first quarter of 2009 (rebounding from the −4.5 percent recorded in the previous quarter). As global financial markets slowly stabilized, with the risk factors phasing out, the Korean economy accelerated with a surprising quarter-on-quarter growth rate of 2.4 percent in the second quarter of 2009.

Increasing demand from major trade partners such as China alleviated the severe contraction in exports and was another major factor in the recovery from the second quarter of 2009. Although the stability of

Korea's foreign exchange market was low, Korean exports gained a competitive edge because of the depreciation of the won. Moreover, the current account surplus along with the fall of oil and raw material prices reduced the tension of supply and demand in foreign exchange transactions. The rapid improvement in the economy was boosted by the real purchasing power of domestic income (which gained strength from the improvement in terms of trade), the recovery of asset prices (including stocks) and the stabilized inflation (which alleviated concerns about further contraction of domestic demand).

The Korean economy continued to enjoy fast recovery in the second half of 2009, with the improvement in export demand and domestic demand and with stable employment. The quarter-on-quarter GDP growth rate increased to 3.2 percent in the third quarter. It appears that expansionary monetary and fiscal policies successfully buffered the negative impacts of the global financial crisis on domestic Korean demand. In addition, the fiscal expenditure in late 2008 and early 2009 enhanced the self-sustainability and viability of the private sector, albeit with some lags through dynamic equilibrium channels.

Expansionary Fiscal Policy and its Consequences

When the global financial crisis brought the sharp economic downturn to Korea, the government responded with a large fiscal stimulus of 50 trillion won (more than 5 percent of nominal 2008 GDP). The OECD (2010) subsequently estimated the magnitude of the package implemented or announced at 6.1 percent of GDP, which was the highest level among OECD member countries adopting explicit crisis driven stimulus programs (Table 9.1).

Such a large fiscal stimulus made significant contributions to Korea's economic recovery. However, as the government carried out its "front-loading" of fiscal expenditure during the first half of 2009, its capacity to cover the additional fiscal expenditure grew weaker, triggering concerns that the recovery might slow sharply during the second half of the year.[11] These concerns were rooted in worries that the growth potential of the private sector had not recovered sufficiently. This concern can be examined by measuring the contribution of the fiscal stimulus to the recovery of the GDP growth rate and by estimating the extent of the private sector recovery.

Generally, in a simple dynamic general equilibrium model, it is expected that the effect of expanded fiscal expenditure will be realized with some lags. Using the quarterly macroeconomic model of the Korea Development Institute, KDI (2009) simulated the dynamic effects of

Table 9.1 *Composition of fiscal packages in selected countries 2008–10 as shares of 2008 GDP*

	Canada	France	Germany	Italy	Japan	Korea	United Kingdom	United States	OECD average
Net effect	−4.1	−0.7	−3.2	0.0	−4.7	−6.1	−1.9	−5.6	−3.9
Tax measures									
Individuals	−0.8	−0.1	−0.6	0.0	−0.1	−1.4	−0.5	−2.4	–
Firms	−0.3	−0.1	−0.3	0.0	−0.1	−1.1	−0.2	−0.8	–
Consumption	−1.1	0.0	0.0	0.1	−0.1	−0.2	−0.6	0.0	–
Social contributions	−0.1	0.0	−0.7	0.0	−0.2	0.0	0.0	0.0	–
Total	−2.4	−0.2	−1.6	0.3	−0.5	−2.8	−1.5	−3.2	−1.9
Spending measures									
Final consumption	0.1	0.0	0.0	0.3	0.2	0.0	0.0	0.7	–
Investment	1.3	0.2	0.8	0.0	1.2	1.2	0.4	0.3	–
Transfers to households	0.3	0.3	0.3	0.2	0.6	0.7	0.2	0.5	–
Transfers to firms	0.1	0.0	0.3	0.1	1.5	1.0	0.0	0.0	–
Transfers to subnational government	–	0.0	0.0	0.0	0.6	0.3	0.0	0.9	–
Total	1.7	0.6	1.6	0.3	4.2	3.2	0.4	2.4	−2.1

Notes:
The data represent packages announced or implemented during 2008–10. The amounts shown in the totals do not always match the sums of the columns, because some components either have not been clearly specified or are not classified in this breakdown.
OECD data are weighted averages of countries that adopted positive stimulus programs.

Source: OECD (2010).

Table 9.2 Macroeconomic effects of fiscal expansion by 1 percent of Korean GDP: KDI simulation in 2009 (%)

Item	1st quarter	2nd quarter	3rd quarter	4th quarter	5th quarter	6th quarter	7th quarter	8th quarter
Real GDP	0.49	0.21	0.20	0.15	0.11	0.08	0.05	0.03
Private consumption	0.50	0.53	0.43	0.32	0.24	0.17	0.12	0.09
Equipment investment	1.31	1.09	0.91	0.70	0.48	0.28	0.11	−0.03
Construction investment	0.53	0.53	0.52	0.50	0.46	0.42	0.38	0.33

Note: Data for each quarter represent the changes in growth rate from the respective baseline quarter-to-quarter growth rates.

Korea's fiscal expenditure on GDP for several quarters.[12] The results reported in Table 9.2 imply that a temporary increase in fiscal expenditure of 1 percent of annual GDP (about 10 trillion won) in a given quarter will raise the real GDP growth rate by 0.49 percentage point from the baseline for the same quarter and 0.26 percentage point for the period of four quarters (that is, during the year immediately following the stimulus).[13] It should be noted that the positive effect of fiscal expenditure will weaken after the fifth quarter and will turn negative in later quarters, so that the long-run effect of the increase in fiscal expenditure will be negated. Table 9.2 also shows the effects of the increase in fiscal expenditure on other macroeconomic variables.[14]

To measure the macroeconomic effects of the fiscal stimulus package executed since the fourth quarter of 2008, the numbers in Table 9.2 can be used as multipliers that can be combined with the temporarily expanded fiscal expenditure under the discretionary stimulus policy. It is assumed first that the entire supplementary budget of 4.6 trillion won determined in September 2008 was spent during the fourth quarter of 2008. For the first half of 2009, 34.6 trillion won is estimated to be the temporarily expanded discretionary fiscal expenditure, including the increased expenditure during the first half of 2009 under the original budget and the amount spent under the supplementary budget during the same period. For the second half of 2009, a similar calculation shows that discretionary fiscal expenditure decreased by 4.4 trillion won from the baseline, due to front-loading in the first half, despite the increased expenditure under the supplementary budget. Also, due to the limitations of data, it is assumed that the temporarily expanded discretionary fiscal expenditure in each half

Table 9.3 Contribution of fiscal stimulus to the GDP growth rate in Korea, 2008–10 (%)

Item	2008	2009				2010			
	Q4	Q1	Q2	Q3	Q4	Q1	Q2	Q3	Q4
Real GDP growth (A)	−4.5	0.2	2.4	3.2	0.2	2.1	1.5	1.0	1.2
Contribution of fiscal stimulus (B)	0.4	1.2	1.8	1.2	1.0	0.8	0.5	0.3	0.2
A−B	−4.9	−1.0	0.6	2.0	−0.8	1.3	1.0	0.7	1.0

Notes: Data for each quarter represent the changes in growth rate from the respective baseline quarter-to-quarter growth rates. Estimated growth rates for the third and fourth quarters of 2010 are from KDI's *Economic Outlook*.

of 2009 was equally distributed in the relevant two quarters. It is assumed that half of the tax reduction in the second half of 2008 (6.6 trillion won) was executed in the fourth quarter of 2008 and that one-fourth of the tax reduction in 2009 (11.7 trillion won) was executed in each quarter of 2009. In this way, the "temporary expansion" of total fiscal stimulus is calculated to be 46.5 trillion won during the period from the fourth quarter of 2008 to the fourth quarter of 2009.

Table 9.3 shows the accumulated contribution of fiscal stimulus executed in each quarter, considering the dynamic effect of fiscal expenditure shown by the numbers in the second row of Table 9.2. Table 9.3 indicates that the fiscal stimulus contributed significantly in buffering the Korean economy against the falling growth rate in the first half of 2009. In other words, the expansion in fiscal expenditure and the tax reduction enabled the growth rate to increase by an estimated 1.2 percentage points in the first quarter of 2009 and by 1.8 percentage points in the second quarter. Without such fiscal stimulus, the growth rate would have been negative (−1.0 percent) in the first quarter and only 0.6 percent in the second quarter.

Furthermore, Table 9.3 shows that the contribution of the fiscal stimulus was sustained in the second half of 2009, even though the fiscal expenditure was decreasing sharply in that period.[15] Subsequently, the GDP growth rate remained above the total contribution of the fiscal stimulus, which implies an acceleration in the recovery pace of demand in the private sector during the time when the effects of the fiscal 2008–09 stimulus were being phased out. In particular, exports and domestic demand in the private sector appear to be the lead drivers in the strong recovery, helping to sustain economic growth. Therefore, the fiscal stimulus played a successful role in priming the pump during the crisis.

Low Interest Rate Policy and its Consequences

In August 2008, only one month before the Lehman shock, the Bank of Korea raised its base interest rate (the target call rate) to 5.25 percent. It quickly reversed its course. Between September 2008 and February 2009, the Bank cut the base interest rate six times, ultimately to a record low of 2 percent. It remained at that level until July 2010, when the Bank raised it by 0.25 percentage point (Figure 9.4). In addition, the Bank of Korea provided 27.8 trillion won (2.7 percent of GDP) through its open market operations, the Aggregate Ceiling Credit Program, and contributions to the Bond Market Stabilization Fund and the Bank Recapitalization Fund (OECD 2010).

This proactive monetary policy response, together with the strong fiscal stimulus, contributed to successfully buffering the negative impact of the global financial crisis on the Korean economy. That is, the low interest rate and increasing money growth, supplemented by the discretionary fiscal stimulus, played a role as a powerful countercyclical policy. However, after holding interest to a super-low rate for some time, concerns began to arise about the potential side effects of this monetary policy stance, such as asset market bubbles and fast inflation. In particular, as seen in Figure 9.6, the target call rate has been significantly lower than the rate implied by the Taylor rule since the second quarter of 2009, implying excessively loose monetary policy.

For example, the appropriate deleveraging in any sector of the Korean economy may have been delayed as a result of the super-low interest rate policy. In fact, in advanced economies, no significant debt adjustment of households and companies can be easily observed. In the case of households in Korea, the debt ratio against GDP rose even after the crisis to 80 percent in 2009, meaning that it would be difficult to exclude the possibility of growing pressure for repayment and insolvency risks, when the rapid rise in household debt continues, although the possibility of an outbreak of a massive default problem was low. In the case of corporations, the debt ratio against GDP in Korea was above 110 percent, higher than it was in the crisis epicenter countries, meaning that a full-scale deleveraging is required, centering on loans to small and medium-size enterprises and the construction sector, which posted a sharp rise from 2005.

Despite the excessively loose monetary policy, consumer price inflation stabilized. Headline CPI inflation fell from a peak of nearly 6 percent (year-on-year) in mid-2008 to 2 percent in the third quarter of 2009 (Figure 9.10). Contrary to concerns about actual or potential deflation, inflation in Korea then remained above 2 percent, reflecting, in part, the base effect related to the higher starting point. Such relatively high inflation during

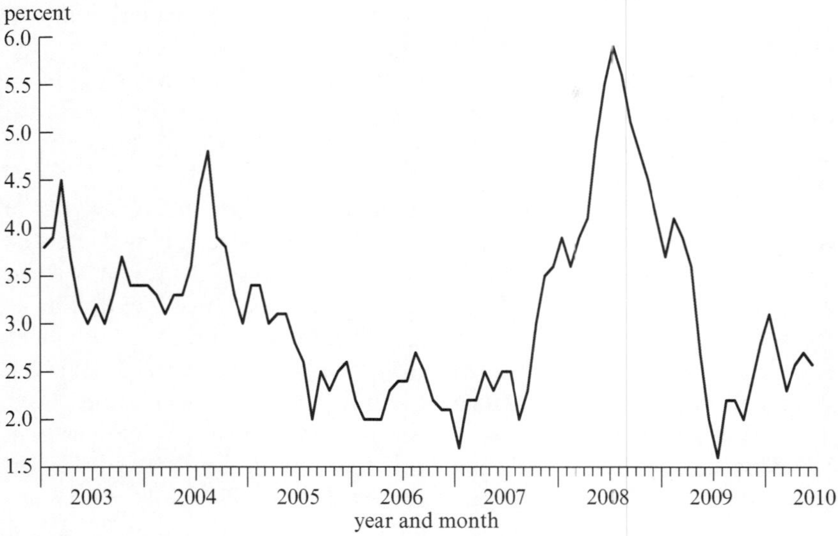

Source: Bank of Korea.

Figure 9.10 Headline CPI inflation in Korea, 2003–10

the crisis period in Korea also reflects the large depreciation of the won, which boosted import prices. After bottoming out in the third quarter of 2009, inflation subsequently picked up, although remaining below the mid-point of the inflation target zone.

The stabilization of the inflation rate is mostly attributable to the stabilization of the exchange rate. Inflationary pressure built up with the overall economic recovery, and the increased prices of imports (particularly oil) also continuously maintained upward pressure. However, Korea's exchange rate flexibility served well, and the appreciation of the won since 2009 has been successfully offsetting the upward inflationary pressure.

POLICIES FOR EXITING FROM THE CRISIS

The proactive fiscal and monetary policy contributed significantly to the recovery from the recent crisis. But questions were raised about the appropriate timing and speed of the exit from such exceptional macroeconomic policy stances, considering that Korea's strong recovery from the global financial crisis was expected to continue. One concern was that excessive macroeconomic stimulus implemented during the crisis might have negative effects, such as an asset price bubble or an overheated economy, unless these macroeconomic policies were normalized in a timely manner. Further, to lead the economic recovery pace into stable and steady growth, it was suggested that macroeconomic policies need to be implemented with a focus on improving economic efficiency while gradually normalizing contingency measures.

Worries arose continuously about the fiscal policy and whether the rapidly expanded fiscal stimulus measures—intended to alleviate the impact of the crisis and overcome economic recession—might instead undermine fiscal soundness. Korea has not yet faced fiscal conditions as severe as those in some advanced economies, and Korea's government debt (currently around 35 percent of GDP) seems manageable. But the specter of growing government debt still looms in the near future. And from a longer-term perspective, several factors with potentially negative consequences (such as population aging and reunification of the Korean peninsula) pose a threat to Korea's future fiscal soundness.

Judging from the fiscal impulse indicators, the budget for 2010 had already become relatively tight when compared with the previous year, and thus the normalization process in the fiscal policy was already under way. Given the pace of the upturn in the economy, the plan for withdrawing the fiscal stimulus in 2010 appears to have been appropriate. But it needs to be followed by more spending restraint compared with the past, with a policy focus on reinforcing fiscal soundness. Not only should temporary measures of fiscal incentives be phased out as scheduled, but also revenue bases should be expanded, for example by reducing tax exemptions. Additional revenue could be obtained by broadening tax bases without making distortions worse. In addition, some structural changes are needed in the fiscal policy framework, such as stricter medium-term budget planning and a reduction in discretionary components.

Given Korea's outlook for strong output growth led by private-sector demand, the Bank of Korea should begin withdrawing from the monetary policy of a super-low interest rate, to keep inflation firmly anchored at its recent level of 3 percent. While there is uncertainty, it is important not to let inflationary expectations and pressures build for too long, which makes it important to begin withdrawing the monetary stimulus. Such preemptive action would avoid another run-up in inflation, which would likely require a significant tightening that could undermine the expansion.

There are yet other concerns that should be mentioned. It should be noted that normalizing the super-low interest rate will take a considerable amount of time. On the other hand, a sudden upward adjustment of policy interest rates could impose unnecessary burdens on the recovery. Therefore, as a way to normalize the current macroeconomic policy stances at a gradual pace, it seems natural to start the adjustment of the interest rate before the potential side effects are realized. In other words, now is the time to start steering the monetary policy toward stable growth.

It is necessary, moreover, to consider the international spillover effect of the change in the macroeconomic policy stance. That is, policy change in one nation can have significant impacts on other countries through trade and financial channels, and therefore a certain degree of international cooperation may be required. In particular, implementing an exit strategy without considering such spillover effects is likely to bring about some unexpected negative impact on the global demand, which in turn will hinder the stable recovery of the global economy. Reflecting on these possibilities, world leaders in the G20 Summit reached an agreement on the principles of global cooperation in implementing exit strategies, but no unified restrictions were made to determine the time schedule and the scale of the exit strategy of each country.[16]

Individual exit strategies could differ, depending on the country, in terms of the implementation time and scale. Each country must recognize the need for an independent policy that fits its unique conditions, such as independent decisionmaking by central banks to raise policy interest rates. Nevertheless, for each government to carry out correct policies, an accurate understanding of global economic conditions is of great significance. In that sense, the sharing of information about macroeconomic conditions and policy stances among countries is particularly important in terms of global cooperation.

NOTES

1. Despite the continued weakening of the dollar from 2003, the Korean government took action to maintain the value of the won at a low level. Then, when a significant appreciation of the won occurred in the fourth quarter of 2004, export companies called for government intervention in the foreign exchange market. However, the government was already under increased pressure for handling the cost of sustaining the over-accumulation of foreign exchange reserves, which at that time were even larger than Korea's total debt. Thus there was little room for the government to initiate an active foreign exchange policy.
2. Considering the fact that the increased supply of foreign exchange was largely through the increase in short-term borrowing, it is, of course, naive or incorrect to argue that the Korean government's foreign exchange policy posed no problems. The rapid increase in short-term external liability was a main culprit that caused a large and abrupt outflow and subsequent sharp depreciation of the Korean won, rapidly infecting the Korean economy with the global financial crisis.
3. The aggregate market value of houses was nearly double that of the stock exchange in 2005. The standard deviation of the monthly year-on-year growth rate of the stock exchange index (KOSPI) from January 2000 to December 2007 was 28.7 percent, whereas it was only 5.6 percent for the house price index.

4. The Taylor rule specifies how a central bank might have altered its targeted short-term interest rate (the target call rate or base rate in Korea) in response to evolving macroeconomic fundamentals—specifically, the divergence of current output from potential output and of current inflation from the desired rate of inflation.
5. In fact, since 2005, competition among Korean banks strengthened further, leading to a sharp increase in loans. As a means of financing the loans, banks have dramatically expanded nondeposit liabilities. Together with the rise in household loans, the loans to small and medium-size enterprises increased at a fast pace. Above all, as the balance sheet adjustment of households was drawing to an end, the rate of increase of household credit began to pick up again from 2005 onward. This renewed acceleration is largely attributable to the continuous expansion of mortgage loans, as the upward trend of housing prices persisted unabated along with the intensified competition among financial institutions to expand their loan books.
6. Despite the increases in the call rate target since October 2005, the growth rate of M2 (unlike that of M1) picked up sharply, reflecting the enlargement of the private sector's financial investments in the nondeposit financial products of banks and nonbank financial institutions.
7. The depreciation of the dollar in the wake of the subprime mortgage crisis in the United States pushed up oil and raw materials prices, which were already showing an upward trend due to the global demand pressure. For example, the price of Dubai oil soared from $70 per barrel on average in 2007 to US$140 per barrel in mid-July 2008. Figure 9.1 shows that the sharp rise in import prices caused the year-on-year GDI growth rate to fall from 3.9 percent in 2007 to −0.8 percent during the first three quarters in 2008, while the year-on-year GDP growth rate dropped only slightly from 5.0 percent in 2007 to 4.8 percent during the first three quarters in 2008.
8. The degree of exchange rate pass-through to export prices in Korea also declined due to firms' cost cutting efforts. See Kim and Lee (2009) for more discussion.
9. Considering that Korea already had foreign reserves of more than US$250 billion, it is hard to see how the currency swap of US$30 billion could be very meaningful. Obstfeld et al. (2009) suggest that the swap lines could be interpreted as signals. In fact, the stabilizing effect of the currency swap contract did not last very long. Only after the US Federal Reserve Board announced that it would renew the swap agreement, did foreign investors' confidence in the Korean economy improve, and only then could stability in the foreign exchange market be secured.
10. Emergency economy meetings were held 40 times in 2009.
11. The Korean government announced that 65 percent of the budget (167 trillion won out of 258 trillion won) was front-loaded in the first half of 2009.
12. The numbers in the second row of Table 9.2 can be considered as the fiscal multiplier. As reported in Spilimbergo et al. (2008), existing studies provide a wide range of values for the short-term fiscal multiplier from less than zero to larger than four, depending on the identifying assumptions, the type of fiscal policy and the country of interest. Similarly for Korea, Huh (2007) found that the fiscal multiplier is not significantly different from zero, or even negative, while most other studies indicate that the fiscal multiplier is positive but less than 1, like those found in this study. Hong (2010) suggested that the fiscal multiplier is likely to have been larger in the current crisis, because the effectiveness of a stimulus package depends on the severity of a recession, especially when there is large slack in the economy.
13. In the model used for the estimation, interest rates are endogenously determined so that an increase in fiscal expenditure leads to upward pressure on interest rates, which partially crowds out the effects on the GDP growth rate. However, as experienced in 2009 and the first half of 2010, when interest rates remain at a low level due to expansionary monetary policy, the effect of fiscal expenditure would be bigger than that shown here. Still, there remains the issue that the leakage of demand through imports and the effects of fiscal expansion on the exchange rate also have the "crowding-out" effect.

14. Numbers in Table 9.2 show the magnitude of the change in the growth rates of each macroeconomic variable triggered by the temporary expansion of fiscal expenditure. The effects on macroeconomic variables could turn out differently when the type of fiscal expenditure—such as final consumption, investment or transfer—is considered. This table reports the weighted average of simulated numbers for each type of fiscal expenditure, considering the composition of fiscal stimulus in 2008 and 2009.
15. There were concerns that the pace of recovery of the Korean economy might slow down significantly in the second half of 2009, since there was not much room left for additional fiscal expenditure.
16. In particular, the G20 Summit discussed different exit strategies depending on the economic conditions of each country and the proactive attitudes of each government.

REFERENCES

Adrian, Tobias and Hyun Song Shin. 2008. "Liquidity, Monetary Policy, and Financial Cycles". *Current Issues in Economics and Finance*, **14** (1): 1–7.

Blanchard, Olivier, Giovanni Dell'Ariccia and Paolo Mauro. 2010. "Rethinking Macroeconomic Policy". Paper presented at the Conference on Reconstructing the World Economy, organized by the Korea Development Institute and the International Monetary Fund, Seoul, 25 February 2010. Also published as IMF Staff Position Note SPN/10/03 (Washington: International Monetary Fund).

Hong, Kiseok. 2010. *Fiscal Policy Issues in Korea after the Current Crisis*. ADBI Working Paper 225. Tokyo: Asian Development Bank Institute.

Huh, Seok-Kyun. 2007. "On the Efficacy of Fiscal Policy in Korea during 1979–2000". *Korea Development Review*, **29** (2): 1–40. In Korean.

Kim, Hyeon-Wook. 2009. *Short-term Liquidity Expansion and Implications for Monetary Policy in Korea*. KDI Policy Forum 217 (200–10). Seoul: Korea Development Institute. In Korean.

Kim, Hyeon-Wook and Hangyong Lee. 2009. "Declines in Exchange Rate Pass-through to Export Prices in Korea". *Korea Development Review*, **31** (2): 235–66. In Korean.

Korea Development Institute (KDI). 2009. "Macroeconomic Effects of Fiscal Stimulus". Unpublished paper, Korea Development Institute. In Korean.

Obstfeld, Maurice, Jay C. Shambaugh and Alan M. Taylor. 2009. "Financial Instability, Reserves, and Central Bank Swap Lines in the Panic of 2008". *American Economic Review*, **99** (2): 480–86.

Organisation for Economic Co-operation and Development (OECD). 2010. *2010 Economic Review: Korea*. Paris: Economic and Development Review Committee, Organisation for Economic Co-operation and Development.

Reinhart, Carmen and Kenneth S. Rogoff. 2009a. "The Aftermath of Financial Crisis". *American Economic Review*, **99** (2): 466–72.

Reinhart, Carmen and Kenneth S. Rogoff. 2009b. *This Time Is Different: Eight Centuries of Financial Folly*. Princeton, New Jersey, and Oxford: Princeton University Press.

Spilimbergo, Antonio, Steve Symansky, Olivier Blanchard and Carlo Cottarelli. 2008. *Fiscal Policy for the Crisis*. IMF Staff Position Note SPN/08/01. Washington: International Monetary Fund.

10. Are all emerging market crises alike?

Marcos Chamon, Atish Ghosh and Jun Il Kim

INTRODUCTION

Are all emerging market economies' (EMEs) crises alike? Yes and no. While countries have experienced balance of payments crises since time immemorial, the more spectacular "capital account" crises first came to the fore with Mexico's devaluation in December 1994. Setting the stage for subsequent crises in East Asia and Latin America, Mexico's crisis was characterized by a sharp correction of the currency and the current account, together with a collapse of output and economic activity. Broadly similar outcomes were observed following Russia's 1998 devaluation cum default, Brazil's abandonment of its peg in 1999 and both Turkey's 2001 and Argentina's 2002 crises.

But while the *consequences* of these crises show characteristic similarities (output and exchange rate collapse, sharp reversal of the current account as private financing is withdrawn, see Figure 10.1), their *causes* appear bewilderingly different. Thus Mexico and Russia's crises stemmed from difficulties in funding the public sector. In Brazil (1998–99), Turkey (2000–01) and Argentina (2002) public sector debt dynamics played a key role—in the latter two cases, accompanied by a banking crisis. On the other hand, Uruguay (2002) was a banking crisis—caused by withdrawals of Argentine deposits—that spilled into a public sector debt problem and a balance of payments crisis.

Nor has the academic literature been particularly successful at developing a unified theory of currency crises. In the early models (Krugman 1979; Flood and Garber 1984), the peg was undermined by the government money-financing its deficit. Following the European exchange rate mechanism crises in 1992–93, theoretical models focused on the possibility of multiple equilibria whereby a self-fulfilling expectation of policy loosening could engender a speculative attack (Obstfeld 1986). The East Asian crisis in 1997–98 gave rise to yet a third generation of crisis models, emphasizing balance sheet effects of unhedged foreign-currency debt exposure (Aghion et al. 2001). But Argentina's 2002 crisis harkened back

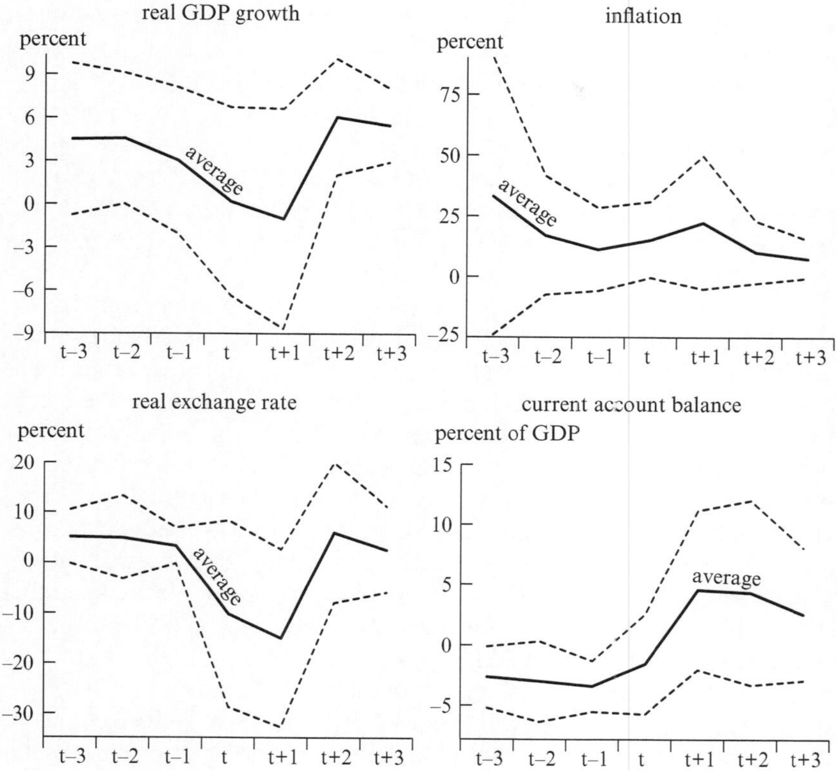

Notes:
The sample comprises 12 crises in 11 countries: Argentina (1995 and 2002), Brazil (1999), Indonesia (1997), Korea (1997), Malaysia (1997), Mexico (1995), the Philippines (1997), Russia (1998), Thailand (1997), Turkey (2000) and Uruguay (2002).
Time *t* marks the onset of crisis and withdrawal of private finance.
The upper and lower dotted lines represent respectively the average plus one standard deviation and the average minus one standard deviation.

Figure 10.1 Selected macroeconomic indicators during capital account crises

to the first-generation models in which financing the budget was the root cause of the crisis (even though the currency board itself largely ruled out money-financing the deficit).

All this suggests the need for a more unified approach to understanding EME crises (some of which, recently, have occurred in advanced economies). Drawing on earlier work by Ghosh and Ghosh (2003) and Ghosh et al. (2008), this chapter proposes a general framework for modeling crises: as the confluence of an underlying vulnerability plus a specific crisis trigger. The vulnerability is typically a balance sheet mismatch (maturity, currency, capital) that may persist for many years until a crisis is triggered by a particular event. Such vulnerabilities can therefore be readily identified. By contrast, the event that triggers the crisis may take many different forms—economic or political, domestic or external—and is likely to be highly unpredictable. If this view of crises is correct, then it has important implications for crisis prevention efforts, namely that policy efforts should be directed at addressing underlying vulnerabilities rather than at trying to predict crises.

But while previous EME crises appear to fit this framework, actually testing the idea that crises are the confluence of underlying vulnerabilities and a specific trigger is difficult, because the triggering event may be endogenous to the underlying vulnerabilities. Indeed, the recent theoretical models suggest that a small change in the balance sheet or liquidity position of a country may trigger a sudden stop if creditors are unable to coordinate among themselves (Morris and Shin 2006; Corsetti et al. 2006). The global financial crisis in 2007–08—whose epicenter was advanced, not emerging market, economies—provides a natural experiment in this regard. If the crisis in advanced economies, including the consequent deleveraging by financial institutions, is taken to be the triggering event, then how EMEs fared during the crisis should be correlated to their preexisting vulnerabilities (those at the end of 2007). In this chapter we use the global financial crisis to test whether countries that were more vulnerable indeed suffered larger output declines (relative to their respective historical growth performance) once the crisis was triggered.

The second section of the chapter elaborates on the analytical framework for considering crises as the confluence of an underlying vulnerability and a specific crisis trigger. In the absence of full sectoral balance sheets, the third section develops some simple indicators of vulnerabilities across key sectors of the economy. The fourth section applies these indicators to identify underlying vulnerabilities in emerging market economies on the eve of the global financial crisis, treating the crisis (whose epicenter was the advanced economies) as the triggering event for the subsequent performance of EMEs during 2008–09. The key hypothesis is that EMEs that suffered the worst performance (that is, experienced their own crises in 2008–09) were indeed those that had underlying vulnerabilities. By contrast, EMEs that were hit hard by the global financial crisis (through trade or financial links with advanced economies) nevertheless came through relatively unscathed if they did not have these vulnerabilities.

UNDERLYING VULNERABILITIES AND CRISIS TRIGGERS

Prior to the onset of the "capital account" crises of the 1990s, most analyses of financial crises focused on flow disequilibria: a budget or current account deficit that could no longer be financed. With the onset of the East Asian crises in 1997–98, however, balance sheet mismatches gained prominence as an important source of vulnerability. Balance sheet analysis typically analyses four main sectoral balance sheets: the government sector (including the central bank), the private financial sector, the private nonfinancial sector (households and corporations) and the external sector (or "rest of the world").

This sectoral decomposition can reveal important vulnerabilities that are hidden when considering the country's consolidated balance sheet (or its net position vis-à-vis the rest of the world). In particular, weaknesses in one sector's balance sheet may interact with others, eventually spilling into a countrywide balance of payments crisis even though the original mismatch was not evident in the country's aggregate balance sheet. A prime example is the foreign currency debt *between* residents, which of course gets netted out of the aggregate balance sheet, but may nevertheless contribute to a balance of payments crisis. For example, if the government has foreign currency debt to residents and faces a funding crisis, it will need to draw down the central bank's foreign exchange reserves, possibly leading to a balance of payments crisis.

More generally, a loss of confidence or a re-evaluation of risks in one sector can prompt sudden and large scale portfolio adjustments, such as massive withdrawals of bank deposits, panic sales of securities or abrupt halts in debt rollovers. As the exchange rate, interest rates and other prices adjust, other balance sheets can sharply deteriorate, in turn provoking creditors to shift toward safer foreign assets—resulting in capital outflows and further pressure on the exchange rate and reserves, until there is a full-blown capital account crisis. Various case studies of capital account crises illustrate how currency and maturity mismatches in sectoral balance sheets (and linkages between them) can contribute to the likelihood that a capital account crisis could be (and ultimately was) triggered.[1] At the same time, given emerging market countries' limited ability to borrow in their own currencies ("original sin"), there must be foreign exchange (FX) exposure in some sectoral balance sheet in the economy. This also means that any "hedging" will either be incomplete or that, in effect, the country is not a net recipient of capital from the rest of the world. Therefore, the key to reducing vulnerability is to try to limit currency, maturity and capital structure mismatches and ensure that risks—including risks to real shocks—are ultimately contained by strong balance sheets within the economy.[2]

Balance sheet analysis of past financial crises in EMEs provides some useful insights, as shown by the following examples.

The banking system often acts as a key transmission channel of balance sheet problems from one sector into another. If a shock in the corporate sector (Asian crisis countries) or the public sector (Russia 1998, Turkey 2001, Argentina 2002) results in that sector being unable to meet its liabilities, then another sector (typically the banking sector) loses its claims. In turn, this can cause a deposit run, sparking a banking crisis, especially if the government's own balance sheet is too weak to provide credible deposit insurance or lacks international reserves to provide liquidity support in foreign exchange. By the same token, if banks tighten their lending to prevent their portfolios from deteriorating, their action further complicates the situation of the corporate or public sector that is facing financing difficulties.

If the government's balance sheet is sufficiently strong, it can serve as a "circuit breaker", halting the propagation of shocks across domestic balance sheets. In some crises (such as Argentina 2002), however, the government balance sheet was the main source of weakness, precluding such a role. Indeed, banks typically want to hold government securities, because they may be the only liquid assets denominated in the domestic currency. However, if (as in Argentina) the government defaults on its debt, then the default can be a source of vulnerability to the banking sector.

Foreign exchange reserves or contingent financing may be especially valuable in reducing the economy's balance sheet vulnerabilities as they can be used to cover short-term financing needs of the public sector, to provide a partial lender of last resort function in dollarized economies or to help close the private sector's foreign currency mismatch—insulating the economy from the impact of a devaluation—by providing liquidity to banks. However for contingent financing to be useful, it must be very quickly accessible.

Maturity and currency mismatches are sometimes hidden in indexed or floating rate instruments. For instance, liabilities may be formally denominated in a local currency but linked to the exchange rate. Likewise, an asset may have a long maturity but carry a floating interest rate. Such indexation often creates the same mismatches, as though the debt were denominated in foreign currency or as though the maturity were as short as the frequency of the interest rate adjustments.

Balance sheet linkages can *transform* one type of risk into another without necessarily *reducing* that risk, which was the case in both Thailand and Argentina. For example, the banking system may try to close its FX mismatch on foreign currency deposits by lending to domestic corporations in foreign currency. However, if the nonfinancial sector recipients of those loans do not have natural hedges (such as export revenues), then the banking system's currency risk is simply transformed into credit risk.

Off-balance sheet items can substantially alter the overall risk exposure, reducing or increasing balance sheet exposures according to whether an underlying position is being hedged or the entity is taking a speculative position in the derivatives markets. However, such transactions can also mask vulnerabilities, for instance as risk from a balance sheet mismatch is transformed into counterparty risk. In aggregate, a sectoral balance sheet may appear hedged through the derivative markets but may still be exposed to the risk if the counterparties are connected.[3] For example, in Turkey 2000, the open FX exposure of the banking system was small when forward transactions were included, but the main counterparties in these forward transactions were other Turkish banks.

The ultimate buffer for private sector balance sheet mismatches (such as the currency-FX ratio) is capital. A major source of vulnerability in the East Asian crises was the very high debt–equity ratios.

Pegged exchange rate regimes, by offering an implicit exchange rate guarantee, might encourage greater risk-taking in the form of open (mismatched) FX positions. As noted above, to the extent that emerging market countries' ability to borrow in their own currency is limited, there must be aggregate foreign currency exposure associated with foreign liabilities (that is, obligations to nonresidents). Nevertheless, pegged exchange rates might exacerbate foreign currency risk. By providing an implicit guarantee, they may encourage more "carry trade" (arbitrage between low-cost foreign currency borrowing and higher domestic interest rates at a given exchange rate), resulting in either greater total foreign borrowing or a bias toward shorter maturity foreign liabilities (as in Thailand 1997 and Turkey 2001–02).

Although mismatches may represent important sources of vulnerability, they do not imply that the country will necessarily experience a crisis. In particular, crises require some triggering event. Table 10.1 lists the major emerging market crises as well as the underlying vulnerabilities and (plausible) crisis triggering events. What is striking from the list is the similarity of the underlying vulnerabilities—and the dissimilarity of the specific crisis triggers. The underlying vulnerabilities are nearly always maturity or currency mismatches on public or private sector balance sheets. By contrast, the specific event that triggers the crisis varies widely, including political uncertainty (Mexico 1994), external shocks (Argentina 1995, Korea and Indonesia 1997, Uruguay 2002) and perceptions about policy inconsistencies or insufficient political will (Russia 1998, Brazil 1999, Turkey 2000, Argentina 2002).

Table 10.1 Selected emerging market economy crises prior to 2008

Country and year	Balance sheet vulnerability	Crisis trigger
Mexico (1994)	government's short-term external (and foreign-exchange-denominated) liabilities	US monetary policy; political shocks (Chiapas; assassination)
Argentina (1995)	banking system short-term external and peso- and foreign-exchange-denominated liabilities	contagion from Mexico's 1994 "Tequila" crisis
Thailand (1997)	financial and nonfinancial corporate sector external liabilities; concentrated exposure of finance companies to real estate	terms of trade deterioration; asset price deflation
Korea (1997)	financial sector external liabilities (with substantial maturity mismatch) and concentrated exposure to *chaebols*; high coporate debt/equity ratio	terms of trade deterioration; profitability of *chaebols*; contagion from Thailand's crisis
Indonesia (1997)	corporate sector external liabilities; concentration of banking system assets in real estate lending; high corporate debt/equity ratio	contagion from Thailand's crisis; banking crisis
Russia (1998)	government's short-term external financing needs	failure to implement budget deficit targets; terms of trade deterioration
Brazil (1999)	government's short-term external liabilities	doubts about ability to implement budget cuts; current account deficit; contagion from Russian default
Argentina (2002)	public and private sector external and foreign-exchange-denominated liabilities	inconsistency between currency board arrangement and fiscal policy; Russian default
Uruguay (2002)	banking system short-term external liabilities	Argentine deposit freeze leading to mass withdrawals from Uruguayan banks
Turkey (2001)	government short-term liabilities, banking system foreign exchange and maturity mismatches	current account deficit, real exchange rate appreciation, uncertainty about political will to undertake financial sector reforms

Source: Ghosh et al. (2008).

VULNERABILITY INDICATORS

While balance sheet analysis can be revealing about potential vulnerabilities in the economy, it is also data intensive, requiring detailed information on sectoral balance sheets and their interaction. A simpler approach, therefore, is to create indicators of vulnerability that are broadly related to currency and maturity mismatches and that can then be related to crisis risk.

Definition of Crisis

The first step in this exercise is to define the type of crisis for whose vulnerability we are trying to explain. We follow the crisis definition used in Chamon et al. (2007) and consider capital account crises, which involve sudden stops in capital flows that are likely to be associated with currency, sovereign, banking or corporate crises.

While there is no standard definition of a sudden stop, we define such episodes as a year in which one of the following holds (where means and standard deviations are computed based on the 1993–2007 values deflated by the US consumer price index):

- ratios of net private capital flows to GDP have declined by at least 3 percent from the previous year and 2 percent from two years before;
- or net private capital flows are at least 1.5 standard deviations below their mean and have declined by at least 0.75 standard deviation from the previous year;
- or net private capital flows have declined by at least 1.5 standard deviations from the previous year and at least 0.75 standard deviation from two years before;
- or net private capital flows have declined by at least 0.75 standard deviation from the previous year and at least 1.5 standard deviations from two years before.

Table 10.2 lists the resulting crisis episodes for the 50 countries in our sample.[4]

Explanatory Variables

There are many possible candidate explanatory variables for underlying vulnerabilities. For each of the three "sectors" (external, public, financial), we consider five potential explanatory variables.

Table 10.2 Emerging market crises in the sample, 1997–2006

Country	Crises	
Algeria	1994	
Argentina	1995	2001
Brazil	1999	2002
Bulgaria	1994	
Colombia	1999	2002
Dominican Republic	2003	
Ecuador	1999	
Hungary	1994	
Indonesia	1997	
Israel	1997	2002
Jamaica	2003	
Kazakhstan	2007	
Korea	1997	
Lebanon	2001	2006
Lithuania	1999	
Malaysia	1997	
Mexico	1994	
Pakistan	1998	
Philippines	1997	
Romania	1999	
Russia	1998	
South Africa	2001	
Thailand	1997	
Turkey	1994	2001
Ukraine	1998	
Uruguay	2002	
Venezuela	1994	2001

Note: Countries with no crisis year indicated in the table are Bosnia and Herzegovina, Chile, China, Costa Rica, Croatia, Egypt, El Salvador, Estonia, Georgia, Guatemala, India, Jordan, Latvia, Macedonia, Morocco, Panama, Peru, Poland, Serbia, Sri Lanka and Tunisia.

- External sector: reserve cover (dummy for reserves covering short-term debt and current account deficit), current account balance/GDP, external debt/GDP, external debt/exports and exchange rate overvaluation.[5]
- Fiscal sector: public debt/GDP, public debt exposed to roll-over risk (short-term debt at remaining maturity/GDP), public debt exposed to currency risk (foreign currency denominated debt/GDP), government overall balance and primary gap (difference between primary balance and the level that would stabilize debt/GDP).

- Financial sector: nonperforming loans (NPLs) as a share of total loans, capital adequacy ratio, return on assets, private sector credit growth over the previous year (change in private sector credit/GDP) and private sector credit growth over the previous three years.

Estimation Approach

Given the wide variety of candidate explanatory variables, any estimation will inevitably give rise to data mining concerns. The traditional approach would involve a "horse race" between variables to see which ones seem more relevant for inclusion in the explanatory set. But there are a number of possible concerns. First, even a variable that performs weakly may still play a useful role by complementing other variables (that is, a "weaker" predictor in isolation may still be more useful than a "stronger" predictor if it helps identify crises that are often missed by the other explanatory variables). Any horse race exercise is prone to "over-fitting" concerns, and while the hand-picked combination may perform well in sample, it could perform poorly out of sample.

Since our main goal is to identify whether underlying vulnerabilities can indeed explain the occurrence of crises, any use of a "hand-picked" regression that works well in sample is subject to the criticism that the approach is not robust. Instead, therefore, we consider (all) possible combinations of the explanatory variables. Specifically, we estimate a series of probit equations (for the probability of crisis), each time choosing one external, one fiscal and one financial variable—yielding a total of 125 probit equations. We also consider regressions where only two of these three sectors are used, which yield an additional 75 combinations. The probits are estimated using data through 2006 to predict probabilities for 2007; these are used to see whether existing vulnerabilities helped to determine how emerging market countries fared in the 2008–09 global financial crisis.

Estimation Results

Given the large number of probit regressions estimated, we present only summary information on the statistical significance of the explanatory variables. To this end, Table 10.3 reports the percentage of probit estimations for which each variable is statistically significant (at the 10 percent significance level or higher) and is of the expected sign. The results suggest that the factors most robustly related to underlying vulnerabilities are the real exchange rate overvaluation and the debt–export ratio (in the external sector), the primary gap (the budget surplus required to stabilize the public debt ratio) and the maturing debt (in the fiscal sector), and that

Table 10.3 Statistical significance of variables in crisis probits

Sector	All 3 sectors		External and fiscal only		External and financial only		Financial and fiscal only	
	N	S	N	S	N	S	N	S
External sector								
reserve cover >100%	25	48	5	80	5	60	–	–
external debt/GDP	25	0	5	0	5	40	–	–
external debt/exports	25	100	5	100	5	100	–	–
current account balance/GDP	25	28	5	60	5	60	–	–
exchange rate overvaluation	25	72	5	80	5	100	–	–
Fiscal sector								
debt/GDP	25	4	5	0	–	–	5	40
maturing debt/GDP	25	44	5	60	–	–	5	80
foreign exchange debt/GDP	25	16	5	0	–	–	5	0
primary gap	25	28	5	20	–	–	5	60
overall balance	25	0	5	0	–	–	5	20
Financial sector								
credit growth (1 year)	25	0	–	–	5	0	5	0
nonperforming loans ratio	25	0	–	–	5	0	5	0
return on assets	25	68	–	–	5	0	5	100
capital adequacy	25	0	–	–	5	0	5	0
credit growth (3 years)	25	0	–	–	5	0	5	0
Total regressions	175		25		25		25	

Notes:
N = number of regressions. S = significant percentage.
The table reports the frequency at which variable had the "right" sign and was statistically significant at the 10 percent level or above.
Among the regressions, 175 include all 3 sectors, and 75 include only 2 sectors (25 for each sector pairing).

in the financial sector, only the return on bank assets seems to matter. In general, the external sector variables capture the most important vulnerabilities.

VULNERABILITIES ON THE EVE OF THE GLOBAL FINANCIAL CRISIS

To what extent were EMEs vulnerable on the eve of the global financial crisis? Over the past decade, many emerging market economies have strengthened their economic fundamentals through both structural reforms and improved policies. Nevertheless, during this decade in some countries, balance sheet vulnerabilities remained—and, for example in Eastern Europe, worsened.

The framework developed above can help quantify these vulnerabilities. In general, crises are rare events, and in our sample (up to 2007) correspond to only 5.2 percent of observations. By 2008, EMEs were somewhat less vulnerable to crisis than in the past, with an average crisis probability of 4.6 percent in 2008 (compared with 5.2 percent for the sample through 2007). Of course, there was also variation across countries, and the 25th, 50th, 75th and 95th percentiles of the sample's crisis probabilities in 2008 were 2.6, 4.0, 5.6 and 8.8 percent, respectively. The time series evolution of the sample's average crisis probabilities is plotted in Figure 10.2, differentiating by region. The regional time series confirms anecdotal evidence of declining vulnerabilities in Asia (post-2000) and in Latin America, but increasing vulnerabilities in Eastern Europe (which peaked just before the global financial crisis triggered the EME crises). The general perception is that, in Latin America, it was mainly improvement of the public finances that was responsible for the lower vulnerability (and in East Asia, it was mainly improvement of external indicators). A decomposition of the factors explaining the falling vulnerability scores, however, points mainly to improved external indicators in both regions (while, in Europe, it was mainly deterioration of the external indicators that resulted in higher estimated vulnerability). The average fitted probability for Emerging Europe was 5.7 percent, compared with 4.2 percent for Latin America and 3.3 percent for Asia.

Accepting the paradigm proposed in this chapter (that crises are the conjuncture of an underlying vulnerability and a crisis trigger), and assuming that the financial crisis whose epicenter was in the advanced economies constituted the crisis trigger, we would expect to see a correlation between the extent of preexisting vulnerabilities and how emerging market countries have fared in the past couple of years. Table 10.4 therefore reports the results from the regression of the change in real GDP growth during the

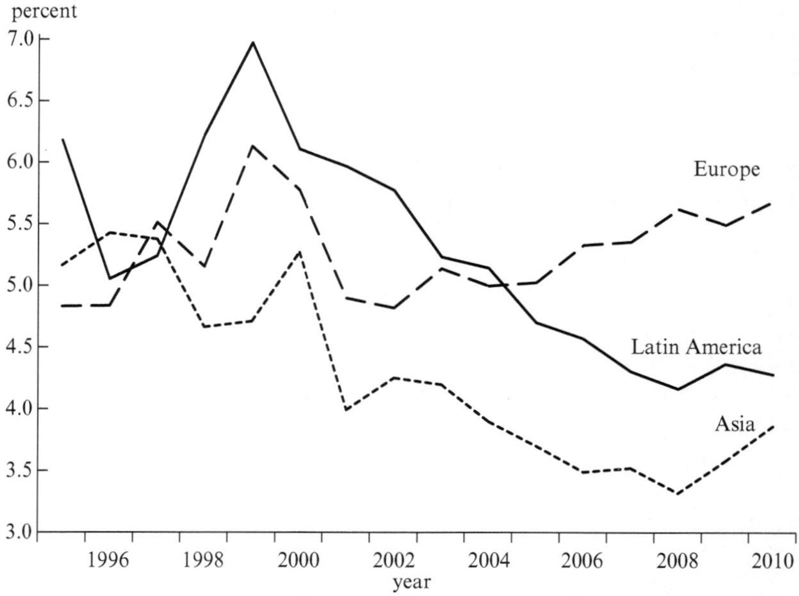

Source: Authors' calculations.

Figure 10.2 Crisis probability: estimated vulnerability in Asia, Europe, and Latin America, 1995–2010

crisis on our vulnerability index (that is, the estimated probability of crisis in 2008, which is the average probability implied by the 200 probit regressions estimated above). The change in real GDP growth is measured as average growth in 2008–09 relative to the country's historical performance (taken here as average growth in 2003–07); other controls in the regression are the terms of trade and growth in advanced economy trading partners.

Ignoring other explanatory variables, our vulnerability index yields a statistically and economically significant coefficient of −1.82 (the first column in Table 10.4). This means that each percentage point increase in the vulnerability index's predicted crisis probability for 2008 would have lowered growth by 1.82 percentage points in 2008–09 relative to the country's normal growth performance. Therefore, moving from a 2.6 to a 5.6 probability of having a crisis (the interquartile range of our vulnerability index) would have lowered growth by 5.4 percentage points during the global financial crisis.

Of course, preexisting vulnerabilities were not the only factor determining economic performance during the crisis: the external environment

Table 10.4 Growth change during the 2008–09 crisis as a function of estimated vulnerability

Item	(1)	(2)	(3)
Vulnerability index	−1.823***	−1.356***	−1.073***
	[0.523]	[0.481]	[0.308]
Terms of trade change	–	0.125	0.076
		[0.106]	[0.088]
Growth of trade partners	–	0.031***	0.026*
		[0.010]	[0.013]
Net private capital flows/ GDP (2009)	–	–	0.234***
			[0.070]
Constant	3.093	1.7	0.519
	[2.186]	[2.127]	[1.396]
Observations	43	42	42
R-squared	0.34	0.499	0.618

Notes:
Growth change during the crisis corresponds to GDP growth in 2008–09 minus the average for 2003–07.
The vulnerability index is the average fitted value for each country of the crisis probability averaged across 200 probits described in Table 10.3.
Growth of trade partners is the real GDP growth of partner countries (weighted by export share).
Symbols *, ** and *** denote statistical significance at the 10, 5 and 1 percent levels.

mattered as well. To this end, we add the change in the terms of trade (positive but statistically insignificant) and output growth in the country's advanced economy trading partners (positive and significant). Even controlling for these factors, the vulnerability index continues to be highly significant (the second column in Table 10.4).

The relationship between the vulnerability index and individual countries' performance during the crisis is shown in Figure 10.3, where the strong correlation between vulnerability and the subsequent output decline is clearly visible. What is also evident from the figure is that the Baltic states (and Ukraine) suffered disproportionately more than their very large vulnerability would imply. But the regression results are not driven by these "outliers". Excluding Ukraine, Lithuania, Latvia and Estonia still yields a coefficient of −0.83 on the vulnerability index.

A further factor affecting how EMEs fared during the crisis was the behavior of capital flows. The deleveraging by advanced economy banks and the general increase in risk aversion led to significant capital outflows from EMEs. Figure 10.4 and the third column in Table 10.4 show that these capital outflows had a significant negative impact on the

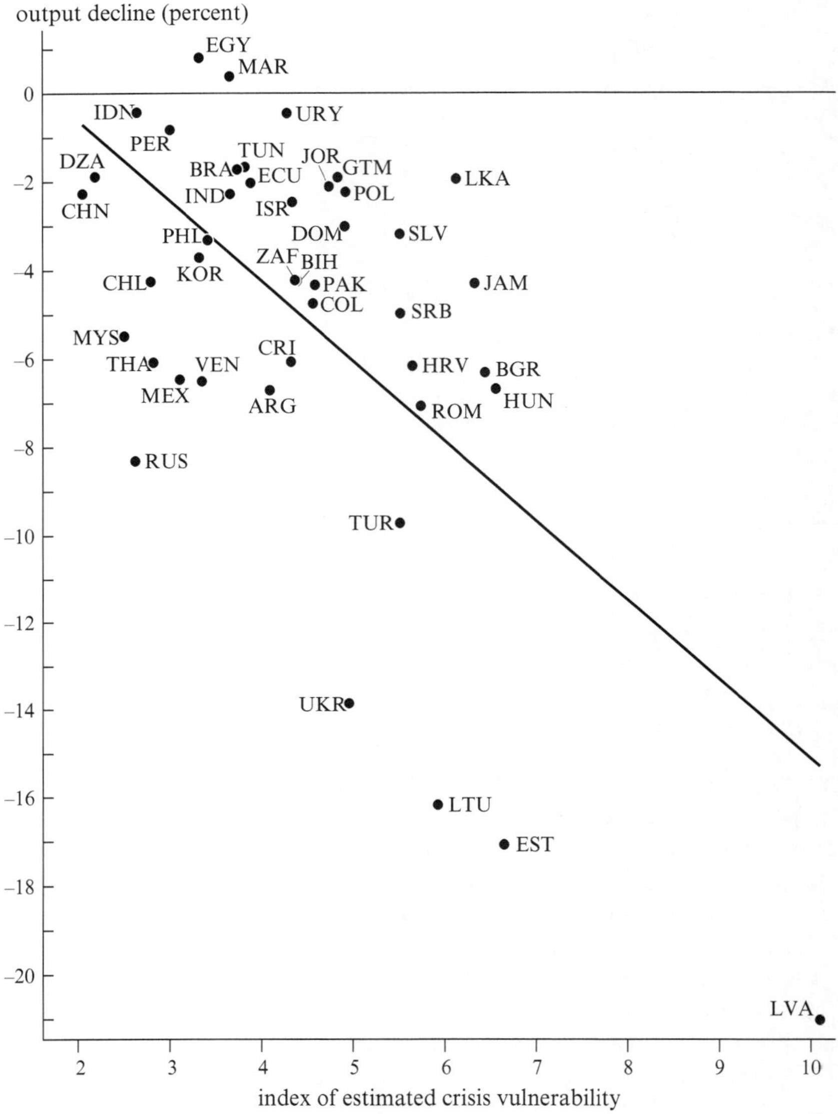

Note: Decline is calculated as average real GDP growth for 2008–09 minus average real GDP growth for 2002–07.

Source: Authors' calculations.

Figure 10.3 Estimated crisis vulnerability and output decline in selected countries, 2008–09

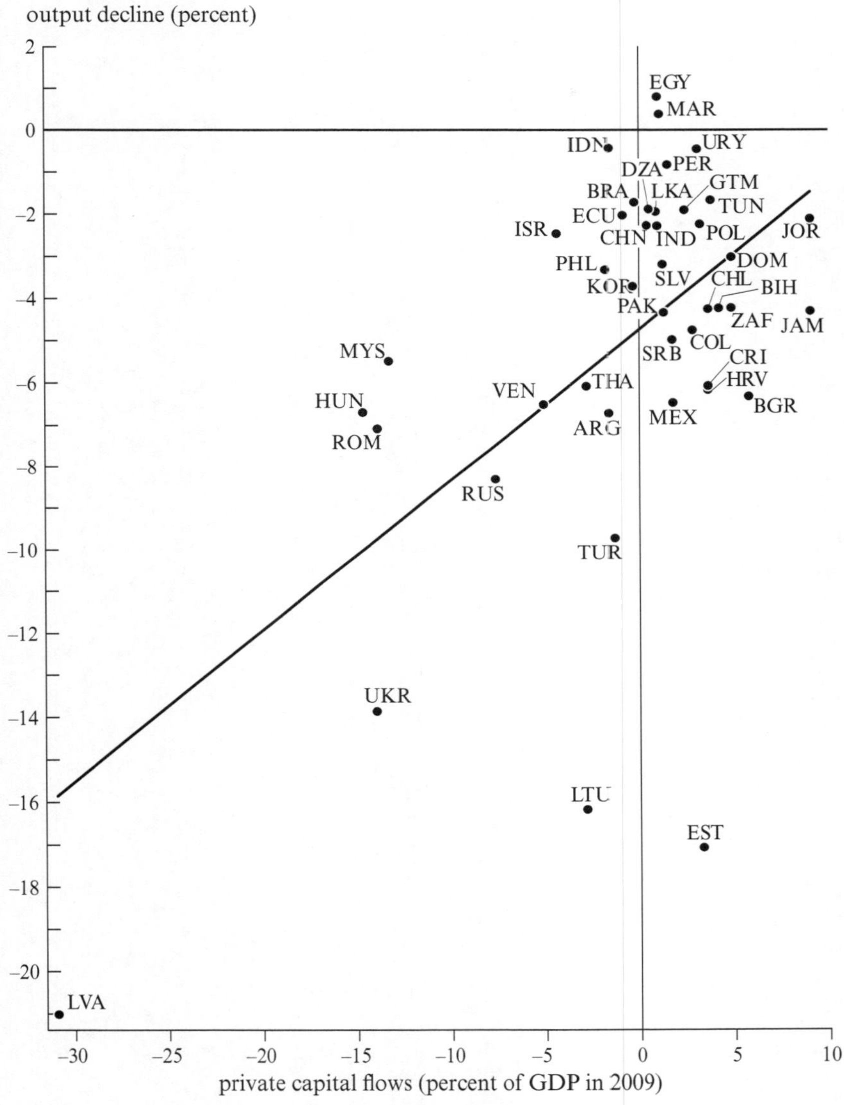

Note: Decline is calculated as average real GDP growth for 2008–09 minus average real GDP growth for 2002–07.

Source: Authors' calculations.

Figure 10.4 Capital flows and output decline in selected countries, 2008–09

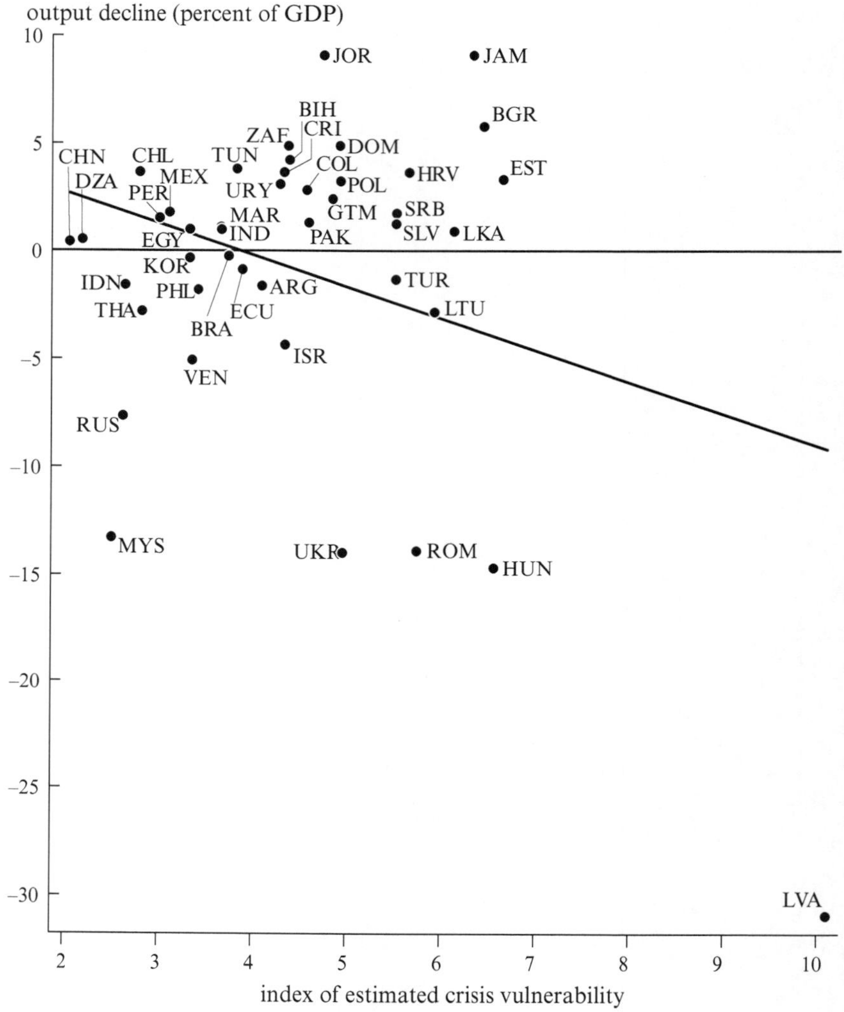

Source: Authors' calculations.

Figure 10.5 Crisis vulnerability and capital flows in selected countries including Latvia, 2009

growth performance of EMEs during the crisis. The outflows themselves, however, seem to have been largely indiscriminate. While there is a relationship between higher precrisis vulnerability and larger outflows (Figure 10.5), it turns out that this relationship is driven entirely by Latvia. By excluding this observation, it is evident that the extent of capital outflows

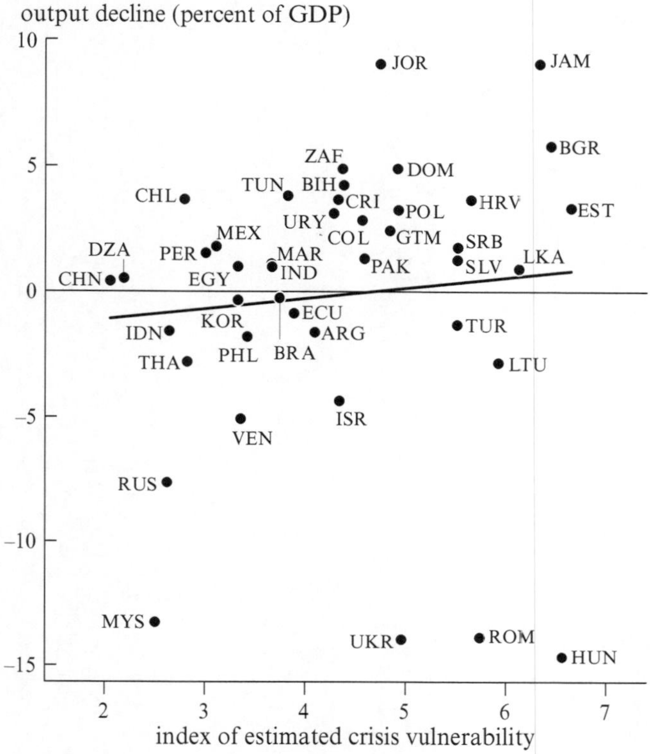

Source: Authors' calculations.

Figure 10.6 Crisis vulnerability and capital flows in selected countries excluding Latvia

was largely unrelated to precrisis vulnerabilities (Figure 10.6). This is also borne out in some anecdotal evidence of large capital outflows from Korea and Brazil—not because investors were worried about vulnerabilities, but because the larger and more liquid markets in these countries allowed investors to withdraw funds from them more easily. Whether this "indiscriminate" pattern of outflows is unique to the current global crisis, or holds more generally, is an open question. But it is at least plausible, inasmuch as most of the outflows were driven by deleveraging in advanced economies rather than concerns about the individual emerging markets (as is usually the case in sudden stops).

Finally, Figure 10.7 plots the conditional relationship beween the output decline and the estimated precrisis vulnerability (that is, controlling for the effect of other explanatory variables, including capital outflows).

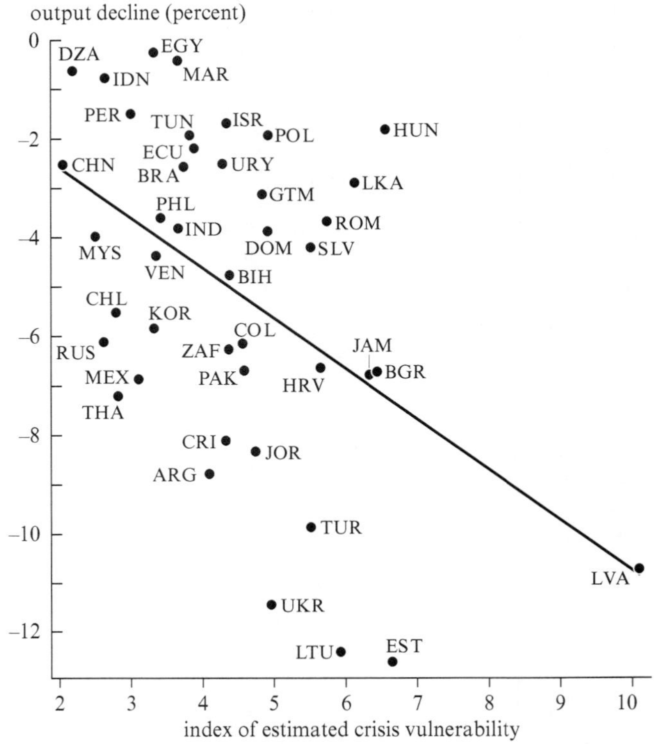

Note: Decline is calculated as average real GDP growth for 2008–09 minus average real GDP growth for 2002–07.

Source: Authors' calculations.

Figure 10.7 Conditional relationship between estimated crisis vulnerability and output decline, 2008–09

Consistent with the regression results (the third column of Table 10.4), it is evident that precrisis vulnerabilities, as captured by our index, are strongly related to how EMEs fared during the global financial crisis.

CONCLUSIONS

Are all emerging market economy crises alike? Yes and no. Superficially, they differ markedly, ranging from public funding and sovereign debt crises to banking and corporate sector problems. But a more general framework, in which crises are viewed as the conjuncture of an underlying vulnerability and a specific trigger, can help explain the diversity—and similarities—of EME crises.

In this chapter, in the absence of full sectoral balance sheet data, we develop some simple indicators of vulnerability that are likely to be related to foreign currency and maturity mismatches on domestic balance sheets. Since the precise interaction of the various sectoral vulnerabilities is unknown, we use robust estimation techniques. Using this framework, we are able to trace how vulnerabilities have evolved in different countries and regions. Consistent with anecdotal evidence, we find that Asia and Latin America became more resilient in the run-up to the 2008–09 global financial crisis, whereas Emerging Europe becomes vulnerable. We then find a strong correlation between how emerging market countries fared during the global financial crisis and their estimated vulnerability on the eve of the crisis. Other factors were also at play. Korea, for example, had low vulnerability but suffered large capital outflows as the global financial crisis unfolded (in part because its liquid markets provided easy exit to foreign banks trying to deleverage and reduce exposure to all EMEs). But the pre-global crisis vulnerability is the most important determinant of how EMEs fared once the crisis had been triggered.

This way of viewing financial crises—as the conjuncture of an underlying vulnerability and a specific crisis trigger—also has important implications for early warning systems and crisis prevention. In particular, it implies that crisis prediction ("calling crises") is a fool's errand, because specific events that trigger the crisis (which can be domestic or external, economic or political) are likely to be impossible to predict.[6] Instead, therefore, policy efforts should be directed at eliminating (or at least reducing) the underlying vulnerabilities, because the crisis cannot be triggered if there are no vulnerabilities. And indeed, this is very much the approach of current efforts at crisis prevention, such as the International Monetary Fund and Financial Stability Board's early warning exercise (see Ghosh et al. 2009).

NOTES

This chapter should not be reported as representing the views of the IMF. The views expressed in this chapter are those of the authors and do not necessarily represent those of the IMF or IMF policy.

1. See, for example, Allen et al. (2002) and Rosenberg et al. (2005).
2. To use an analogy, lightning strikes might leave a house at risk of burning down, and whereas measures can be taken to reduce that risk (for example by installing a lightning

conductor), some risk may be unavoidable. By purchasing insurance, however, the homeowner transfers the associated financial risk from his own relatively weak, undiversified balanced sheet to that of the insurance company, which is much stronger in that it holds diversified risks.
3. For example, a bank may be closing its spot FX exposure through a derivative transaction with its parent conglomerate. Such practices apparently occurred in Turkey prior to the 2000 crisis.
4. This selection of the list of crises is the result of a concerted effort by the IMF Working Group on Vulnerability Indicators, whose aim was to develop new criteria for rating countries' vulnerabilities. The following two-stage procedure was followed. First, a set of potential crisis episodes was identified on the basis of various definitions of crises, including two measures of a sudden stop in net private capital flows, years of high exchange rate pressure as indicated by early warning systems, sovereign defaults, IMF programs (but only years with positive net disbursements), a banking indicator and a corporate crisis indicator. Second, the final set of crisis years was chosen taking into consideration comments from the IMF's desk economists. Their suggestions helped resolve remaining ambiguities.
5. The exchange rate overvaluation measure is based on a methodology that follows the IMF's Consultative Group on Exchange Rates Macroeconomic Balance approach for countries covered by that exercise, and deviations from a long-term average (beginning in 1980) for countries where such estimates are not available.
6. This also explains why initial "early warning" models, which tried to predict the timing of crises, generally performed poorly (see Berg and Pattillo 2005).

REFERENCES

Aghion, P., P. Bacchetta and A. Banerjee. 2001. "Currency Crises and Monetary Policy in an Economy with Credit Constraints". *European Economic Review*, **45** (7): 1121–50.

Allen, M., C. Rosenberg, C. Keller, B. Setser and N. Roubini. 2002. *A Balance Sheet Approach to Financial Crisis*. IMF Working Paper 02/210. Washington: International Monetary Fund.

Berg, Andrew and Catherine Pattillo. 2005. "Assessing Early Warning Systems: How Have They Worked in Practice?". *IMF Staff Papers*, **52** (3): 462–502.

Chamon, Marcos, Paolo Manasse and Alessandro Prati. 2007. "Can We Predict the Next Current Account Crisis?". *IMF Staff Papers*, **54** (2): 270–305.

Corsetti, G., B. Guimaraes and N. Roubini. 2006. "International Lending of Last Resort and Moral Hazard: A Model of the IMF's Catalytic Finance". *Journal of Monetary Economics*, **53** (3): 441–71.

Flood, R. and P. Garber. 1984. "Collapsing Exchange Rate Regime: Some Linear Examples". *Journal of International Economics*, **17**: 1–13.

Ghosh, A. and S. Ghosh. 2003. "Structural Vulnerabilities and Currency Crises". *IMF Staff Papers*, **50** (7): 481–507.

Ghosh, A., B. Joshi, J. Kim, U. Ramakrishnan, A. Thomas and J. Zalduendo. 2008. *IMF Support and Crisis Prevention*. IMF Occasional Paper 262. Washington: International Monetary Fund.

Ghosh, A., J.D. Ostry and N. Tamirisa. 2009. "Anticipating the Next Crisis". *Finance and Development*, (September): 35–37.

Krugman, Paul. 1979. "A Model of Balance of Payments Crises". *Journal of Money, Credit, and Banking*, **11**: 311–25.

Morris, S. and H. Shin. 2006. "Catalytic Finance: When Does It Work?". *Journal of International Economics*, **70** (1): 161–77.

Obstfeld, Maurice. 1986. "Rational and Self-fulfilling Balance-of-Payments Crises". *American Economic Review*, **76** (1): 72–81.

Rosenberg, C., I. Halikias, B. House, C. Keller, J. Nystedt, A. Pitt and B. Setser. 2005. *Debt-related Vulnerabilities and Financial Crises: An Application of the Balance Sheet Approach to Emerging Market Countries*. IMF Occasional Paper 240. Washington: International Monetary Fund.

11. Structural fundamentals of Korean corporations: this time was different

Kyung-Mook Lim

INTRODUCTION

The financial crisis of 2008 affected the world economy at the most far-reaching level of any crisis since the Great Depression of the 1930s. At the beginning of the crisis, Korea was hit severely, owing in part to high exposure to outside demand, and the won depreciated deeply, reflecting pessimistic views about the Korean economy. Criticism arose in the popular media and from other commentators that Korea had not learned essential lessons from the financial crisis of 1997.

In spite of the bleak initial outlook, the Korean economy recovered relatively well. Many factors enabled this robust recovery. Government action, such as an expansionary fiscal and monetary policy, was taken promptly and turned out to be very effective. The early recovery of developing countries including China created ample external demand.

Moreover, the fundamentals such as financial soundness of financial institutions and corporations notably improved after the financial crisis in 1997. In particular, the large Korean corporate groups (*chaebols* in Korean), which had routinely pursued growth and market shares at the expense of profitability and shareholder's value,[1] experienced a full scale restructuring (financial and nonfinancial) and improved their corporate governance after 1997. These fundamental changes were mainly due to the law and regulation reform driven by the outbreak of the crisis and to the market monitoring mechanism that grew out of these policy reforms. The notoriously high debt–equity ratios declined significantly, and corporate liquidity (the cash holding ratios) increased.

Thanks to these improved fundamentals, the Korean corporations were able to absorb the huge external shock of 2008 effectively. Thus, domestic demand (such as private consumption and investment) did not collapse as much in 2008–09 as it did during 1997–98.[2] Figure 11.1 compares fixed investment in Korea during and after the two crises. In 1997, fixed investment plummeted more than 20 percent after the outbreak of the crisis, and

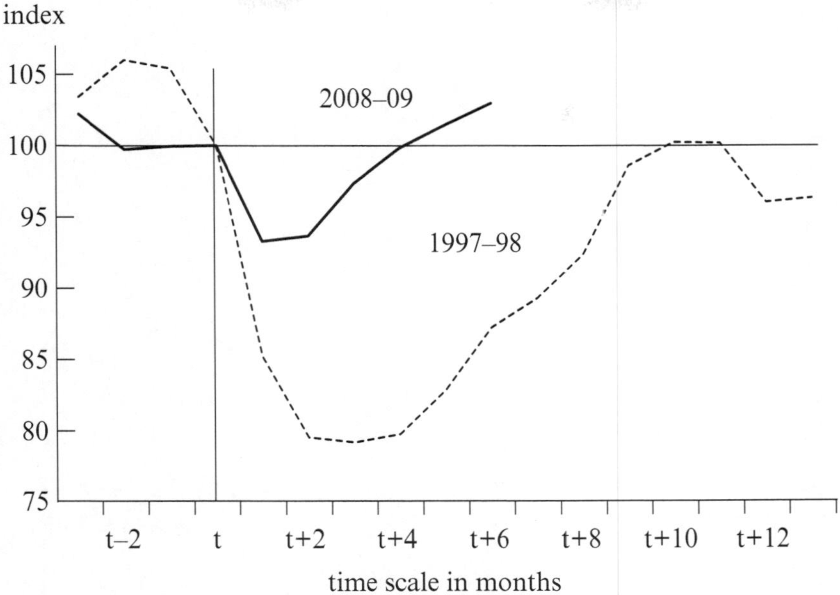

Note: Seasonally adjusted quarterly data are used. The bases of the index are 100 in the fourth quarter of 1997 for the first crisis and 100 in the third quarter of 2008 for the second crisis.

Source: Bank of Korea.

Figure 11.1 Fixed investment in Korea: comparison of 1997–98 and 2008–09 crises

it took more than two years to recover to the precrisis level. By contrast, the decline in 2008–09 was much more modest and the recovery was quick (less than a year). In 1997–98 there were massive lay-offs in the labor market, due to bankruptcies and restructuring pressure, and the employment level had not fully recovered even two years later. Again by contrast, the employment adjustment process was relatively benign in 2009 (Figure 11.2).[3]

This chapter investigates the financial restructuring process of Korean corporations after the 1997–98 crisis, which seems to have prevented the propagation of the external shock to domestic sectors a decade later. The chapter examines the overall changes in the financial structure, such as cash-holding, profitability and investment behavior, and then provides detailed analysis concentrating on debt–equity ratio changes. Before the 2008–09 global crisis, there were hot debates in Korea regarding the pros and cons of these changes in financial structure and corporate behavior.

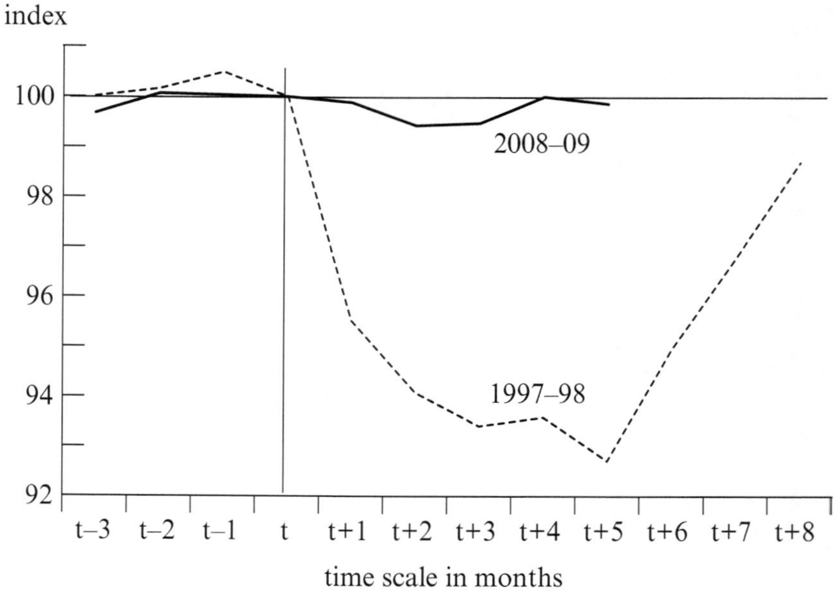

Note: Seasonally adjusted quarterly data are used. The bases of the index are 100 in the fourth quarter of 1997 for the first crisis and 100 in the third quarter of 2008 for the second crisis.

Source: National Statistical Office.

Figure 11.2 Employment in Korea: comparison between 1997–98 and 2008–09 crises

Some have argued that this sound and relatively conservative financial management is not only natural, given the memory of the financial crisis, but also desirable, given the increasing competition and uncertainty, whereas others have claimed that the new financial management scheme is too conservative for adequate investment for the future. The latter argument gained momentum because investment in the postcrisis period, especially equipment investment, was very sluggish compared with the precrisis period. The supporters of the latter view have continuously criticized many of the reforms and have urged a reversal or relaxation of some measures (such as the defensive schemes for hostile take-overs and the elimination of cross equity investment within group affiliates), along with relaxing regulations on bank shareholding by nonfinancial companies.[4]

Given the controversy about the corporate reform in Korea since 1997, the second crisis and its effects provide an appropriate juncture for reviewing the policy changes and the process of balance sheet restructuring. The outcome of the second crisis is also an opportunity for examining whether this time was different for Korean corporations.

The next section of this chapter provides a brief overview of related research. The third section examines the impact of the 1997–98 financial crisis on corporate behavior, the trends of key financial variables (such as cash holding ratios and debt–equity ratios) and the determinants of debt–equity ratios in Korea. The final section explores some policy implications arising from these changes in the structural fundamentals of Korean corporations.

RELATED LITERATURE

Many studies have analyzed the origins of the 1997–98 crisis. Most of them point to the deteriorated corporate financial status as one of the major sources of the financial crisis, or at least as the key channel for propagating the crisis to the Korean economy. In particular, the chaebols, which are conglomerates of many companies in diversified industries, were at the center of lax financial management. Considering themselves too big to fail, the chaebols pursued size-oriented strategies through heavy borrowing from financial institutions.

Many studies have examined the inefficient investment behavior of Korean chaebols prior to the crisis. Most showed that chaebol-affiliated companies, in comparison with stand-alone companies, were investing either too aggressively or inefficiently through huge external financing.[5]

Some studies have examined the effects of the financial crisis on the behavior of Korean corporations. Borensztein and Lee (2002) show that chaebol-affiliated companies have lost the preferential access to credit that they enjoyed in the precrisis period, and credit appears to have been reallocated in favor of more efficient companies. Hong et al. (2007) show that the difference in investment behavior between chaebol and nonchaebol firms disappeared after the financial crisis and that the sharp reduction in investment by chaebols in the postcrisis period can be attributed mainly to the need to reduce their debt burden.

Lee et al. (2009) show that internal capital markets operated prior to the crisis but lost their significance after it, while Kim (2009) argues that the role of internal capital markets faded after the crisis but has not yet fully faded away.

Lim and Choi (2007), exploring changes in the financial structure of Korean companies, analyse changes in cash holding patterns. They show that most of the increase in the cash holding ratio is due to the accumulation of cash by large corporations, which were starting from a very low level in the precrisis period. Also, they show that the increase in cash holding itself cannot explain the investment slowdown.

Closely related to the present study is Fattouh et al. (2005). The authors use 1992–2001 data to show that government efforts to reduce the debt–equity ratio were concentrated on the larger corporations and argue that the government policy, which focused on the chaebols, was successful and can be justified. Their analysis is concentrated, however, on the period when the restructuring process was driven mainly by the government policy. It also does not explore how the debt–equity ratio changed over time. The present study encompasses a much longer period (1990–2009), analyses in detail the changes in the debt–equity ratio and their effects on investment and employment, and takes other key variable changes into account.

STRUCTURAL CHANGES OF KOREAN CORPORATIONS

Impacts of the 1997 Financial Crisis

The financial crisis in 1997 became the cornerstone of government policy for the restructuring of many Korean corporations, including the chaebols, which dramatically improved not only their financial soundness but also their corporate governance. At first, these changes were driven mainly by the government policies. After the crisis the government proposed a comprehensive policy reform package for corporate governance,[6] accounting and disclosure practices, financial structure, regulations for mergers and acquisitions (M&A) and so on. The most notable changes with respect to corporate debt management were the elimination of cross-guarantees among group-affiliated companies and the consolidation of chaebol accounts.

Some of the measures listed above were implemented through the enactment of new laws and regulations, whereas other measures for corporate restructuring were implemented by means of pressure from government officials.[7] Among the top 30 chaebols, 17 were forced to undertake some form of corporate restructuring (Table 11.1), and most of the founders lost control of the companies.[8] In addition, for debt–equity ratios, the government imposed a target of 200 percent, which initially seemed to be a mission-impossible for the major chaebols. This decisive but hasty restructuring pressure created a credit crunch for most companies, especially the chaebols.

In addition to the government policies, other factors affected the financial structure of the Korean corporations. First, the corporations

Table 11.1 Corporate rehabilitation procedures post-1997 among the top 30 chaebols

Chaebol	End of 1997		Corporate rehabilitation procedure and date
	Number of affiliates	Total borrowing (billion won)	
Daewoo	250	25,347	workout (1999.8.26)
Kia	40	5,819	corporate reorganization (1998.4.15)
Ssangyong	75	9,004	workout (Ssangyong Construction 1998.11.1)
Halla	36	4,501	composition (1998.3.20)
Kohab	25	3,384	workout (1998.7.14)
DongAh	42	3,696	corporate reorganization (DongAh Construction: discontinuance of corporate reorganization 2001.3.9)
Jinro	32	1,443	composition (1998.2.3)
Hanil	20	1,578	corporate reorganization (1999.1.19)
Anam	34	2,217	workout (Anan Semiconductor: 1998.10.30)
Haitai	37	3,254	corporate reorganization (2001.4.11)
Shinho	33	1,569	workout (1998.7.16)
Tongil	18	1,373	corporate reorganization (1999.4.23)
New Core	18	691	corporate reorganization (1998.11.16)
Dongkuk	24	1,091	workout (1998.10.27)
Saehan	24	1,805	workout (2000.5.27)
Kabeul	23	832	workout (1998.7.24)
Keopyong	20	1,960	workout (1998.7.23)
Total of 17 chaebols	751	69,564	

themselves realized the need for more conservative balance sheet management. The following quotation from an interview illustrates in retrospect the desperation of top managers during this credit crunch.

> During the foreign exchange crisis, on more than a few occasions, I walked out of a bank weeping, as it refused to provide the company with any loan . . . Reflecting on these experiences, Samsung Electronics lowered its debt–equity ratio to below 100 percent and started the nonborrowing management system, since it yielded profits over a trillion won. As it can manage a situation comparable to the foreign exchange crisis with about 12 trillion won, Samsung Electronics currently possesses 8 to 10 trillion won in cash.[9]

Second, market pressure was more actively in play especially by foreign investors. The outbreak of the crisis expedited the capital market liberalization process, since there was an urgent need to induce foreign capital. The ceiling on shares owned by foreign investors was gradually lifted and, by 2006, the proportion of foreign ownership of listed companies amounted to 37 percent (up from only 13 percent in 1996). The increased share of foreign investors and relaxed regulations regarding M&As[10] created sound checks and balances between incumbent managers (or major shareholders) and institutional investors. Foreign institutional investors actively presented their view on corporate policies and closely monitored decisions of companies. The most striking event for the major shareholders (or founding families) was the attempt by Sovereign Fund at a hostile take-over of the SK group, one of the top five chaebols in Korea. In 2004, Sovereign Fund purchased a significant proportion of the shares of the SK Corporation, the de facto holding company of the SK group, by taking advantage of a drop in share prices due to an accusation against the chief executive officer (a question of accounting manipulation to hide an affiliated company's financial trouble). This attempt gained momentum since the Fund claimed that it could improve the corporate governance and value for shareholders. The founding family barely managed to defend the chaebol from this hostile take-over attempt, with some help from domestic institutional investors.[11] Even though this ambitious attempt failed, this episode made a strong impression on Korean corporations.

Data and Descriptive Statistics

The data used in this study were obtained from WISEfn, which refined the dataset originally constructed by the Korea Listed Companies Association. (The WISEfn Corporation was established in 1996 with support from Korea's Ministry of Information and Communication, as a capital market information provider at www.wisefn.com.) The announcements

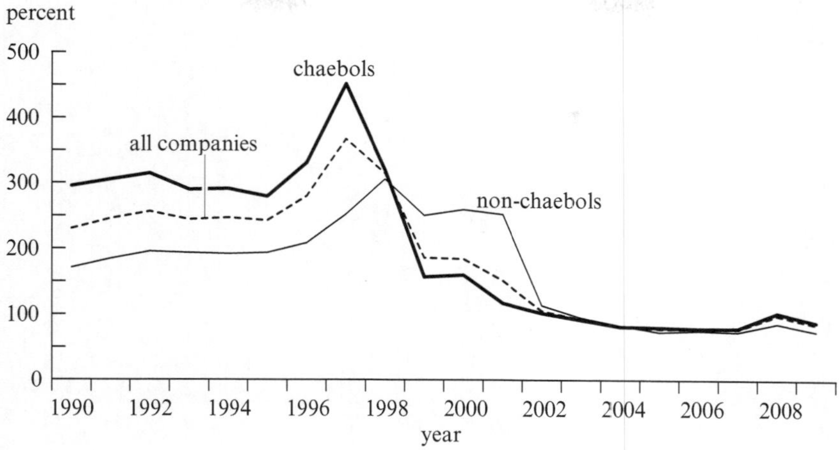

Note: Data represent asset weighted average value.

Source: WISEfn Corporation.

Figure 11.3 *Debt–equity ratio of the listed companies in Korea, 1990–2008*

of the Korea Fair Trading Commission were used to identify the chaebols involved.[12] Throughout the analysis, the service sector is excluded, because it has a balance sheet structure very different from that of the financial sector and because many industries (such as gas, telecommunications and electricity) are highly regulated. Firms with negative capital ratios are also excluded from the sample.

The financial crisis created a credit crunch for most Korean corporations, which came under both government and market pressures to improve their debt–equity ratios. The government pushed the major corporations to reduce the ratios to below 200 percent, which they had done by the end of 1999 (Figure 11.3). Considering that their debt–equity ratios had been around 400 percent, this was a daunting task for most companies. While reducing the debt level gradually, most companies tackled this task in two ways. First, they issued seasoned equity aggressively after the financial crisis. Since stock market conditions were improving as the economy recovered, and since the capital market was opened to foreign investors, most companies were able to issue seasoned equity successfully. Through these new issues in equity, the paid-in capital and the capital surplus increased 66 percent and 115 percent, respectively, between 1997 and 1999.

Before the 1997–98 financial crisis, Korea's accounting practices were consistent with Germany's and Japan's. The corporations relied on historic

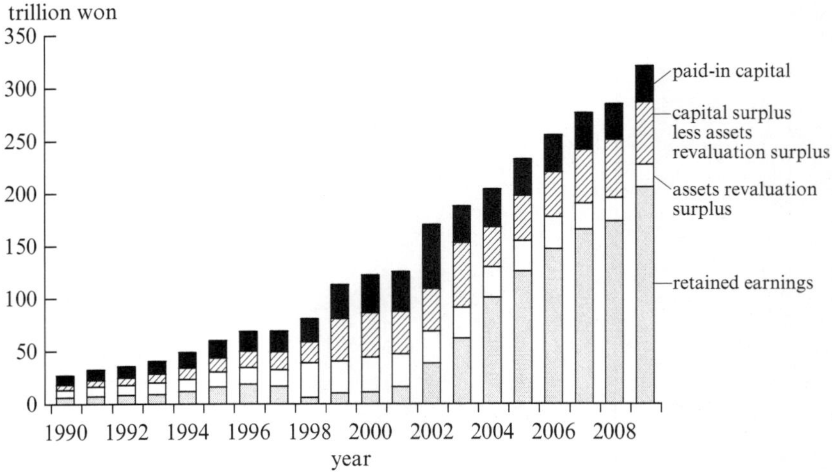

Source: WISEfn Corporation.

Figure 11.4 Capital structure of the listed companies in Korea, 1990–2009

cost accounting, rather than the fair market value that is used in the North American Generally Accepted Accounting Principles (GAAP).[13] Since most tangible assets, especially land and other real estate, had appreciated significantly over time since the initial purchases, the change in accounting practices and consequent reappraisals of these assets boosted the size of equity, which increased by 94 percent between 1997 and 1999 (Figure 11.4). Such reappraisals helped the corporations achieve the "policy goal" of a 200 percent debt–equity ratio, and the ratio declined from 367 percent to 186 percent, even though the total debt decreased by only 10 percent.[14]

Even after achieving the guideline set by the government, the Korean companies continuously lowered their debt–equity ratios by reducing debt and increasing equity. In fact, the reduction of the debt level continued very aggressively until 2003 (Figure 11.5). Although the total debt level of the listed companies began to increase after 2004, the debt–equity ratio did not change much, mainly due to the improved profitability of the listed companies.[15] Throughout the period of financial and nonfinancial restructuring, the net profit margin jumped (Figure 11.6). Since 2000 the major factor that held the lowered debt–equity ratio stable was retained earnings, reflecting improved profitability. That is, the speed of accumulation of retained earnings was fast enough to hold the debt–equity ratio at the new low level, although the level of debt was increasing continuously.

When the sample is divided into chaebol-affiliated companies and

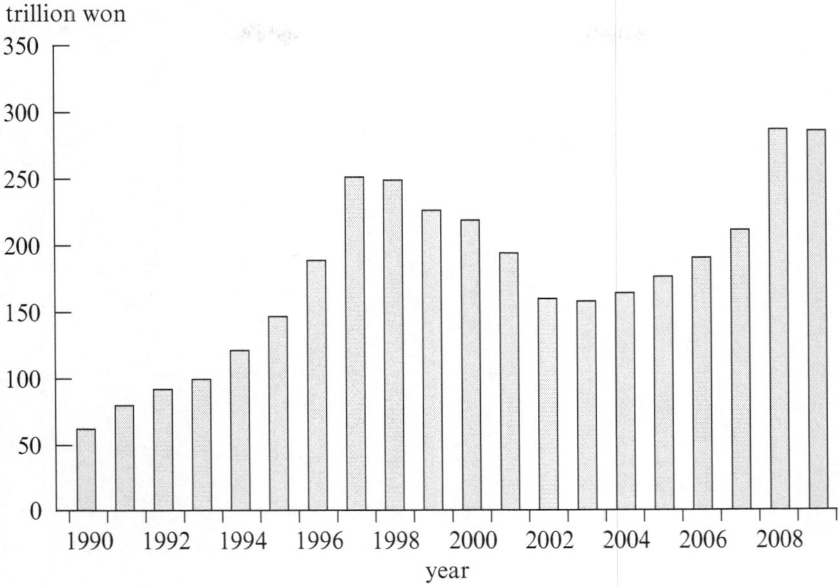

Source: WISEfn Corporation.

Figure 11.5 Total debt of the listed companies in Korea, 1990–2009

other companies, some interesting points emerge (as seen in Figure 11.3). First, the debt–equity ratio of the chaebol-affiliated companies was higher than that of other companies.[16] Second, the chaebol-affiliated companies started the debt–equity ratio reduction process earlier than other companies, probably because the government pushed the 200 percent rule for the top 30 chaebols first. Last, and more interestingly, the ratios of both chaebol and nonchaebol companies converged to a very similar level after 2002. This implies that the "too big to fail" legacy is no longer valid in Korea and that the size-oriented strategy has lost its ground. Figure 11.7 divides the debt–equity ratios into company asset size by quartile. The result is very similar to the case of the chaebol and nonchaebol analysis. That is, the debt–equity ratio of the highest quartile is very similar to that of the chaebols.

Before the financial crisis, most companies (especially chaebol affiliates) did not have enough incentive to reserve cash or cash equivalent assets,[17] since they not only had easy access to the financial market but also could rely on the financial resources of other affiliates. As soon as the crisis occurred, the corporations realized the true value of holding liquid assets, since it was almost impossible to find easy money, given the comprehensive

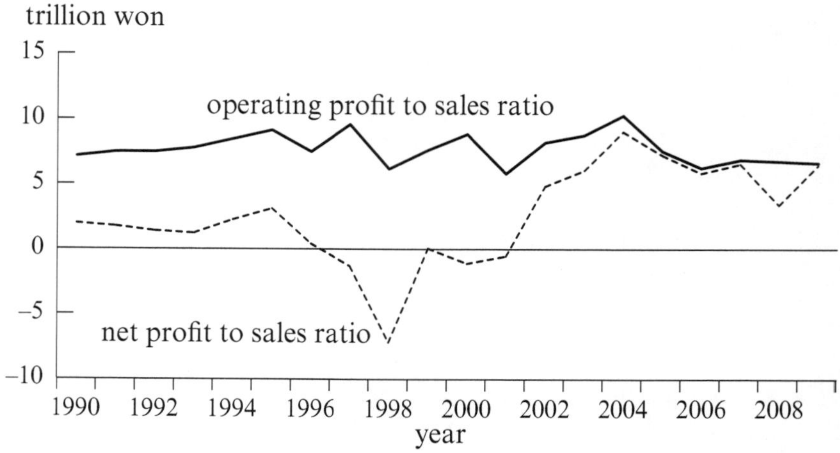

Note: Data represent asset weighted average value.

Source: WISEfn Corporation.

Figure 11.6 Operating and net profit of listed companies in Korea, 1990–2009

restructuring process in both the financial and nonfinancial sectors.[18] Cash management was a more serious issue for chaebol-affiliated companies. Before the crisis, an affiliate that was in urgent need of credit could get help from other affiliates, either by equity injection or by loan guarantees.[19] These two channels of the internal capital market were no longer available after the postcrisis reforms. Under this new environment, chaebol affiliates had to accumulate a new optimal level of cash. Figure 11.8 reveals that the increase in the overall cash holding ratio was driven mainly by the increase of the cash holding ratio of the chaebol-affiliated companies.[20] Figure 11.9 shows cash holding ratios in greater detail, dividing them into asset size by quartile. Similar to the case of the debt–equity ratio, the highest quartile was the main driver of the overall change.

Determinants of Financial Structure of Korean Corporations

A simple empirical test should demonstrate whether there was a significant change in the financial structure of Korean corporations after the 1997–98 crisis. Since many studies of the changes in investment and cash holding have already been made, the focus here is on the changes in the debt–equity ratio after the crisis, controling the analysis with commonly used variables in capital structure literature. There are well established

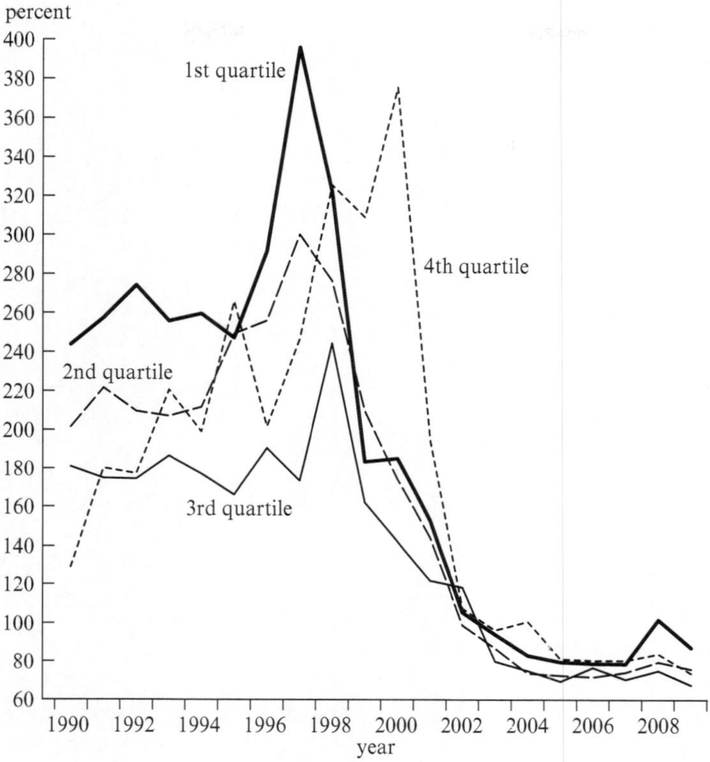

Source: WISEfn Corporation.

Figure 11.7 Corporate debt to equity ratios by asset size quartile in Korea, 1990–2009

factors that affect the financial structure (debt and equity) of corporations.[21] In this study we consider the following variables as determinants of the debt–equity ratio.

Empirical evidence on the standard model from many countries, such as Booth et al. (2001), has shown that size, asset tangibility, growth opportunity, profitability and nondebt tax shields are the main determinants of a firm's capital structure.

Larger firms (in terms of asset or sales) could have better access to capital markets and borrow at lower rates, because they are relatively well known and more diversified in their investments, and therefore information asymmetry and default risk are more favorable to these firms than to smaller ones. For the present study, logarithms of both total assets and

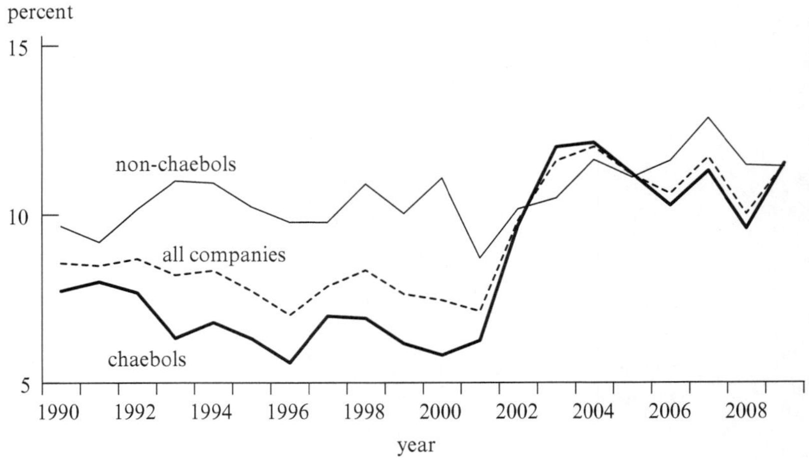

Note: Data represent asset weighted average value and cash as a share of total assets.

Source: WISEfn Corporation.

Figure 11.8 Cash holding ratio of the listed companies in Korea, 1990–2009

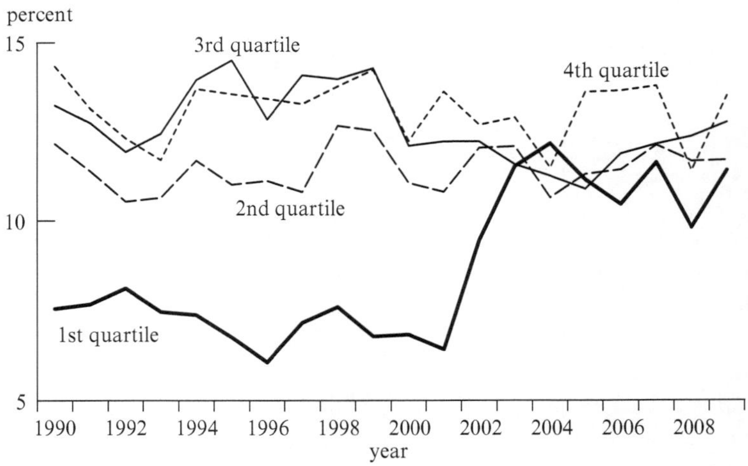

Source: WISEfn Corporation.

Figure 11.9 Corporate cash-holding by asset size quartile in Korea, 1990–2009 sales were tried. Since there was no significant difference, only the case of total assets is reported here.

Most capital structure theories argue that the types of assets owned by a firm can affect its capital structure choice. In particular, firms with a large proportion of tangible assets are likely to obtain financing at a lower cost because of the collateral value of their tangible assets. For tangibility, the ratio of tangible assets to total assets is used here.

In contrast, growth opportunities represent noncollateralizable assets (intangible assets, R&D). Firms with a high proportion of noncollateralizable assets find it more difficult to obtain credit because of information asymmetry and the agency problem. For growth opportunities, the ratio of R&D expenses to sales is used here.

To identify the impact of the crisis and the policy reforms, two dummy variables and one interaction term were created. First, "crisis" is a periodic dummy which takes the value of 1 if the year is greater than 1997; otherwise it is zero. Second, "groupdum" represents whether a company is an affiliate of the top 30 chaebols. Third, "cgroupdum" is an interaction term between "crisis" and "groupdum". Box 11.1 summarizes the definitions of the variables used in the regression, and Table 11.2 reports basic statistics of these variables.

The regression results are reported in Table 11.3.[22] Case (1) shows that the overall debt–equity ratio has declined about 80 percentage points. Case (2) shows that the top 30 chaebols had a debt–equity ratio about 45 percentage points higher over the whole period. Case (3) shows that the difference between the debt–equity ratios of chaebol and nonchaebol companies was about 100 percentage points in the precrisis period, that this difference nearly disappeared after the financial crisis, and that there was an overall debt–equity ratio reduction in both groups. Case (4) shows that the results of case (3) are robust to the inclusion of the usual control variables. Moreover, the estimated coefficients of control variables show the signs expected, with the exception of "tratio".

This simple empirical analysis confirms that there was a significant change in the debt–equity ratios of the listed companies. That is, the overall debt–equity ratio declined significantly, and the "too big to fail" legacy is no longer valid in Korea. Although it is almost impossible to pinpoint factors, it seems that both chaebol-specific and more broadly targeted changes in regulations have affected the capital structure of listed companies in Korea to a considerable degree.

BOX 11.1 DEFINITIONS OF REGRESSION VARIABLES

variable	name	definition
dratio2	debt to equity ratio	total liabilities / (total assets – total liabilities)
crisis	crisis	after 1997: 1, 1997 and before: 0
groupdum	group dummy	top 30 chaebols: 1, the rest: 0
cgroupdum	interaction term between crisis and groupdum	crisis × groupdum
size2	size	log of total assets
tratio	tangible assets to total assets ratio	tangible assets / total assets
roa	return on assets	operating profit / total assets
rndratio	R&D to sales ratio	R&D expenses / sales
dpratio	depreciation to assets ratio	depreciation / total assets

Table 11.2 Basic regression data

Variable	Observations	Average	Standard deviation	Minimum	Maximum
dratio2	8807	1.951	2.456	0.117	27.557
crisis	8807	0.591	0.492	0.000	1.000
groupdum	8807	0.178	0.383	0.000	1.000
cgroupdum	8807	0.091	0.288	0.000	1.000
size2	8807	18.937	1.398	15.206	25.178
tratio	8807	0.361	0.160	0.004	0.918
roa	8807	0.050	0.075	−1.163	0.550
rndratio	8807	0.005	0.013	0.000	0.270
dpratio	8746	0.004	0.005	0.000	0.091

Source: WISEfn.

Table 11.3 Regression results: 1990–2009 panel data

Variable	(1) dratio2	(2) dratio2	(3) dratio2	(4) dratio2
crisis	−0.837***	−0.817***	−0.640***	−0.925***
	(0.0474)	(0.0476)	(0.0527)	(0.0609)
groupdum	–	0.458***	1.029***	0.945***
		(0.122)	(0.142)	(0.143)
cgroupdum	–	–	−0.998***	−0.991***
			(0.129)	(0.130)
size2	–	–	–	0.342***
				(0.0500)
tratio	–	–	–	−0.543**
				(0.221)
roa	–	–	–	−4.507***
				(0.364)
rndratio	–	–	–	−7.448***
				(2.501)
dpratio	–	–	–	39.29***
				(7.348)
constant	2.445***	2.351***	2.236***	−3.760***
	(0.0350)	(0.0429)	(0.0453)	(0.945)
Observations	8807	8807	8807	8746
R-squared	0.037	0.039	0.046	0.072

Notes:
Standard errors are in parentheses.
*** = $p<0.01$, ** = $p<0.05$, * = $p<0.1$.

Reactions to the Two Different Crises

This subsection examines two key spending components of companies—capital expenditure and employment—and how they reacted to the outbreaks of the two crises. Figures 11.3 and 11.5 show that neither the debt–equity ratio nor the debt level changed significantly in 2009, despite the global crisis. This implies that there was no urgent need to reduce the debt burden in this period.

Figure 11.10 shows the trends of capital expenditure of listed companies. Capital expenditure collapsed after the financial crisis in 1997. It declined by about 35 percent in 1998 and did not recover to the precrisis level until the mid-2000s. This period coincides with the sharp debt–equity ratio adjustment discussed earlier. This decline in investment due to debt-adjustment has been pointed out by several studies

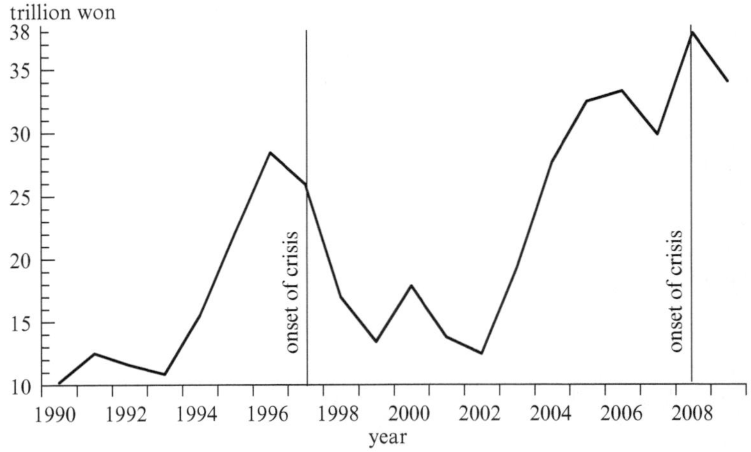

Source: WISEfn Corporation.

Figure 11.10 Capital expenditure of listed companies in Korea, 1990–2009

(see Lim 2005 and Hong 2006). After the debt–equity ratio had "fully" adjusted, the capital expenditure of listed companies increased continuously. The growth rate of capital expenditure of the listed companies was much bigger than that of nonlisted (mostly small and medium-size) companies.

By contrast, the capital expenditure decline in 2009 was much more modest. In fact, the quarterly financial statement in 2010 showed that capital expenditure had already picked up by that time, as the economy recovered.

The change in employment was much more dramatic after the first crisis than after the second one (Figure 11.11). Employment had peaked in 1996, then plummeted by more than 30 percent in two years and never reached the precrisis level, whereas capital expenditure during the same period fell initially but then exceeded the precrisis level. By contrast, the employment level in 2009 did not decline at all.

These well controlled reactions in the corporate sector were probably the main factors that prevented the huge external shocks in 2008 from being propagated to other domestic sectors. It seems that the improved financial soundness has helped to prove that this time was different for major Korean corporations.

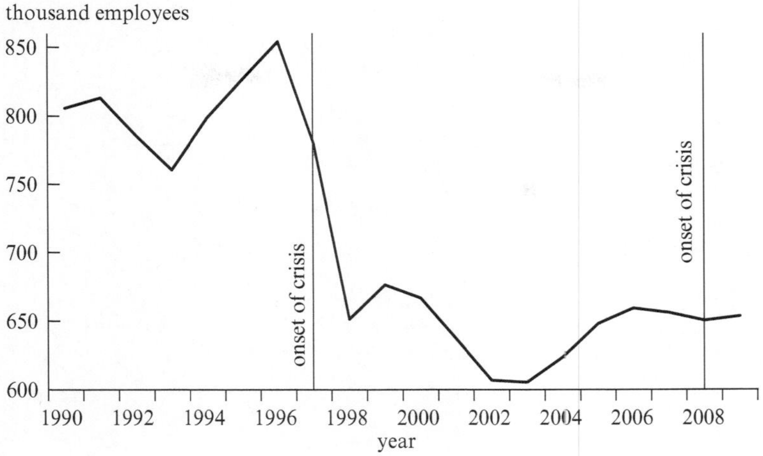

Source: WISEfn Corporation.

Figure 11.11 Employment in listed companies in Korea, 1990–2009

SUMMARY AND REMAINING ISSUES

The fundamentals in Korea's corporate sector improved significantly after the financial crisis of 1997–98. In particular, the chaebols up to that time had routinely pushed growth and market share at the expense of profitability and shareholder's value, but since 1997 they have undergone a full scale restructuring and have improved their corporate governance. Also during this period, the notoriously high debt–equity ratio in the corporate sector declined significantly, and liquidity (the cash holding ratios of corporations) increased. These fundamental changes were mainly the results of changes in the law and government regulations—a process of policy reform driven first by the outbreak of the crisis and then by the market monitoring mechanism that emerged from the changes. The improved financial soundness helped to prove that this time was different for major Korean corporations. In sum, the corporate restructuring in Korea is a great success story in terms of absorbing the external shock successfully.

The lower debt–equity ratio in Korea is still a subject of controversy. Some analysts are concerned about this new capital structure, arguing that dynamic growth would no longer be possible under such a conservative financial management regime.[23] Some analysts argue, moreover, that the debt–equity ratios of companies in Korea are relatively too low,

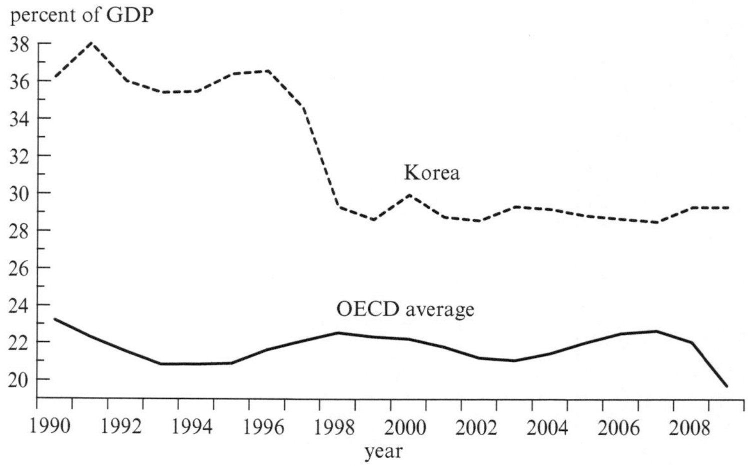

Note: The OECD average is for 30 member countries: Australia, Austria, Belgium, Canada, Czech Republic, Denmark, Finland, France, Germany, Greece, Hungary, Iceland, Ireland, Italy, Japan, Korea, Luxembourg, Mexico, the Netherlands, New Zealand, Norway, Poland, Portugal, Slovak Republic, Spain, Sweden, Switzerland, Turkey, the United Kingdom and the United States. Missing observations are omitted.

Source: OECD STAN database.

Figure 11.12 Corporate investment as a percentage of GDP: Korea and the OECD average, 1990–2009

in comparison with companies elsewhere. Even Lee and Rhee (2007), who acknowledge the positive aspects of the comprehensive reforms, express concern about the lower investment to GDP ratio.[24] Even though they admit that this ratio could be a natural response, given the over-investment in the precrisis period, they claim that the current investment rates are lower than the optimal level.

It is not easy to demonstrate, through direct evidence, that these concerns are not valid. Some plausible counter-arguments can nonetheless be made. First, the investment ratio in Korea (around 30 percent) is still very high in comparison with other major economies (Figure 11.12). It is very unclear whether any further increase in investment ratio in Korea is either possible or desirable. Second, any international comparison of debt–equity ratios should be treated with caution, given different accounting practices across countries. Most notably, the basic corporate financial statement is not a consolidated one but an individual statement, which does not reflect the status of any subsidiary companies.[25] If the debt–equity ratio in Korea is recalculated on the basis of consolidated financial

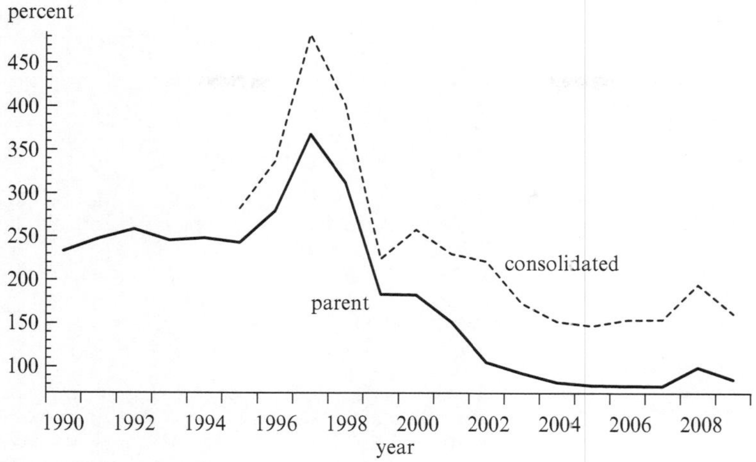

Source: WISEfn Corporation.

Figure 11.13 Corporate debt to equity ratios: individual and consolidated financial statements in Korea, 1990–2009

statements, the ratio for 2009 increases from around 100 percent to 160 percent (Figure 11.13), which is not low in comparison with other countries.[26] Third, the investment growth rates in Korea after 2003 were much higher for listed companies than for nonlisted ones, which implies that the overall sluggish investment growth rate was due mainly to the performance of nonlisted companies.

In fact, the listed companies in the present analysis are relatively large and sound in comparison with nonlisted ones, which are mostly small and medium-size companies (SMEs). While the fundamentals of listed companies have improved, as we have seen, the restructuring process in the SME sector has not been actively pursued. Since most of the labor force is employed by the SMEs, the restructuring of the SMEs has been politically burdensome for the government. Under political pressure, subsidies to SMEs increased dramatically after 1997 and increased further in 2009.[27] In addition, bank lending to SMEs increased considerably until 2008. Under these circumstances, an appropriate entry and exit process in the SME sector, which is one of the key factors for enhancement of productivity, has been hampered. Fostering a proper restructuring process for the SMEs is one of the major remaining tasks for the Korean government regarding corporation related matters.

NOTES

1. Such mismanagement was sustainable only because there was no checking mechanism available to restrain reckless business diversification, excessive borrowing and dogmatic decisionmaking by the controlling shareholders.
2. Cho (2009) provides a detailed explanation of the impact of the 2008 crisis on the Korean economy.
3. This benign decline in employment was due partly to the major public job creation efforts of the government. Even if we control for the effect of this program, the adjustment process in the labor market was still very mild.
4. Some even argued that this conservative behavior was due to antichaebol sentiment in Korea.
5. See Shin and Park (1999) and Hahn (1999).
6. For more detailed discussion regarding reforms on corporate governance, see Kim and Kim (2008) and Cho and Youn (2008).
7. In 1998, the government and the chief executive officers of the top five chaebols announced an "agreement" on mergers and business swaps, referred to as the "Big Deal". The Big Deal was intended to help the economy by resolving two main problems in the corporate sector: excess capacity from overinvestment and high leverage. The Big Deal turned out to be a big failure, with which most participants were not satisfied.
8. While formal insolvency procedures were also applied to a few troubled chaebols, it was the informal workout program that played a far more important role in corporate restructuring.
9. Extract from a media interview in 2005 with Choi Do-seok, the chief executive officer of Samsung Electronics.
10. Before the financial crisis, most of the M&A related regulations were intended to protect the founding owners of corporations. In those times, a hostile M&A was generally considered to be an improper appropriation of someone else's property, so there were very few hostile M&A attempts. After the financial crisis, most of the regulations that worked against hostile M&As were abolished.
11. After this attempt to take over the SK group, there were more cases of hostile takeovers of major Korean corporations. This created a debate about whether to introduce some defensive schemes, known popularly as poison pills, golden parachutes, golden shares and so on.
12. Every year the Korea Fair Trade Commission announces a list of business groups that will be regulated by certain laws and regulations. This list is mainly determined by the total asset size of the business group.
13. Booth et al. (2001) point out this accounting practice difference.
14. Haggard et al. (2003) offer the criticism that the reduction in the debt–equity ratio does not represent a genuine improvement in capital structure, because it was achieved mainly through increasing equity rather than reducing debt.
15. In general, improved quality from more intensive R&D, lower interest payments (due to both lower interest rate and lower debt level) and profit from overseas subsidiaries were considered as main sources of profitability improvements in Korea.
16. Since our definition of "chaebol" is restricted to the top 30 chaebols, there are some chaebol companies in our nonchaebol sample that are affiliates of chaebols but are ranked below the top 30.
17. Cash in this study is defined as the sum of cash and cash-equivalents such as short-term financial assets and short-term security, as in other studies.
18. Increased cash holding is not a phenomenon unique to Korea, but has recently been observed in most countries (see IMF 2006).
19. In some cases, they were even able to access credit from affiliated financial companies.
20. For a more detailed analysis on the cash holding pattern changes of the Korean corporations, see Lim and Choi (2007).

21. For general empirical analyses on the capital structure, see Titman and Wessels (1988), Rajan and Zingales (1995) and Booth et al. (2001).
22. The reported results are based on a random-effects panel estimation. A fixed-effects estimation does not change the results qualitatively.
23. For example, Shin and Chang (2003) argue that the reforms were ill designed and imposed too much "transitional" cost on the Korean economy.
24. The investment ratio was lowered to around 30 percent after the crisis in 1997, which is far lower than the level of 36 percent in the precrisis period.
25. Since the listed companies were required to prepare a consolidated financial statement in 1996, individual based financial statements had to be used here for making comparisons.
26. In 2008, the debt to equity ratios in the United States and Japan were 147 percent and 139 percent, respectively.
27. Most of the subsidies have been given in the form of credit guarantees.

REFERENCES

Booth, Laurence, Varouj Aivazian, Asli Demirguc-Kunt and Vojislav Maksimovic. 2001. "Capital Structure in Developing Countries". *Journal of Finance*, **56**: 87–130.

Borensztein, Eduardo and Jong-Wha Lee. 2002. "Financial Crisis and Credit Crunch in Korea: Evidence from Firm-level Data". *Journal of Monetary Economics*, **49**: 853–75.

Cho, Dongchul. 2009. "The Korean Economy in the Swirl of Global Crisis". Paper presented at the ADB Institute Conference on Global Financial Crisis: Impacts, Lessons and Growth Rebalancing, Tokyo, 22–23 April 2009.

Cho, Sungbin and Taehoon Youn. 2008. "Changes in Corporate Governance of Korean Enterprises after the Financial Crisis". In *Government Policies and Corporate Strategies under Structural Changes and Dynamism: The Cases of Korea and China*, edited by Dongsoo Kang, pp.15–38. Seoul: KDI Press.

Fattouh, Bassam, Pasquale Scaramozzino and Laurence Harris. 2005. "Capital Structure in South Korea: A Quantile Regression Approach". *Journal of Development Economics*, **76** (1): 231–50.

Haggard, Stephan, Won-hyuk Lim and Euysung Kim. 2003. "Conclusion: Whither the Chaebol?". In *Economic Crisis and Corporate Restructuring in Korea: Reforming the Chaebol*, edited by Stephan Haggard, Won-hyuk Kim and Euysung Kim, pp. 312–18. Cambridge: Cambridge University Press.

Hahn, Chinhee. 1999. "Implicit Loss-Protection and Investment Behavior of Korean Chaebols: An Empirical Analysis". *KDI Journal of Economic Policy*, **21** (1): 3–52. In Korean.

Hong, Kiseok. 2006. *A Micro Analysis of Recent Corporate Investment in Korea*. Economic Analysis Report. Seoul: Bank of Korea. In Korean.

Hong, Kiseok, Jong-wha Lee and Young Soo Lee. 2007. "Investment by Korean Conglomerates before and after the Crisis". *Japan and World Economy*, **19** (3): 347–73.

International Monetary Fund (IMF). 2006. "Awash with Cash: Why Are Corporate Savings So High?". In *World Economic Outlook 2006*, pp. 135–59. Washington: International Monetary Fund.

Kim, E. Han and Woochan Kim. 2008. "Changes in Korean Corporate Governance: A Response to Crisis". *Journal of Applied Corporate Finance*, **20**: 47–58.

Kim, Joon-Kyung. 2009. *Post-Crisis Corporate Reform and Internal Capital Markets in Chaebols*. Working Paper 09-15. Seoul: KDI School of Public Policy and Management.

Lee, Jong-Wha and Changyong Rhee. 2007. "Crisis and Recovery: What We Have Learned from the South Korean Experience?". *Asian Economic Policy Review*, **2** (1): 146–64.

Lee, Sangwoo, Kangwoo Park and Hyun-Han Shin. 2009. "Disappearing Internal Capital Markets: Evidence from Diversified Business Groups in Korea". *Journal of Banking and Finance*, **33** (2): 326–34.

Lim, Kyung-Mook. 2005. *An Analysis on Changes of Equipment Investment Patterns of Korean Firms Using Micro and Macro Data*. KDI Policy Studies. Seoul: KDI Press. In Korean.

Lim, Kyung-Mook and Yong-Seok Choi. 2007. "A Study on the Pattern Changes and Determinants of Corporate Cash Holding". *KDI Journal of Economic Policy*, **29** (2): 75–116. In Korean.

Rajan, Raghuram and Luigi Zingales. 1995. "What Do We Know about Capital Structure? Some Evidence from International Data". *Journal of Finance*, **50** (5): 1421–60.

Shin, Hyun-Han and Young S. Park. 1999. "Financing Constraints and Internal Capital Markets: Evidence from Korean Chaebols". *Journal of Corporate Finance*, **5** (2): 169–91.

Shin, Jang-Sup and Ha-Joon Chang. 2003. *Restructuring Korea Inc*. London and New York: Routledge Curzon.

Titman, S. and R. Wessels. 1988. "The Determinants of Capital Structure Choice". *Journal of Finance*, **43** (1): 1–19.

Index